ASPEN PUBLISHERS

& Strategies Tactics for the MBE 2

(Multistate Bar Exam)

Steven L. Emanuel, J.D.

Founder & Editor in Chief, Emanuel Bar Review
Member, NY, CT, MD, and VA bars

Wolters Kluwer

Law & Business

AUSTIN   BOSTON   CHICAGO   NEW YORK   THE NETHERLANDS

Aspen Publishers
Attn: Permissions Department
76 Ninth Avenue, 7th Floor
New York, NY 10011-5201

To contact Customer Care, e-mail customer.care@aspenpublishers.com, call 1-800-234-1660, fax 1-800-901-9075, or mail correspondence to:

Aspen Publishers
Attn: Order Department
P.O. Box 990
Frederick, MD 21705

Printed in the United States of America.

3 4 5 6 7 8 9 0

ISBN 978-0-7355-9408-1

This book is intended as a general review of a legal subject. It is not intended as a source for advice for the solution of legal matters or problems. For advice on legal matters, the reader should consult an attorney.

Siegel's, Emanuel, the judge logo, Law in a Flash and design, CrunchTime and design, Strategies & Tactics and design, and The Professor Series are registered trademarks of Aspen Publishers.

SUMMARY OF CONTENTS

TABLE OF CONTENTS

Contracts

Criminal Law and Procedure
CRIMINAL LAW

Evidence

Real Property

Torts

PREFACE

Thank you for buying this book. Its sole purpose is to help you excel on the MBE.

Here's how I prepared this book, and why I think it will help you:

- I've selected over 300 MBE-format questions — none of which appears in *Strategies & Tactics for the MBE*, and the vast majority of which are **actual past** MBE questions released by the MBE's drafters.

- I've put the questions into a **subtopic-by-subtopic hierarchy**. So, for instance, within Contracts, suppose you wanted to review just questions dealing with the Parol Evidence Rule. You'd look in the Table of Contents for the Contracts portion, then the Chapter on Parol Evidence, then the part called "II. SITUATIONS WHERE PAROL EVIDENCE RULE DOES NOT APPLY," then the sub-part called "A. Existence of a condition on effectiveness of contract." In that sub-part, you'd find multiple questions turning on this sub-issue, i.e., the effect of an oral provision that the writing won't become effective until some condition (e.g., "My architect's approval") has been satisfied.

- Because I've arranged the questions by subtopic, you can **spot the "hot topics"** on the MBE by seeing where the questions are **clustered**. So, for instance, if you're studying the Parol Evidence Rule, you could see at a glance — by the number of questions devoted to it — that the examiners like to focus on fact patterns where the Parol Evidence Rule does *not* apply.

- I **personally wrote and edited the answers** to each of these questions.

- For most all answer explanations, I tell you not just why the right choice is right, but also **why each wrong choice is wrong**. During my many years of helping students prepare for the MBE, I've learned that the MBE examiners exploit a pool of common student misconceptions over and over. So focusing on why a given wrong choice from a past question is wrong will help you a lot in spotting the examiners' use of that same trap on your actual exam.

- My discussion of each answer choice is **extensively researched and annotated**. When I did this research, I was often surprised to learn intricacies of law that I hadn't been aware of before. And one thing I can promise you based on my review of over 1,000 past MBE questions: when the MBE drafters write a question, they look carefully at Restatements, treatises, technical statutory provisions (e.g., subtleties of UCC Article 2 that you probably never covered in class), semi-obscure court decisions, and other authorities. The MBE is a very technical exam, and to do your best on it you need choice-by-choice analysis that focuses on the same authorities as those the drafters rely on; that's what I've given you here.

- Some of the questions are ones to which the National Conference of Bar Examiners (the drafters of the MBE) has released its own "annotations." But the answer discussions in this book are my own independently-researched ones, and I believe that my analysis is generally **significantly more complete** than the ones released by the National Conference of Bar Examiners.

All of these questions and answers have been used by hundreds of bar-prep students in major markets as part of Emanuel Bar Review materials. These students then passed their state's bar exam at a rate ten percentage points higher than the state-wide average.*

Good luck on the MBE. I hope this book helps.

Steve Emanuel
Larchmont, NY
May, 2009

*Based on passage rate of students who used Emanuel Bar Review materials in California and New York for bar exams in 2008 and 2009.

CONSTITUTIONAL LAW

CONSTITUTIONAL LAW Q&A BY TOPIC

All cases cited are U.S. Supreme Court cases unless otherwise noted.

CHAPTER 1

THE SUPREME COURT'S AUTHORITY AND THE FEDERAL JUDICIAL POWER

I. THE SUPREME COURT'S AUTHORITY AND THE FEDERAL JUDICIAL POWER

A. Supreme Court review of state court decision

1. "Independent and adequate state grounds"

a. Violations of state and federal constitutions

i. How to tell

Question 1: A state constitution provides that in every criminal trial "the accused shall have the right to confront all witnesses against him face to face." A defendant was convicted in state court of child abuse based on testimony from a six-year-old child. The child testified while she was seated behind one-way glass, which allowed the defendant to see the child but did not allow the child to see the defendant. The defendant appealed to the state supreme court claiming that the inability of the witness to see the defendant while she testified violated both the United States Constitution and the state constitution. Without addressing the federal constitutional issue, the state supreme court reversed the defendant's conviction and ordered a new trial. The state supreme court held that "the constitution of this state is clear, and it requires that while testifying in a criminal trial, a witness must be able to see the defendant." The state petitioned the United States Supreme Court for a writ of certiorari.

On which ground should the United States Supreme Court DENY the state's petition?

(A) A state may not seek appellate review in the United States Supreme Court of the reversal of a criminal conviction by its own supreme court.

(B) The decision of the state supreme court was based on an adequate and independent state ground.

(C) The Sixth Amendment to the United States Constitution does not require that a witness against a criminal defendant be able to see the defendant while the witness testifies.

(D) The state supreme court's decision requires a new trial, and therefore it is not a final judgment.

[Q7025]

Answer 1: Choice **(B)** is correct. The Supreme Court may not review a judgment by the highest court of a state if that judgment is supported entirely by state law and is wholly independent of the interpretation and application of federal law. In this case, although the defendant claimed a violation of the Sixth Amendment of the U.S. Constitution, the state supreme court based its decision entirely on the state constitution without addressing the federal constitutional issue.

(A) is wrong because the Supreme Court *may* review a judgment of the highest court of a state reversing a criminal conviction, if the state high court's decision turns on a question arising under federal law. (But what happened here was that the state court decision was based entirely on state, not federal, law.)

(C) is wrong for two reasons. First, the Sixth Amendment right of a criminal defendant (even in a state-court rather than federal-court proceeding) to confront the witnesses against him *does* usually include the right to view the witness, so this choice is wrong as a matter of law. Second, the Supreme Court would not reach even the merits of the defendant's Sixth Amendment claim, for the reason stated in (B) above.

(D) is wrong because although the Supreme Court may only review final judgments and decrees from the highest state courts, this judgment qualifies because it finally settled the confrontation issue (i.e., that issue would not arise again on re-trial, so the present petition provided the U.S. Supreme Court its only opportunity to review the confrontation issue).

Question 2: Plaintiff challenged the constitutionality of a state tax law, alleging that it violated the equal protection clauses of both the United States Constitution and the state constitution. The state supreme court agreed and held the tax law to be invalid. It said: "We hold that this state tax law violates the equal protection clause of the United States Constitution and also the equal protection clause of the state constitution because we interpret that provision of the state constitution to contain exactly the same prohibition against discriminatory legislation as is contained in the equal protection clause of the Fourteenth Amendment to the United States Constitution."

The state sought review of this decision in the United States Supreme Court, alleging that the state supreme court's determination of the federal constitutional issue was incorrect.

How should the United States Supreme Court dispose of the case if it believes that this interpretation of the federal Constitution by the state supreme court raises an important federal question and is incorrect on the merits?

(A) Reverse the state supreme court decision, because the equal protection clause of a state constitution must be construed by the state supreme court in a manner that is congruent with the meaning of the equal protection clause of the federal Constitution.

(B) Reverse the state supreme court decision with respect to the equal protection clause of the federal Constitution and remand the case to the state supreme court for further proceedings, because the state and federal constitutional issues are so intertwined that the federal issue must be decided so that this case may be disposed of properly.

(C) Refuse to review the decision of the state supreme court, because it is based on an adequate and independent ground of state law.

(D) Refuse to review the decision of the state supreme court, because a state government may not seek review of decisions of its own courts in the United States Supreme Court.

[Q1010]

Answer 2: Choice **(B)** is correct. Although the state supreme court made a finding about what the state constitution required, this decision was not truly "independent" of federal constitutional law, because the facts make it clear that the state court was first determining what the federal constitution required, and only then concluding that the state constitution required the same thing. Therefore, the Supreme Court can and should correct the state court's error in federal constitutional law. Once the Supreme Court has done this, it should then remand in order to give the state court the opportunity to conclude, after further reflection, that the state constitution's ban on discriminatory legislation goes further than the federal ban.

Choice (A) is wrong as a pure matter of law: even where provisions of a state and the federal constitution contain identical language, the state court is always free to interpret the state constitution as imposing different requirements than the apparently-identical federal provision.

Choice (C) is wrong because, for the reasons described above, the state court's decision was not in fact based on an adequate and independent state ground.

Choice (D) is wrong as a pure matter of law: nothing prevents a state government from seeking review of the decisions of its own courts in the U.S. Supreme Court, as long as the decision poses some serious question of federal law.

II. CONGRESS'S CONTROL OF FEDERAL JUDICIAL POWER

A. Congress's power to decide

1. Limits by Congress

Question 3: Assume that Congress passed and the President signed the following statute:

"The appellate jurisdiction of the United States Supreme Court shall not extend to any case involving the constitutionality of any state statute limiting the circumstances in which a woman may obtain an abortion, or involving the constitutionality of this statute."

The strongest argument against the constitutionality of this statute is that

(A) Congress may not exercise its authority over the appellate jurisdiction of the Supreme Court in a way that seriously interferes with the establishment of a supreme and uniform body of federal constitutional law.

(B) Congress may only regulate the appellate jurisdiction of the Supreme Court over cases initially arising in federal courts.

(C) the appellate jurisdiction of the Supreme Court may only be altered by constitutional amendment.

(D) the statute violates the equal protection clause of the Fourteenth Amendment.
[Q2097]

Answer 3: The correct choice is **(A)**. In cases not falling within the Supreme Court's original jurisdiction (e.g., cases in which a state is a party), the Supreme Court has "appellate Jurisdiction, both as to Law and Fact, with such Exceptions, and under such Regulations as the Congress shall make." (Article III, Sec. 2, Cl. 2.) So Congress, acting under this clause, has the power to regulate (including limit) the appellate jurisdiction of the Supreme Court. However, the Court held in *U.S. v. Klein* that Congress cannot use this power to specify jurisdiction as a "mean to an end" to make a particular substantive question come out a certain way. Choice (A) best captures this limitation, by suggesting that Congress was attempting to freeze then-current abortion law and to prevent a future Supreme Court from developing constitutional law in this area as the Court sees fit. This argument might not succeed, but it is the only choice that could even theoretically work.

(B) is simply wrong — Congress can under Article III, Sec. 2, Cl. 2 regulate the appellate jurisdiction of the Supreme Court whether the case originally arose in federal court or state court (and the only significance of where the case arose is that in those rare cases falling within the original jurisdiction of the Supreme Court itself, no "appellate jurisdiction" is necessary, so that there is no appellate jurisdiction which Congress might limit.)

(C) is also simply wrong — as discussed in (A) above, Article III, Sec. 2, Cl. 2 lets Congress, acting without a constitutional amendment, change the appellate jurisdiction of the Supreme Court.

(D) is wrong because the Fourteenth Amendment's Equal Protection Clause protects only against classifications made by state governments, and if there is any classification being made here (doubtful), it is being made by Congress, not a state.

Question 4: Which of the following acts by the United States Senate would be constitutionally IMPROPER?

(A) The Senate decides, with the House of Representatives, that a disputed state ratification of a proposed constitutional amendment is valid.

(B) The Senate determines the eligibility of a person to serve as a senator.

(C) The Senate appoints a commission to adjudicate finally a boundary dispute between two states.

(D) The Senate passes a resolution calling on the President to pursue a certain foreign policy.
[Q1087]

Answer 4: Choice **(C)** is correct. Art. III, Sec. 2, says that the federal judicial power extends "to controversies between two or more States." Art. III, Sec. 3 then says that "in all cases ... in which a State shall be a Party, the supreme Court shall have original jurisdiction." That same article says that the Supreme Court's "appellate jurisdiction" shall be "with such exceptions, and under such regulations as the Congress shall make." There is no similar provision allowing Congress to make exceptions to (i.e., restrictions on) the Supreme Court's original jurisdiction, so Congress can't restrict the Supreme Court's original jurisdiction. Since a boundary dispute between two states is a dispute in which "a State shall be a party," since the Supreme Court has original jurisdiction over cases involving a party, and since Congress is not authorized to limit the Supreme Court's original jurisdiction, it follows that Congress cannot "adjudicate finally" (i.e., remove the Supreme Court's right to adjudicate) the boundary dispute.

Choice (A) is wrong because, under *Coleman v. Miller* (1939), the House and Senate together *do* have the right (indeed, the exclusive right) to determine whether a disputed state ratification of an amendment is valid.

Choice (B) is incorrect because the Senate *does* have the power to determine the eligibility of its members — Art. I, Sec. 5, Cl. 1 says that "each House shall be the judge of the Elections, Returns, and *Qualifications* of its own Members."

Choice (D) is wrong because Art. I, Sec. 7, Cl. 3 says that "Every Order, *Resolution*, or Vote to which the Concurrence of the Senate and House of Representatives may be necessary ... shall be presented to the President of the United States[.]" This clause implicitly gives each house the power to adopt resolutions; a resolution will not become law unless signed by the President, but the clause means that either house's adoption of a resolution is proper.

CHAPTER 2
POWERS OF THE FEDERAL GOVERNMENT; THE SEPARATION OF POWERS

I. POWERS OF THE THREE FEDERAL BRANCHES

A. Powers of the three branches

1. Congress

a. Federal property

Question 5: The National Ecological Balance Act prohibits the destruction or removal of any wild animals located on lands owned by the United States without express permission from the Federal Bureau of Land Management. Violators are subject to fines of up to $1,000 per offense.

After substantial property damage was inflicted on residents of a state by hungry coyotes, the state legislature passed the Coyote Bounty Bill, which offers $25 for each coyote killed or captured within the state. A National Forest, owned by the federal government, is located entirely within that state. Many coyotes live in the National Forest.

Without seeking permission from the Bureau of Land Management, a hunter shot several coyotes in the National Forest and collected the bounty from the state. As a result, he was subsequently tried in federal district court, convicted, and fined $1,000 for violating the National Ecological Balance Act. The hunter appealed his conviction to the United States Court of Appeals.

On appeal, the Court of Appeals should hold the National Ecological Balance Act, as applied to the hunter, to be

(A) constitutional, because the property clause of Article IV, Section 3, of the Constitution authorizes such federal statutory controls and sanctions.

(B) constitutional, because Article I, Section 8, of the Constitution authorizes Congress to enact all laws necessary and proper to advance the general welfare.

(C) unconstitutional, because Congress may not use its delegated powers to override the Tenth Amendment right of the state to legislate in areas of traditional state governmental functions, such as the protection of the property of its residents.

(D) unconstitutional, because Congress violates the full faith and credit clause of Article IV when it punishes conduct that has been authorized by state action.

[Q2079]

Answer 5: Choice **(A)** is correct. Art. IV, Sec. 3, Cl. 2 gives Congress the power to "make all needful Rules and Regulations respecting the Territory or other Property belonging to the United States[.]" Since the National Forest is federally-owned property, this clause gives Congress the power to pass regulations governing it. Under the supremacy clause, those regulations would take precedence over any conflicting state regulations, such as the right to kill coyotes implied by the state bounty bill.

(B) is wrong because it suggests that there is an independent congressional power to act to advance "the general welfare." This is not so — there's a power to "*tax and spend* ... for the general welfare," but that's not what's at issue here (because Congress is doing pure regulating, not taxing or spending).

(C) is wrong because if Congress has been given an explicit power in a certain area (here, the power to regulate on federal lands), Congress can indeed override whatever right the state might otherwise have to legislate in areas of traditional state governmental functions.

(D) is wrong because the Full Faith and Credit clause does not block Congress from punishing conduct that has been authorized by a state; the clause merely requires one state to enforce every other state's judgments.

2. President

a. CEO of the U.S., and "Executive Orders"

i. Direction to private party

Question 6: The president issued an executive order in an effort to encourage citizens to use the metric (Celsius) system of temperatures. Sec. 1 of the executive order requires the United States Weather Bureau, a federal executive agency, to state temperatures only in Celsius in all weather reports. Sec. 2 of the executive order requires all privately owned federally licensed radio and television stations giving weather reports to report temperatures only in Celsius. No federal statute is applicable.

Is the president's executive order constitutional?

(A) Sec. 1 is constitutional, but Sec. 2 is not.

(B) Sec. 2 is constitutional, but Sec. 1 is not.

(C) Sections 1 and 2 are constitutional.

(D) Sections 1 and 2 are unconstitutional.

[Q7064]

Answer 6: Choice **(A)** is correct. Sec. 1 of the executive order is constitutional, because the President, as the chief executive officer of the U.S. government, has authority to direct the actions of federal executive agencies, so long as the President's directives are not inconsistent with an act of Congress. (The facts state that there is no applicable statute here.) Sec. 2 of the executive order is unconstitutional. At least as a general rule, the President does not have authority to direct the actions of persons outside the executive branch unless the President's direction is authorized by an act of Congress. There are no circumstances presented in the facts (such as a sudden attack on the U.S.) that might justify an exception to this general rule.

(B), (C) and (D) are wrong because each is inconsistent with the above analysis.

b. Pardons

Question 7: Congress passed a bill prohibiting the President from granting a pardon to any person who had not served at least one-third of the sentence imposed by the court which convicted that person. The President vetoed the bill, claiming that it was unconstitutional. Nevertheless, Congress passed it over his veto by a two-thirds vote of each house.

This act of Congress is

(A) constitutional, because it was enacted over the President's veto by a two-thirds vote of each house.

(B) constitutional, because it is a necessary and proper means of carrying out the powers of Congress.

(C) unconstitutional, because it interferes with the plenary power of the President to grant pardons.

(D) unconstitutional, because a Presidential veto based upon constitutional grounds may be overridden only with the concurrence of three-fourths of the state legislatures.

[Q1179]

Answer 7: The correct choice is **(C)**. The President's pardon power is indeed plenary. Therefore, when Congress purported to place conditions on that power, those conditions were ineffective. For the same reason, Choices (A), (B), and (D) are wrong. (By the way, Choice (D) is also grossly incorrect as a statement of the law of vetoes: where the President vetoes a bill passed by Congress, Article I, Sec. 7, Cl. 2 says that the veto can be overwritten by a two-thirds vote of both houses. There is no procedure by which the concurrence of three-fourths of state legislatures can act as an overriding method.)

II. THE FEDERAL COMMERCE POWER

A. Summary of modern view

1. "Substantially affecting" commerce

a. Activity is commercial

Question 8: A federal statute prohibits the sale or resale, in any place in this country, of any product intended for human consumption or ingestion into the human body that contains designated chemicals known to cause cancer, unless the product is clearly labeled as dangerous.

The constitutionality of this federal statute may most easily be justified on the basis of the power of Congress to

(A) regulate commerce among the states.

(B) enforce the Fourteenth Amendment.

(C) provide for the general welfare.

(D) promote science and the useful arts.

[Q1026]

Answer 8: Choice **(A)** is correct. The key point is that Congress can use its commerce powers to regulate even entirely *intrastate* transactions, on the theory that such transactions are being regulated as part of a broader regulation of interstate transactions, and excluding purely intrastate transactions from the overall scheme would be unwieldy. So, for instance, Congress here can forbid a farmer's sale, at a roadside stand adjacent to his farm, of a tomato that he had raised, where the farmer sprayed a cancer-causing substance produced inside that same state onto the tomato — even though this is an entirely intrastate transaction, it is still a "commercial" transaction, and can be regulated pursuant to Congress's broader interstate-commerce regulatory scheme.

(B) is wrong for several reasons; most importantly, the Fourteenth Amendment protects only against various conduct (e.g., denials of equal protection and due process) involving "state action," and while Congress has the power to enforce that Amendment by appropriate legislation, Congress here is not focused on attempting to prohibit any state from violating the Amendment.

(C) is wrong because there is no general congressional power to "provide for the general welfare"; there is only a power to *tax and spend* for the general welfare.

(D) is similarly incorrect because there is no general congressional power to "promote science and the useful arts"; there is only the limited power in Art. I, Sec. 8, Cl. 8 to "promote the progress of science and useful arts" by "securing for limited times to authors and inventors the exclusive right to their respective writings and discoveries" (i.e., the power to issue *patents* and *copyrights*).

Question 9: "Look-alike drugs" is the term used to describe nonprescription drugs that look like narcotic drugs and are sold on the streets as narcotic drugs. After extensive hearings, Congress concluded that the sale of look-alike drugs was widespread in this country and was creating severe health and law enforcement problems. To combat these problems, Congress enacted a comprehensive statute that regulates the manufacture, distribution, and sale of all nonprescription drugs in the United States.

Which of the following sources of constitutional authority can most easily be used to justify the authority of Congress to enact this statute?

(A) The spending power.

(B) The commerce clause.

(C) The general welfare clause.

(D) The enforcement powers of the Fourteenth Amendment.

[Q1029]

Answer 9: Choice **(B)** is correct. All of the activities being regulated by Congress here — manufacturing, distribution and sale of drugs — pertain to commerce. Therefore, Congress's power to regulate commerce is an ample source of authority for the regulatory scheme here. That is true even though the overall objectives being sought by Congress — the protection of health and the enforcement of law at the local level — are arguably "local" concerns traditionally left to the states.

(A) is wrong because the congressional statute here is essentially regulatory, and does not involve significant spending of federal funds.

(C) is wrong because there *is* no "general welfare" clause in the sense of a freestanding congressional power to legislate for the general welfare; there is, instead, only the power to tax and spend to achieve the general welfare, and Congress is not doing meaningful taxing or spending in the regulation at issue here.

(D) is wrong because the Fourteenth Amendment protects only against various conduct (e.g., denials of equal protection and due process) involving "state action," and while Congress has the power to enforce that Amendment by appropriate legislation, Congress here is not focused on attempting to prohibit states from violating the Amendment; for instance, there is no indication that Congress is trying to prevent the states from discriminating in the sale of nonprescription drugs or from denying anyone due process as to such drugs.

B.   The Tenth Amendment as a limit on Congress's power

Question 10: A federal law provides that all motor vehicle tires discarded in this country must be disposed of in facilities licensed by the federal Environmental Protection Agency. Pursuant to this federal law and all proper federal procedural requirements, that agency has adopted very strict standards for the licensing of such facilities. As a result, the cost of disposing of tires in licensed facilities is substantial. The state of East Dakota has a very large fleet of motor vehicles, including trucks used to support state-owned commercial activities and police cars. East Dakota disposes of used tires from both kinds of state motor vehicles in a state-owned and -operated facility. This state facility is unlicensed, but its operation in actual practice meets most of the standards imposed by the federal Environmental Protection Agency on facilities it licenses to dispose of tires.

Consistent with United States Supreme Court precedent, may the state of East Dakota continue to dispose of its used tires in this manner?

(A) No, because a state must comply with valid federal laws that regulate matters affecting interstate commerce.

(B) No, because some of the tires come from vehicles that are used by the state solely in its commercial activities.

(C) Yes, because some of the tires come from vehicles that are used by the state in the performance of core state governmental functions such as law enforcement.

(D) Yes, because the legitimate needs of the federal government are satisfied by the fact that the unlicensed state disposal scheme meets, in actual practice, most of the federal standards for the licensing of such facilities.

[Q1046]

Answer 10: The correct choice is **(A)**. The federal law on tire disposal was a proper exercise of Congress's power to regulate interstate commerce, so the law was validly enacted. The fact that Congress has chosen to regulate the actions of state governments does not prevent an otherwise-valid statute from being constitutional. There is one major exception — the Tenth Amendment prevents Congress from "commandeer[ing] the legislative processes of the states" by directly compelling states to enact or enforce a federal regulatory program [*New York v. U.S.*] But here, although Congress is regulating the states, it is not forcing the states to enact or enforce any federal regulatory program (merely forcing the states to obey the federal program in the state's own internal operations), so the exception does not apply.

Choice (B) is wrong because, although it reaches the correct conclusion, it does so for the wrong reasons; even if none of the tires came from vehicles used by the state in commercial activities, the federal regulation would still be valid.

Choice (C) is wrong because Congress has power to regulate interstate commerce in a way that binds the states, and there is no exception to this power for regulation of "core state governmental functions" (although as noted above, if Congress were actually ordering the state to enact or enforce a regulatory program, this *would* be beyond Congress's commerce powers).

Choice (D) is wrong because the fact that the unlicensed state disposal facility meets most federal standards is irrelevant; Congress has the power to insist that the state strictly obey the federal requirement that only licensed disposal facilities be used.

1. Not a source of state authority

Question 11: Widgets are manufactured wholly from raw materials mined and processed in the state of Green. The only two manufacturers of widgets in the United States are also located in that state. However, their widgets are purchased by retailers located in every state. The legislature of the state of Green is considering the adoption of a statute that would impose a tax solely on the manufacture of widgets. The tax is to be calculated at 3% of their wholesale value.

Which of the following arguments would be LEAST helpful to the state in defending the constitutionality of this proposed state tax on widgets?

(A) At the time widgets are manufactured and taxed they have not yet entered the channels of interstate commerce.

(B) The economic impact of this tax will be passed on to both in-state and out-of-state purchasers of widgets and, therefore, it is wholly nondiscriminatory in its effect.

(C) Because of the powers reserved to them by the Tenth Amendment, states have plenary authority to construct their tax system in any manner they choose.

(D) A tax on the manufacture of widgets may be imposed only by the state in which the manufacturing occurs and, therefore, it is not likely to create the danger of a multiple tax burden on interstate commerce.

[Q2020]

Answer 11: Choice **(C)** is correct. If this tax scheme has a problem, the problem is likely to have to do with the fact that Green is imposing a tax on widgets that are shipped throughout the U.S., and that tax may be a burden on commerce. The Tenth Amendment does not solve this problem for Green — if Green is unduly burdening commerce, the Tenth Amendment won't save it. And it's certainly inaccurate to say that the states "have plenary authority to construct their tax system in any manner they choose" — for instance, if a state intentionally designs its tax system so as to put most of the burden on out-of-staters who derive some revenue from customers in the state and who don't vote in state elections, the scheme would clearly violate the dormant commerce clause.

(A), (B), and (D) each arguably helps the state rebut the plaintiff's argument that the tax is an undue burden on commerce and that it thus violates the dormant commerce clause. Therefore, each of these arguments might help the state.

III. THE TAXING AND SPENDING POWERS

A. Taxing power

1. Regulation

a. Adverse economic consequences no problem

Question 12: The Sports Championship Revenue Enhancement Act is a federal statute that was enacted as part of a comprehensive program to eliminate the federal budget deficit. That act imposed, for a period of five years, a 50% excise tax on the price of tickets to championship sporting events. Such events included the World Series, the Super Bowl, major college bowl games, and similar championship sports events.

This federal tax is probably

(A) constitutional, because the compelling national interest in reducing the federal budget deficit justifies this tax as a temporary emergency measure.

(B) constitutional, because an act of Congress that appears to be a revenue raising measure on its face is not rendered invalid because it may have adverse economic consequences for the activity taxed.

(C) unconstitutional, because a 50% tax is likely to reduce attendance at championship sporting events and, therefore, is not rationally related to the legitimate interest of Congress in eliminating the budget deficit.

(D) unconstitutional, because Congress violates the equal protection component of the Fifth Amendment by singling out championship sporting events for this tax while failing to tax other major sporting, artistic, or entertainment events to which tickets are sold.

[Q2033]

Answer 12: Choice **(B)** is correct; a federal tax that will raise revenue is not rendered invalid by virtue of the fact that it has regulatory consequences, including a lessening of demand for the product or activity being taxed. (That's true, by the way, whether or not Congress intended that lessening of demand.)

(A) is incorrect because the tax would be valid as a revenue-raising measure even in the absence of a compelling national interest.

(C) is incorrect for the same reason that Choice (B) is correct — as long as the tax is on its face a revenue-raiser, it does not even have to be rationally related to some broader federal interest like deficit-reduction (and in any event the tax probably *is* rationally related to def-icit-reduction even though sporting attendance may go down — the rational-relation test is very easy to satisfy, and you should beware of any choice that requires you to conclude that a means chosen by government is not rationally related to a particular governmental goal).

(D) is incorrect because where, as here, a legislative classification involves economics and does not implicate any suspect class or fundamental right, equal protection is satisfied as long as the classification is rationally related to the achievement of some legitimate gov-ernmental objective; here, the objective is revenue-raising, and the fact that other similar activities are spared the tax does not prevent the tax from being rationally-related to that objective.

b. No relation needed between activity taxed and how funds are spent

Question 13: In order to provide funds for a system of new major airports near the ten largest cities in the United States, Congress levies a tax of $25 on each airline ticket issued in the United States. The tax applies to every airline ticket, even those for travel that does not originate in, terminate at, or pass through any of those ten large cities.

As applied to the issuance in the United States of an airline ticket for travel between two cities that will not be served by any of the new airports, this tax is

(A) constitutional, because Congress has broad discretion in choosing the subjects of its taxation and may impose taxes on subjects that have no relation to the purpose for which those tax funds will be expended.

(B) constitutional, because an exemption for the issuance of tickets for travel between cit-ies that will not be served by the new airports would deny the purchasers of all other tickets the equal protection of the laws.

(C) unconstitutional, because the burden of the tax outweighs its benefits for passengers whose travel does not originate in, terminate at, or pass through any of the ten largest cities.

(D) unconstitutional, because the tax adversely affects the fundamental right to travel.

[Q1124]

Answer 13: Choice **(A)** is correct. This choice accurately restates the fundamental rule about Congress's power to tax: as long as Congress can rationally be said to be pursuing the general welfare (not a meaningful constraint), Congress can pick pretty much any activity it wishes as the subject of taxation, and can then spend the funds for a purpose that has no relation to the activity taxed. So here, the fact that Congress is taxing trips that do not involve the 10 large cities, and then spending the funds solely for the benefit of pas-sengers whose travel does involve those 10 cities, makes no difference.

(B) is wrong because, although the main conclusion is correct (that the tax is constitu-tional), giving an exemption for cities that would not be served would certainly not deny any other purchasers equal protection. In the case of economic regulation not involving a suspect class or fundamental right, the classification scheme merely needs to withstand easy-to-satisfy mere-rationality review, and giving an exemption for travel between cities not involving the new airports would certainly pass this easy test.

(C) is wrong because the burden/benefit analysis used here would not be the proper test for a federally-imposed tax; the burden/benefit analysis would be a proper way to analyze a *state* regulation that might burden interstate travel and thus violate the dormant Commerce Clause, but the regulation here is not by a state.

(D) is wrong because, while the Supreme Court has occasionally recognized a fundamental "right to travel" for equal protection purposes, these cases have involved what would better be called the right to "migrate interstate," (e.g., the right to change one's state of residence and still receive welfare benefits), not the right to take a trip from one state to another.

B. Spending power

1. General welfare

Question 14: A newly enacted federal statute appropriates $100 million in federal funds to support basic research by universities located in the United States. The statute provides that "the ten best universities in the United States" will each receive $10 million. It also provides that "the ten best universities" shall be "determined by a poll of the presidents of all the universities in the nation, to be conducted by the United States Department of Education." In responding to that poll, each university president is required to apply the well-recognized and generally accepted standards of academic quality that are specified in the statute. The provisions of the statute are inseverable.

Which of the following statements about this statute is correct?

(A) The statute is unconstitutional, because the reliance by Congress on a poll of individuals who are not federal officials to determine the recipients of its appropriated funds is an unconstitutional delegation of legislative power.

(B) The statute is unconstitutional, because the limitation on recipients to the ten best universities is arbitrary and capricious and denies other high-quality universities the equal protection of the laws.

(C) The statute is constitutional, because Congress has plenary authority to determine the objects of its spending and the methods used to achieve them, so long as they may reasonably be deemed to serve the general welfare and do not violate any prohibitory language in the Constitution.

(D) The validity of the statute is nonjusticiable, because the use by Congress of its spending power necessarily involves political considerations that must be resolved finally by those branches of the government that are closest to the political process.

[Q2145]

Answer 14: Choice (C) is correct. Although Congress, when it spends, must spend "for the general welfare," this test is extremely easy to satisfy — as the choice correctly states, all that is required is that the spending be "reasonably deemed to serve the general welfare," and that it not violate some specific constitutional ban (e.g., the Establishment Clause's ban on spending for the purpose of advancing religion). Since Congress could rationally have believed that rewarding the "best universities" would promote the country's general welfare, and that determining the "ten best" by this kind of vote was a rational way to go about attaining that end, the spending is constitutional.

(A) is wrong because the statute here is an acceptable exercise of legislative delegation: Congress has made it reasonably clear to the Dept. of Education what they are to do, and how they are to do it, so there is no "unconstitutional delegation" despite the fact that non-federal officials will be somehow involved in the process.

(B) is wrong, because when a governmental classification does not involve a suspect or semi-suspect class or fundamental right, equal protection requires only a rational relation between the means chosen and a legitimate governmental objective, and the means and end here meet this easy-to-satisfy standard. (To put it another way, limiting the money to the "top ten," and picking the top ten this way, are *not* "arbitrary and capricious" methods.)

(D) is wrong because the mere fact that Congress's use of its spending power is being challenged does not make the matter a nonjusticiable political question.

IV. THE SEPARATION OF POWERS

A. Separation of powers generally

1. President can't make the laws

a. Delegation

i. Requirements for delegation

Question 15: Congress passed a statute directing the United States Forest Service, a federal agency, to issue regulations to control campfires on federal public lands and to establish a schedule of penalties for those who violate the new regulations. The statute provided that the Forest Service regulations should "reduce, to the maximum extent feasible, all potential hazards that arise from campfires on Forest Service lands." The Forest Service issued the regulations and the schedule of penalties directed by Congress. The regulations include a rule that provides for the doubling of the fine for any negligent or prohibited use of fire if the user is intoxicated by alcohol or drugs.

Which of the following is the best argument for sustaining the constitutionality of the Forest Service's rule providing for the fines?

(A) The executive branch of government, of which the Forest Service is part, has inherent rule-making authority over public lands.

(B) The rule is issued pursuant to a valid exercise of Congress's power to delegate rule-making authority to federal agencies.

(C) The rule is justified by a compelling governmental interest in safeguarding forest resources.

(D) The rule relates directly to law enforcement, which is an executive rather than legislative function, and hence it does not need specific congressional authorization.

[Q7036]

Answer 15: Choice **(B)** is correct. Congress can only delegate powers it possesses, so you first have to determine whether Congress itself has power to regulate federal lands. The answer is "yes," because Art. I, Sec. 8, Clause 17 gives Congress power to regulate federal lands. Next, you have to determine whether Congress validly delegated this power that it possesses. Here, too, the answer is "yes." Congress may delegate rule-making authority to federal agencies through statutes that set concrete objectives for the agency, and that list adequate criteria for carrying out those objectives. The Supreme Court has been very deferential in applying these "concrete objectives" and "adequate criteria" requirements. The objective being pursued here (control of campfires on federal lands) is quite concrete, and the criteria specified by Congress for achieving that objective (use of a penalty schedule for rule violators) seem quite adequate. Therefore, the statute's provision of authority to the Forest Service would likely be held to satisfy the requirements.

(A) is incorrect, because the executive branch does not have inherent rule-making authority over public lands. The only source of federal power to regulate public lands is the grant in Art. I, Sec. 8, Cl. 17, to *Congress* to regulate such lands, as discussed above. So the executive's rule-making authority over public lands comes from delegation by Congress, not from any inherent authority.

(C) is wrong because the compelling nature of the government's regulatory interest is neither necessary nor sufficient to justify the Forest Service's regulation. The constitutional requirement is merely that the regulation be pursuant to a valid act of Congress, and that it not violate any specific constitutional prohibition. Since the act is a valid exercise of Congress's power to regulate federal lands, and since the delegation was validly done (as described in (B) above), that's the end of the matter, and the strength of the federal interest never becomes relevant.

(D) is wrong because, although law enforcement is an executive function, the constitutional exercise of that function requires that the executive act pursuant to congressional authorization provided by law.

2. Presidential Commissions

Question 16: The vaccination of children against childhood contagious diseases (such as measles, diphtheria, and whooping cough) has traditionally been a function of private doctors and local and state health departments. Because vaccination rates have declined in recent years, especially in urban areas, the President proposes to appoint a Presidential Advisory Commission on Vaccination which would be charged with conducting a national publicity campaign to encourage vaccination as a public health measure. No federal statute authorizes or prohibits this action by the President. The activities of the Presidential Advisory Commission on Vaccination would be financed entirely from funds appropriated by Congress to the Office of the President for "such other purposes as the President may think appropriate."

May the President constitutionally create such a commission for this purpose?

(A) Yes, because the President has plenary authority to provide for the health, safety, and welfare of the people of the United States.

(B) Yes, because this action is within the scope of executive authority vested in the President by the Constitution, and no federal statute prohibits it.

(C) No, because the protection of children against common diseases by vaccination is a traditional state function and, therefore, is reserved to the states by the Tenth Amendment.

(D) No, because Congress has not specifically authorized the creation and support of such a new federal agency.

[Q3109]

Answer 16: Choice (B) is correct. The setting up of a presidential advisory commission, such as the one here, falls within the President's executive powers — nothing in the facts indicates that the commission will have legislative or judicial powers, so the commission is a proper delegation by the President of his executive power. As to funding: Congress has the right to earmark specified federal monies to be spent as the President shall determine. Therefore, nothing about this arrangement violates any constitutional provision.

(A) is wrong, because the President does *not* have "plenary power to provide for the health, safety, and welfare of the people..." For instance, the President does not have power to spend federal money for what he determines to be the health needs of "the people." This answer ignores both the source of the President's authority (which is limited to the executive power, that is, the power to see that the laws are carried out) and the need for all funding to be appropriated by Congress.

(C) is wrong because it incorrectly states the effect of the Tenth Amendment. The Tenth Amendment states that the powers not delegated to the federal government by the Constitution, and not prohibited to the states, are reserved to the states. The Tenth Amendment has relatively little force today as a limit on federal power. (About the only force it has as a limit on federal powers is to prevent Congress from directly forcing the states to enact or enforce federal policies.) The Amendment does not mean that the federal government may not exercise power over a "traditional state function." So the fact that vaccination has traditionally been a function handled by the states does not mean that the Tenth Amendment bars the federal government from taking action with respect to vaccinations.

(D) is wrong, because Congress does not need to authorize the creation of a temporary commission. An Advisory Commission on Vaccination is not a new federal agency — it is an advisory group, set up for a specific purpose and having a temporary existence. The President does not need congressional approval to create such an organization. Nor has Congress prohibited its creation (which if it had happened might bar creation of the Commission), because as the facts state no federal statute authorizes or prohibits this action.

CHAPTER 3

TWO LIMITS ON STATE POWER: THE DORMANT COMMERCE CLAUSE AND CONGRESSIONAL ACTION

I. THE DORMANT COMMERCE CLAUSE

A. Dormant Commerce Clause generally

1. Protectionism

Question 17: A toy manufacturer that has its headquarters and sole manufacturing plant in the state of Green developed a "Martian" toy that simulates the exploration of Mars by a remote-controlled vehicle. It accurately depicts the Martian landscape and the unmanned exploratory vehicle traversing it. The toy is of high quality, safe, durable, and has sold very well. Other toy manufacturers, all located outside Green, developed similar toys that are lower in price. These manufacturers have contracts to sell their Martian toys to outlets in Green. Although these toys are safe and durable, they depict the Martian landscape less realistically than the toys manufactured in Green. Nevertheless, because of the price difference, sales of these toys have cut severely into the sales of the Martian toys manufactured in Green. The Green legislature subsequently enacted a law "to protect the children of Green from faulty science and to protect Green toy manufacturers from unfair competition." This law forbids the sale in Green of any toy that purports to represent extraterrestrial objects and does not satisfy specified scientific criteria. The Martian toy manufactured in Green satisfies all of these criteria; none of the Martian toys of the competing manufacturers meets the requirements.

Is the Green law constitutional?

A) No, because it abrogates the obligations of the contracts between the other toy manufacturers and their Green outlets who have agreed to sell their Martian toys.

(B) No, because it imposes an undue burden on interstate commerce.

(C) Yes, because it deals only with a local matter, the sale of toys in Green stores.

(D) Yes, because the state's interest in protecting the state's children from faulty science justifies this burden on interstate commerce.

[Q7008]

Answer 17: Choice **(B)** is correct. The Commerce Clause gives Congress the power to regulate commerce among the states and, by negative implication, restricts the regulatory power of the states with respect to interstate commerce. Any state law that has a substantial effect on interstate commerce must not be protectionist (i.e., must not benefit in-state interests at the expense of out-of-state interests) or otherwise impose an undue burden on interstate commerce. A state law that discriminates against interstate commerce is protectionist unless it serves a legitimate local interest that cannot be served by nondiscriminatory legislation. By barring the sale in Green of the Martian toys manufactured in other states, the state law here has a substantial negative effect on interstate commerce. Although the law does not explicitly discriminate against the out-of-state toy manufacturers, it has a purely discriminatory effect against them, and the state has less discriminatory alternatives available to protect the legitimate interests cited in the law (e.g., better public education about the nonsensicality of extra-terrestrialism). The state law therefore violates the negative implications of the Commerce Clause.

(A) is wrong because, while it is true that the Green law is unconstitutional, this answer misstates the basis for this conclusion. The contracts clause (Article I, Section 10, Clause 1 of the Constitution) does not forbid state laws affecting contractual relations between private parties so long as they are reasonably related to a legitimate state interest. Because the courts typically defer to state regulations of private contracts as reasonable, the statute at issue here is not likely to be found unconstitutional under the contracts clause.

(C) is wrong because the fact that the matter being regulated is arguably a "local matter" is not a defense to a dormant Commerce Clause claim, if the state's form of regulation discriminates against out-of-state producers. So the fact that education is arguably a "local" state matter won't protect the obviously-protectionist statute here.

(D) is wrong because it is not a defense to protectionist legislation (i.e., legislation that intends to protect in-state economic interests at the expense of out-of-staters, or has that clear effect) that the state is also attempting to achieve some otherwise-permissible state objective. So here, although the state's interest in protecting children from faulty science is legitimate, that interest does not justify the law's intentional discrimination against out-of-staters where the state has less discriminatory alternatives available to protect that interest (e.g., better science education).

Question 18: Small retailers located in the state of Yellow were concerned about the loss of business to certain large retailers located nearby in bordering states. In an effort to deal with this concern, the legislature of Yellow enacted a statute requiring all manufacturers and wholesalers who sell goods to retailers in Yellow to do so at prices that are no higher than the lowest prices at which they sell them to retailers in any of the states that border Yellow. Several manufacturers and wholesalers who are located in states bordering Yellow and who sell their goods to retailers in those states and in Yellow bring an action in federal court to challenge the constitutionality of this statute.

Which of the following arguments offered by these plaintiffs is likelym to be most persuasive in light of applicable precedent?

The state statute

(A) deprives them of their property or liberty without due process of law.

(B) imposes an unreasonable burden on interstate commerce.

(C) deprives them of a privilege or immunity of national citizenship.

(D) denies them the equal protection of the laws.

[Q1190]

Answer 18: Choice **(B)** is correct. This is a classic case of protectionism: the in-state retailers have persuaded the legislature to strengthen the in-staters' economic position vis-a-vis out-of-state retailers (since small in-state retailers now get an advantage that small out-of-state retailers don't get, and get an unearned cost-equality with large out-of-state retailers). So out-of-state retailers are being discriminated against (treated less favorably by virtue of their out-of-state status). This sort of protectionism is virtually a per se violation of the dormant commerce clause, and is certainly an undue burden on commerce.

(A) is wrong because economic regulation that does not involve a suspect class or fundamental right (and the regulation here involves neither) will receive only mere-rationality review under the Due Process Clause, and the measure here would pass that review.

(C) is wrong because the privileges and immunities of "national" (as opposed to state) citizenship are guaranteed by the Fourteenth Amendment, Sec. 1; that P&I Clause would not protect the plaintiffs because only a few rights have been recognized as rights of national citizenship for purposes of the clause (e.g., the right to travel physically from state to state, to move from state to state, and to vote in national elections), and the right of an out-of-stater to be free of economic discrimination is not one of them. (The plaintiffs might win with an argument based on Art. *IV*'s P&I Clause, which protects against discrimination by a state against out-of-staters; however, that clause doesn't protect the rights of "national citizenship," but rather, the rights of state citizenship.)

(D) is wrong because economic regulations that do not involve a suspect or semi-suspect class or fundamental right receive only easy-to-satisfy mere-rationality review under the equal protection clause, and the statute here would pass that review (since the legislature could reasonably have believed that its citizens would fare better, overall, if small local retailers were not at a disadvantage to large out-of-state retailers).

2. Discrimination against foreign commerce

Question 19: In response to massive layoffs of employees of automobile assembly plants located in the state of Ames, the legislature of that state enacted a statute which prohibits the parking of automobiles manufactured outside of the United States in any parking lot or parking structure that is owned or operated by the state or any of its instrumentalities. This statute does not apply to parking on public streets.

Which of the following is the strongest argument with which to challenge the constitutionality of this statute?

(A) The statute imposes an undue burden on foreign commerce.

(B) The statute denies the owners of foreign-made automobiles the equal protection of the laws.

(C) The statute deprives the owners of foreign-made automobiles of liberty or property without due process of law.

(D) The statute is inconsistent with the privileges and immunities clause of the Fourteenth Amendment.

[Q2069]

Answer 19: The correct choice is **(A)**. Ames is making foreign cars materially less attractive to Ames residents, so residents are likely to buy fewer of them. Therefore, Ames is discriminating against foreign imports and in favor of U.S.-made cars. Since such a rule would clearly be held to be an undue burden on "domestic" interstate commerce if it were applied to the parking of cars made in U.S. states other than Ames, it will found to be an undue burden here, since restraints on foreign commerce are if anything scrutinized more strictly than restraints on domestic interstate commerce.

(B) is wrong because this is an economic regulation not involving a suspect class or fundamental right (there's no fundamental right to park in state-operated parking facilities), so it will be upheld as long as it's rationally related to achievement of a legitimate state objective; the measure here would meet this easy-to-satisfy test, since it's at least rational to believe that making it harder to park will cut down on the number of foreign cars sold in Ames and thus make in-state-produced cars more economically viable.

(C) is wrong, because (1) it's not clear that a person has *any* liberty or property interest in being able to park in a state-owned facility; and (2) even if there is such an interest, the interest is not "fundamental" (parking in state-owned facilities has not been held to be a fundamental right for due process purposes — only some privacy/autonomy-related rights have this status), so the measure would merely need to satisfy the easy rational-relation test, which it does.

(D) is wrong because the Fourteenth Amendment P&I Clause protects only the rights of "national citizenship," and the right to park in a state-owned facility is certainly not a right of national citizenship.

II. CONGRESSIONAL PRE-EMPTION AND CONSENT; THE SUPREMACY CLAUSE

A. The Supremacy Clause and federal pre-emption

1. Direct conflict

a. Congress forbids, state allows

Question 20: Congressional hearings determined that the use of mechanical power hammers is very dangerous to the persons using them and to persons in the vicinity of the persons using them. As a result, Congress enacted a statute prohibiting the use of mechanical power hammers on all construction projects in the United States. Subsequently, a study conducted by a private research firm concluded that nails driven by mechanical power hammers have longer-lasting joining power than hand-driven nails. After learning about this study, the city council of the city of Green enacted an amendment to its building safety code requiring the use of mechanical power hammers in the construction of all buildings intended for human habitation.

This amendment to the city of Green's building safety code is

(A) unconstitutional, because it was enacted subsequent to the federal statute.

(B) unconstitutional, because it conflicts with the provisions of the federal statute.

(C) constitutional, because the federal statute does not expressly indicate that it supersedes inconsistent state or local laws.

(D) constitutional, because the long-term safety of human habitations justifies some additional risk to the people engaged in their construction.

[Q1016]

Answer 20: The correct choice is **(B)**. This is a relatively easy case in which Congress is forbidding action X (use of mechanical power hammers) and the state is purporting to allow that very same action X. So this is about as simple a case of preemption by operation of the Supremacy Clause as could be imagined.

(A) is wrong because where federal and state rules conflict, the Supremacy Clause causes the state regulation to be invalid even if it was enacted subsequent to the federal rule.

(C) is wrong because state rules that directly conflict with federal rules are invalid even though the federal pronouncement does not expressly indicate that it supersedes inconsistent state or local laws.

(D) is wrong because whether or not a state regulation might represent a better balance of risk and reward than a directly-conflicting federal regulation, the state law must yield on account of the Supremacy Clause.

b. Conflict between aims

Question 21: The United States Department of the Interior granted the plaintiff the food and drink concession in a federal park located in the state of Purple. The plaintiff operated his concession out of federally owned facilities in the park. The federal statute authorizing the Interior Department to grant such concessions provided that the grantees would pay only a nominal rental for use of these federal facilities because of the great benefit their concessions would provide to the people of the United States.

The legislature of the state of Purple enacted a statute imposing an occupancy tax on the occupants of real estate within that state that is not subject to state real estate taxes. The statute was intended to equalize the state tax burden on such occupants with that on people occupying real estate that is subject to state real estate taxes. Pursuant to that statute, the Purple Department of Revenue attempted to collect the state occupancy tax from the plaintiff because the federal facilities occupied by the plaintiff were not subject to state real estate taxes. The plaintiff sued to invalidate the state occupancy tax as applied to him.

The strongest ground upon which the plaintiff could challenge the occupancy tax is that it violates the

(A) commerce clause by unduly burdening the interstate tourist trade.

(B) privileges and immunities clause of the Fourteenth Amendment by interfering with the fundamental right to do business on federal property.

(C) equal protection of the laws clause of the Fourteenth Amendment because the tax treats him less favorably than federal concessionaires in other states who do not have to pay such occupancy taxes.

(D) supremacy clause of Article VI and the federal statute authorizing such concessions.

[Q2150]

Answer 21: Choice **(D)** is correct. The federal concession statute, by requiring a nominal rental on account of the great public benefit from concessions, shows a federal intent to keep the total occupancy costs for concessionaires low. The state occupancy tax has the effect (and purpose) of making occupancy costs higher for the affected taxpayers than it would otherwise be. This fact is coupled with the fact that the state is singling out taxpayers on non-state-taxed property, including federally-owned property, so the interference with federal interests is especially acute. Therefore, a court might well hold that the state law so undermines the federal purposes as to be invalid under the Supremacy Clause. The court would not *necessarily* reach this conclusion, but this is the most powerful of the four arguments.

(A) is wrong because the occupancy tax does not discriminate against interstate commerce (since the effect on tourists from inside Purple is the same as on out-of-state tourists), and it is unlikely that subjecting the plaintiff to the same overall level of overall taxation as businesses located in state-taxable facilities would be found to be an "undue burden."

(B) is wrong because the Fourteenth Amendment's Privileges and Immunities Clause protects only certain very limited rights of "national citizenship" (mostly the right to travel from state to state), and the Clause has never been interpreted to protect a "fundamental right to do business on federal property." (It's true that the P&I Clause of Art. *IV* protects the fundamental right to pursue one's business or profession, but the examiners have tried to trick you here by using the Fourteenth Amendment's P&I Clause, not the Art. IV Clause.)

(C) is wrong because the Fourteenth Amendment Equal Protection Clause protects only against a given state's unfair classification of multiple persons, not against one state's treating a person less favorably than other states treat similarly-situated persons. (Also, any classification being done by Purple here does not involve a suspect or semi-suspect class or a fundamental right, so the classification merely has to be rationally related to the achievement of a legitimate state objective, and the occupancy tax here meets this easy-to-satisfy standard.)

Question 22: Road Lines is an interstate bus company operating in a five-state area. A federal statute authorizes the Interstate Commerce Commission (ICC) to permit interstate carriers to discontinue entirely any unprofitable route. Road Lines applied to the ICC for permission to drop a very unprofitable route through the sparsely populated Shaley Mountains. The ICC granted that permission even though Road Lines provided the only public transportation into the region.

Foley is the owner of a mountain resort in the Shaley Mountains, whose customers usually arrived on vehicles operated by Road Lines. After exhausting all available federal administrative remedies, Foley filed suit against Road Lines in the trial court of the state in which the Shaley Mountains are located to enjoin the discontinuance by Road Lines of its service to that area. Foley alleged that the discontinuance of service by Road Lines would violate a statute of that state prohibiting common carriers of persons from abandoning service to communities having no alternate form of public transportation.

The state court should

(A) dismiss the action, because Foley lacks standing to sue.

(B) direct the removal of the case to federal court, because this suit involves a substantial federal question.

(C) hear the case on its merits and decide for Foley because, on these facts, a federal agency is interfering with essential state functions.

(D) hear the case on its merits and decide for Road Lines, because a valid federal law preempts the state statute on which Foley relies.

dards. WeTest sues appropriate Magenta officials in federal court claiming that Magenta may not constitutionally exclude WeTest from performing the required radon tests in Magenta.

In this suit, the court will probably rule in favor of

(A) WeTest, because the full faith and credit clause of the Constitution requires Magenta to respect and give effect to the action of the EPA in including WeTest on its list of testers that use reasonably accurate methods.

(B) WeTest, because the supremacy clause of the Constitution requires Magenta to respect and give effect to the action of the EPA in including WeTest on its list of testers that use reasonably accurate methods.

(C) Magenta, because the federal statute and the action of the EPA in including WeTest on its list of testers that use reasonably accurate methods are not inconsistent with the more rigorous Magenta licensing requirement, and that requirement is reasonably related to a legitimate public interest.

(D) Magenta, because radon exposure is limited to basement areas, which, by their very nature, cannot move in interstate commerce.

[Q2170]

Answer 24: The correct choice is **(C)**. The question, of course, is whether the federal regulation on radon detectors preempts the state regulation. The issue is always one of intent: if the federal government did not intend to preempt the state, or to occupy the entire field, then the state regulation will survive if it does not violate any independent constitutional prohibition. Here, there are strong clues that neither Congress nor the EPA intended to displace more-rigorous state regulation of radar detection: the federal government has not chosen to actually license radon testers, and the EPA is merely purporting to give useful information to the public, not to "regulate." Furthermore, it appears that a radon tester can comply simultaneously with both the federal "reasonably accurate" standard and the more-rigorous Magenta standard. All of this justifies the conclusion that the EPA's maintenance of its reasonably-accurate-methods list was not intended to displace more-rigorous state licensing standards.

(A) is wrong because (among other reasons) the Full Faith and Credit Clause applies only to require a state to honor the statutes and judgments of *another state*, not those of the federal government.

(B) is wrong because, for the reasons described above, the EPA's list was not intended to displace or preempt more-rigorous state licensing methods, so the supremacy clause never came into action.

(D) is wrong because the fact that what is being regulated cannot "move in interstate commerce" does not dispose of the issue of whether federal regulation has preempted the state regulation. For instance, Congress could have (but did not) authorized the EPA to enact radon-testing regulations that would displace any more-stringent state regulation; in doing so Congress could have used its commerce power based on the fact that radon *detectors* move in or affect interstate commerce even though the basement areas being measured do not themselves move in interstate commerce.

B. Consent by Congress

Question 25: A state legislature conducted an investigation into a series of fatal accidents in the state involving commercial trucks with trailer exteriors made of polished aluminum. The investigation revealed that the sun's glare off of these trucks blinded the drivers of other vehicles. The state's legislature then enacted a law prohibiting commercial trucks with polished aluminum trailer exteriors from traveling on the state's highways.

Litigation over the state law resulted in a final decision by the United States Supreme Court that the law impermissibly burdened interstate commerce and, therefore, was unconstitutional. Congress later enacted a statute permitting any state to enact a law regulating the degree of light reflectiveness of the exteriors of commercial trucks using the state's highways.

Is this federal statute constitutional?

(A) No, because the U.S. Supreme Court has already determined that state laws of this type impermissibly burden interstate commerce.

(B) No, because Article III vests the judicial power in the federal courts, the essence of judicial power is the ability to render a final judgment, and this statute overrules a final judgment of the federal Supreme Court.

(C) Yes, because Article I, Section 8 grants Congress authority to enact statutes authorizing states to impose burdens on interstate commerce that would otherwise be prohibited.

(D) Yes, because Article I, Section 8 grants Congress authority to enact statutes for the general welfare, and Congress could reasonably believe that state laws regulating the light reflectiveness of the exteriors of trucks promote the general welfare.

[QA047]

Answer 25: Choice **(C)** is correct. Congress has the power to consent to state conduct that would, in the absence of congressional consent, violate the dormant commerce clause. That's what has happened here. And the usual rule prohibiting Congress from enacting a statute overruling a constitutional decision of the U.S. Supreme Court does not apply here: Congress is not "overruling" the Court's judgment, it's simply changing the law for future cases, which is an action that is within the legislative power of Congress and that doesn't encroach on the Court's power to decide cases.

(A) is wrong because this is one area in which Congress may reverse the impact of prior Supreme Court decisions. In many areas of constitutional law (e.g., the meaning of the equal protection, due process and free speech guarantees), Congress does not have power to prospectively overrule decisions of the Supreme Court. But that is not true of the Court's decisions in some other areas. In particular, Congress has the power to authorize state conduct that would otherwise violate the dormant commerce clause, and the fact that the Supreme Court has already held that particular state conduct violates the dormant commerce clause does not negate this power.

(B) is wrong because it mischaracterizes what the statute did. The congressional statute permitting any state to regulate the degree of light reflectiveness of the exteriors of trucks using the state's highways did not overrule the U.S. Supreme Court's judgment. If the Court had, for example, awarded damages or attorney's fees to the prevailing party in that earlier suit, those awards would remain in effect after Congress enacted the statute, and Congress would not have had the power to reverse those litigant-specific outcomes. But here, Congress's statute simply changed the law for *future cases*, which is an action that is within the legislative power of Congress and that does not encroach on the Court's judicial power to decide cases within its jurisdiction.

(D) is wrong because it relies on a non-existent source of congressional power. While the Constitution gives Congress the power to *appropriate money* to promote the general welfare of the United States (i.e., to "tax and spend" for the general welfare), it does not give Congress the power generally to enact *regulatory*-type statutes on the basis that they promote the general welfare. Since there is no taxing or spending being done by the statute here, the concept of "general welfare" is irrelevant.

Question 26: A federal statute provides that the cities in which certain specified airports are located may regulate the rates and services of all limousines that serve those airports, without regard to the origin or destination of the passengers who use the limousines.

The cities of Redville and Greenville are located adjacent to each other in different states. The airport serving both of them is located in Redville and is one of those airports specified in the federal statute. The Redville City Council has adopted a rule that requires any limousines serving the airport to charge only the rates authorized by the Redville City Council.

Airline Limousine Service has a lucrative business transporting passengers between Greenville and the airport in Redville, at much lower rates than those required by the Redville City Council. It transports passengers in interstate traffic only; it does not provide local service within Redville. The new rule adopted by the Redville City Council will require Airline Limousine Service to charge the same rates as limousines operating only in Redville.

Must Airline Limousine Service comply with the new rule of the Redville City Council?

(A) Yes, because the airport is located in Redville and, therefore, its city council has exclusive regulatory authority over all transportation to and from the airport.

(B) Yes, because Congress has authorized this form of regulation by Redville and, therefore, removed any constitutional impediments to it that may have otherwise existed.

(C) No, because the rule would arbitrarily destroy a lucrative existing business and, therefore, would amount to a taking without just compensation.

(D) No, because Airline Limousine Service is engaged in interstate commerce and this rule is an undue burden on that commerce.

[Q3079]

Answer 26: The correct choice is **(B)**. The Redville rule, by requiring higher limo prices for interstate trips than would be set by the market, might well be an undue burden on interstate commerce (and thus a violation of the dormant Commerce Clause) if there were no federal legislation on the subject. But Congress has the power to allow state regulation that would otherwise violate the dormant Commerce Clause, and that's what happened here: Congress gave the city containing the airport the right to set limo rates without respect to the rates' effect on commerce, so there is no dormant Commerce Clause problem.

(A) is wrong because it incorrectly explains the correct result. If Congress had not specifically allowed the city in which any specified airport is located to regulate limos serving that city, Redville would be acting unconstitutionally by burdening interstate commerce. That is, as a general principle it is not correct to say that a city has exclusive regulatory authority over all transportation to and from an airport located within the city. (Under the dormant commerce clause, no city or state may intentionally discriminate against, or unduly burden, interstate commerce, even if that commerce relates to a facility located within the city or state that's doing the regulating.) Only the special congressional authorization validates the Redville regulation.

(C) is wrong because what Redville is doing here is regulating, not "taking." Only if a regulation destroys all economic value of a business will it be deemed to be a Fifth Amendment "taking" for which compensation must be paid. And there's no evidence here that the regulation here will destroy all economic value of the plaintiff's business. Furthermore, even in the exceptionally unlikely event that a court would conclude that there had been a taking, the proper remedy would be an order that Redville pay "just compensation," not a decree holding the regulation itself invalid.

(D) is wrong because Congress has authorized the regulation in question. If Congress had not expressly authorized the type of regulation at issue here (limo rates for airport traffic, imposed by the city where the airport is located), this choice would likely be correct, because the uniform-rate regulation probably would unduly burden (and discriminate against) out-of-state-based limo companies. But Congress always has the power to authorize what would otherwise be a violation of dormant-commerce-clause principles, and that's what it has done here.

Question 27: The United States Congress enacted a federal statute providing that any state may "require labeling to show the state or other geographic origin of citrus fruit that is imported into the receiving state." Pursuant to the federal statute, a state that produced large quantities of citrus fruit enacted a law requiring all citrus fruit imported into the state to be stamped with a two-letter postal abbreviation signifying the state of the fruit's origin. The law did not impose any such requirement for citrus fruit grown within the state. When it adopted the law, the state legislature declared that its purpose was to reduce the risks of infection of local citrus crops by itinerant diseases that have been found to attack citrus fruit. A national association of citrus growers sued to have the state law declared unconstitutional. The association claims that the law is prohibited by the negative implications of the commerce clause of the Constitution.

Which of the following is the best argument in favor of the state's effort to have this lawsuit dismissed?

(A) Any burden on interstate commerce imposed by the state law is outweighed by a legitimate state interest.

(B) Congress has the authority to authorize specified state regulations that would otherwise be prohibited by the negative implications of the commerce clause, and it has done so in this situation.

(C) The state law does not discriminate against out-of-state citrus growers or producers.

(D) The state law furthers a legitimate state interest, the burden it imposes on interstate commerce is only incidental, and the state's interest cannot be satisfied by other means that are less burdensome to interstate commerce.

[Q7084]

Answer 27: Choice **(B)** is correct. In the absence of congressional action, the state rule here probably would be a violation of the dormant Commerce Clause (what the question calls the "negative implications of the commerce clause"), because it discriminates against out-of-state growers. But Congress may use its commerce power to permit states to discriminate against interstate commerce. The federal statute here explicitly authorizes states to enact state-of-origin labeling requirements on imported citrus fruit.

(A) is incorrect, because the balancing argument would work only if: (1) Congress had not enacted a statute authorizing the state regulation at issue; and (2) the state law did not discriminate against interstate commerce. In this case, however, neither of these conditions is satisfied: Congress *has* authorized state-of-origin labeling requirements on imported citrus fruit, and the state law *is* discriminatory.

(C) is incorrect, because the state law *does* discriminate against out-of-state citrus growers, in that the law requires that all citrus fruit "imported" into the state be stamped with the state of origin, while the law imposes no such requirement on citrus fruit grown within the state.

(D) is incorrect, because although this argument correctly paraphrases the burden on the state to justify a law that discriminates against interstate commerce, the argument would be less likely to succeed than the "Congress authorized it" argument: in the absence of congressional authorization, the burden on a state to justify its discriminatory regulation is a heavy one, and states only rarely succeed in carrying it. Here, the availability of less-discriminatory alternatives (e.g., requiring in-state growers, not just out-of-staters, to stamp the state's two-letter code on the fruit) makes it unlikely that the state would win with this argument.

CHAPTER 4

INTERGOVERNMENTAL IMMUNITIES; INTERSTATE RELATIONS

I. TAX AND REGULATORY IMMUNITIES

A. Several types of immunities

1. Federal immunity from state regulation

a. Applies to generally-applicable rules

Question 28: A federally owned and operated office building in the state of Red is heated with a new, pollution-free heating system. However, in the coldest season of the year, this new system is sometimes insufficient to supply adequate heat to the building. The appropriation statute providing the money for construction of the new heating system permitted use of the old, pollution-generating system when necessary to supply additional heat. When the old heating system operates (only about two days in any year), the smokestack of the building emits smoke that exceeds the state of Red's pollution-control standards.

May the operators of the federal office building be prosecuted successfully by Red authorities for violating that state's pollution control standards?

(A) Yes, because the regulation of pollution is a legitimate state police power concern.

(B) Yes, because the regulation of pollution is a joint concern of the federal government and the state and, therefore, both of them may regulate conduct causing pollution.

(C) No, because the operations of the federal government are immune from state regulation in the absence of federal consent.

(D) No, because the violations of the state pollution-control standards involved here are so *de minimis* that they are beyond the legitimate reach of state law.

[Q1195]

Answer 28: Choice **(C)** is correct. The operations of the federal government are indeed immune from state regulation, no matter how reasonable the state regulation, and even though the regulation is a generally-applicable one that treats the federal government no differently than anyone else. Since the office building is owned by and operated by the federal government, this regulatory immunity applies.

(A) is wrong, because even though the regulation of pollution may be a legitimate state police power concern, that regulation must give way to federal regulatory immunity.

(B) is wrong because, even if regulation of pollution is a joint concern of the federal and state governments, and even though both governments can regulate private parties (assuming that the state regulation is not inconsistent with the federal regulation), it does not follow that the state can regulate the federal government — under the principles of regulatory immunity, the state cannot do so.

(D) is wrong because there is no "de minimis" exception to the principle that states may regulate pursuant to their inherent police power. (The sole problem here is the federal immunity from regulation, which applies whether the asserted violation of the state's regulation is de minimis or not.)

Question 29: The United States Department of Energy regularly transports nuclear materials through Centerville on the way to a nuclear weapons processing plant it operates in a nearby state. The city of Centerville recently adopted an ordinance prohibiting the transportation of any nuclear materials in or through the city. The ordinance declares that its purpose is to protect the health and safety of the residents of that city.

May the Department of Energy continue to transport these nuclear materials through the city of Centerville?

(A) No, because the ordinance is rationally related to the public health and safety of Centerville residents.

(B) No, because the Tenth Amendment reserves to the states certain unenumerated sovereign powers.

(C) Yes, because the Department of Energy is a federal agency engaged in a lawful federal function and, therefore, its activities may not be regulated by a local government without the consent of Congress.

(D) Yes, because the ordinance enacted by Centerville is invalid because it denies persons transporting such materials the equal protection of the laws.

[Q2049]

Answer 29: Choice **(C)** is correct — the federal government, including the operations of federal agencies, are essentially immune from state regulation. Notice that the answer does not use the word "immunity" — it's up to you to recognize that when the choice says "may not be regulated," what's being referred to is the concept of immunity.

(A) is incorrect, because of federal immunity; note that if there were no federal immunity involved (e.g., the entity being regulated was a private company pursuing its own interests), this choice would be correct, at least if the regulation were challenged on equal protection grounds.

(B) is wrong because the Tenth Amendment has no relevance here. The Tenth Amendment does not restrict the powers of the federal government as long as the latter is not purporting to require the state to enact laws or regulations. Here, the Dept. of Energy isn't requiring the state to enact a federal regulatory program — the DOE is merely pursuing its own regulatory program. And the Tenth Amendment doesn't limit DOE's ability to do that.

(D) is wrong because the equal protection clause would not invalidate this ordinance. The ordinance is an economic regulation, and clearly satisfies the applicable rational-basis test (see the discussion of Choice (A) above). It's only federal immunity from state regulation that causes the ordinance not to be enforceable against the DOE's activities.

II.   THE FULL FAITH AND CREDIT CLAUSE

A. How tested on the MBE

1.   Effect of Clause

a.   Collection of money judgments

Question 30: The state of Red sent three of its employees to a city located in the state of Blue to consult with a chemical laboratory there about matters of state business. While in the course of their employment, the three employees of Red negligently released into local Blue waterways some of the chemical samples they had received from the laboratory in Blue.

Persons in Blue injured by the release of the chemicals sued the three Red state employees and the state of Red in Blue state courts for the damages they suffered. After a trial in which all of the defendants admitted jurisdiction of the Blue state court and fully participated, plaintiffs received a judgment against all of the defendants for $5 million, which became final.

Subsequently, plaintiffs sought to enforce their Blue state court judgment by commencing a proper proceeding in an appropriate court of Red. In that enforcement proceeding, the state of Red argued, as it had done unsuccessfully in the earlier action in Blue state court, that its liability is limited by a law of Red to $100,000 in any tort case. Because the three individual employees of Red are able to pay only $50,000 of the judgment, the only way the injured persons can fully satisfy their Blue state court judgment is from the funds of the state of Red.

Can the injured persons recover the full balance of their Blue state court judgment from the state of Red in the enforcement proceeding they filed in a court of Red?

(A) Yes, because the final judgment of the Blue court is entitled to full faith and credit in the courts of Red.

(B) Yes, because a limitation on damage awards against Red for tortious actions of its agents would violate the equal protection clause of the Fourteenth Amendment.

(C) No, because the Tenth Amendment preserves the right of a state to have its courts enforce the state's public policy limiting its tort liability.

(D) No, because the employees of Red were negligent and, therefore, their actions were not authorized by the state of Red.

[Q3151]

Answer 30: Choice **(A)** is correct. The Blue court issued a valid judgment against the plaintiffs. Therefore, the Red state court was required by the Full Faith and Credit Clause to enforce that judgment, even though the only solvent defendant in the Blue proceeding is the state of Red itself. The constitutional requirement of Full Faith and Credit does not recognize any exception just because the state in which enforcement is sought happens to itself be the defendant against which the original judgment was issued. (By the way, it's important that all the defendants admitted jurisdiction in the original Blue proceedings — if the Blue courts had not had jurisdiction, the defendants could make a "collateral attack" on the original judgment in Red court, and Full Faith and Credit would not have applied.)

(B) is wrong because it gives an incorrect reason for the current result. A state may, without violating the equal protection clause, cap (or even abolish entirely) its liability for torts by its employees or agents. The correct reason Red must pay the judgment is as given in (A).

(C) is wrong because (1) although a state does, as a general rule, have the right to enforce a public policy limiting its tort liability, this right does not derive from the Tenth Amendment; and (2) in any event, a state's obligation to enforce an out-of-state judgment under the Full Faith and Credit clause takes priority over the state's own public policy, at least where the out-of-state judgment came after all defendants had a full and fair opportunity to litigate in a court that had jurisdiction over them.

(D) is wrong because the Red courts must enforce the Blue court's judgment, regardless of whether a Red court would have reached the same conclusion on the merits as the Blue court did about whether Red as employer is liable for these torts by its agents.

b.   First state's error of law

Question 31: A man bought an antique car from a car dealer in State A. Under State A law, a person who buys from such a dealer acquires good title, even if the property was stolen from a previous owner. The man showed the car at an antique car show in State B. A woman recognized the car as having been stolen from her. Under State B law, a person whose property is stolen may reclaim it, even if the current possessor is an innocent purchaser. The woman sued the man in a State B court to reclaim the car. The man defended, claiming that he had good title under the law of State A. Nevertheless, the State B court applied State B law, and the woman prevailed. The man did not appeal. The sheriff gave the woman possession of the car. Several months later, the woman drove the car to State A. The man brought a new suit against the woman, claiming that the State B court in the prior suit should have applied the State A law, which protected innocent purchasers. The woman appeared and moved to dismiss the suit.

What should the State A court do?

(A) Apply the federal law of sale of goods, because the car has moved in interstate commerce.

(B) Apply the State A law, because the car is currently located in State A.

(C) Dismiss the suit, because the State A court must give full faith and credit to the State B judgment.

(D) Remove the case to federal court, because the car has moved in interstate commerce, and therefore the case raises a federal question.

[Q7051]

Answer 31: Choice **(C)** is correct. The Full Faith & Credit (FF&C) clause prohibits state courts from re-litigating cases in which the courts of another state have rendered final judgment. Even if the first court should have applied the second court's laws under standard conflict rules, the FF&C clause bars the second court from re-hearing the case. (If the State B courts had not had jurisdiction over the man, and the jurisdiction issue had not been litigated or waived, the FF&C clause might not bar the State A courts from hearing the new suit. But the facts tell us that the man "defended" on the merits, thus waiving any claim he might have had that the State B courts lacked jurisdiction over him.) Accordingly, the court in State A was required to dismiss the suit.

(A) is incorrect, because the FF&C clause prevents the court in State A from relitigating the merits, and the fact that the woman drove the car to State A has no effect on the constitutional analysis.

(B) is, similarly, wrong because the location of the car has no effect on the constitutional analysis.

(D) is wrong because the movement of the car across state lines did not create a federal question.

THE DUE PROCESS CLAUSE

I. SUBSTANTIVE DUE PROCESS — ECONOMIC AND SOCIAL WELFARE REGULATION

A. Economic and social-welfare regulation

1. Easy to satisfy

Question 32: A state statute requires each insurance company that offers burglary insurance policies in the state to charge a uniform rate for such insurance to all of its customers residing within the same county in that state. So long as it complies with this requirement, a company is free to charge whatever rate the market will bear for its burglary insurance policies.

An insurance company located in the state files suit in federal district court against appropriate state officials to challenge this statute on constitutional grounds. The insurance company wishes to charge customers residing within the same county in the state rates for burglary insurance policies that will vary because they would be based on the specific nature of the customer's business, on its precise location, and on its past claims record.

In this suit, the court should

(A) hold the statute unconstitutional, because the statute deprives the insurance company of its liberty or property without due process of law.

(B) hold the statute unconstitutional, because the statute imposes an undue burden on interstate commerce.

(C) hold the statute constitutional, because the statute is a reasonable exercise of the state's police power.

(D) abstain from ruling on the merits of this case until the state courts have had an opportunity to pass on the constitutionality of this state statute.

[Q2008]

Answer 32: Choice **(C)** is correct. This is a classic illustration of a state regulation in the economic or social-welfare area, where no fundamental right is involved. (Insurers don't have a fundamental right to adopt any particular pricing mechanism.) Since the "one price for all" scheme is rationally related to achieving one or more legitimate state objectives (e.g., promoting a sense of fairness and non-discrimination among insurance customers living in a particular county, or avoiding race-based redlining), the scheme does not violate the insurer's due process rights.

(A) is wrong for the same reason (C) is right — the company may have a due process right not to be irrationally deprived of its desired pricing mechanism, but the requirement of uniform pricing here is not irrational.

(B) is wrong, because the statute does not unduly burden interstate commerce (it only applies to policies written in-state, and it does not discriminate against out-of-state insurers).

(D) is wrong because federal courts do not have a duty to abstain from passing on the case until the state courts have had an opportunity to pass on the constitutionality of this state statute. When a litigant believes that a state statute violates the federal constitution, the litigant may sue immediately in federal court for a determination that this is so, as long as the requirements of justiciability (e.g., ripeness, actual injury to the plaintiff, etc.) are met. In other words, there is no sense in which state courts get "first shot" to determine the federal constitutionality of a state statute.

II. SUBSTANTIVE DUE PROCESS — REGULATIONS AFFECTING FUNDAMENTAL RIGHTS

A. Abortion

1. Consent

a. Parental consent

i. Emancipation or maturity

Question 33: A state statute requires, without exception, that a woman under the age of 18 notify one of her parents at least 48 hours before having an abortion. A proper lawsuit challenges the constitutionality of this state statute.

In that suit, should the court uphold the constitutionality of the statute?

(A) No, because a 48-hour waiting period is excessively long and, therefore, it imposes an undue burden on a woman's right to procure an abortion.

(B) No, because the state law does not provide a bypass procedure that would allow a court to authorize a minor to obtain an abortion without prior parental notification under appropriate circumstances.

(C) Yes, because parents' rights to supervise their minor daughter's health care outweighs any individual right she may have.

(D) Yes, because such parental notification and waiting-period requirements do not impose an undue burden on a minor's right to procure an abortion.

[Q7056]

Answer 33: Choice **(B)** is correct. The Supreme Court has held that parental notification requirements constitute an undue burden on the minor's right to abortion, and thus violate the minor's due substantive right to due process, unless there is a satisfactory judicial bypass procedure. Such a procedure must allow a court to approve an abortion for a minor without parental notification if the court finds either that: (1) the minor is sufficiently mature and informed to make an independent decision to obtain an abortion; or (2) the abortion would be in the minor's best interest. Because no such bypass procedure is included in the statute at issue, the court will hold the statute unconstitutional.

(A) is wrong because although it is true that the statute at issue is unconstitutional, this answer misstates the basis for this conclusion — the Supreme Court has held that a short waiting period does not constitute an undue burden on a woman's right to an abortion.

(C) is incorrect, because the rights of parents to supervise the health care of their minor children do not always prevail over the individual rights of their children — as discussed above, the Court has held that parental notification requirements violate a minor's right to an abortion unless there is a satisfactory judicial bypass procedure, which is not included in the statute at issue.

(D) is incorrect, because the Court has held that parental notification requirements are an undue burden, and violate a minor's right to an abortion, unless there is a satisfactory judicial bypass procedure.

2. Public funding

Question 34: A state statute prohibits the use of state-owned or state-operated facilities for the performance of abortions that are not "necessary to save the life of the mother." That statute also prohibits state employees from performing any such abortions during the hours they are employed by the state.

A woman was in her second month of pregnancy. She sought an abortion at a state-owned and state-operated hospital. The woman did not claim that the requested abortion was necessary to save her life. The officials in charge of the hospital refused to perform the requested abortion solely on the basis of the state statute. The woman immediately filed suit against those officials in an appropriate federal district court. She challenged the constitutionality of the state statute and requested the court to order the hospital to perform the abortion she sought. In this case, the court will probably hold that the state statute is

(A) unconstitutional, because a limit on the availability of abortions performed by state employees or in state-owned or state-operated facilities to situations in which it is necessary to save the life of the mother impermissibly interferes with the fundamental right of the woman to decide whether to have a child.

(B) unconstitutional, because it impermissibly discriminates against poor persons who cannot afford to pay for abortions in privately owned and operated facilities and against persons who live far away from privately owned and operated abortion clinics.

(C) constitutional, because it does not prohibit a woman from having an abortion or penalize her for doing so, it is rationally related to the legitimate governmental goal of encouraging childbirth, and it does not unduly burden the voluntary performance of abortions by private physicians in private facilities.

(D) constitutional, because the use of state-owned or state-operated facilities and access to the services of state employees are privileges and not rights and, therefore, a state may condition them on any basis it chooses.

[Q2162]

Answer 34: Choice **(C)** is correct. The Court held in *Webster v. Reproductive Health Services* (1989) that a state could constitutionally forbid the use of all public facilities and publicly-employed staff in abortions, without thereby violating the substantive due process right to abortion. If the state forbade all facilities in the state — public or private — from performing abortions, that would be an unconstitutional "undue burden" on abortion, but the availability of private-facility abortions here prevents an undue burden from occurring. And the fact that the state here is allowing the use of public facilities for those abortions necessary to save the life of the mother makes it even more clear that the regulation is constitutional. (Probably under *Webster* such an exception is not even required.)

(A) is wrong because the Court has held (in *Webster*, supra) that the availability of private-facility abortions means that a ban on the use of public facilities does not impermissibly interfere with the right of abortion.

(B) is wrong because the Court has held (in *Harris v. McRae* (1980)) that government's refusal to fund abortions for patients who cannot afford them does not constitute an interference with the constitutionally-protected right to abortion.

(D) is wrong because the Court no longer uses the privilege/right distinction in deciding cases involving the exercise of the important constitutional interests, and it is certainly not the case that the state may condition access to public facilities for an abortion "on any basis it chooses." (For instance, the state could not say that it will fund abortions at state-owned facilities for white women but not black women.)

III. PROCEDURAL DUE PROCESS

A. Process required

1. Time for hearing

> **Question 35:** A state statute declares that after five years of continuous service in their positions all state employees, including faculty members at the state university, are entitled to retain their positions during "good behavior." The statute also contains a number of procedural provisions. Any state employee who is dismissed after that five-year period must be given reasons for the dismissal before it takes effect. In addition, such an employee must, upon request, be granted a post-dismissal hearing before an administrative board to seek reinstatement and back pay. The statute precludes any other hearing or opportunity to respond to the charges. That post-dismissal hearing must occur within six months after the dismissal takes effect. The burden of proof at such a hearing is on the state, and the board may uphold the dismissal only if it is supported by a preponderance of the evidence. An employee who is dissatisfied with a decision of the board after a hearing may appeal its decision to the state courts. The provisions of this statute are inseverable.
>
> A teacher who had been employed continuously for seven years as a faculty member at the state university was dismissed. A week before the dismissal took effect, she was informed that she was being dismissed because of a charge that she accepted a bribe from a student in return for raising the student's final grade in her course. At that time she requested an immediate hearing to contest the propriety of her dismissal.
>
> Three months after her dismissal, she was granted a hearing before the state administrative board. The board upheld her dismissal, finding that the charge against her was supported by a preponderance of the evidence presented at the hearing.
>
> The faculty member did not appeal the decision of the state administrative board to the state courts. Instead, she sought a declaratory judgment in federal district court to the effect that the state statute prescribing the procedures for her dismissal is unconstitutional.
>
> In this case, the federal district court should
>
> (A) dismiss the suit, because a claim that a state statute is unconstitutional is not ripe for adjudication by a federal court until all judicial remedies in state courts provided for by state law have been exhausted.
>
> (B) hold the statute unconstitutional, because the due process clause of the Fourteenth Amendment requires a state to demonstrate beyond a reasonable doubt the facts constituting good cause for termination of a state employee.
>
> (C) hold the statute unconstitutional, because a state may not ordinarily deprive an employee of a property interest in a job without giving the employee an opportunity for some kind of predismissal hearing to respond to the charges against that employee.

(D) hold the statute constitutional, because the due process clause of the Fourteenth Amendment entitles state employees who have a right to their jobs during good behavior only to a statement of reasons for their dismissal and an opportunity for a post-dismissal hearing.

[Q1152]

Answer 35: Choice **(C)** is correct. Since the government had previously agreed that the teacher could only be fired if she were shown not to have had "good behavior," she had a due process "property" interest in maintaining her job. The Supreme Court has held that once a person has a property interest in a job or benefit, only the courts, not the government, may prescribe the procedures that are to be used to terminate that job or benefit. So the fact that the statute provides only for a post-discharge hearing does not mean that this is all the teacher is due. Instead, the Court has held that the job holder is entitled to a hearing before the termination (or at least before the termination of salary). *Cleveland Bd. of Ed. v. Loudermill* (1985). Since the statute here did not give the teacher such a pre-termination hearing, the statute was unconstitutional. And the statute did not get saved by the government's holding a hearing three months after the termination.

(A) is wrong because it is not true that a claim that a state statute is unconstitutional is not ripe until all state-court remedies have been exhausted. When a litigant believes that a state statute violates the federal constitution, the litigant may sue immediately in federal court for a determination that this is so, as long as the requirements of justiciability are met. And although it's true that one of the requirements of justiciability is that the case be "ripe," ripeness merely means that the plaintiff has already suffered, or imminently faces, actual injury.

(B) is wrong for at least two reasons: (1) not all state employees have the right not to be dismissed except for good cause (and this choice implies that all of them do); and (2) even if an employee such as the teacher here had a right not to be dismissed except for good cause, the burden of proof on the government would be just a preponderance-of-the-evidence standard, not the hard-to-satisfy "beyond a reasonable doubt" standard.

(D) is wrong because the Supreme Court has held that, where a state employee has a right to hold her job during good behavior, the employee is entitled not only to a pre-dismissal statement of reasons but a pre-dismissal hearing (and the fact that the statute provides only for a post-dismissal hearing does not change the constitutional requirement of a pre-dismissal one). Cf. *Loudermill, supra.*

CHAPTER 6

EQUAL PROTECTION

I. ECONOMIC AND SOCIAL LAWS — THE "MERE RATIONALITY" TEST

A. Non-suspect, non-fundamental rights (economic and social legislation)

1. "Grandfather clause" as rational classification

Question 36: A city has had a severe traffic problem on its streets. As a result, it enacted an ordinance prohibiting all sales to the public of food or other items by persons selling directly from trucks, cars, or other vehicles located on city streets. The ordinance included an inseverable grandfather provision exempting from its prohibition vendors who, for 20 years or more, have continuously sold food or other items from such vehicles located on the streets of the city.

A retail ice cream vendor qualifies for this exemption and is the only food vendor that does. A yogurt company is a business similar to the ice cream company, but the yogurt company has been selling to the public directly from trucks located on the streets of the city only for the past ten years. The yogurt company filed suit in an appropriate federal district court to enjoin enforcement of this ordinance on the ground that it denies the yogurt company the equal protection of the laws.

In this case, the court will probably rule that the ordinance is

(A) constitutional, because it is narrowly tailored to implement the city's compelling interest in reducing traffic congestion and, therefore, satisfies the strict scrutiny test applicable to such cases.

(B) constitutional, because its validity is governed by the rational basis test, and the courts consistently defer to economic choices embodied in such legislation if they are even plausibly justifiable.

(C) unconstitutional, because the nexus between the legitimate purpose of the ordinance and the conduct it prohibits is so tenuous and its provisions are so underinclusive that the ordinance fails to satisfy the substantial relationship test applicable to such cases.

(D) unconstitutional, because economic benefits or burdens imposed by legislatures on the basis of grandfather provisions have consistently been declared invalid by courts as per se violations of the equal protection clause of the Fourteenth Amendment.

[Q1021]

Answer 36: Choice **(B)** is correct. The city here is engaging in economic regulation, and no suspect class or fundamental right is involved. The "even plausibly justifiable" standard is a good summary of the extreme deference that courts give to government choices in the economic-regulatory area where no suspect class or fundamental right is at issue. Grandfather schemes in which people with longtime track records of pursuing an activity are treated more favorably than newcomers to that activity are a good illustration of classifications that are very likely to be upheld.

(A) is wrong because it incorrectly applies strict scrutiny; strict scrutiny would be appropriate for a regulation that intentionally disfavored a suspect class (e.g., persons of a particular race) or substantially impaired a fundamental right (e.g., the right to vote), but the classification here does not do either of these things.

(C) is wrong because the grandfather scheme here would not be found to be so "tenuous" or "underinclusive" as to fail the easy-to-satisfy rational-basis test.

(D) is wrong as a statement of law; so long as no suspect class or fundamental right is impaired, grandfather clauses are usually found valid, and are certainly not "per se violations" of equal protection.

2. **Non-suspect classes**

a. **Status as convicted criminal**

Question 37: A city zoning ordinance requires anyone who proposes to operate a group home to obtain a special use permit from the city zoning board. The zoning ordinance defines a group home as a residence in which four or more unrelated adults reside. An individual applied for a special use permit to operate a group home for convicts during their transition from serving prison sentences to their release on parole. Although the proposed group home met all of the requirements for the special use permit, the zoning board denied the individual's application because of the nature of the proposed use. The individual sued the zoning board seeking declaratory and injunctive relief on constitutional grounds.

Which of the following best states the appropriate burden of persuasion in this action?

(A) Because housing is a fundamental right, the zoning board must demonstrate that denial of the permit is necessary to serve a compelling state interest.

(B) Because the zoning board's action has the effect of discriminating against a quasi-suspect class in regard to a basic subsistence right, the zoning board must demonstrate that the denial of the permit is substantially related to an important state interest.

(C) Because the zoning board's action invidiously discriminates against a suspect class, the zoning board must demonstrate that denial of the permit is necessary to serve a compelling state interest.

(D) Because the zoning board's action is in the nature of an economic or social welfare regulation, the individual seeking the permit must demonstrate that the denial of the permit is not rationally related to a legitimate state interest.

[Q7041]

Answer 37: Choice **(D)** is correct. Note that the only plausible ground for plaintiff's attack is the equal protection clause — government is saying that certain groups of four or more people can live together without a permit and others can't. Persons convicted of crimes have not been held to constitute either a suspect or a quasi-suspect class for equal protection purposes. Therefore, the zoning board's denial of the permit discriminated against neither a suspect class nor a quasi-suspect class. Nor did it unduly burden the exercise of a fundamental right (since housing has not been held to be a fundamental right for equal protection purposes). The denial therefore triggers rational basis scrutiny.

(A) is wrong because housing has been held not to be a fundamental right for equal protection purposes. *Lindsey v. Normet* (1972). Therefore, the strict scrutiny standard articulated in this choice would not be appropriate.

(B) is wrong because convicts have never been held to be a semi-suspect class. (The only semi-suspect class is recognized by the court to date are gender and illegitimacy.) Nor does housing have any special equal protection status as a "basic subsistence right." Therefore, the intermediate standard of review (which this choice correctly describes as the "substantially related to an important state interest" test) would not apply here.

(C) is wrong because convicts do not constitute a suspect class for equal protection purposes. Therefore, while this would be the correct test if the legislative classification involved a suspect class (e.g., race or national origin), it is not the correct test for this case.

II. SUSPECT CLASSIFICATIONS, ESPECIALLY RACE

A. Suspect classifications

Question 38: The United States government demonstrated that terrorist attacks involving commercial airliners were perpetrated exclusively by individuals of one particular race. In response, Congress enacted a statute imposing stringent new airport and airline security measures only on individuals of that race seeking to board airplanes in the United States.

Which of the following provides the best ground for challenging the constitutionality of this statute?

(A) The commerce clause of Article I, Section 8.

(B) The due process clause of the Fifth Amendment.

(C) The privileges and immunities clause of Article IV.

(D) The privileges or immunities clause of the Fourteenth Amendment.

[QA041]

Answer 38: Choice **(B)** is correct. What makes this question slightly challenging is that you're expecting a choice that uses the phrase "equal protection" (since the government is treating members of one race differently than those of other races). But the key is that the way equal protection principles apply to the federal government is via the Fifth Amendment's Due Process Clause — the Supreme Court held, in *Bolling v. Sharpe* (1954), that the equal protection principles of the Fourteenth Amendment apply to actions of the federal government through incorporation into the Due Process Clause of the Fifth Amendment. The new security measures presumptively violate equal protection because they contain a racial classification: the new measures apply only to individuals of one race. A court therefore would uphold the measures only if the government could prove that they are necessary to serve a compelling public interest, a standard that the government typically cannot meet and would be very unlikely to meet here.

(A) is wrong because the statute here would be a proper exercise of the commerce power, if it did not violate the Due Process Clause. The commerce clause grants Congress plenary power to regulate the safety of air travel because airlines are instrumentalities of interstate commerce. (Instead, the problem is that the new security measures presumptively violate equal protection, as made applicable to the states via the Fifth Amendment's Due Process Clause. See Choice (B) for more details.)

(C) is wrong because the privileges and immunities clause of Article IV prohibits only actions by states that improperly discriminate against the citizens of other states. The clause does not apply to actions of the federal government.

(D) is wrong because the privileges or immunities clause of the Fourteenth Amendment prohibits *states* from depriving individuals of the privileges or immunities of United States citizenship. The U.S. Supreme Court has never applied the clause to actions of the federal government. (Furthermore, even where state rather than federal action is at issue, be skeptical of any choice that finds a governmental action unconstitutional on the grounds that it violates the Fourteenth Amendment P&I Clause. That clause protects only the privileges and immunities of "national citizenship." There are very few privileges and immunities of national citizenship, mainly the right to vote in national elections, the right to travel physically from state to state, and the right not to be discriminated against by virtue of one's having recently moved to the state from a different state.)

III. MIDDLE-LEVEL REVIEW (GENDER, ILLEGITIMACY AND ALIENAGE)

A. Gender

1. Male or female plaintiff

Question 39: A public high school has had a very high rate of pregnancy among its students. In order to assist students who keep their babies to complete high school, the high school has established an infant day-care center for children of its students, and also offers classes in child care. Because the child-care classes are always overcrowded, the school limits admission to those classes solely to students at the high school who are the mothers of babies in the infant day-care center.

A male student at the high school has legal custody of his infant son. The school provides care for his son in the infant day-care center, but will not allow the male student to enroll in the child-care classes. He brings suit against the school challenging, on constitutional grounds, his exclusion from the child-care classes.

Which of the following best states the burden of persuasion in this case?

(A) The student must demonstrate that the admission requirement is not rationally related to a legitimate governmental interest.

(B) The student must demonstrate that the admission requirement is not as narrowly drawn as possible to achieve a substantial governmental interest.

(C) The school must demonstrate that the admission policy is the least restrictive means by which to achieve a compelling governmental interest.

(D) The school must demonstrate that the admission policy is substantially related to an important governmental interest.

[Q2155]

Answer 39: Choice **(D)** is correct. The issue here is the validity of the school's gender-based classification, under which students who are mothers of an infant can use the day-care center but students who are fathers of an infant cannot. For such a gender-based classification, the court uses intermediate-level scrutiny, under which, as Choice (D) recites, the defendant (the government) bears the burden of showing that its classification is "substantially related" to the fulfillment of an "important governmental interest." *Craig v. Boren* (1976). Notice that the standard is the same for a male plaintiff who is disadvantaged by the classification as it would be for a female plaintiff who was disadvantaged.

(A) would be correct if the classification were one that did not involve a suspect or semi-suspect class or fundamental interest (e.g., a garden-variety economic or social-welfare regulation); but since gender is a semi-suspect category, the standard in Choice (A) is insufficiently demanding.

(B) is incorrect mainly because, when the classification is based on gender, the use of semi-strict scrutiny means that the government bears the burden of persuasion. (Also, the key phrases "narrowly drawn as possible" and "substantial governmental interest" are not quite right.)

(C) is wrong because, while it correctly places the burden of persuasion on the government defendant, this choice recites the standard for strict rather than semi-strict scrutiny.

IV. FUNDAMENTAL RIGHTS

A. Voting rights

1. Fifteenth Amendment

Question 40: Twenty percent of the residents of Green City are members of minority racial groups. These residents are evenly distributed among the many different residential areas of the city. The five city council members of Green City are elected from five single-member electoral districts that are nearly equally populated. No candidate has ever been elected to the city council who was a member of a minority racial group.

A group of citizens who are members of minority racial groups file suit in federal district court seeking a declaratory judgment that the single-member districts in Green City are unconstitutional. They claim that the single-member districting system in that city diminishes the ability of voters who are members of minority racial groups to affect the outcome of city elections. They seek an order from the court forcing the city to adopt an at-large election system in which the five candidates with the greatest vote totals would be elected to the city council. No state or federal statutes are applicable to the resolution of this suit.

Which of the following constitutional provisions provides the most obvious basis for plaintiffs' claim in this suit?

(A) The Thirteenth Amendment.

(B) The due process clause of the Fourteenth Amendment.

(C) The privileges and immunities clause of the Fourteenth Amendment.

(D) The Fifteenth Amendment.

[Q2028]

Answer 40: The correct answer is Choice **(D)**. Direct impairments of the right to vote, based on a person's race or color, may violate the Fifteenth Amendment, even where Congress has not passed a statute banning the impairment.

(A) is wrong because the Thirteenth Amendment bars only slavery. Congress has the power to ban the "badges and incidents" of slavery under this Amendment, and voting rules that have a racially discriminatory impact might qualify as a badge-or-incident, but Congress has not used its power here (since we're told that there is no applicable federal statute).

(B) is wrong because the Due Process Clause does not directly address voting rights, so any due process violation would be far more tenuous than the Thirteenth Amendment claim. (There might be a valid Fourteenth Amendment *equal protection* claim, but *that's not one of the choices*.)

(C) is wrong because the Fourteenth Amendment's P&I Clause is interpreted to protect only the rights of "national" (not state) citizenship, and the right to vote in a local election is not a right of national citizenship, at least where the local government is not discriminating against those who recently moved there.

B. Ballot access

1. Two invalid restrictions

a. Unfair to new parties

Question 41: A state has a statute providing that an unsuccessful candidate in a primary election for a party's nomination for elected public office may not become a candidate for the same office at the following general election by nominating petition or by write-in votes.

A woman sought her party's nomination for governor in the May primary election. After losing in the primary, the woman filed nominating petitions containing the requisite number of signatures to become a candidate for the office of governor in the following general election. The chief elections officer of the state refused to certify the woman's petitions solely because of the above statute. The woman then filed suit in federal district court challenging the constitutionality of this state statute.

As a matter of constitutional law, which of the following is the proper burden of persuasion in this suit?

(A) The woman must demonstrate that the statute is not necessary to achieve a compelling state interest.

(B) The woman must demonstrate that the statute is not rationally related to a legitimate state interest.

(C) The state must demonstrate that the statute is the least restrictive means of achieving a compelling state interest.

(D) The state must demonstrate that the statute is rationally related to a legitimate state interest.

[Q1122]

Answer 41: Choice **(C)** is correct. Ballot restrictions that are so severe that minor-party and independent candidates have no realistic opportunity to get on the ballot are given strict scrutiny, under both the equal protection clause and the First Amendment's freedom of association clause. *Williams v. Rhodes* (1968). The statute here is such a restriction, because it makes it completely impossible (not just somewhat harder) for someone who fails to get a major-party nomination to then run as an independent or minor-party candidate in the general election, no matter how much public support that person can demonstrate. Consequently, the choice here, by articulating strict scrutiny as the standard, is correct.

(A) is incorrect because, although it correctly articulates the strict-scrutiny standard, it incorrectly says that the plaintiff who is challenging the government bears the burden of persuasion; in those scenarios triggering strict scrutiny, the burden of persuasion is on the government.

(B) is wrong because it incorrectly uses the easy-to-satisfy mere-rationality standard, when what is at issue is a serious impairment of the fundamental right to be a candidate (and the right of voters to choose the best candidate).

(D) is wrong because, for the reasons stated above, the court would apply the strict scrutiny standard on these facts.

C. Necessities

1. Education

Question 42: Public schools in a state are financed, in large part, by revenue derived from real estate taxes imposed by each school district on the taxable real property located in that district. Public schools also receive other revenue from private gifts, federal grants, student fees, and local sales taxes. For many years, the state has distributed additional funds, which come from the state treasury, to local school districts in order to equalize the funds available on a per-student basis for each public school district. These additional funds are distributed on the basis of a state statutory formula that considers only the number of students in each public school district and the real estate tax revenue raised by that district. The formula does not consider other revenue received by a school district from different sources.

The school boards of two school districts, together with parents and schoolchildren in those districts, bring suit in federal court to enjoin the state from allocating the additional funds from the state treasury to individual districts pursuant to this formula. They allege that the failure of the state, in allocating this additional money, to take into account a school district's sources of revenue other than revenue derived from taxes levied on real estate located there violates the equal protection clause of the Fourteenth Amendment. The complaint does not allege that the allocation of the additional state funds based on the current statutory formula has resulted in a failure to provide minimally adequate education to any child.

Which of the following best describes the appropriate standard by which the court should review the constitutionality of the state statutory funding formula?

(A) Because classifications based on wealth are inherently suspect, the state must demonstrate that the statutory formula is necessary to vindicate a compelling slate interest.

(B) Because the statutory funding formula burdens the fundamental right to education, the state must demonstrate that the formula is necessary to vindicate a compelling state interest.

(C) Because no fundamental right or suspect classification is implicated in this case, the plaintiffs must demonstrate that the funding allocation formula bears no rational relationship to any legitimate state interest.

(D) Because the funding formula inevitably leads to disparities among the school districts in their levels of total funding, the plaintiffs must only demonstrate that the funding formula is not substantially related to the furtherance of an important state interest.

[Q1073]

Answer 42: Choice **(C)** is correct. First, education is not a fundamental right for equal protection purposes. *San Antonio Sch. Dist. v. Rodriguez* (1973). Second, wealth classifications are not a suspect category. This choice therefore correctly asserts that (1) no fundamental right or suspect classification is involved in this case; and (2) where this is true, the plaintiff must bear the very difficult burden of proving that there is no rational relationship between the classification being used and any legitimate state interest. (By the way, it is very unlikely that the plaintiffs would win under this test; a school-funding scheme relying principally on local property taxes was upheld against rational-basis equal protection attack in *San Antonio v. Rodriguez*, *supra*.)

(A) is wrong because classifications based on wealth are not "inherently suspect" for equal protection purposes, so such classifications do not have to satisfy the strict scrutiny standard that this choice articulates.

(B) is wrong because the Court has held that education (or at least the right to have a public education that goes beyond minimally-adequate standards) is not a fundamental right for equal protection purposes; therefore, the strict scrutiny standard articulated by this choice would not apply.

(D) is wrong because it articulates an intermediate level of scrutiny, and that level is only used in cases involving semi-suspect classifications (e.g., ones based on gender).

CHAPTER 7
MISCELLANEOUS CLAUSES

I.   *EX POST FACTO* LAWS

A. Constitutional prohibition

1. Criminal only

a. Significance

Question 43: A doctor, a resident of the city of Greenville in the state of Green, is a physician licensed to practice in both Green and the neighboring state of Red. The doctor finds that the most convenient place to treat her patients who need hospital care is in the publicly owned and operated municipal hospital of the city of Redville in the state of Red, which is located just across the state line from Greenville. For many years the doctor had successfully treated her patients in that hospital. Early this year she was notified that she could no longer treat patients in the Redville hospital because she was not a resident of Red, and a newly adopted rule of the Redville hospital, which was adopted in conformance with all required procedures, stated that every physician who practices in that hospital must be a resident of Red.

Which of the following constitutional provisions would be most helpful to the doctor in an action to challenge her exclusion from the Redville hospital solely on the basis of this hospital rule?

(A) The bill of attainder clause.

(B) The privileges and immunities clause of Article IV.

(C) The due process clause of the Fourteenth Amendment.

(D) The ex post facto clause.

[Q3190]

Answer 43: Choice **(B)** is correct. When a state (or subdivision of a state, like a city and its municipally-owned operations) regulates a right that is "fundamental to national unity," and does so in a way that disadvantages out-of-staters, that regulation will essentially be subject to strict scrutiny under the Art. IV Privileges and Immunities clause. (Among other things, the state must show that the discrimination against non-residents bears a "substantial relationship" to the problem the state is attempting to solve.) Practice of one's business or profession is a right "fundamental to national unity" for P&I purposes.

The case here is on all fours with *New Hampshire v. Piper* (1985), where the Court held that New Hampshire's attempt to restrict the right to practice law to state residents violated the Art. IV P&I Clause. Applying *Piper*, since there's no showing that out-of-state doctors are the peculiar source of any special problem that the hospital is trying to solve, the restriction violates the P&I Clause.

(By the way, there's no exception under the P&I Clause for activities in which the city or state is a "market participant," as there is under the dormant Commerce Clause. *United Bldg. and Constr. Trades Counc. v. Camden* (1984). So the fact that the city owns the hospital that's making the rule doesn't help it, as it would against a Commerce Clause attack.)

(A) is wrong because the legislature of state Red was not trying to punish the doctor. A bill of attainder is a legislative act that attempts to inflict punishment without a judicial trial upon individuals who are designated by name or in terms of past conduct. The constitutional prohibition against a bill of attainder would not be helpful to the doctor because the hospital here merely took the purely regulatory action of changing the residency requirement for practicing medicine at the hospital — no public entity named the doctor as a criminal, or attempted to punish or stigmatize him, which is what a bill of attainder would have done.

(C) is wrong because the doctor would have to show that the licensing requirement was not rationally related to a legitimate government interest, a showing the doctor probably couldn't make. The Due Process Clause of the Fourteenth Amendment provides that no state shall make or enforce any law which shall deprive any person of life, liberty, or property, without due process of law. When a fundamental right is not involved, substantive due process requires only that a law be "rationally related" to the achievement of a "legitimate government interest." So to win on due process, the doctor would have to prove that Red's new residency requirement was not rationally related to some legitimate government purpose. This standard is very lenient and easy-to-satisfy. Here, for instance, the hospital could plausibly claim that it wants to have on staff only doctors who live very nearby, and that it's entitled to use state of residence as a proxy for nearby-ness. Although the fit between means and end isn't very tight under this rationale, it's almost certainly tight enough to meet the extremely lenient rational-relation standard.

(D) is wrong because state Red was not legislating against past acts. The Ex Post Facto clauses, Article I, § 9 and § 10, prohibit both the federal government and the state, respectively, from passing legislation that retroactively alters the criminal law as to offenses or punishments, in a substantially prejudicial manner. A retroactive change in civil regulations, such as licensing requirements, cannot violate the prohibition, since the prohibition applies only to "penal," i.e., punitive, measures. Here, the facts make it clear that the hospital was not making a rule penalizing past acts, but was instead making residency a requirement to practice medicine in state Red going forward.

CHAPTER 8

THE "STATE ACTION" REQUIREMENT; CONGRESS'S ENFORCEMENT OF THE CIVIL WAR AMENDMENTS

I. STATE ACTION

A. "State involvement" doctrine

1. Entanglement or entwinement

a. Licensing

Question 44: Insurance is provided in a particular state only by private companies. Although the state insurance commissioner inspects insurance companies for solvency, the state does not regulate their rates or policies. A particular insurance company charges higher rates for burglary insurance to residents of one part of a county in the state than to residents of another section of the same county because of the different crime rates in those areas.

A resident of that county was charged the higher rate by the insurance company because of the location of her residence. The resident sues the insurance company, alleging that the differential in insurance rates unconstitutionally denies her the equal protection of the laws.

Will the resident's suit succeed?

(A) Yes, because the higher crime rate in the resident's neighborhood demonstrates that the county police are not giving persons who reside there the equal protection of the laws.

(B) Yes, because the insurance rate differential is inherently discriminatory.

(C) No, because the constitutional guarantee of equal protection of the laws is not applicable to the actions of these insurance companies.

(D) No, because there is a rational basis for the differential in insurance rates.
[Q1114]

Answer 44: Choice **(C)** is correct. Although the state does some regulation of the insurance industry (for solvency), the state is not sufficiently involved with the operations of the insurance company here to satisfy the requirement — applicable to any equal protection claim — that there be "state action." Notice that the choice never uses the phrase "state action" — it's up to you to spot the state action issue and to notice that this choice's use of the phrase "not applicable to the actions of these ... companies" captures the state-action concept.

(A) is wrong for several reasons, including most basically the fact that it ignores the state-action requirement for any equal protection claim. (The fact that the *state police* are arguably failing to give equal protection is irrelevant, since the police aren't a party and aren't tightly associated with a party.)

(B) and (D) are wrong, similarly, because they too ignore the state-action requirement for equal protection claims. (If the state-action requirement were satisfied — if, for instance, the state expressly required burglary-insurance rates to be adjusted based on local crime rates — then (D) would be the best answer because it correctly expresses the idea that a governmental classification that does not involve a suspect class or fundamental right needs to be supported only by a rational basis.)

II. CONGRESSIONAL ENFORCEMENT OF CIVIL RIGHTS

A. Congress's power to reach private conduct

1. Thirteenth Amendment

a. "Badges of slavery"

Question 45: A proposed federal statute would prohibit all types of discrimination against black persons on the basis of their race in every business transaction executed anywhere in the United States by any person or entity, governmental or private.

Is this proposed federal statute likely to be constitutional?

(A) Yes, because it could reasonably be viewed as an exercise of Congress's authority to enact laws for the general welfare.

(B) Yes, because it could reasonably be viewed as a means of enforcing the provisions of the Thirteenth Amendment.

(C) No, because it would regulate purely local transactions that are not in interstate commerce.

(D) No, because it would invade the powers reserved to the states by the Tenth Amendment.

[Q2101]

Answer 45: Choice **(B)** is correct. The Thirteenth Amendment permits Congress to forbid the "badges and incidents" of slavery. This power has been interpreted by the Court to include the power to forbid even private acts of racial discrimination against black people, on the theory that such discrimination is the relic of slavery.

(A) is wrong because Congress does not have any "authority to enact laws for the general welfare" (only the power to "tax and spend" for the general welfare).

(C) is wrong because this might be an explanation of why the statute couldn't be supported by Congress's commerce power, but the Thirteenth Amendment power allows Congress to forbid even purely local racial discrimination (i.e., discrimination that does not involve interstate commerce).

(D) is wrong because if Congress's action falls within a specific grant of power (here, the Thirteenth Amendment grant), the Tenth Amendment acts as a limitation only in the highly specialized case of Congress's attempt to take over state lawmaking mechanisms.

CHAPTER 9
FREEDOM OF EXPRESSION

I. GENERAL THEMES

A. Analysis of content-based government action

1. Protected category

a. "Viewpoint neutrality" not enough

Question 46: The Federal Family Film Enhancement Act assesses an excise tax of 10% on the price of admission to public movie theaters when they show films that contain actual or simulated scenes of human sexual intercourse.

Which of the following is the strongest argument against the constitutionality of this federal act?

(A) The act imposes a prior restraint on the freedom of speech protected by the First Amendment.

(B) The act is not rationally related to any legitimate national interest.

(C) The act violates the equal protection concepts embodied in the due process clause of the Fifth Amendment because it imposes a tax on the price of admission to view certain films and not on the price of admission to view comparable live performances.

(D) The act imposes a tax solely on the basis of the content of speech without adequate justification and, therefore, it is prohibited by the freedom of speech clause of the First Amendment.

[Q1099]

Answer 46: Choice **(D)** is correct. The tax applies only to films that show some form of sexual intercourse. This means that the regulation is content-based (it treats different forms of expression differently depending solely on the message being conveyed). Therefore, the court will apply strict scrutiny to it. (Notice, by the way, that the tax is not limited to films that would be "obscene" — not all portrayals of sexual intercourse would be obscene; if only obscene films were taxed, probably strict scrutiny would *not* be used.)

Choice (A) is wrong because a tax is not a "prior restraint"; a legislative act imposes a prior restraint only where government forbids the doing of the act in advance (e.g., a statute forbidding showing of a film without first paying a license fee). Since the tax here kicks in only after the showing of the film, it is not a prior restraint.

Choice (B) is wrong because the regulation here is a content-based regulation on expression, and such a restraint is evaluated based on strict scrutiny, not the easy-to-satisfy rational-relation test.

Choice (C) is wrong because an equal protection attack on a legislative classification that does not involve a suspect or semi-suspect class or fundamental right is evaluated based on the easy-to-satisfy rational-relation standard, and the tax here would likely pass that standard.

II. DEFAMATION AND INVASION OF PRIVACY

A. Other state-law tort claims

1. Can't take whole performance

Question 47: Roberts, a professional motorcycle rider, put on a performance in a privately owned stadium during which he leaped his motorcycle over 21 automobiles. Spectators were charged $55 each to view the jump and were prohibited from using cameras. However, the local television station filmed the whole event from within the stadium without the knowledge or consent of Roberts and showed the film in its entirety on the evening newscast that day. Roberts thereafter brought suit to recover damages from the station for the admittedly unauthorized filming and broadcasting of the act. The television station raised only constitutional defenses.

The court should

(A) hold against Roberts, because the First and Fourteenth Amendments authorize press coverage of newsworthy entertainment events.

(B) hold against Roberts, because under the First and Fourteenth Amendments news broadcasts are absolutely privileged.

(C) find the station liable, because its action deprives Roberts of his property without due process.

(D) find the station liable, because the First and Fourteenth Amendments do not deprive an entertainer of the commercial value of his or her performances.

[Q1159]

Answer 47: Choice **(D)** is correct. While the First Amendment does indeed give the media a privilege to cover newsworthy events, that privilege does not extend to the broadcasting of a performance where this would deprive the performer of the commercial value of that performance. The fact pattern here is on all fours with *Zacchini v. Scripps-Howard Broadcasting* (1997).

(A) is wrong, because while the First Amendment does give a privilege for press coverage of newsworthy events, that privilege does not extend to a broadcast that takes so much of an act that it deprives the performer of much of the commercial value of the act.

(B) is wrong because news broadcasts are not "absolutely privileged"; rather, they receive a qualified privilege, subject to a number of limits (including, here, the limit that the broadcast not appropriate so much of a performance that the commercial value of the performance is taken from the performer).

(C) is wrong, because the Due Process Clause of the Fourteenth Amendment protects only against a taking by a government, and any taking here was by a private party (the TV station), not by the government.

III. OBSCENITY

A. Regulating secondary effects of adult speech

1. Regulation of red-light districts

Question 48: A city has an ordinance that prohibits the location of "adult theaters and bookstores" (theaters and bookstores presenting sexually explicit performances or materials) in residential or commercial zones within the city. The ordinance was intended to protect surrounding property from the likely adverse secondary effects of such establishments. "Adult theaters and bookstores" are freely permitted in the areas of the city zoned industrial, where those adverse secondary effects are not as likely. A storekeeper is denied a zoning permit to open an adult theater and bookstore in a building owned by him in an area zoned commercial. As a result, the storekeeper brings suit in an appropriate court challenging the constitutionality of the zoning ordinance.

Which of the following statements regarding the constitutionality of this city ordinance is most accurate?

(A) The ordinance is valid, because a city may enforce zoning restrictions on speech-related businesses to ensure that the messages they disseminate are acceptable to the residents of adjacent property.

(B) The ordinance is valid, because a city may enforce this type of time, place, and manner regulation on speech-related businesses, so long as this type of regulation is designed to serve a substantial governmental interest and does not unreasonably limit alternative avenues of communication.

(C) The ordinance is invalid, because a city may not enforce zoning regulations that deprive potential operators of adult theaters and bookstores of their freedom to choose the location of their businesses.

(D) The ordinance is invalid, because a city may not zone property in a manner calculated to protect property from the likely adverse secondary effects of adult theaters and bookstores.

[Q2193]

Answer 48: Choice **(B)** is correct. The Supreme Court has repeatedly held that even if a city is using its zoning powers to limit or prohibit a speech-related activity, the regulation is acceptable if the city is reasonably targeting the secondary effects of that speech (e.g., crime or lower property values) rather than targeting the expressive content of that speech. See, e.g., *Erie v. Pap's A.M.* (2004) (city may completely ban "nude dancing" to combat the bad secondary effects of such). Since the government is targeting the secondary effects rather than the message, the regulation is to be evaluated based on the test for content-neutral time, place and manner regulations, which as this choice suggests makes such regulations valid as long as they are designed to serve a substantial governmental interest and do not unreasonably limit alternative avenues of expression. Since the interest in preventing blight is "substantial," and since adult uses are permitted in alternative venues (areas zoned commercial), these requirements are easily satisfied.

(A) is wrong because it falsely asserts that the city may use its zoning powers to forbid particular messages based on their content. Such a content-based regulation would have to be strictly scrutinized, and would almost certainly be struck down.

(C) is wrong because it badly misstates the law: cities may indeed use their zoning regulations to prevent operators of adult theaters and the like from choosing their location, as long as the city is acting reasonably to combat the perceived negative secondary effects of the business, rather than out of distaste for the content of the messages transmitted by the business.

(D) is wrong because it exactly misstates present law; cities may (not "may not") "zone property in a manner calculated to protect property from the likely adverse secondary effects of adult theaters and bookstores." *Erie v. Pap's, supra.*

IV. FREEDOM OF ASSOCIATION, AND DENIAL OF PUBLIC BENEFITS OR JOBS

A. Denial of public benefit or job

1. Some exceptions

a. Speech critical of superiors or otherwise inappropriate

i. Non-policy-making role

Question 49: A clerical worker has been employed for the past two years in a permanent position in the Public Records Office of a county. The clerk has been responsible for copying and filing records of real estate transactions in that office. The clerk works in a non-public part of the office and has no contact with members of the public. However, state law provides that all real estate records in that office are to be made available for public inspection.

On the day an attempted assassination of the governor of the state was reported on the radio, the clerk remarked to a coworker, "Our governor is such an evil man, I am sorry they did not get him." The clerk's coworker reported this remark to the clerk's employer, the county recorder. After the clerk admitted making the remark, the county recorder dismissed him stating that "there is no room in this office for a person who hates the governor so much."

The clerk sued for reinstatement and back pay. His only claim is that the dismissal violated his constitutional rights.

In this case, the court should hold that the county recorder's dismissal of the clerk was

(A) unconstitutional, because it constitutes a taking without just compensation of the clerk's property interest in his permanent position with the county.

(B) unconstitutional, because in light of the clerk's particular employment duties his right to express himself on a matter of public concern outweighed any legitimate interest the state might have had in discharging him.

(C) constitutional, because the compelling interest of the state in having loyal and supportive employees outweighs the interest of any state employee in his or her job or in free speech on a matter of public concern.

(D) nonjusticiable, because public employment is a privilege rather than a right and, therefore, the clerk lacked standing to bring this suit.

[Q2184]

Answer 49: The correct choice is **(B)**. The facts here are very similar to those of *Rankin v. McPherson*, where the Court held that: (1) the clerk's statement supporting a recent assassination attempt (of President Reagan) was indeed on a matter of "public concern"; and (2) the fact that the clerk had no policy-making role and that his statement had little negative impact on his job effectiveness made it unreasonable to dismiss him for that statement.

Choice (A) is wrong because even a "permanent" public employee (i.e., one with a property right in his post) may have his job taken without just compensation, as long as procedures constituting due process are followed. In other words, what the Due Process Clause guarantees on these facts is that Clerk's job won't be taken arbitrarily or capriciously, not that the job won't be taken "without just compensation" (a standard that would more properly be applied to the taking of tangible real or personal property rather than a job). Choice (C) is wrong because the Court has held (in *Rankin, supra*) that although the government has an interest in having loyal and supportive employees, this interest does not outweigh the employee's interest in commenting on matters of public concern, where the comment does not undermine the employee's effectiveness in light of the non-policy-making and limited scope of the employee's job (which, like the job here, was clerical). Choice (D) is wrong because: (1) the Court does not use the right/privilege distinction in First Amendment public employment cases; and (2) even if the Court did believe that public employment was a "privilege" rather than a "right," the Court would almost certainly view the case as justiciable.

ii. Interferes with job

Question 50: A city ordinance makes the city building inspector responsible for ensuring that all buildings in that city are kept up to building code standards, and requires the inspector to refer for prosecution all known building code violations. Another ordinance provides that the city building inspector may be discharged for "good cause." The building inspector took a newspaper reporter through a number of rundown buildings in a slum neighborhood. After using various epithets and slurs to describe the occupants of these buildings, the building inspector stated to the reporter: "I do not even try to get these buildings up to code or to have their owners prosecuted for code violations because if these buildings are repaired, the people who live in them will just wreck them again." The reporter published these statements in a story in the local newspaper. The building inspector admitted he made the statements.

On the basis of these statements, the city council discharged the building inspector.

Is the action of the city council constitutional?

(A) Yes, because the statements demonstrate that the building inspector has an attitude toward a certain class of persons that interferes with the proper performance of the obligations of his job.

(B) Yes, because the building inspector is a government employee and a person holding such a position may not make public comments inconsistent with current governmental policy.

(C) No, because the statements were lawful comments on a matter of public concern.

(D) No, because the statements were published in a newspaper that is protected by the First and Fourteenth Amendments.

[Q1103]

Answer 50: Choice **(A)** is correct. When a public employee speaks on a matter that is arguably one of public concern, the employee gets limited protection against dismissal or discipline. However, where the content of the speech interferes with the speaker's proper performance of his job (or indicates that the speaker has underlying attitudes that would interfere with job performance), the balance is tipped heavily toward the employer's right to discharge or discipline the employee. Here, given that the inspector is required to enforce the building codes, and given that he has publicly stated that he does not even try to do this core job function on account of his attitudes towards slumdwellers, the city council was clearly justified in firing him.

Choice (B) is wrong because it is overbroad; even a government employee may make public comments inconsistent with current governmental policy, if the speaker is not in a public role and/or the comments do not interfere with the speaker's ability to perform his job adequately.

Choice (C) is wrong because, although the comments may have been "lawful" and on a "matter of public concern," these two facts do not give the speaker immunity from being punished for the comments, for the reasons given above in the discussion of the correct choice.

Choice (D) is wrong because the fact that the comments were published in a newspaper that was in turn protected by the First and Fourteenth Amendments, is irrelevant to the question of whether the speaker may be punished; as described above, government may discharge a government employee for making statements (even ones published in a First-Amendment-protected newspaper) that seriously interfere with the employee's proper performance of her job.

CHAPTER 10
FREEDOM OF RELIGION

I. THE ESTABLISHMENT CLAUSE

A. Three-part test

1. Incidental benefit not fatal

Question 51: A city operates a cemetery pursuant to a city ordinance. The ordinance requires the operation of the city cemetery to be supported primarily by revenues derived from the sale of cemetery lots to individuals. The ordinance further provides that the purchase of a cemetery lot entitles the owner to perpetual care of the lot, and entitles the owner to erect on the lot, at the owner's expense, a memorial monument or marker of the owner's choice, subject to certain size restrictions. The ordinance requires the city to maintain the cemetery, including mowing the grass, watering flowers, and plowing snow, and provides for the expenditure of city tax funds for such maintenance if revenues from the sale of cemetery lots are insufficient. Although cemetery lots are sold at full fair market value, which includes the current value of perpetual care, the revenue from the sale of such lots has been insufficient in recent years to maintain the cemetery. As a result, a small amount of city tax funds has also been used for that purpose.

A group of city taxpayers brings suit against the city challenging the constitutionality of the city ordinance insofar as it permits the owner of a cemetery lot to erect a religious memorial monument or marker on his or her lot.

Is this suit likely to be successful?

(A) No, because only a small amount of city tax funds has been used to maintain the cemetery.

(B) No, because the purpose of the ordinance is entirely secular, its primary effect neither advances nor inhibits religion, and it does not foster an excessive government entanglement with religion.

(C) Yes, because city maintenance of any religious object is a violation of the establishment clause of the First Amendment as incorporated into the Fourteenth Amendment.

(D) Yes, because no compelling governmental interest justifies authorizing private persons to erect religious monuments or markers in a city-operated cemetery.

[Q1138]

Answer 51: Choice **(B)** is correct. This choice correctly states the three-part *Lemon v. Kurtzman* (1970) test for government action that is alleged to benefit some religious interest. On the facts here, the statute passes all three parts: there is no evidence that the city's decision to operate the cemetery under these rules was intended to benefit religious groups; the primary effect of the cemetery operation is not to benefit those who put religious monuments on their plot; and the city's work in maintaining the religious monuments is so incidental to the overall operation of the cemetery — and so comparable to the work needed to maintain non-religious monuments — that there is no excessive entanglement between government and religion.

(A) is wrong because the amount of government funds spent is not dispositive; if the city was intending to benefit only religion (e.g., by providing a $20 reimbursement to the first 100 people who bought a piece of religious jewelry), the fact that only a "small amount" of city funds was spent would not save the expenditure from being a violation of the Establishment Clause.

(C) is wrong because it misstates the test for Establishment Clause violations; a city may maintain a "religious object" if the maintenance is part of a religiously-neutral program that is not intended to, and does not have the primary effect of, benefiting religion.

(D) is wrong because, if the government acts neutrally as to religion (as it has done here), there is no Establishment Clause violation whether the government has pursued a compelling interest or not.

II.   THE FREE EXERCISE CLAUSE

A. Generally-applicable laws

1.   State need not tolerate serious impairment of important state interest

Question 52: Members of a religious group believe in Lucifer as their Supreme Being. The members of this group meet once a year on top of Mt. Snow, located in a U.S. National Park, to hold an overnight encampment and a midnight dance around a large campfire. They believe this overnight encampment and all of its rituals are required by Lucifer to be held on the top of Mt. Snow. U.S. National Park Service rules that have been consistently enforced prohibit all overnight camping and all campfires on Mt. Snow because of the very great dangers overnight camping and campfires would pose in that particular location. As a result, the park Superintendent denied a request by the group for a permit to conduct these activities on top of Mt. Snow. The park Superintendent, who was known to be violently opposed to cults and other unconventional groups had, in the past, issued permits to conventional religious groups to conduct sunrise services in other areas of that U.S. National Park.

The group brought suit in Federal Court against the U.S. National Park Service and the Superintendent of the park to compel issuance of the requested permit.

As a matter of constitutional law, the most appropriate result in this suit would be a decision that denial of the permit was

(A) invalid, because the free exercise clause of the First Amendment prohibits the Park Service from knowingly interfering with religious conduct.

(B) invalid, because these facts demonstrate that the action of the Park Service purposefully and invidiously discriminated against the group.

(C) valid, because the establishment clause of the First Amendment prohibits the holding of religious ceremonies on federal land.

(D) valid, because religiously motivated conduct may be subjected to nondiscriminatory time, place, and manner restrictions that advance important public interests.

[Q2112]

Answer 52: Choice (D) is correct. Government may take generally-applicable actions that advance important public interests, without giving an exemption to those whose religious beliefs are thereby burdened. The facts tell us that the rules against overnight camping and campfires are "consistently enforced" because of "very great dangers," so the "generally applicable" and "advancement of important public interests" standards are met here. The fact that the Superintendent doesn't like cults doesn't matter, because there is no indication that his decision to deny the permit here was motivated by anything other than a desire to enforce these generally-applicable rules.

(A) is wrong, for the same reason that (D) is right: government may impose a generally-applicable rule to promote an important interest, even if government knows that its enforcement of that rule will interfere with religious conduct.

(B) is wrong because the Park Service's action did not "purposely and invidiously discriminate" against the group — what was being enforced was a generally-applicable rule that was not enacted for anti-religious purposes.

(C) is wrong because it misstates the law governing the Establishment Clause as well as the facts — if non-religious groups were permitted to take the same general type of action in question (here, overnight camping and campfires), which they are not, then it would not be a violation of the Establishment Clause for the government to allow a religious group to do the same thing (and, indeed, it would probably be a violation of the Free Exercise Clause for the government *not* to allow the religious group to do the same thing that the non-religious are permitted to do).

CHAPTER 11
JUSTICIABILITY

I. STANDING

A. Cases not based on taxpayer or citizen status

1. "Injury in fact"

a. Imminent harm

i. P hasn't made relevant decision

Question 53: An ordinance of a city requires that its mayor must have been continuously a resident of the city for at least five years at the time he or she takes office. The plaintiff, who is thinking about running for mayor in an election that will take place next year, will have been a resident of the city for only four and one-half years at the time the mayor elected then takes office. Before he decides whether to run for the position of mayor, the plaintiff wants to know whether he could lawfully assume that position if he were elected. As a result, the plaintiff files suit in the local federal district court for a declaratory judgment that the five-year-residence requirement is unconstitutional and that he is entitled to a place on his political party's primary election ballot for mayor. He names the chairman of his political party as the sole defendant but does not join any election official. The chairman responds by joining the plaintiff in requesting the court to declare the residence requirement invalid.

In this case, the court should

(A) refuse to determine the merits of this suit, because there is no case or controversy.

(B) refuse to issue such a declaratory judgment, because an issue of this kind involving only a local election does not present a substantial federal constitutional question.

(C) issue the declaratory judgment, because a residency requirement of this type is a denial of the equal protection of the laws.

(D) issue the declaratory judgment, because the plaintiff will have substantially complied with the residency requirement.

[Q2153]

Answer 53: Choice **(A)** is correct. The plaintiff does not meet the requirement of "injury in fact." He clearly has not been injured yet; the real question is whether he faces sufficiently imminent injury from the residency requirement. A court would likely hold that because the plaintiff has not yet even made the decision to run, and could not be injured unless he decided to run, any threatened injury to him is too uncertain and speculative to meet the requirement that prospective injury be reasonably concrete and imminent. The fact that the chairman has joined the suit does not change this, since the chairman (and the chairman's party) would not be injured unless some actual candidate was blocked by the residency requirement, and there is no such candidate now.

(B) is wrong because: (1) the absence of a case or controversy would prevent the court even from getting to the issue of whether there was a substantial federal constitutional question in the case; and (2) the fact that something is a local election does not prevent it from presenting a substantial federal constitutional question (for instance, an unduly long residency require- ment probably *would* constitute a violation of an actual candidate's equal protection rights).

(C) is wrong because, while the residency restriction might well constitute an equal protection violation of the rights of an actual candidate, the plaintiff's lack of actual-candidate status pre- vents him from raising a case or controversy.

(D) is wrong because there is no basis (certainly not a federal constitutional basis) for the court to conclude that "substantially complying," rather than fully complying, with the residency requirement here would be sufficient.

B. Third-party standing

Question 54: City police officers shot and killed the plaintiff's friend as he attempted to escape arrest for an armed robbery he had committed. The plaintiff brought suit in federal dis- trict court against the city police department and the city police officers involved, seeking only a judgment declaring unconstitutional the state statute under which the police acted. That newly enacted statute authorized the police to use deadly force when necessary to apprehend a person who has committed a felony. In his suit, the plaintiff alleged that the police would not have killed his friend if the use of deadly force had not been authorized by the statute.

The federal district court should

(A) decide the case on its merits, because it raises a substantial federal question.

(B) dismiss the action, because it involves a nonjusticiable political question.

(C) dismiss the action, because it does not present a case or controversy.

(D) dismiss the action, because the Eleventh Amendment prohibits federal courts from decid- ing cases of this type.

[Q1133]

Answer 54: Choice **(C)** is correct. Because the only person whose rights have been arguably affected by the new statute is the friend, who is not a claimant, there is no live case or contro- versy between the litigants, so standing rules prevent the court from hearing it.

(A) is wrong because the lack of standing prevents the court from deciding the case on its merits even though the plaintiff is claiming that the Constitution has been violated (which would of course raise a federal question if there were a case or controversy before the court).

(B) is wrong because, if there were not any standing problem, the question of the constitutionality of the statute would not be a nonjusticiable political question (a category limited to a few special situations, none of which applies here).

(D) is wrong, because the Eleventh Amendment bars only suits seeking money damages against states, and the suit here is seeking a declaratory judgment rather than money damages.

II. RIPENESS

A. Reasonable probability of harm required

1. Specificity required

Question 55: The legislature of the state of Gray recently enacted a statute forbidding public utilities regulated by the Gray Public Service Commission to increase their rates more than once every two years. Economy Electric Power Company, a public utility regulated by that commission, has just obtained approval of the commission for a general rate increase. Economy Electric has routinely filed for a rate increase every 10 to 14 months during the last 20 years. Because of uncertainties about future fuel prices, the power company cannot ascertain with any certainty the date when it will need a further rate increase; but it thinks it may need such an increase sometime within the next 18 months.

Economy Electric files an action in the federal district court in Gray requesting a declaratory judgment that this new statute of Gray forbidding public utility rate increases more often than once every two years is unconstitutional. Assume no federal statute is relevant.

In this case, the court should

(A) hold the statute unconstitutional, because such a moratorium on rate increases deprives utilities of their property without due process of law.

(B) hold the statute constitutional, because the judgment of a legislature on a matter involving economic regulation is entitled to great deference.

(C) dismiss the complaint, because this action is not ripe for decision.

(D) dismiss the complaint, because controversies over state-regulated utility rates are outside of the jurisdiction conferred on federal courts by Article III of the Constitution.

[Q2175]

Answer 55: The correct choice is **(C)**. This is a classic ripeness issue: Economy does not know that it will certainly (or even more-probably-than-not) need another rate increase in less than the now-required two-year minimum. All we know is that Economy "may" need the increase sometime in the next 18 months. Therefore, it is highly uncertain for now whether Economy will ever be harmed by the statute, making it likely that the court would dismiss the action as unripe.

(A) is wrong because the case is not ripe for decision (see the discussion of Choice (C)), so the court will never reach the constitutional merits. (Also, its highly doubtful that a relatively brief moratorium on rate increases would violate the due process rights of a utility.)

(B) is wrong for the same reason as (A): the case is not ripe for decision (see the discussion of Choice (C)), so the court will never reach the constitutional merits.

(D) is wrong, because the federal judicial power extends to any case raising an issue under the federal Constitution or a federal statute, and the fact that the controversy involves state-regulated utility rates does not prevent that controversy from raising a federal issue. For example, if a state utility commission were to prevent a utility from ever raising its rates again, this would raise a serious taking-without-just-compensation constitutional issue.

III. THE ELEVENTH AMENDMENT AND SUITS AGAINST THE STATES

A. The Eleventh Amendment generally

1. Congress can't override

a. Exception for remedial powers

Question 56: A federal statute enacted pursuant to the power of Congress to enforce the Fourteenth Amendment prohibits any state from requiring any of its employees to retire from state employment solely because of their age. The statute expressly authorizes employees required by a state to retire from state employment solely because of their age to sue the state government in federal district court for any damages resulting from that state action. On the basis of this federal statute, a retiree who had worked for State X sues the state in federal district court. State X moves to dismiss the suit on the ground that Congress lacks authority to authorize such suits against a state.

Which of the following is the strongest argument that the retiree can offer in opposition to the state's motion to dismiss this suit?

(A) When Congress exercises power vested in it by the Fourteenth Amendment, Congress may enact appropriate remedial legislation expressly subjecting the states to private suits for damages in federal court.

(B) When Congress exercises power vested in it by any provision of the Constitution, Congress has unlimited authority to authorize private actions for damages against a state.

(C) While the Eleventh Amendment restrains the federal judiciary, that amendment does not limit the power of Congress to modify the sovereign immunity of the states.

(D) While the Eleventh Amendment applies to suits in federal court by citizens of one state against another state, it does not apply to such suits by citizens against their own states.

[Q1027]

Answer 56: Choice **(A)** is correct. The Eleventh Amendment generally forbids the federal courts from entertaining damage suits against states, and Congress cannot override this ban even when it is acting pursuant to some enumerated power (e.g., the Commerce Clause). But there is one exception: when Congress is using its special powers to enforce the post-Civil War amendments (the Thirteenth, Fourteenth and Fifteenth), it may authorize damage suits against the states that would otherwise be barred by the Eleventh Amendment. That is what's happening here.

(B) is wrong because it is overbroad. As a general rule Congress, even where it is acting pursuant to some power given to it by a specific provision in the Constitution, may not override the state immunity from federal-court damage suits conferred by the Eleventh Amendment; enforcement of the post-Civil War amendments represents the only exception to this rule.

(C) is wrong for essentially the same reason: the Eleventh Amendment *does* generally limit the power of Congress (not just the power of the federal judiciary) to modify the sovereign-immunity of the states, but the Supreme Court has held that in the special case in which Congress is enforcing the post-Civil War amendments this general limitation on Congress's power does not apply. *Fitzpatrick v. Bitzer* (1976).

(D) is wrong because it is a flat misstatement of law: the Supreme Court has held that the Eleventh Amendment protects a state from federal-court damage suits even where the suit is brought by a citizen of a different state. *Hans v. Louisiana* (1890).

CONTRACTS

CONTRACTS Q&A BY TOPIC

References to "Rest. 2d" are to the *Second Restatement of Contracts*, to "Farnsworth" are to E.A. Farnsworth, *Contracts* (3d Ed. Aspen, 1999), and to "W&S" are to White & Summers, *Uniform Commercial Code* (5th Ed. West, 2000).

CHAPTER 1

OFFER AND ACCEPTANCE

I.   THE ACCEPTANCE

A. Method of acceptance

1. Offer invites either promise or performance

a. Shipment of goods

i.   Acceptance by shipment of non-conforming goods

Question 1: A retailer ordered from a produce wholesaler 500 bushels of No. 1 Royal Fuzz peaches, at a specified price, "for prompt shipment." The wholesaler promptly shipped 500 bushels, but by mistake shipped No. 2 Royal Fuzz peaches instead of No. 1. The error in shipment was caused by the negligence of the wholesaler's shipping clerk.

Which of the following best states the retailer's rights and duties upon delivery of the peaches?

(A) The wholesaler's shipment of the peaches was a counteroffer and the retailer can refuse to accept them.

(B) The wholesaler's shipment of the peaches was a counteroffer but, since peaches are perishable, the retailer, if it does not want to accept them, must reship the peaches to the wholesaler in order to mitigate the wholesaler's losses.

(C) The retailer must accept the peaches because a contract was formed when the wholesaler shipped them.

(D) Although a contract was formed when the wholesaler shipped the peaches, the retailer does not have to accept them.

[Q1141]

Answer 1: Choice **(D)** is correct. The retailer's order was an offer. The wholesaler's shipment of goods in response to the offer was an acceptance, even though what the wholesaler shipped was non-conforming goods. That's so because § 2-206(1)(b) says that "an order or other offer to buy goods for prompt or current shipment shall be construed as inviting *acceptance* ... by the prompt or current *shipment* of conforming or *non-conforming goods*[.]" A buyer who receives non-conforming goods has the right to reject those goods, sending them back to the seller or holding them for the seller's pickup. That's because § 2-601 says that, subject to some limitations not applicable here, "If the goods or the tender of delivery fail in any respect to conform to the contract, the buyer may (a) reject the whole; or (b) accept the whole; or (c) accept any commercial unit or units and reject the rest." So the retailer could reject all or some of the bushels.

(A) is wrong because the wholesaler's shipment was not a counteroffer, since that nothing in the facts surrounding the shipment indicated that the wholesaler was rejecting the retailer's offer (its order). Instead, the wholesaler's shipment was an acceptance (as well as a breach).

(B) is wrong because: (1) the wholesaler's shipment was not a counteroffer (for the reason described in the analysis of Choice (A)); and (2) under § 2-602(2), if the retailer wants to reject rather than accept the peaches, it is merely required "after rejection to hold [the goods] with reasonable care at the seller's disposition for a time sufficient to permit the seller to remove them." So despite the peaches' perishability, all the retailer has to do is to promptly notify the wholesaler, "We don't want the peaches because they don't conform; we'll hold them for you to pick up."

(C) is wrong because, although a contract was indeed formed when the wholesaler shipped the peaches, their non-conformity to the retailer's order entitled the retailer to reject the goods rather than accept them.

b. Accommodation shipment

Question 2: A retailer faxed the following signed message to his long-time widget supplier: "Urgently need blue widgets. Ship immediately three gross at your current list price of $600." Upon receipt of the fax, the supplier shipped three gross of red widgets to the retailer, and faxed to retailer the following message: "Temporarily out of blue. In case red will help, am shipping three gross at the same price. Hope you can use them."

Upon the retailer's timely receipt of both the shipment and the supplier's fax, which of the following best describes the rights and duties of the retailer and the wholesaler?

(A) The retailer may accept the shipment, in which case he must pay the wholesaler the list price, or he must reject the shipment and recover from the wholesaler for total breach of contract.

(B) The retailer may accept the shipment, in which case he must pay the wholesaler the list price, or he may reject the shipment, in which case he has no further rights against the wholesaler.

(C) The retailer may accept the shipment, in which case he must pay the wholesaler the list price, less any damages sustained because of the nonconforming shipment, or he may reject the shipment and recover from the wholesaler for total breach of contract, subject to the wholesaler's right to cure.

(D) The retailer may accept the shipment, in which case he must pay the wholesaler the list price, less any damages sustained because of the nonconforming shipment, or he may reject the shipment provided that he promptly covers by obtaining conforming widgets from another supplier.

[Q2111]

Answer 2: Choice **(B)** is correct. This was an accommodation shipment under UCC § 2-206(1)(b) — in the words of that section, the supplier "seasonably notifie[d] the buyer that the shipment [was] offered only as an accommodation to the buyer." Therefore, the supplier's shipment did not constitute an acceptance. Instead, it was a counteroffer to sell three gross of red widgets. At that point, the retailer could choose between accepting the red and paying for them, or rejecting the red, in which case there would be no contract (because there never was an accepted offer).

(A) is wrong because when a seller makes an accommodation shipment, the buyer has the right to reject the shipment but does not have the right to recover for breach. That's because the shipment is not an acceptance but instead a counteroffer, and the buyer's rejection of the goods constitutes a rejection of the counteroffer, with the result that there is no breach by the seller for which the buyer could recover.

(C) is wrong for two reasons: (1) if the retailer accepts the shipment, he cannot deduct any damages because of the nonconformity (since this type of accommodation shipment constitutes a counteroffer rather than acceptance, making the buyer's decision to keep the goods an acceptance of the goods as shipped, meaning that the nonconformity to the original order is irrelevant); and (2) if the retailer rejects the shipment, he has simply rejected the supplier's counteroffer, and there is no breach for which the retailer can deduct.

(D) is wrong for two reasons: (1) if the retailer accepts the shipment, he cannot deduct any damages because of the nonconformity (for the reasons described in the analysis of Choice (C) above); and (2) if the retailer rejects the shipment, he may do so without covering by obtaining conforming widgets from someone else. (He may, for instance, decide that he doesn't need widgets of any color after all.)

2. Notice of acceptance of unilateral contract

a. Suretyship contracts

Question 3: A hardware distributor located on the West Coast gave its customer, a hardware retailer who was relocating to the East Coast, the following signed "letter of introduction" to a hardware manufacturer based on the East coast:

> This will introduce you to my good friend and former customer, who is a retailer and will be seeking to arrange the purchase of hardware inventory from you on credit. If you will let him have the goods, I will make good any loss up to $25,000 in the event of his default.

The retailer presented the letter to the manufacturer, who then sold and delivered $20,000 worth of hardware to the retailer on credit. The manufacturer promptly notified the distributor of this sale.

Which of the following is NOT an accurate statement concerning the arrangement between the distributor and the manufacturer?

(A) It was important to enforceability of the distributor's promise to the manufacturer that it be embodied in a signed writing.

(B) By extending the credit to the retailer, the manufacturer effectively accepted the distributor's offer for a unilateral contract.

(C) Although the distributor received no consideration from the retailer, the distributor's promise is enforceable by the manufacturer.

(D) The distributor's promise is enforceable by the manufacturer whether or not the manufacturer gave the distributor seasonable notice of the extension of credit to the retailer.

[Q2174]

Answer 3: Choice **(D)** is correct (i.e., the statement in this chioce is *not* accurate). When the distributor wrote the letter and induced the customer to present the letter to the manufacturer, the distributor was making an offer for a unilateral contract — that is, it's clear that the distributor was expecting the manufacturer to accept (if he accepted at all) by extending the credit, rather than promising the distributor that he would extend the credit. When the manufacturer extended the credit, this was an acceptance of the distributor's offer by performance, so the distributor's guarantee of repayment came into effect. However, because of the requirement that an offeree who accepts an offer for unilateral contract must ordinarily give prompt notice of acceptance to the offeror, if the manufacturer had not given the distributor prompt notice of the sale (which the facts say he did), the distributor's guarantee duty would have been discharged. Notice that it was up to you to spot the fact that this was an offer for unilateral contract — the facts don't highlight this, and if you hadn't noticed it yourself, you would probably not have seen why notice by the manufacturer was important.

(A) is wrong because the statement is correct: the distributor's promise would not have been enforceable had it not been embodied in a signed writing. That's because the distributor's offer was a promise to "answer for the debt of another." As such, it fell within the suretyship provision of the Statute of Frauds, and was therefore required to be in a writing signed by the party to be charged (the distributor).

(B) is wrong because the statement is correct: as the discussion of Choice (D) describes, the distributor's offer was an offer for a unilateral contract (i.e., one to be accepted by performance rather than return promise), and the manufacturer accepted that offer by doing the requested act, i.e., extending credit to the retailer.

(C) is wrong because the statement is correct. It's true that the distributor received no consideration from the customer. However, the distributor received consideration *from the manufacturer* — the distributor bargained to have the manufacturer give credit to the customer, and got the performance he bargained for. (The fact that the performance ran to the customer rather than to the distributor [the promisor] does not prevent it from being consideration to support the distributor's promise.)

The customer was a third-party beneficiary of the distributor's promise, and in a third-party beneficiary arrangement the fact that the third-party beneficiary does not give consideration to the promisor does not make any difference.

II. ACCEPTANCE VARYING FROM OFFER

A. UCC view

1. "Additional" term in acceptance

a. Both merchants

i. Materiality

Question 4: On June 1, a wholesaler received a purchase-order form from a retailer and new customer, in which the latter ordered 1,000 anti-recoil widgets for delivery no later than August 30 at a delivered total price of $10,000, as quoted in the wholesaler's current catalog. Both parties are merchants with respect to widgets of all types. On June 2, the wholesaler mailed to the retailer its own form, across the top of which the wholesaler's president had written, "We are pleased to accept your order." This form contained the same terms as the retailer's form except for an additional printed clause in the wholesaler's form that provided for a maximum liability of $100 for any breach of contract by the retailer.

As of June 5, when the retailer received the wholesaler's acceptance form, which of the following is an accurate statement concerning the legal relationship between the wholesaler and the retailer?

(A) There is no contract, because the liability-limitation clause in the wholesaler's form is a material alteration of the retailer's offer.

(B) There is no contract, because the retailer did not consent to the liability-limitation clause in the wholesaler's form.

(C) There is an enforceable contract whose terms include the liability-limitation clause in the wholesaler's form, because liquidation of damages is expressly authorized by the Uniform Commercial Code.

(D) There is an enforceable contract whose terms do not include the liability-limitation clause in the wholesaler's form.

[Q2034]

Answer 4: Choice **(D)** is correct. Under the UCC, a purported acceptance document will not be prevented from operating as a true acceptance even though it states terms that are additional to or different from those in the offer. UCC § 2-207(1). Therefore, the wholesaler's form with the "We are please to accept" language on it operated as an acceptance even though it contained an additional term (the liability cap). On the other hand, the liability cap was an "additional" term (i.e., a term dealing with a subject that was not covered in the retailer's offer). When the offeror and offeree are both merchants, § 2-207(2) says that an additional term is to be construed as a "proposal for addition to the contract," and becomes part of the contract unless (1) "the offer expressly limits acceptance to the terms of the offer" (which didn't happen here), (2) the additional term "materially alter[s]" the contract, or (3) the offeror promptly notifies the offeree that the offeror objects to the additional term. Here, event (2) has occurred: a liability cap would almost certainly be considered by a court to be a "material alteration" of an offer that did not contain any cap. Therefore, a contract was formed but it did not include the liability cap.

(A) is wrong because, as explained in more detail in Choice (D) above, while the liability-limitation clause was indeed a material alteration of the offer, this fact did not prevent the wholesaler's form from constituting an acceptance. (The wholesaler's form meshed sufficiently with the retailer's offer form, and contained sufficient words of acceptance, that it was a "definite ... expression of acceptance" under § 2-207(1) even though it contained the additional term.)

(B) is wrong because a contract was formed as soon as the wholesaler sent its form, and whether the retailer eventually did or did not expressly consent to the liability-limitation clause wouldn't matter to the issue of whether a contract was formed. (As explained in the discussion of Choice (D), the liability-limitation clause, since it was a material alteration, didn't become part of the contract even if the retailer remained silent.)

(C) is wrong because, while it correctly says that a contract is formed, it is incorrect in stating that the liability-limitation clause would become part of the contract. It's true that a liquidation-of-damages clause can, if the parties agree on it and it is reasonable, be enforced under the UCC. But such a clause won't enter the contract unless the parties somehow agree on the clause, and here, because the proposed clause was a material alteration, the retailer won't be presumed to have agreed from the mere fact that the clause was present on the wholesaler's acceptance and the retailer remained silent.

2. Contract by parties' conduct

a. "Acceptance by conduct" can occur in non-UCC contracts

i. Acts during course of extended negotiations

Question 5: A developer, needing a water well on one of his projects, met several times about the matter with a well driller. Subsequently, the driller sent the developer an unsigned typewritten form captioned "WELL DRILLING PROPOSAL" and stating various terms the two had discussed but not agreed upon, including a "proposed price of $5,000." The form concluded, "This proposal will not become a contract until signed by you [the developer] and then returned to and signed by me [the driller]."

The developer signed the form and returned it to the driller, who neglected to sign it but promptly began drilling the well at the proposed site on the developer's project. After drilling for two days, the driller told the developer during one of the developer's daily visits that he would not finish unless the developer would agree to pay twice the price recited in the written proposal. The developer refused, the driller quit, and the developer hired a substitute driller to drill the well to completion for a price of $7,500.

In an action by the developer against the driller for damages, which of the following is the probable decision?

(A) The developer wins, because his signing of the driller's form constituted an acceptance of an offer by the driller.

(B) The developer wins, because the driller's commencement of performance constituted an acceptance by the driller of an offer by the developer and an implied promise by the driller to complete the well.

(C) The driller wins, because he never signed the proposal as required by its terms.

(D) The driller wins, because his commencement of performance merely prevented the developer from revoking his offer, made on a form supplied by the driller, and did not obligate the driller to complete the well.

[Q1041]

Answer 5: Choice **(B)** is correct. The driller's "proposal" was not an offer, because it could not be accepted by the unilateral act of the recipient (since by its terms it could not become a contract until it was not only signed by the developer, the recipient, but also signed by the driller). When the developer signed the form and and returned it to the driller, the developer was making an offer on the terms described in the form. The driller could have accepted the offer by signing, but didn't in fact sign. However, when the driller started work, his conduct of doing the work described in the form, at the appropriate place, constituted an acceptance by conduct. This acceptance-by-conduct included a promise (albeit an implied one) to complete the work as described in the offer document (the form that the driller didn't sign).

(A) is wrong because, although it lists the correct result, it explains it on an incorrect legal theory. The driller's form could not be an offer, because the provision requiring both signatures meant that the unsigned form as dispatched by the driller did not empower the recipient (the developer) to unilaterally complete the deal (i.e., accept) by signing. Therefore, the developer's signature created an offer, not an acceptance. (And acceptance did not occur until the driller accepted by conduct.)

(C) is wrong because, although the driller never accepted by signature, he did accept by his conduct of starting the well drilling.

(D) is wrong because it misstates the effect of the driller's commencement of performance. That commencement of performance served as an acceptance of the contract, and thereby obligated the driller to complete his side of the deal.

III. DURATION OF THE POWER OF ACCEPTANCE

A. Irrevocable offers

1. "Firm offers" under the UCC

Question 6: On December 15, a lawyer received from a stationer an offer consisting of its catalog and a signed letter stating, "We will supply you with as many of the items in the enclosed catalog as you order during the next calendar year. We assure you that this offer and the prices in the catalog will remain firm throughout the coming year." On January 15, having at that time received no reply from the lawyer, the stationer notified the lawyer that, effective February 1, it was increasing the prices of certain specified items in its catalog.

Is the price increase effective with respect to catalog orders the stationer receives from the lawyer during the month of February?

(A) No, because the stationer's original offer, including the price term, became irrevocable under the doctrine of promissory estoppel.

(B) No, because the stationer is a merchant with respect to office supplies; and its original offer, including the price term, was irrevocable throughout the month of February.

(C) Yes, because the stationer received no consideration to support its assurance that it would not increase prices.

(D) Yes, because the period for which the stationer gave assurance that it would not raise prices was longer than three months.

[Q3028]

Answer 6: Choice **(B)** is correct. This was a firm offer that met the requirements of UCC § 2-205, since it was (1) by a merchant; (2) in a letter signed by the offeror; and (3) it promised that the offeror would sell all items at the catalog price for a year (a promise to hold the offer open). It's true that this promise of irrevocability didn't legally extend beyond three months (despite what it said), but the three months was enough to cover February.

(A) is wrong because, while the doctrine of promissory estoppel says that detrimental reliance by the offeree may render an offer temporarily irrevocable, here there is no indication that the lawyer detrimentally relied on the stationer's offer.

(C) is wrong because the UCC does not require consideration for an offer to be irrevocable. The whole point of § 2-205's firm-offer provision is that qualifying offers by merchants will be irrevocable even though not supported by consideration.

(D) is wrong because, while the maximum period of irrevocability for firm orders under UCC § 2-205 is three months, when an offer that otherwise meets the firm-offer requirements promises more than three months' irrevocability, the offer will nonetheless be irrevocable for three months.

a. Effect if not by a merchant

Question 7: On November 1, Debbit, an accountant, and Barrister, a lawyer, contracted for the sale by Debbit to Barrister of the law books Debbit had inherited from his father. Barrister agreed to pay the purchase price of $10,000 when Debbit delivered the books on December 1.

On November 10, Barrister received a signed letter from Debbit that stated: "I have decided to dispose of the book stacks containing the law books you have already purchased. If you want the stacks, I will deliver them to you along with the books on December 1 at no additional cost to you. Let me know before November 15 whether you want them. I will not sell them to anyone else before then." Debbit was not a merchant with respect to either law books or book stacks.

On November 12 Debbit told Banister that he had decided not to part with the stacks. Will this communication operate as a legally effective revocation of his offer to deliver the stacks?

(A) Yes, because Barrister had a pre-existing obligation to pay $10,000 for the law books.

(B) Yes, because Debbit was not a merchant with respect to book stacks.

(C) No, because Debbit had given a signed assurance that the offer would be held open until November 15.

(D) No, because by delaying his acceptance until November 14, Barrister detrimentally relied on Debbit's promise not to sell the stacks to anyone else in the meantime.

[Q2134]

Answer 7: Choice **(B)** is correct. An offer is revocable unless some special circumstance makes it irrevocable. The contract here is covered by the UCC, making §2-205's firm-offer provision potentially applicable. However, §2-205 applies only to "an offer by a merchant." We are told that Debbit is not a merchant with respect to either lawbooks or book stacks. Therefore, his offer was not a firm offer and could be revoked at any time. Consequently, his statement on November 12 that he had decided not to part with the stacks was a legally operative revocation.

(A) is wrong because Barrister's pre-existing obligation to pay $10,000 for the law books is irrelevant on the issue of whether Debbit's offer about the stacks was irrevocable. Debbit's offer was an offer to modify the contract, and that offer was not rendered irrevocable merely because Barrister had previously given consideration (his promise to pay $10,000) to support Debbit's prior promise to sell the law books.

(C) is wrong because an offer is not rendered irrevocable merely because the offer is signed and states that it is irrevocable. Under the UCC, a signed offer that says it will be irrevocable will be so under some circumstances, but as explained above those circumstances include a requirement that the offeror be a merchant.

(D) is wrong because Barrister did not in fact detrimentally rely. If Barrister *had* detrimentally relied on Debbit's promise not to sell the stacks to someone else, this reliance might indeed have caused the offer to become temporarily irrevocable. But a mere delay in accepting is not the sort of detrimental reliance that will suffice for temporary irrevocability.

2. Part performance or detrimental reliance

a. Offer for unilateral contract

Question 8: While waiting in line to open an account with a bank, a customer read a poster on the bank's wall that said, "New Customers! $25 FOR 5 MINUTES. If you stand in line for more than five minutes, we will pay you $25! We like happy customers! (This offer may be withdrawn at any time.)" The customer started timing his wait and just as five minutes was about to pass, the bank manager tore the poster down and announced, "The $25 stand-in-line promotion is over." The customer waited in line for 10 more minutes before being served.

In the customer's action against the bank for $25, will the customer prevail?

(A) No, because the bank withdrew its offer before the customer completed the requested performance.

(B) No, because the bank's statement was a nonbinding gift promise.

(C) Yes, because the bank could not revoke its offer once the customer had commenced performance.

(D) Yes, because the customer's presence in line served as notice to the bank that he had accepted.

[QA036]

Answer 8: Choice **(C)** is correct. Where an offer invites acceptance by performance, the offeree's beginning of performance creates an option contract, which precludes the offeror from revoking its offer. See Rest. 2d, § 45. The customer's beginning to wait in line created the option contract, which couldn't be revoked as long as the customer continued to wait. Notice that this fact pattern is exactly like the famous law-school hypothetical, "I'll pay you $10 if you cross the Brooklyn Bridge," where once the offeree starts to cross, the offeror can't revoke while the offeree is still trying to finish. You might think that the "This offer may be withdrawn at any time" language would change the result; but a court would likely interpret this to apply only to customers who hadn't yet started to wait on line at the moment the offer was withdrawn. See, e.g., Rest. 2d § 45, Comment b, saying that the "option contract" effect "yields to a manifestation of intention which makes reliance unjustified. A reservation of power to revoke *after performance has begun* means that as yet there is no promise and no offer"; the reservation of power to revoke here was not a reservation to revoke "after performance [i.e., waiting on line] has begun," so the right-to-withdraw language would be interpreted to be inapplicable to the customer here.

(A) is wrong because the bank's offer was an offer for a unilateral contract (i.e., an offer that was to be accepted by a performance rather than by a promise), and an offer for a unilateral contract becomes temporarily irrevocable once the offeree has begun to perform. See Choice (C).

(B) is wrong because the consideration required for an enforceable contract is present. The bank's promise to pay the customer $25 and the customer's standing in line constituted a bargained-for exchange. See Rest. 2d, § 71: a performance is consideration if it is "bargained for," and a performance is bargained for if it is "sought by the promisor [here, the bank] in exchange for his promise and is given by the promisee [the customer] in exchange for that promise."

(D) is wrong because it misstates the legal significance of the customer's presence in line. The offer here was an offer for a unilateral contract, that is, an offer that was to be accepted by performance (waiting in line for more than 5 minutes). Therefore, while the customer's mere presence in line constituted the *beginning* of performance, it did not constitute full performance (i.e., standing in line for more than five minutes), which was the only way the customer could accept. It's true that one who accepts an offer for a unilateral contract must sometimes give notice of acceptance-by-performance; but that's true only where the offeror would not otherwise know of the performance (which is not the case here). And in any event, the required notice would be notice of completed performance, not notice of the beginning of performance.

CHAPTER 2

CONSIDERATION

I. THE BARGAIN ELEMENT

A. Promises to make gifts

1. Existence of condition

a. Mixture of bargain and gift

Question 9: Rollem, an automobile retailer, had an adult daughter, Betsy, who needed a car in her employment but had only $3,000 with which to buy one. Rollem wrote to her, "Give me your $3,000 and I'll give you the car on our lot that we have been using as a demonstrator." Betsy thanked her father and paid him the $3,000. As both Rollem and Betsy knew, the demonstrator was reasonably worth $10,000. After Betsy had paid the $3,000, but before the car had been delivered to her, one of Rollem's sales staff sold and delivered the same car to a customer for $10,000. Neither the salesperson nor the customer was aware of the transaction between Rollem and Betsy.

Does Betsy, after rejecting a tendered return of the $3,000 by Rollem, have an action against him for breach of contract?

(A) Yes, because Rollem's promise was supported by bargained-for consideration.

(B) Yes, because Rollem's promise was supported by the moral obligation a father owes his child as to the necessities of modern life.

(C) No, because the payment of $3,000 was inadequate consideration to support Rollem's promise.

(D) No, because the salesperson's delivery of the car to the customer made it impossible for Rollem to perform.

[Q2024]

Answer 9: Choice **(A)** is correct. Where a transaction is a mixture of a bargain and a gift, the consideration requirement is satisfied. That is the case where, as here, one party promises to sell the other an item at a deep discount from market. Since Rollem was unquestionably bargaining for Betsy's payment of $3,000, the fact that this payment was much less than the market price does not prevent Betsy's payment from being consideration for Rollem's promise.

(B) is wrong as a matter of consideration doctrine, because a promise that is made on account of moral obligation is not supported by consideration. Furthermore, it is doubtful that contract law would regard a father as having any sort of obligation, even a moral one, to supply his adult daughter with a car.

(C) is wrong because contract law does not consider the adequacy of consideration, as long as the bargain and detriment of elements are satisfied. So here, since Rollem clearly bargained for Betsy's $3,000, the fact that this amount was arguably "inadequate" won't matter.

(D) is wrong because the defense of impossibility would not apply on these facts. Where a seller, acting through his agent, sells the contracted-for goods to someone else, this action will be viewed as being voluntary on the seller's part, and therefore not the sort of involuntary event to which the impossibility doctrine applies.

II. THE "DETRIMENT" ELEMENT

A. Generally

1. Motives irrelevant

Question 10: A small-business owner encourages "wellness" on the part of his employees and supports various physical-fitness programs to that end. Learning that one of his employees was a dedicated jogger, the business owner promised to pay the jogger a special award of $100 if she could and would run one mile in less than six minutes on the following Saturday. The jogger thanked him, and did in fact run a mile in less than six minutes on the day specified. Shortly thereafter, however, the business owner discovered that for more than a year the jogger had been running at least one mile in less than six minutes every day as a part of her personal fitness program. He refused to pay the $100.

In an action by the jogger against the business owner for breach of contract, which of the following best summarizes the probable decision of the court?

(A) The business owner wins, because it is a compelling inference that the business owner's promise did not induce the jogger to run the specified mile.

(B) The business owner wins, because the jogger's running of the specified mile was beneficial, not detrimental, to her in any event.

(C) The jogger wins, because running a mile in less than six minutes is a significantly demanding enterprise.

(D) The jogger wins, because she ran the specified mile as requested, and her motives for doing so are irrelevant.

[Q2029]

Answer 10: Choice **(D)** is correct. The only way the business owner can conceivably win is if he can show that his promise was not supported by consideration. But the business owner bargained for the jogger's act of running the six-minute mile. Since the business owner received the bargained act, the consideration requirement was satisfied. The jogger's motives in doing the act — including the fact that she would have done the act anyway without the business owner's request — are indeed irrelevant, as this choice states.

(A) is wrong because it would not matter even if the business owner's promise did not induce the jogger to run the mile. The business owner bargained for a six-minute mile to be run by the jogger, and got it; that's all that matters. So the fact that the jogger would have run that mile on that day anyway is irrelevant.

(B) is wrong because even in courts still interpreting the consideration doctrine to include a requirement that the promisee undergo a "detriment," all that is required is a "legal detriment." "Legal detriment" is really shorthand for "any act, forbearance or promise." The fact that the requested act, forbearance or promise would be of "benefit" to the promisee is irrelevant. Since the jogger performed the requested act, the fact that the doing of that act may have been a benefit to her health therefore doesn't matter.

(C) is wrong because it explains the correct result with incorrect reasoning. Since the jogger performed the requested act, she satisfies the "act, forbearance or promise" aspect of the consideration requirement whether or not the requested act was "significantly demanding" for her.

B. Pre-existing duty rule

1. Modification

Question 11: An accountant entered into a contract with a painter by the terms of which the painter was to paint the accountant's office for $1,000 and was required to do all of the work over the following weekend so as to avoid disruption of the accountant's business.

If the painter had started to paint on the following Saturday morning, he could have finished before Sunday evening. However, he stayed home that Saturday morning to watch the final game of the World Series on TV, and did not start to paint until Saturday afternoon. By late Saturday afternoon, the painter realized that he had underestimated the time it would take to finish the job if he continued to work alone. The painter phoned the accountant at her home and accurately informed her that it was impossible to finish the work over the weekend unless he hired a helper. He also stated that to do so would require an additional charge of $200 for the work. The accountant told the painter that she apparently had no choice but to pay "whatever it takes" to get the work done as scheduled.

The painter hired a helper to help finish the painting and paid the helper $200. The accountant has offered to pay the painter $1,000. The painter is demanding $1,200.

How much is the painter likely to recover?

(A) $1,000 only, because the accountant received no consideration for her promise to pay the additional sum.

(B) $1,000 only, because the accountant's promise to pay "whatever it takes" is too uncertain to be enforceable.

(C) $1,200, in order to prevent the accountant's unjust enrichment.

(D) $1,200, because the impossibility of the painter's completing the work alone discharged the original contract and a new contract was formed.

[Q1120]

Answer 11: Choice **(A)** is correct. If parties to an existing contract agree to modify the contract for the sole benefit for one of them, the modification will usually be unenforceable in non-UCC cases, for lack of consideration. That's because of the pre-existing duty rule: When one party to an existing contract makes an additional promise, and the other party merely promises to do what she is already required to do, the former's promise is not supported by consideration. A primary function of the pre-existing duty rule is to refuse to reward "hold-up" behavior by a provider of services, who in the middle of the contract refuses to complete performance unless she gets a better price or other improved terms. That's exactly what happened here: The painter has unfairly extracted the $200 promise from the accountant when it's too late for the accountant to get a substitute. So the accountant's promise will be unenforceable unless some exception to the pre-existing duty rule applies. Two common exceptions are that: (1) there were unanticipated circumstances that made the painter's request for more money not unreasonable, or (2) the painter agreed to do some additional duty beyond what he was already required to do. But neither of these exceptions (or any other) applies here, so the pre-existing duty rule applies and the accountant's promise is unenforceable for lack of consideration.

(B) is wrong because the accountant's promise is not too uncertain. The parties were not agreeing to a charge of "whatever it takes" — they were instead agreeing to a charge of $200, with the accountant's "whatever it takes" remark being more in the nature of a side commentary (e.g., "I'm agreeing to the $200 because I would in fact agree to whatever it took to get you to finish the work.").

(C) is wrong because letting the accountant escape from her $200-extra-compensation promise would not lead to her unjust enrichment. The painter is only doing exactly what he always agreed to do for exactly the price the two parties agreed to, so depriving him of his unfairly-extracted extra $200 would not constitute unjust enrichment to the accountant.

(D) is wrong because a party's inability to complete performance due to that party's own delay or poor planning does not constitute the sort of extraordinary and unanticipated occurrence to which the impossibility doctrine applies. In general, only "external" events (e.g., an act of God, a strike, etc.) will qualify for the impossibility defense.

a. Unanticipated circumstances

Question 12: A contractor contracted with a warehouse owner to construct for $500,000 a warehouse and an access driveway at highway level on the owner's property. Shortly after commencing work on the driveway, which required for the specified level some excavation and removal of surface material, the contractor unexpectedly encountered a large mass of solid rock. The contractor informed the owner (accurately) that because of the rock the driveway as specified would cost at least $20,000 more than figured, and demanded for that reason a total contract price of $520,000. Since the owner was expecting warehousing customers immediately after the agreed completion date, he signed a writing promising to pay the additional $20,000. Following timely completion of the warehouse and driveway, which conformed to the contract in all respects, the owner refused to pay the contractor more than $500,000.

What is the maximum amount to which the contractor is entitled?

(A) $500,000, because there was no consideration for the owner's promise to pay the additional $20,000.

(B) $500,000, because the owner's promise to pay the additional $20,000 was exacted under duress.

(C) $520,000, because the modification was fair and was made in the light of circumstances not anticipated by the parties when the original contract was made.

(D) $520,000, provided that the reasonable value of the contractor's total performance was that much or more.

[Q2004]

Answer 12: Choice **(C)** is correct. Although the general rule is that a modification solely benefiting one party is unenforceable due to lack of consideration, there is a very important exception: if the modification is "*fair and equitable* in view of *circumstances not anticipated by the parties* when the contract was made," the modification will be binding without consideration. That is the case here: the large amount of rock was a "circumstance not anticipated by the parties when the contract was made," and the $20,000 seems to have been a fair estimate of the increased cost to the contractor in performing. Therefore, the fact that the contractor gave no consideration for the owner's promise to pay the extra $20,000 (the contractor merely promised to do what he was already obligated to do, i.e., build the warehouse and driveway) is irrelevant.

(A) is wrong because, although it is true that there was no consideration for the owner's promise to pay the additional $20,000, the absence of consideration does not matter for the reason explained in the discussion of Choice (C).

(B) is wrong because the contractor's request for the extra $20,000 would not be deemed by a court to have been constituted duress. If no rock had been discovered, and the contractor had demanded the extra $20,000 merely because he knew that the owner was time-sensitive and vulnerable, this choice would probably be correct in result and reasoning. But because the facts make it clear that the $20,000 *was* merely an adjustment on account of the unanticipated cost of the excavating the rock, no duress will be found.

(D) is wrong because it gives the wrong explanation for the correct result. Even if the reasonable value of the contractor's total performance was $520,000 or greater, the contractor would not receive the extra $20,000 if the increase was due to the owner's desperation to have the project completed on time rather than due to an unanticipated circumstance (the rock) — in that case the requirement of consideration would render the modification unenforceable regardless of the "value" of the total performance.

2. Duty owed to third person rather than to promisor

Question 13: A burglar stole Collecta's impressionist painting valued at $400,000. Collecta, who had insured the painting for $300,000 with Artistic Insurance Co., promised to pay $25,000 to Snoop, a full-time investigator for Artistic, if he effected the return of the painting to her in good condition. By company rules, Artistic permits its investigators to accept and retain rewards from policyholders for the recovery of insured property. Snoop, by long and skillful detective work, recovered the picture and returned it undamaged to Collecta.

If Collecta refuses to pay Snoop anything, and he sues her for $25,000, what is the probable result under the prevailing modern rule?

(A) Collecta wins, because Snoop owed Artistic a pre-existing duty to recover the picture if possible.

(B) Collecta wins, because Artistic, Snoop's employer, had a pre-existing duty to return the recovered painting to Collecta.

(C) Snoop wins, because Collecta will benefit more from return of the $400,000 painting than from receiving the $300,000 policy proceeds.

(D) Snoop wins, because the pre-existing duty rule does not apply if the promisee's (Snoop's) duty was owed to a third person.

[Q2186]

Answer 13: Choice **(D)** is correct. If the promisee merely does or promises to do what the promisee is already legally obligated *to the promisor* to do, under the pre-existing duty rule that performance or return promise does not serve as consideration for the promisor's promise. But this rule does not apply where the promisee does or promises to do something that is already legally owed not to the promisor but to some *third person.* This exception applies here, since Snoop (the promisee) does not owe any contractual duty to the promisor (Collecta), merely to a third party (Artistic).

(A) is wrong because, while Snoop indeed owed Artistic a pre-existing duty to recover the picture if possible, no duty was owed to the promisor (Collecta), and that's what matters, as explained in the discussion of Choice (D) above.

(B) is wrong because the fact that Artistic may have had a pre-existing duty to return the recovered painting to Collecta is irrelevant, since it is not Artistic that was the promisee of Collecta's promise of a bonus (Snoop was). For the pre-existing duty rule to apply it must be the promisee who has the pre-existing duty (and who owes that duty to the promisor).

(C) is wrong because it states an irrelevant fact. The issue is whether the pre-existing duty rule applies, and the fact that the promisor would receive some net benefit if the promisee performed the act he was already legally obligated to perform does not render the pre-existing rule inapplicable. (Virtually *every* time the promisor makes a promise in return for the promisee's performance of an already-owed duty, the promisor expects to do better than if the promisee didn't perform, otherwise the promisor wouldn't be making the promise; yet the pre-existing duty rule applies to these situations.)

3. Agreement to accept part payment of debt

a. Disputed debt

Question 14: In a written contract, an architect agreed to draw up the plans for and to supervise construction of a client's new house. In return, the client agreed to pay the architect a fee of $10,000 to be paid upon the house's completion. After completion, the client claimed erroneously but in good faith that the architect's plans were defective. The client orally offered to pay the architect $7,500 in full settlement of the claim for the fee. The architect orally accepted that offer despite the fact that the reasonable value of his services was in fact $10,000. The client paid the architect $7,500 pursuant to their agreement.

The architect subsequently sued the client for the remaining $2,500. In a preliminary finding, the trier of fact found that there were no defects in the architect's plans.

Will the architect be likely to prevail in his action against the client for $2,500?

(A) Yes, because payment of $7,500 cannot furnish consideration for the architect's promise to surrender his claim.

(B) Yes, because the oral agreement to modify the written contract is not enforceable.

(C) No, because the architect's promise to accept $7,500 became binding when the client made the payment.

(D) No, because the architect's acceptance of partial payment constituted a novation.

[QA017]

Answer 14: Choice **(C)** is correct. It's true that under the pre-existing duty rule, as a general matter a party who promises to accept less than the amount or other performance he is owed has not received consideration for that promise. So, for instance, a creditor with an unquestionably-valid liquidated claim who agrees to accept partial payment won't be bound. But all courts recognize an important exception to this rule, in order to encourage settlements: where either (a) the creditor's claim (or a defense to it) is in fact of *uncertain validity*; or (b) the debtor honestly *believes* that the claim may be invalid (or that the debtor's defense may be valid), then the creditor's agreement to take partial payment *is* supported by consideration, namely the debtor's promise to pay a lesser amount. And that's true even if it later turns out that the claim was valid and/or the defense was invalid. See Rest. 2d, §74. (In this situation, the settlement agreement is an "executory accord," which becomes a completed "accord-and-satisfaction" when the agreed-upon partial payment is made, thereby extinguishing the creditor's original claim for the whole amount.)

That's exactly what happened here: the client believed in good faith (even though, as it turned out, erroneously) that she had a valid defense, based on the defectiveness of the architect's performance. Her agreement to pay the architect's claim in return for a $2,500 discount was thus a surrender of her good-faith potential defense, and that surrender furnished consideration for the architect's return promise to give the discount. Therefore, the architect's promise to give the discount was binding on him, as an executory accord that became a completed accord-and-satisfaction at the moment the client paid the $7,500.

(A) is wrong because of the special rule validating compromises of claims that are disputed in good faith. The rule of *Foakes v. Beer*, which is a specific application of the pre-existing duty rule, provides that a promise to accept partial payment of a liquidated and undisputed debt is invalid for a lack of consideration. The rule does not apply, however, where there is a compromise of a claim disputed in good faith. This exception applies even if it later becomes apparent that the reason for disputing the claim was invalid. See the analysis of Choice (C) for more information.

(B) is wrong for two reasons. First, there is nothing in these facts that makes the Statute of Frauds applicable, as this choice suggests. Oral contracts are valid unless the situation falls within one of the enumerated Statute of Frauds categories, which this one does not. Oral modifications are ordinarily binding as long as neither the original contract nor the contract-as-modified falls within the Statute of Frauds. And the fact that the original contract was in writing does not change this. If the written contract had contained a "No Oral Modifications" clause, then this clause *would* have been enforceable to make an oral modification (such as a modification of the price) unenforceable. But there is no indication in these facts that an N.O.M. clause was present. Furthermore, even if there *was* an N.O.M. clause, it's likely that the court would conclude that full performance (the payment of the agreed-upon lesser sum, and its acceptance by the architect) caused the N.O.M. clause to become ineffective.

Second, even if the original contract *had* been within the Statute of Frauds, full performance by both parties — the architect's doing of the work, and the client's payment to the agreed-upon lesser sum — would have caused the statute of frauds to disappear as a defense anyway. (See Rest. 2d, §145.)

(D) is wrong because the facts here did not involve a novation. A novation arises where either one or both of the parties to a contract is replaced by a *third party*. See Rest. 2d, § 280. The architect's acceptance of payment does not constitute a novation, since neither the client nor the architect was replaced by a third party.

b.   Cashing of check tendered as settlement

i.   How tested on the MBE

Question 15: A client consulted a lawyer about handling the sale of the client's building, and asked the lawyer what her legal fee would be. The lawyer replied that her usual charge was $100 per hour, and estimated that the legal work on behalf of the client would cost about $5,000 at that rate. The client said, "Okay; let's proceed with it," and the lawyer timely and successfully completed the work. Because of unexpected title problems, the lawyer reasonably spent 75 hours on the matter and shortly thereafter mailed the client a bill for $7,500, with a letter itemizing the work performed and time spent. The client responded by a letter expressing his good-faith belief that the lawyer had agreed to a total fee of no more than $5,000. The client enclosed a check in the amount of $5,000 payable to the lawyer and conspicuously marked, "Payment in full for legal services in connection with the sale of [the client's] building." Despite reading the "Payment in full..." language, the lawyer, without any notation of protest or reservation of rights, endorsed and deposited the check to her bank account. The check was duly paid by the client's bank. A few days later, the lawyer unsuccessfully demanded payment from the client of the $2,500 difference between the amount of her bill and the check, and now sues the client for that difference.

What, if anything, can the lawyer recover from the client?

(A) Nothing, because the risk of unexpected title problems in a real-property transaction is properly allocable to the seller's attorney and thus to the lawyer in this case.

(B) Nothing, because the amount of the lawyer's fee was disputed in good faith by the client, and the lawyer impliedly agreed to an accord and satisfaction.

(C) $2,500, because the client agreed to an hourly rate for as many hours as the work reasonably required, and the sum of $5,000 was merely an estimate.

(D) The reasonable value of the lawyer's services in excess of $5,000, if any, because there was no specific agreement on the total amount of the lawyer's fee.

[Q2123]

Answer 15: Choice **(B)** is correct. UCC § 3-311 deals with the effect of a creditor's cashing of an "in full settlement" partial-payment check. To get the protection of § 3-311 (i.e., to have the creditor's cashing of the check constitute full settlement), the debtor must show that: (1) the check or accompanying written communication contained a "conspicuous statement to the effect that the instrument was tendered as full satisfaction of the claim," (2) the underlying claim was either "unliquidated" or "subjected to a bona fide dispute," and (3) the debtor acted in good faith. Here, all of these requirements are met, since: (1) we're told that the check was "conspicuously marked, 'Payment in full' "; (2) the parties had a real dispute about whether the $5,000 initially quoted by the lawyer was merely a non-binding estimate or a binding cap; and (3) we're expressly told that the client's letter expressed his "good-faith belief" that the lawyer had quoted the $5,000 as a cap. Therefore, when the lawyer cashed the check, his doing so constituted an implied agreement to an accord and satisfaction of his claim, under § 3-311. Note that this result would still occur even if the lawyer had placed a notation of protest or of reservation-of-rights on the check before cashing it.

(A) is wrong for two reasons: (1) the "rule of law" it purports to state about the risk of loss probably would not be accurate even in the absence of the lawyer's cashing the partial-payment check; and (2) under UCC § 3-311, the cashing of that check constituted a settlement, for the reasons stated in the discussion of Choice (B) above.

(C) is wrong because it is not clear that the $5,000 figure quoted by the lawyer was merely an estimate — in the absence of the check-cashing, a court might well have found that the client reasonably understood the figure to be a firm cap (i.e., an upper bound) on the amount that the lawyer would charge, in which case the cap would have been deemed part of the contract.

(D) is wrong for two reasons: (1) there may indeed have been a specific agreement on the total amount of the lawyer's fee (the facts are indeterminate about whether this would be true, in the absence of the partial-check-cashing); and (2) when the lawyer cashed the check, the case became governed by UCC § 3-311, not the parties' original agreement, whatever that was.

Question 16: Ames had painted Bell's house under a contract which called for payment of $20,000. Bell, contending in good faith that the porch had not been painted properly, refused to pay anything.

On June 15, Ames mailed a letter to Bell stating, "I am in serious need of money. Please send the $20,000 to me before July 1." On June 18, Bell replied "I will settle for $18,000 provided you agree to repaint the porch." Ames did not reply to this letter.

Thereafter, Bell mailed a check for $18,000 marked "Payment in full on the Ames-Bell painting contract as per letter dated June 18." Ames received the check on June 30. Because he was badly in need of money, Ames cashed the check without objection and spent the proceeds but has refused to repaint the porch.

After cashing the check Ames sued Bell for $2,000. Ames probably will

(A) succeed if he can prove that he had painted the porch according to specifications.

(B) succeed, because he cashed the check under economic duress.

(C) not succeed, because he cashed the check.

(D) not succeed, because he is entitled to recover only the reasonable value of his services.

[Q4006]

Answer 16: Choice **(C)** is correct. Under UCC § 3-311, a creditor who cashes a partial-payment check offered in full settlement will be deemed to have accepted an "accord and satisfaction," and lose his right to sue for the balance, if: (1) the check or accompanying communication contained a "conspicuous statement to the effect that the instrument was tendered as full satisfaction of the claim," (2) the claim was either "unliquidated" or was "subject to a bona fide dispute," and (3) the debtor acted in good faith. (This provision applies even to contracts for services rather than goods.) All 3 requirements imposed by § 3-311 are met here: (1) the "payment in full" legend on the check was a "conspicuous statement" that the check was tendered in full payment; (2) the prior letter shows that there was a dispute about whether the painting was done correctly; and (3) there's no indication that Bell didn't act in good faith.

(A) is not the best response, because Ames' cashing of the check was an accord and satisfaction under UCC § 3-311, as described above. Therefore, Ames can't recover even if he did paint the porch according to specs.

(B) is not the best response, because (1) it ignores the fact that UCC § 3-311 treats the cashing of the check as an agreement to settle; and (2) "economic duress" is not a defense or a relevant factor, at least where the duress does not come from the other party to the contract.

(D) is not the best answer, because it states an irrelevant factor. If Ames had not cashed the check, he could have recovered the $2,000 (the remaining contract price) if he had been able to show he had fulfilled the contract. But by cashing the partial-payment check, he cut off his right to sue for the contract price. And that's true no matter what the relationship was between the contract price and the value of the services rendered. (If you chose this response, you may have been thinking of quasi-contractual recovery, where a non-substantially-performing plaintiff's damages are measured by the reasonable value of his services. But this concept doesn't apply here, not only because of the check-cashing but because there's no indication that Ames indeed failed to substantially perform, or if so, that the services were worth only $18,000.)

III. REQUIREMENTS AND OUTPUT CONTRACTS

A. Requirements and output contracts generally

1. UCC approach

a. How tested on the MBE

Question 17: Responding to County's written advertisement for bids, Tyres was the successful bidder for the sale of tires to County for County's vehicles. Tyres and County entered into a signed, written agreement that specified, "It is agreed that Tyres will deliver all tires required by this agreement to County, in accordance with the attached bid form and specifications, for a one-year period beginning September 1, 2005." Attached to the agreement was a copy of the bid form and specifications. In the written advertisement to which Tyres had responded, but not in the bid form, County had stated, "Multiple awards may be issued if they are in the best interests of County." No definite quantity of tires to be bought by County from Tyres was specified in any of these documents.

In January 2006, Tyres learned that County was buying some of its tires from one of Tyres's competitors. Contending that the Tyres-County agreement was a requirements contract, Tyres sued County for the damages caused by County's buying some of its tires from the competitor.

If the court concludes that the Tyres-County contract is an agreement by County to buy its tire requirements from Tyres, Tyres probably will

(A) recover under the contracts clause of the United States Constitution.

(B) recover under the provisions of the Uniform Commercial Code.

(C) not recover, because the agreement lacks mutuality of obligation.

(D) not recover, because the agreement is indefinite as to quantity.

[Q2017]

Answer 17: Choice **(B)** is correct. The UCC, in § 2-306(1), makes requirements contracts valid, and interprets such agreements to cover "such actual ... requirements as may occur in good faith, except that no quantity unreasonably disproportionate to any stated estimate or in the absence of a stated estimate to any normal or otherwise comparable prior ... requirements may be ... demanded." Given that the question tells you to assume that the Tyres-County contract is interpreted to represent an obligation by County to buy all its requirements for tires from Tyres, the contract is valid as a requirements contract under § 2-306(1).

(A) is wrong because the contracts clause of the U.S. Constitution would not furnish the basis of recovery for Tyres. The contracts clause limits the circumstances in which a government may use its legislative powers to alter the terms of the terms of contracts. But here, County is not trying to alter the terms of its contract; it is merely hoping to persuade the court to find the contract invalid under general contract principles. Such an argument does not implicate the contracts clause.

(C) is wrong because the agreement *does* have mutuality of obligation — Tyres is required to supply all of the reasonable requirements of County for tires at the prices stated in the attachments, and in return County is obligated to purchase all of its tires exclusively from Tyres. (If the agreement were interpreted to mean merely that County would "order whatever tires it decides to order" from Tyres, then the lack-of-mutuality argument might work; but you're told that the contract is interpreted by the court to be a true requirements contract.)

(D) is wrong because the agreement is not indefinite as to quantity. It's true that the contract does not specify a particular number of tires, but a contract that specifies that "all of the buyer's requirements" for a particular type of item are to be purchased from the seller is deemed to be sufficiently definite as to quantity.

b. Good faith obligation

Question 18: Under a written agreement a manufacturer of pastries promised to sell its entire output of baked buns at a specified unit price to a bakery, for one year. The bakery promised not to sell any other supplier's baked buns. Shortly after making the contract, and before the manufacturer had tendered any buns, the bakery decided that the contract had become undesirable because of a sudden, sharp decline in its customers' demand for baked buns. It renounced the agreement, and the manufacturer sues for breach of contract.

Which of the following will the court probably decide?

(A) The bakery wins, because mutuality of obligation was lacking in that the bakery made no express promise to buy any of the manufacturer's baked buns.

(B) The bakery wins, because the agreement was void for indefiniteness of quantity and total price for the year involved.

(C) The manufacturer wins, because the bakery's promise to sell at retail the manufacturer's baked buns exclusively, if it sold any such buns at all, implied a promise to use its best efforts to sell bakery's one-year output of baked buns.

(D) The manufacturer wins, because under the applicable law both parties to a sale-of-goods contract impliedly assume the risk of price and demand fluctuations.

[Q1017]

Answer 18: Choice **(C)** is correct. This was an output contract, as well as a requirements contract. Under UCC § 2-306(2), "A lawful agreement by either the seller or the buyer for exclusive dealing in the kind of goods concerned imposes unless otherwise agreed an obligation by the seller to use best efforts to supply the goods and *by the buyer to use best efforts to promote their sale.*" This was an exclusive-dealing contract (all requirements and output contracts are exclusive-dealing contracts); therefore, since the parties did not otherwise agree, § 2-306(2) imposed on the bakery the "obligation ... to use best efforts to promote [the goods'] sale." When the bakery renounced the agreement without having even bought any buns yet, it breached this best-efforts-to-promote obligation.

(A) is wrong because, even though the bakery made no express promise to buy any of the manufacturer's buns, under § 2-306(2) the bakery was implicitly obligated to make best efforts to promote the sale of buns so that the bakery would need some of them.

(B) is wrong because, under § 2-306(1), "A term which measures the quantity by the output of the seller ... means such actual output ... as may occur in good faith[.]" This section has the effect of providing a quantity (or at least, a method for determining quantity), saving the output contract here from indefiniteness.

(D) is wrong because it does not speak to the main issue in the case. It's essentially true that both buyer and seller "impliedly assume the risk of price and demand fluctuations," but the question here is whether buyer could rely on the sudden reduction in its own customers' demand to escape the contract. UCC § 2-306(2) in effect allocates this risk, by saying that the buyer in both a requirements and output contract must use good faith to promote sale of the goods, effectively negating the bakery's ability to discontinue the product line here without any promotional effort.

CHAPTER 3

PROMISES BINDING WITHOUT CONSIDERATION

I.   PROMISSORY ESTOPPEL

A. Possible applications

1. Promise to perform business service

a. Promise to make a loan

Question 19: Dominique obtained a bid of $10,000 to tear down her old building and another bid of $90,000 to replace it with a new structure in which she planned to operate a sporting goods store. Having only limited cash available, Dominique asked Hardcash for a $100,000 loan. After reviewing the plans for the project, Hardcash in a signed writing promised to lend Dominique $100,000 secured by a mortgage on the property and repayable over ten years in equal monthly installments at 10% annual interest. Dominique promptly accepted the demolition bid and the old building was removed, but Hardcash thereafter refused to make the loan. Despite diligent efforts, Dominique was unable to obtain a loan from any other source.

Does Dominique have a cause of action against Hardcash?

(A) Yes, because by having the building demolished, she accepted Hardcash's offer to make the loan.

(B) Yes, because her reliance on Hardcash's promise was substantial, reasonable, and foreseeable.

(C) No, because there was no bargained-for exchange of consideration for Hardcash's promise to make the loan.

(D) No, because Dominique's inability to obtain a loan from any other source demonstrated that the project lacked the financial soundness that was a constructive condition to Hardcash's performance.

[Q2040]

Answer 19: Choice **(B)** is correct. Hardcash has made a promise, but no contract has come into existence. (If Hardcash's promise is viewed as an offer, it was never accepted, since Dominique never actually bound herself to take the loan, as is further described in the discussion of Choice (A) below.) Therefore, Dominique will have to recover on a promissory estoppel theory or not at all. Under P.E., "A promise which the promisor should *reasonably expect to induce action or forbearance* on the part of the promisee or a third person and which *does induce* such action or forbearance is *binding if injustice can be avoided* only by enforcement of the promise." Rest. 2d, § 90. Dominique meets all of the requirements for promissory estoppel: (1) Hardcash made a promise of the loan; (2) Hardcash should reasonably have expected that Dominique would rely on the availability of the loan, by demolishing the old structure (Hardcash knew that Dominique had gotten both bids, an indication of the likelihood that she would rely by doing the demolition); (3) Dominique did indeed rely by demolishing, and reasonably so; and (4) at least some type of enforcement of the loan promise will be required to avoid injustice, since otherwise Dominique will be left without the use of the old building and with a loss of the funds used for the demolition. (Notice that the phrase "promissory estoppel" is not used in this choice — you have to notice that that's the basis for the choice, something that you're clued in to from the reference to "reliance.")

(A) is wrong because Dominique's act of having a building demolished was not an acceptance of the offer. It's not so clear that Hardcash's promise was an "offer" at all, but even if it was, Hardcash did nothing to authorize Dominique to "accept" the offer by demolishing the old building — any acceptance of a loan offer would under these circumstances have to be by Dominique's taking some action vis-a-vis Hardcash (e.g., signing loan papers and promising to repay the loan, or at least paying some sort of commitment fee).

(C) is wrong because the absence of bargained-for consideration does not matter. The whole point of the promissory estoppel doctrine, which as described above applies here, is that there does not need to be consideration for the promise. In other words, promissory estoppel here is a substitute for consideration.

(D) is wrong because the project's financial soundness was not a constructive condition to Hardcash's obligation to make the loan. Hardcash could of course have made his loan promise conditional upon Dominique's demonstration to his satisfaction that the project was financially sound; but the facts give no suggestion that Hardcash did this, and there is no reason for the court to infer such a condition out of thin air.

CHAPTER 4

MISTAKE

I. REFORMATION AS REMEDY FOR ERROR IN EXPRESSION

A. Generally

1. Not a remedy for underlying disagreement about deal

Question 20: A landowner and a prospective buyer, standing on a parcel owned by the landowner, orally agreed to its sale and purchase for $5,000, and orally marked its bounds as "that line of trees down there, the ditch that intersects them, the fence on the other side, and that street on the fourth side."

In which of the following is the remedy of reformation most appropriate?

(A) As later reduced to writing, the agreement by clerical mistake included two acres that are actually beyond the fence.

(B) The buyer reasonably thought that two acres beyond the fence were included in the oral agreement but the landowner did not. As later reduced to writing, the agreement included the two acres.

(C) The buyer reasonably thought that the price orally agreed upon was $4,500, but the landowner did not. As later reduced to writing, the agreement said $5,000.

(D) The buyer reasonably thought that a dilapidated shed backed up against the fence was to be torn down and removed as part of the agreement, but the landowner did not. As later reduced to writing, the agreement said nothing about the shed.

[Q1128]

Answer 20: Choice **(A)** is correct. If the parties orally agree on a deal, but mistakenly prepare and execute a document which incorrectly reflects that oral agreement, either party may obtain a court order for reformation (i.e., a re-writing of the document). That's what would happen in this choice, since both parties agreed on what acreage was to be covered by the agreement, and a clerical mistake caused the document to diverge from the oral agreement.

Choices (B), (C), and (D) are all wrong for the same reason: the parties did not in fact have a meeting of the minds about a key issue, so reformation to match their "actual" (subjective) agreement is not possible. In this situation, discharge for mutual mistake, rather than reformation, is the appropriate remedy.

PAROL EVIDENCE AND INTERPRETATION

I.   TOTAL AND PARTIAL INTEGRATIONS

A. Statement of rule

1. Summary

Question 21: Stirrup, a rancher, and Equinox, a fancier of horses, signed the following writing: "For $55,000, Stirrup will sell to Equinox a gray horse that Equinox may choose from among the grays on Stirrup's ranch."

Equinox refused to accept delivery of a gray horse timely tendered by Stirrup or to choose among those remaining, on the ground that during their negotiations Stirrup had orally agreed to include a saddle, worth $100, and also to give Equinox the option to choose a gray or a brown horse. Equinox insisted on one of Stirrup's brown horses, but Stirrup refused to part with any of his browns or with the saddle as demanded by Equinox.

If Equinox sues Stirrup for damages and seeks to introduce evidence of the alleged oral agreement, the court probably will

(A) admit the evidence as to both the saddle and the option to choose a brown horse.

(B) admit the evidence as to the saddle but not the option to choose a brown horse.

(C) admit the evidence as to the option to choose a brown horse but not the promise to include the saddle.

(D) not admit any of the evidence.

[Q1160]

Answer 21: Choice **(B)** is correct. The key to this question is to correctly categorize the writing: Is it a complete integration or a partial one? In deciding such a question, courts give a lot of weight to the nature of the document itself: the more extensive and formal, the more likely it is to have been intended to be a complete integration. Here, the fact that the writing consists of just one very informal sentence strongly suggests that it was intended as only a partial integration; since there is no evidence pointing in the other direction, a court would almost certainly conclude that the writing was only a partial integration. Therefore, it can be supplemented, but cannot be contradicted, by a prior or simultaneous oral understanding. The alleged saddle agreement merely supplements the writing, since the writing doesn't purport to cover the issue of accessories; therefore, evidence of the saddle agreement will be admissible. The oral agreement to choose a brown horse, on the other hand, is directly at odds with the writing, since the writing specifies that Equinox is permitted to choose from among gray horses, and does not mention any right to choose a brown horse; therefore, the oral agreement on brown horses will be excluded as a contradiction even though the writing is only a partial integration.

Choices (A), (C) and (D) are wrong because they are inconsistent with the above analysis.

II. SITUATIONS WHERE PAROL EVIDENCE RULE DOES NOT APPLY

A. Existence of a condition on effectiveness of contract

1. Often tested on MBE

Question 22: Buyer, Inc., contracted in writing with Shareholder, who owned all of XYZ Corporation's outstanding stock, to purchase all of her stock at a specified price per share. At the time this contract was executed, Buyer's contracting officer said to Shareholder, "Of course, our commitment to buy is conditioned on our obtaining approval of the contract from Conglomerate, Ltd., our parent company." Shareholder replied, "Fine. No problem."

Later, Shareholder was willing and ready to consummate the sale of her stock to Buyer, but the latter refused to perform on the ground (which was true) that Conglomerate had firmly refused to approve the contract. If Shareholder sues Buyer for breach of contract and seeks to exclude any evidence of the oral condition requiring Conglomerate's approval, the court will probably

(A) admit the evidence as proof of a collateral agreement.

(B) admit the evidence as proof of a condition to the existence of an enforceable obligation, and therefore not within the scope of the parol evidence rule.

(C) exclude the evidence on the basis of a finding that the parties' written agreement was a complete integration of their contract.

(D) exclude the evidence as contradicting the terms of the parties' written agreement, whether or not the writing was a complete integration of the contract.

[Q3039]

Answer 22: Choice **(B)** is correct. When the parties to a written contract agree orally that the enforceability of the contract is subject to a condition, proof of the existence of that condition does not fall within the parol evidence rule.

(A) is wrong because, although there is indeed a "collateral agreement" exception to the parol evidence rule (an exception discussed immediately below in the main text), that exception is not applicable here. The collateral agreement exception allows proof of an oral "side" agreement in which the parties agreed to a separate exchange, as long as the alleged side agreement is not inconsistent with the total integration. But the "approval required" condition here was not a collateral agreement; rather, it was a condition to the enforceability of the main agreement, so the collateral-agreement exception does not apply.

(C) is wrong because, even though the parties' written agreement here was probably a complete integration of their contract, proof of an oral condition to the contract's enforceability is nonetheless allowed, as described in the discussion of Choice (B).

(D) is wrong because, although this formulation is essentially a correct statement of the parol evidence rule on provisions that contradict the writing (under which even a partial rather than complete integration may not be contradicted by a prior or simultaneous oral understanding), the rule does not apply to a condition to the enforceability of the contract.

Question 23: A landowner and a landscape architect signed a detailed writing in which the landscape architect agreed to landscape and replant the landowner's residential property in accordance with a design prepared by the architect and incorporated in the writing. The landowner agreed to pay $10,000 for the work upon its completion. The landowner's spouse was not a party to the agreement, and had no ownership interest in the premises.

Shortly before the agreement was signed, the landowner and the architect orally agreed that the writing would not become binding on either party unless the landowner's spouse should approve the landscaping design. If the landowner's spouse disapproves the design and the landowner refuses to allow the architect to proceed with the work, is evidence of the oral agreement admissible in the architect's action against the landowner for breach of contract?

(A) Yes, because the oral agreement required approval by a third party.

(B) Yes, because the evidence shows that the writing was intended to take effect only if the approval occurred.

(C) No, because the parol evidence rule bars evidence of a prior oral agreement even if the latter is consistent with the terms of a partial integration.

(D) No, because the prior oral agreement contradicted the writing by making the parties' duties conditional.

[Q1044]

Answer 23: Choice **(B)** is correct. Ordinarily, the parol evidence rule bars proof of an oral clause offered to supplement or contradict a completely integrated writing (which the writing here probably was). But an oral agreement that the writing will simply *not be legally enforceable at all* unless some condition precedent is satisfied is *not* barred by the parol evidence rule. This exception applies here: the owner's spouse's approval of the design was a condition precedent to the enforceability of the agreement, so that oral condition, and its non-satisfaction, may be proved.

(A) is wrong because it gives an incorrect reason for the correct result. It is not the fact that a third party's approval was required that makes evidence of the oral agreement admissible in the face of the parol evidence rule; it's the fact that the oral agreement established a condition precedent to the writing's enforceability that exempts proof of the oral agreement from the rule.

(C) is wrong for two reasons: (1) it misstates the "partial integration" branch of the parol evidence rule (under which an oral agreement that supplements rather than contradicts a partial integration *is* admissible); and (2) the parol evidence rule simply doesn't apply to an orally-agreed-upon condition to the writing's enforceability, as analyzed in Choice (B) above.

(D) is wrong because, while it correctly summarizes the branch of the parol evidence rule that bars oral understandings that contradict any sort of integration (partial or complete), it fails to reflect the fact that the parol evidence rules simply doesn't apply to an orally-agreed-upon condition to the writing's enforceability, as analyzed in Choice (B) above.

III. INTERPRETATION

A. Modern view

1. Extrinsic evidence in the case of ambiguous terms

a. Evidence of parties' own pre-contract negotiations

Question 24: Responding to County's written advertisement for bids, Tyres was the successful bidder for the sale of tires to County for County's vehicles. Tyres and County entered into a signed, written agreement that specified, "It is agreed that Tyres will deliver all tires required by this agreement to County, in accordance with the attached bid form and specifications, for a one-year period beginning September 1, 2005." Attached to the agreement was a copy of the bid form and specifications. In the written advertisement to which Tyres had responded, but not in the bid form, County had stated, "Multiple awards may be issued if they are in the best interests of County." No definite quantity of tires to be bought by County from Tyres was specified in any of these documents.

In January 2006, Tyres learned that County was buying some of its tires from one of Tyres's competitors. Contending that the Tyres-County agreement was a requirements contract, Tyres sued County for the damages caused by County's buying some of its tires from the competitor.

If County defends by offering proof of the advertisement concerning the possibility of multiple awards, should the court admit the evidence?

(A) Yes, because the provision in the written agreement, "all tires required by this agreement," is ambiguous.

(B) Yes, because the advertisement was in writing.

(C) No, because of the parol evidence rule.

(D) No, because it would make the contract illusory.

[Q2016]

Answer 24: Choice **(A)** is correct. All courts agree that if a term is found by the trial court to be ambiguous — capable of more than one meaning — extrinsic evidence on the meaning the parties attached to the term must be allowed, notwithstanding the parol evidence rule. The phrase "all tires required by this agreement" is indeed ambiguous, as this choice suggests: a reader looking only at the contract document itself (including the attachments) would not know whether the phrase meant merely "whatever quantities of tires that County decides to order during the contract term" or instead the far meatier "all

County's tire requirements during the contract term." Since the advertisement was effectively part of the parties' negotiations — it disclosed to Tyres what County was thinking at the outset — it fairly bears on what the parties intended by the ambiguous phrase.

(B) is wrong because the fact that the advertisement was in writing is irrelevant. This choice incorrectly implies that the only materials barred by the parol evidence rule are prior or simultaneous oral understandings between the parties. Prior *writings* agreed to or exchanged between the parties are also excluded by the parol evidence rule, if offered to add terms to, or contradict terms in, a final writing.

(C) is wrong because of the "ambiguity" exception to the parol evidence rule, described in the discussion of Choice (A) above.

(D) is wrong because it makes a conclusion that does not logically follow from its premise. It is true that if County is permitted to put in proof of the advertisement, the consequence will likely be that the contract would be held illusory (since County would be promising only to "buy whatever we decide to buy"), and County's illusory promise would not furnish consideration for Tyres' return promise. But the fact that an item of proffered evidence would if admitted tend to prove that a contract is unenforceable does not mean that the parol evidence rule requires exclusion of that piece of evidence.

IV. TRADE USAGE, COURSE OF PERFORMANCE, AND COURSE OF DEALING

A. Used to interpret even a complete integration

Question 25: A radio manufacturer and a retailer, after extensive negotiations, entered into a final, written agreement in which the manufacturer agreed to sell and the retailer agreed to buy all of the retailer's requirements of radios, estimated at 20 units per month, during the period January 1, 2004, and December 31, 2006, at a price of $50 per unit. A dispute arose in late December, 2006, when the retailer returned 25 undefective radios to the manufacturer for full credit after the manufacturer had refused to extend the contract for a second three-year period.

In an action by the manufacturer against the retailer for damages due to the return of the 25 radios, the manufacturer introduces the written agreement, which expressly permitted the buyer to return defective radios for credit but was silent as to the return of undefective radios for credit. The retailer seeks to introduce evidence that during the three years of the agreement it had returned, for various reasons, 125 undefective radios, for which the manufacturer had granted full credit. The manufacturer objects to the admissibility of this evidence.

The trial court will probably rule that the evidence proffered by the retailer is

(A) inadmissible, because the evidence is barred by the parol evidence rule.

(B) inadmissible, because the express terms of the agreement control when those terms are inconsistent with the course of performance.

(C) admissible, because the evidence supports an agreement that is not within the relevant statute of frauds.

(D) admissible, because course-of-performance evidence, when available, is considered the best indication of what the parties intended the writing to mean.

[Q1108]

Answer 25: Choice **(D)** is correct. Even where the writing is a complete integration, as it is here, the court will look to course-of-performance evidence to determine what the parties meant as to a point on which the writing is ambiguous. This is true in both sales and non-sales cases. Thus in sales governed by UCC Article 2, § 2-208(1) says that "Where the contract for sale involves repeated occasions for performance by either party with knowledge of the nature of the performance and opportunity for objection to it by the other, any course of performance *accepted or* *acquiesced in without objection* shall be *relevant to determine the meaning* of the agreement." Here, the evidence proffered by the retailer — that the manufacturer permitted him to return undamaged radios for credit earlier during the course of the present contract — fits § 2-208(1) exactly, since the retailer is claiming that the manufacturer's knowing acquiescence in the retailer's repeated requests for a credit for non-defective returned goods was a course of performance, admissible to show that the parties intended the writing to mean that such returns are allowed.

(A) is wrong because, as further explained in Choice (D) above, even though the writing here is a complete integration, the proffered evidence is course-of-performance evidence, which is admissible notwithstanding the parol evidence rule to show the meaning of the agreement.

(B) is wrong because it states an irrelevant point. It's true that the express terms control if those terms are inconsistent with the course of performance; thus UCC § 2-208(2) says that "The express terms of an agreement and any ... course of performance, as well as any course of dealing and usage of trade, shall be construed wherever reasonable as consistent with each other; but when such construction is unreasonable, *express terms shall control course of performance* and course of performance shall control both course of dealing and usage of trade[.]" But here, there *is* no express term dealing with the retailer's right to return non-defective goods for credit (the writing is silent on this point), so the priority of express terms over the course of performance simply doesn't apply.

(C) is wrong because it relies on an irrelevant fact. The retailer is not trying to show an "agreement" to modify the original agreement — if he were, then there might be a Statute of Frauds issue. Instead, he's trying to show what the original written agreement *meant* (by the use of course-of-performance evidence), and his ability to do that has nothing to do with the Statute of Frauds.

CHAPTER 6
CONDITIONS, BREACH, AND OTHER ASPECTS OF PERFORMANCE

I. EXPRESS CONDITIONS

A. Check whose duty was conditional

1. Right to waive condition

a. Frequently tested on MBE

Question 26: In a writing signed by both parties on December 1, a buyer agreed to buy from a seller a gasoline engine for $1,000, delivery to be made on the following February 1. Through a secretarial error, the writing called for delivery on March 1, but neither party noticed the error until February 1. Before signing the agreement, the buyer and seller orally agreed that the contract of sale would be effective only if the buyer should notify the seller in writing not later than January 2 that the buyer had arranged to resell the engine to a third person. Otherwise, they agreed orally, "There is no deal." On December 15, the buyer entered into a contract with a third person to resell the engine to the third person at a profit.

On December 16, the buyer notified the seller by telephone of the buyer's resale agreement with the third person, and explained that a written notice was unfeasible because the buyer's secretary was ill. The seller replied, "That's okay. I'll get the engine to you on February 1, as we agreed." Having learned, however, that the engine had increased in value about 75% since December 1, the seller renounced the agreement on February 1.

If the buyer sues the seller on February 2 for breach of contract, which of the following concepts best supports the buyer's claim?

(A) Substantial performance.

(B) Nonoccurrence of a condition subsequent.

(C) Waiver of condition.

(D) Novation of buyers.

[Q2052]

Answer 26: Choice **(C)** is correct. It was a condition precedent to the enforceability of the contract that the buyer give written notice to the seller by Jan. 2 that the buyer had found a buyer. However, when the buyer explained the difficulty with a written notice to the seller on Dec. 16, the seller's "That's okay" response clearly indicated to the buyer that the seller would not insist on the written notice. This oral response constituted a waiver of the condition, i.e., a knowing intent to abandon the benefit of the condition.

(A) is wrong because the requirement of a writing by Jan. 2 was an express condition to the enforceability of the contract. Complete, not just substantial, compliance with an express condition is normally required. Since the oral notice did not completely comply with the requirement of a written notice, the fact that it may have constituted substantial performance will not help the buyer.

(B) is wrong because: (1) the condition here was a condition precedent (the condition had to be satisfied before the contract would ever become enforceable), not a condition subsequent (i.e., something that if not satisfied would "unenforce" the previously-enforceable contract); and (2) even in the unlikely event that the condition was found to be a condition subsequent, its nonoccurrence could only help the seller, not the buyer.

(D) is wrong because the concept of a novation has nothing to do with these facts. A novation occurs when the two original parties to a contract — an obligor and an obligee — agree that a stranger can be substituted for the original obligor. So, for instance, if the seller and the buyer agreed that the third person would substitute for the buyer as the party who was under contract to buy the engine from the seller, a novation would have occurred. But on the actual facts here, no substitution of either of the original parties to the contract has occurred, so there is no novation.

[Q2052]

b.   Waiver by receiving and keeping benefit

i.   MBE tip

Question 27: Ohner and Planner signed a detailed writing in which Planner, a landscape architect, agreed to landscape and replant Ohner's residential property in accordance with a design prepared by Planner and incorporated in the writing. Ohner agreed to pay $50,000 for the work upon its completion.

At Ohner's insistence, the written Ohner-Planner agreement contained a provision that neither party would be bound unless Ohner's law partner, an avid student of landscaping, should approve Planner's design. Before Planner commenced the work, Ohner's law partner, in the presence of both Ohner and Planner, expressly disapproved the landscaping design. Nevertheless, Ohner ordered Planner to proceed with the work, and Planner reluctantly did so. When Planner's performance was 40% complete, Ohner repudiated his duty, if any, to pay the contract price or any part thereof.

If Planner now sues Ohner for damages for breach of contract, which of the following concepts best supports Planner's claim?

(A) Substantial performance.

(B) Promissory estoppel.

(C) Irrevocable waiver of condition.

(D) Unjust enrichment.

[Q1045]

Answer 27: Choice **(C)** is correct. When the circumstances indicate that a condition is intended for the protection of just one party, that party is always free to waive the condition. Such a waiver can occur by implication. That's what happened here: the "partner must approve" provision was an express condition intended for the benefit of Ohner, and Ohner had the power to waive it, expressly or implicitly. When Ohner ordered Planner to proceed notwithstanding the partner's disapproval, this was an implied waiver of the condition. At the moment the waiver occurred, Ohner had the power to retract it (i.e., reinstate the condition). But once Planner began the work, this was a material change in position by Planner in reliance on the waiver, and that reliance made the waiver non-retractable, i.e., irrevocable.

(A) is wrong because: (1) the doctrine of substantial performance helps a plaintiff recover "on the contract," and here there would *be* no contract if the non-occurrence of the partner-approval condition is not somehow excused (which it is by operation of the doctrine of waiver, as described in the analysis of Choice (C) above); and (2) Planner has done only 40% of the work, and such a small portion would not be considered "substantial performance."

(B) is wrong because the promissory estoppel doctrine, even where it applies, makes the promise enforceable only to the extent "necessary to avoid injustice," and here, injustice could be avoided by awarding Planner just the value of 40% partial performance (a reliance or restitution measure). Planner is suing for breach of the contract, and would like to be able to recover his full "contract," i.e., expectation, damages, which would give him a greater recovery than the reliance or restitution damages that are all that promissory estoppel would allow.

(D) is wrong because unjust enrichment would yield a lesser recovery than a waiver-of-condition theory, since unjust enrichment will get Planner just the relatively small amount by which he has increased the value of Ohner's property, whereas waiver will permit recovery "on the contract," i.e., for full expectation damages.

II. CONSTRUCTIVE CONDITIONS

A. Waiver

Question 28: Bitz, an amateur computer whiz, agreed in writing to design for the Presskey Corporation, a distributor of TV game systems, three new games a year for a five-year period. The writing provided, in a clause separately signed by Bitz, that "No modification shall be binding on Presskey unless made in writing and signed by Presskey's authorized representative."

Because of family problems, Bitz delivered and Presskey accepted only two game-designs a year for the first three years; but the games were a commercial success and Presskey made no objection. Accordingly, Bitz spent substantial sums on new computer equipment that would aid in speeding up future design work. In the first quarter of the fourth year, however, Presskey terminated the contract on the ground that Bitz had breached the annual-quantity term.

In Bitz's suit against Presskey for damages, the jury found that the contract had been modified by conduct and the trial court awarded Bitz substantial compensatory damages.

Is this result likely to be reversed on appeal?

(A) Yes, because the contract's no-oral-modification clause was not expressly waived by Presskey.

(B) Yes, because the contract's no-oral-modification clause was a material part of the agreed exchange and could not be avoided without new consideration.

(C) No, because the contract's no-oral-modification clause was unconscionable as against an amateur designer.

(D) No, because Presskey by its conduct waived the annual-quantity term and Bitz materially changed his position in reasonable reliance on that waiver.

[Q2171]

Answer 28: Choice **(D)** is correct. The beneficiary of a constructive condition may be found to have waived the condition. Such a waiver may be implied rather than express. Here, when Presskey accepted the two game-designs a year without protest for three years, this constituted an implied waiver of the minimum-quantity term, at least as to the already-completed three years. Then, when Bitz spent the substantial sums on new computer equipment, this probably constituted a material change of position in reasonable reliance on this waiver. While it is probably not the case that no reasonable jury could have found for *Presskey* on these facts (for instance, a reasonable jury could probably have found that Bitz's reliance expenditure was not reasonable), a reasonable jury could have found for Bitz, so an appellate affirmance would be proper. (Note that the question doesn't ask you to predict who would win at trial, merely to predict whether Presskey could get a reversal of the jury verdict, a harder task for Presskey to accomplish.)

(A) is wrong because, while a no-oral-modification clause will normally be enforced, such a clause does not prevent enforcement of an oral or implicit waiver where the conditions for waiver are satisfied, as they are here. (The difference between modification and waiver is that a true modification — which was forbidden by the N.O.M. clause — could not have been prospectively retracted, whereas Presskey's waiver could have been retracted by it until Bitz changed position in reasonable reliance on it.)

(B) is wrong because it does not apply on these facts — as described in the discussion of Choice (A) above, what happened here was a waiver rather than an avoidance of the no-oral-modification clause's effect, and a waiver is not prevented by a N.O.M. clause.

(C) is wrong because the no-oral-modification clause would not be unconscionable on these facts. It is rare for a clause in a commercial (as opposed to consumer) contract to be ruled unconscionable. To be unconscionable, the clause would have to either be shockingly unfair substantively, or very unfair from a procedural perspective. N.O.M. clauses are quite routine, and the one here would not be found to be either substantively or procedurally unfair. The fact that Bitz was supposedly an "amateur" designer would not change this result, especially since what he was performing was a series of commercial services.

III. SUBSTANTIAL PERFORMANCE

A. Material breach in contracts for the sale of goods

1. "Perfect tender" rule

a. Not so strict

i. Trade usage or course of dealing as "wiggle room"

Question 29: Computers, Inc., contracted in writing with Bank to sell and deliver to Bank a mainframe computer using a new type of magnetic memory, then under development but not perfected by Computers, at a price substantially lower than that of a similar computer using current technology. The contract's delivery term was "F.O.B. Bank, on or before July 31." Computers tendered the computer to Bank on August 15, and Bank rejected it because of the delay.

If Computers sues Bank for breach of contract, which of the following facts, if proved, will best support a recovery by Computers?

(A) The delay did not materially harm Bank.

(B) Computers believed, on the assumption that Bank was getting a "super deal" for its money, that Bank would not reject because of the late tender of delivery.

(C) Computers' delay in tender was caused by a truckers' strike.

(D) A usage in the relevant trade allows computer sellers a 30-day leeway in a specified time of delivery, unless the usage is expressly negated by the contract.

[Q3156]

Answer 29: Choice **(D)** is correct. For one-shot (i.e., non-installment) sales contracts like the one here, UCC § 2-601 states what is, in effect, a perfect tender rule: "[I]f the goods or the tender of delivery fail *in any respect* to conform to the contract, the buyer may (a) reject the whole[.]" So Computers will lose unless it finds a defense that is not inconsistent with the perfect-tender rule of § 2-601. § 1-205(3) says that "[A]ny usage of trade in the vocation or trade in which [the parties] are engaged or of which they are or should be aware *give[s] particular meaning to and sup-*

plement[s] or qualif[ies] terms of an agreement." So if Computers can indeed show that under trade usage in the purchase of computers, an apparently fixed delivery date really means "plus or minus 30 days on either side of the specified date," the contract will be interpreted in light of this usage. In other words, § 2-601 will still entitle Bank to reject if delivery were untimely, but the delivery won't in fact be deemed untimely because of the trade usage.

(A) is wrong because as described in the analysis of Choice (D) above, the UCC essentially requires tenders to be perfect (and "perfect" includes timely delivery), so that a defense based on lack of material harm won't work.

(B) is wrong because the goodness of the deal Bank was getting would not entitle Computers to relief from the perfect-tender rule. As described further in Choice (D) above, UCC § 2-601 essentially applies the perfect tender rule to non-installment contracts. Under § 2-601, there is no room for an argument that because the deal was an unusually good one for the buyer, the buyer loses its right to reject for late delivery or other non-conformity.

(C) is wrong because a trucker's strike would not give Computers a cause of action for breach. The fact that the contract stated "F.O.B. Bank" hurts Computers' ability to rely on the truckers' strike. § 2-319(1)(b) says that "when the [shipment] term is F.O.B. the place of destination, the seller must at his own expense *and risk* transport the goods to that place and there tender delivery of them..." So a court would probably hold that use of the F.O.B. destination clause shifted to Computers the risk of a problem with Computers' choice of delivery methods. The defense of commercial impracticability might conceivably help Computers escape *monetary liability* (a damages award against it) for breach, but the section wouldn't allow it to insist that Bank must take delivery late; the best that Computers could reasonably hope for is for both parties to be *discharged*, not for an affirmative recovery for breach against Bank.

2. Cure

a. Beyond contract

Question 30: In a signed writing, a buyer contracted to purchase a 25-foot travel trailer from an RV dealer for $15,000, cash on delivery no later than June 1. The buyer arrived at the dealer's sales lot on Sunday, May 31, to pay for and take delivery of the trailer, but refused to do so when he discovered that the spare tire was missing.

The dealer offered to install a spare tire on Monday when its service department would open, but the buyer replied that he did not want the trailer and would purchase another one elsewhere.

Which of the following is accurate?

(A) The buyer had a right to reject the trailer, but the dealer was entitled to a reasonable opportunity to cure the defect.

(B) The buyer had a right to reject the trailer and terminate the contract under the perfect tender rule.

(C) The buyer was required to accept the trailer, because the defect could be readily cured.

(D) The buyer was required to accept the trailer, because the defect did not substantially impair its value.

[Q2106]

Answer 30: Choice **(A)** is correct. The case is governed by the UCC, since a trailer, though large, is still an item of personal property and thus constitutes "goods," the sale of which is covered by Article 2. To begin our analysis, if we assume that the contracted-for trailer was one with a spare tire, the buyer was permitted to reject the tendered trailer for lack of the tire. That's because § 2-601 says that in a single-shot (non-installment) contract, "unless otherwise agreed ... if the goods or the tender of delivery fail *in any respect* to conform to the contract, the buyer may (a) reject the whole [.]" So no matter how minor the defect, the buyer was entitled to insist that it be cured before he was required to accept the trailer. But it does not follow that the defect entitled the buyer to cancel the contract. That's because § 2-508(1) says that "where any tender or delivery by the seller is rejected because non-conforming and the time for performance has not yet expired, the seller may seasonably notify the buyer of his intention to cure and may then within the contract time make a conforming delivery." Here, the time for performance would not expire until the end of business on Monday, June 1, and the dealer was proposing to cure the problem on Monday, i.e., within the contract time. Therefore, the dealer met the notification requirement of § 2-508(1), and had the right to try to make the actual cure up until the end of June 1.

(B) is wrong because, while § 2-601 in theory applies the perfect tender rule — which would allow the buyer to reject and terminate immediately — that rule is subject to the seller's right under § 2-508(1) to give notice of intent to cure within the contract period and to then make the cure.

(C) is wrong because the buyer was not required to accept the trailer on May 31, with the defect still uncured. And that was true no matter how easy and probable a timely cure appeared to be. Instead, the buyer was permitted to suspend his performance (i.e., his acceptance and payment), wait and see whether the dealer promptly cured the defect as promised, and if it didn't, make a final rejection.

(D) is wrong because the buyer was *not* required to accept the trailer given the defect, despite the fact that the defect did not substantially impair the trailer's value. If the tendered goods are defective, no matter how small the defect is (assuming it indeed amounts to a true "defect" as opposed to a permissible variation under relevant trade usage), the buyer may reject the goods if the defect is not cured. To put it another way, there is no doctrine of "substantial performance" with respect to the seller's obligations under a single-shot (non-installment) contract for the sale of goods.

CHAPTER 7

ANTICIPATORY REPUDIATION AND OTHER ASPECTS OF BREACH

I.   ANTICIPATORY REPUDIATION

A. What constitutes repudiation

1. Statement

a. Grudging willingness to perform

Question 31: Broker needed a certain rare coin to complete a set that he had contracted to assemble and sell to Collecta. On February 1, Broker obtained such a coin from Hoarda in exchange for $1,000 and Broker's signed, written promise to re-deliver to Hoarda "not later than December 31 this year" a comparable specimen of the same kind of coin without charge to Hoarda. On February 2, Broker consummated sale of the complete set to Collecta.

On October 1, the market price of rare coins suddenly began a rapid, sustained rise; and on October 15 Hoarda wrote Broker for assurance that the latter would timely meet his coin-replacement commitment. Broker replied, "In view of the surprising market, it seems unfair that I should have to replace your coin within the next few weeks."

Having received Broker's message on October 17, Hoarda sued Broker on November 15 for the market value of a comparable replacement-coin as promised by Broker in February. The trial began on December 1.

If Broker moves to dismiss Hoarda's complaint, which of the following is Broker's best argument in support of the motion?

(A) Broker did not repudiate the contract on October 17, and may still perform no later than the contract deadline of December 31.

(B) Even if Broker repudiated on October 17, Hoarda's only action would be for specific performance because the coin is a unique chattel.

(C) Under the doctrine of impossibility, which includes unusually burdensome and unforeseen impracticability, Broker is temporarily excused by the market conditions from timely performance of his coin-replacement obligation.

(D) Even if Broker repudiated on October 17, Hoarda has no remedy without first demanding in writing that Broker retract his repudiation.

[Q2177]

Answer 31: Choice **(A)** is correct. To constitute a repudiation, a party must clearly bring home to the other party that he will be unable or unwilling to perform. Mere expression of doubts about performance, or statements that performance would be burdensome or unfair, will usually not constitute a sufficiently clear indication of an impending non-performance. Therefore, Broker's statement that it "seems unfair" that he should have to honor the contract in a timely manner probably did not constitute a repudiation. It is not certain that Broker will succeed with this argument, but of the four presented, it is the one that has by far the best chance of success for him.

(B) is wrong because it is a flat misstatement of law. While Honda would probably be *entitled* to seek specific performance due to the coin's status as a unique chattel, the plaintiff is always free to decline to seek a remedy of specific performance and to instead seek money damages if these can be proved with sufficient certainty (and there is no indication here that they could not be).

(C) is wrong because the facts here would not support the temporary impossibility defense. The defense of impossibility is not available to a party if a court would conclude that the agreement implicitly placed on that party the risk of the type of event that has occurred. The market prices of rare coins are constantly fluctuating, sometimes severely, and a court would almost certainly conclude that Broker, when he undertook to replace Hoarda's coin within a defined period, implicitly took the risk that the price of doing so would increase sharply. This result is especially likely in view of the fact that Broker was in the business of buying and selling such coins.

(D) is wrong because when one party repudiates, the other is not required to demand (in writing or otherwise) that the repudiation be retracted. It is true that the repudiatee has the *right* to demand a retraction, but the repudiatee may instead elect to treat the repudiation as final and immediately sue upon it.

II. OTHER ASPECTS OF REPUDIATION

A. Retraction of repudiation

1. Final acts

a. Cancellation and new contract with someone else

i. Real estate

Question 32: On June 1, a seller and a buyer contracted in writing for the sale and purchase of the seller's cattle ranch, and to close the transaction on December 1. The buyer unequivocally repudiated the contract on August 1. On August 15, the seller urged the buyer to change her mind and proceed with the scheduled closing on December 1. On October 1, having heard nothing further from the buyer, the seller sold and conveyed his ranch to a third party — a rancher — without notice to the buyer. On December 1, the buyer attempted to close under the June 1 contract by tendering the full purchase price to the seller. The seller rejected the tender.

If the buyer sues the seller for breach of contract, the buyer will probably

(A) win, because the seller failed seasonably to notify the buyer of any pending sale to the rancher.

(B) win, because the seller waived the buyer's August 1 repudiation by urging her to retract it on August 15.

(C) lose, because the buyer did not retract her repudiation before the seller materially changed his position in reliance thereon by selling the ranch to the rancher.

(D) lose, because acceptance of the purchase price by the seller was a concurrent condition to the seller's obligation to convey the ranch to the buyer on December 1.

[Q3143]

Answer 32: Choice **(C)** is correct. A repudiation may be retracted until the aggrieved party has either (i) sued for breach, (ii) changed his position materially in reliance on the repudiation, or (iii) stated that he regards the repudiation as final. Rest. 2d § 256(1). Under these facts, the buyer had from August 1, when she unequivocally repudiated the contract, to October 1 to retract her unequivocal repudiation. The buyer didn't do so. The buyer's right to retract her repudiation and perform under the contract ended when the seller materially changed his position in reliance on the repudiation, by selling to the rancher. The fact that the seller initially urged the buyer to change her mind does not alter the analysis — under the modern view, the repudiatee's exhortation to the repudiator to perform does not "reinstate the contract," and does not impair the repudiatee's subsequent right to cancel the contract or change position in reliance on the repudiation.

(A) is wrong because the seller had no obligation to notify the buyer that the seller was viewing the contract as being in material breach. A repudiation may be retracted until the aggrieved party has done any of three things (see the discussion of Choice (C) above), one of which is to materially change position in reliance on the repudiation. While the seller had the *right* to notify the buyer that the seller was viewing the contract as terminated and preparing to sell to someone else (and such a notice would have immediately ended the buyer's right to retract the repudiation, under the third branch of the Restatement test cited above), the seller did not have the *obligation* to give this notice before changing position.

(B) is wrong because the seller did not waive the repudiation by urging performance. Under the modern view, the repudiatee's exhortation to the repudiator to perform does not "reinstate the contract," and does not impair the repudiatee's right to cancel the contract or change position in reliance on the repudiation.

(D) is wrong because this choice misstates the law both as to a repudiation and a non-repudiation scenario. For instance, suppose that the buyer never repudiated and tendered the contract price on December 1, and the seller refused either to accept the money or convey the ranch — in that scenario the buyer would win, whereas the language of Choice (D) says that the buyer would lose. Beyond that, of course, the fact that the buyer had repudiated long before Dec. 1 entitled the seller to cancel the contract and convey to someone else, making the buyer's later tender of the contract price (and whether the seller accepted that tender) irrelevant.

B. Special UCC rules

1. Party has choice of remedies

Question 33: Broker needed a certain rare coin to complete a set that he had contracted to assemble and sell to Collecta. On February 1, Broker obtained such a coin from Hoarda in exchange for $1,000 and Broker's signed, written promise to re-deliver to Hoarda "not later than December 31 this year" a comparable specimen of the same kind of coin without charge to Hoarda. On February 2, Broker consummated sale of the complete set to Collecta.

On October 1, the market price of rare coins suddenly began a rapid, sustained rise; and on October 15 Hoarda wrote Broker for assurance that the latter would timely meet his coin-replacement commitment. Broker replied, "In view of the surprising market, it seems unfair that I should have to replace your coin within the next few weeks."

After receiving Broker's message on October 17, Hoarda telephoned Broker, who said, "I absolutely will not replace your coin until the market drops far below its present level." Hoarda then sued Broker on November 15 for the market value of a comparable replacement-coin as promised by Broker in February. The trial began on December 1.

If Broker moves to dismiss Hoarda's complaint, which of the following is Hoarda's best argument in opposing the motion?

(A) Hoarda's implied duty of good faith and fair dealing in enforcement of the contract required her to mitigate her losses on the rising market by suing promptly, as she did, after becoming reasonably apprehensive of a prospective breach by Broker.

(B) Although the doctrine of anticipatory breach is not applicable under the prevailing view if, at the time of repudiation, the repudiatee owes the repudiator no remaining duty of performance, the doctrine applies in this case because Hoarda, the repudiatee, remains potentially liable under an implied warranty that the coin advanced to Broker was genuine.

(C) When either party to a sale-of-goods contract repudiates with respect to a performance not yet due, the loss of which will substantially impair the value of the contract to the other, the aggrieved party may in good faith resort to any appropriate remedy for breach.

(D) Anticipatory repudiation, as a deliberate disruption without legal excuse of an ongoing contractual relationship between the parties, may be treated by the repudiatee at her election as a present tort, actionable at once.

[Q2178]

Answer 33: Choice **(C)** is correct. This is a sale-of-goods case, so the UCC's special anticipatory repudiation provision, § 2-610, applies. That section says that "when either party repudiates the contract with respect to a performance not yet due the loss of which will substantially impair the value of the contract to the other, the aggrieved party may ... (b) resort to any remedy for breach[.]" This section applies to these facts, and almost perfectly matches the phrasing in Choice (C): Broker has repudiated his obligation to deliver a replacement coin by Dec. 31; this repudiation has substantially impaired the value of the contract to Hoarda (since Broker's insistence on waiting for prices to come down means that the delay may be infinite, and will expose Hoarda to an ever-increasing financial loss if prices continue to mount); and a suit for the market value of the promised coin is an authorized "remedy for breach" in the circumstances.

(A) is wrong because Hoarda had no duty to mitigate her losses in the rising market by suing promptly. UCC § 2-610(a) gives Hoarda the right to "for a commercially reasonable time await performance by the repudiating party." So Hoarda could have waited a while, and didn't *have to* mitigate her damages by bringing suit immediately (although for the reasons described in Choice (C) she had the *right* to bring such an immediate suit).

(B) is wrong because, while it is true that in non-UCC cases, the repudiatee cannot bring suit prior to the time for the performance if the repudiatee has no remaining duty of performance, this special rule does not apply to UCC cases. Therefore, it wouldn't matter whether Hoarda did or did not have a surviving implied warranty that the coin she advanced to Broker was genuine.

(D) is wrong because, while this choice correctly states that the repudiatee may bring suit at once, the choice incorrectly states that this action would be for a "present tort." When the doctrine of anticipatory repudiation allows suit, the suit is a form of breach-of-contract action, not a tort suit.

CHAPTER 8

STATUTE OF FRAUDS

I.   SURETYSHIP

A. Main purpose rule

1.   Often tested on MBE

a.   Question may not mention Statute of Frauds

Question 34: A father and his adult daughter encountered an old family friend on the street. The daughter said to the friend, "How about lending me $1,000 to buy a used car? I'll pay you back with interest one year from today." The father added, "And if she doesn't pay it back as promised, I will." The friend thereupon wrote out and handed to the daughter his personal check, payable to her, for $1,000, and the daughter subsequently used the funds to buy a used car. When the debt became due, both the daughter and the father refused to repay it, or any part of it.

In an action by the friend against the father to recover $1,000 plus interest, which of the following statements would summarize the father's best defense?

(A) He received no consideration for his conditional promise to the friend.

(B) His conditional promise to the friend was not to be performed in less than a year from the time it was made.

(C) His conditional promise to the friend was not made for the primary purpose of benefiting himself (the father).

(D) The loan by the friend was made without any agreement concerning the applicable interest rate.

[Q1089]

Answer 34: Choice **(C)** is correct. The daughter is the primary obligor on the debt to the friend. The father, by promising to make the payment if the daughter doesn't, has promised to "answer for the debt of another," making him a surety. Since the father's promise is oral, it is rendered unenforceable by the suretyship provision of the Statute of Frauds, unless some exception makes it inapplicable. The most important exception to the suretyship provision is the main purpose rule. But here, the fact that the father's promise was not made for the "primary purpose" (i.e., "main purpose") of benefiting the father's own economic interests means that the main purpose rule does not apply, making the suretyship provision applicable. (Notice that nowhere in this choice do the examiners mention either the Statute of Frauds, the concept of suretyship, or the significance of the fact that the promise was oral — it's up to you to notice that the reference to the absence of "primary purpose" means that the suretyship provision will apply.)

(A) is wrong because the father *did* receive consideration for his conditional promise — the friend's making of the loan to the daughter. Consideration need not be given to the promisor, but can instead be given to a third party, as long as the promisor bargained for it.

(B) is wrong because it refers to the not-performable-within-one year provision of the Statute of Frauds, and that provision does not apply to the father's promise here. The reason is that there is a special exception under which "the one-year provision does not apply to a contract which is *performed on one side at the time it is made, such as a loan of money*, nor to any contract which has been fully performed on one side, whether the performance is completed within a year or not." Rest. 2d, § 130, Comment d. Since the friend has fully performed on his side by making the loan, the full performance removed the entire contract from the one-year provision.

(D) is wrong because the law will supply a reasonable interest rate under the circumstances, so that the contract (and the father's promise) will not be void for indefiniteness. As long as the term omitted by the parties' agreement is not so basic as to prevent them from having had a meeting of the minds, the court will supply the missing term by implication. Here, since the friend cares mainly about getting his principal back, he can stipulate that the interest rate was 0%, and the court will certainly be willing to apply that rate to save the contract from indefiniteness.

II. SATISFACTION BY A MEMORANDUM

A. UCC

1. Confirmation

Question 35: A skiing retailer, in a telephone conversation with a glove manufacturer, ordered 12 pairs of vortex-lined ski gloves at the manufacturer's list price of $600 per dozen "for delivery in 30 days." The manufacturer orally accepted the offer, and immediately faxed to the ski shop this signed memo: "Confirming our agreement today for your purchase of a dozen pairs of vortex-lined ski gloves for $600, the shipment will be delivered in 30 days." Although the retailer received and read the manufacturer's message within minutes after its dispatch, she changed her mind three weeks later about the purchase and rejected the conforming shipment when it timely arrived.

On learning of the rejection, does the manufacturer have a cause of action against the retailer for breach of contract?

(A) Yes, because the gloves were identified to the contract and tendered to the retailer.

(B) Yes, because the manufacturer's faxed memo to the retailer was sufficient to make the agreement enforceable.

(C) No, because the agreed price was $600 and the retailer never signed a writing evidencing a contract with the manufacturer.

(D) No, because the retailer neither paid for nor accepted any of the goods tendered.

[Q2185]

Answer 35: Choice **(B)** is correct. Normally, a contract for the sale of goods having a value of more than $500 is not enforceable unless memorialized in a writing signed by the party against whom enforcement is sought, here, the retailer. However, there is an important exception for confirmations sent between merchants. According to UCC § 2-201(2), "Between merchants if within a reasonable time a writing in confirmation of the contract and sufficient against the sender is received and the party receiving it has reason to know its contents, it satisfies the requirements of [the Statute of Frauds] against such party unless written notice of objection to its contents is given within 10 days after it is received." So here, even though the retailer didn't sign anything, the confirmation makes the contract good against her under § 2-201(2), because: (1) the retailer and the manufacturer are both merchants; (2) the manufacturer signed the confirmation, so that the confirmation would have been binding against the manufacturer; (3) the retailer had "reason to know [the confirmation's] contents" (because she read it); and (4) the retailer did not indicate her objection to the memorandum's contents within 10 days after receiving it.

(A) is wrong because the fact that the goods were "identified to the contract" is irrelevant to the enforceability of the contract — even if the retailer had canceled before the goods were shipped (or even before the goods were identified within the manufacturer's plant as being the ones that would be shipped to the retailer), the manufacturer would still have been entitled to sue for breach if more than 10 days had passed since the retailer received the confirmation. (The MBE examiners are probably trying to fool you into thinking of § 2-709, under which the fact that the goods have been identified to the contract will entitle the seller to sue for the full contract price if the seller cannot resell them at a reasonable price — but this provision doesn't turn an otherwise-unenforceable contract into an enforceable one, it merely governs the measure of damages for an already-enforceable contract.)

(C) is wrong because the retailer is liable despite never having signed a writing, due to her receipt of a confirmation and her lack of objection to it, as described in the discussion of Choice (B) above.

(D) is wrong because the fact that the retailer never paid for or accepted any of the goods is irrelevant — the retailer is bound by virtue of the fact that she received a signed confirmation and failed to object to it, and this is true regardless of whether she paid for or accepted any of the goods.

CHAPTER 9
REMEDIES

I.   EQUITABLE REMEDIES

A. Limitations on equitable remedies

1.   Inadequacy of damages

Question 36: Elda, the aged mother of Alice and Barry, both adults, wished to employ a live-in companion so that she might continue to live in her own home. Elda, however, had only enough income to pay one-half of the companion's $2,000 monthly salary. Learning of their mother's plight, Alice and

Barry agreed with each other in a signed writing that on the last day of January and each succeeding month during their mother's lifetime, each would give Elda $500. Elda then hired the companion.

Alice and Barry made the agreed payments in January, February, and March. In April, however, Barry refused to make any payment and notified Alice and Elda that he would make no further payments.

Assume that there is a valid contract between Alice and Barry and that Elda has declined to sue Barry. Will Alice succeed in an action against Barry in which she asks the court to order Barry to continue to make his payments to Elda under the terms of the Alice-Barry contract?

(A) Yes, because Alice's remedy at law is inadequate.

(B) Yes, because Alice's burden of supporting her mother will be increased if Barry does not contribute his share.

(C) No, because a court will not grant specific performance of a promise to pay money.

(D) No, because Barry's breach of contract has caused no economic harm to Alice.

[Q1065]

Answer 36: Choice **(A)** is correct. Alice's request that the court order Barry to continue making his payments is a request for a decree of specific performance. The principal requirement that Alice must satisfy in order to get this (or any) form of equitable relief is to show that legal relief — i.e. an award of money damages — would not be adequate to protect her. One reason for which an award of money damages might not be adequate is that the amount of the damage award cannot be computed with reasonable accuracy. Here, we don't know how long Elda will live, so the number of payments that Barry will end up being legally obligated to make is unknown. Therefore, the court cannot accurately assess a single amount as a damage award that represents the certain present value of Barry's obligation, and an award of "$500 per month for the rest of Elda's life" is a more accurate solution.

(B) is wrong because, while the burden on Alice will indeed increase by virtue of Barry's non-performance, this fact alone would not entitle Alice to a decree of specific performance rather than an award of damages. Alice will have to show that money damages are not inadequate remedy, and the reason that this is true is as discussed in the analysis of Choice (A).

(C) is wrong because it is a misstatement of law — there simply is no rule that courts will not grant specific performance of a promise to pay money. (Indeed, where the contract calls for a series of payments in return for some sort of ongoing performance, a decree that the payments be made as scheduled is likely to be *preferable* to a one-shot award of money damages, because the decree better protects the defendant's interest in getting the ongoing return performance in exchange for his payments.)

(D) is wrong because there is no requirement that a plaintiff show economic harm from the defendant's breach. Often the promisee in a third-party beneficiary scenario does not suffer economic harm if the promisor fails to render the promised performance to the third-party, but such promises are nonetheless enforceable by the promisee. It's true that there is a requirement that the defendant's promise have been supported by *consideration*; but here, the consideration for Barry's promise was Alice's return promise to pay her half of each monthly payment, so the fact that Alice herself is suffering no economic harm from Barry's breach of his payment obligation does not mean that Barry's promise lacked consideration.

2. Difficulty of enforcement

a. Personal service contract

Question 37: On November 15, a carpenter in a signed writing contracted with a homeowner for an agreed price to personally remodel the homeowner's kitchen according to specifications provided by the homeowner, and to start work on December 1. The carpenter agreed to provide all materials for the job in addition to all of the labor required.

On November 26 the carpenter without legal excuse repudiated the contract, and the homeowner, after a reasonable and prolonged effort, could not find anyone to remodel his kitchen for a price approximating the price agreed to by the carpenter. If one year later the homeowner brings an action for specific performance against the carpenter, which of the following will provide the carpenter with the best defense?

(A) An action for equitable relief not brought within a reasonable time is barred by laches.

(B) Specific performance is generally not available as a remedy to enforce a contractual duty to perform personal services.

(C) Specific performance is generally not available as a remedy in the ease of an anticipatory repudiation.

(D) Specific performance is not available as a remedy where even nominal damages could have been recovered as a remedy at law.

[Q2141]

Answer 37: Choice **(B)** is correct. Courts will usually not grant specific performance of an individual's duty to perform personal services, because of the difficulties in supervising the defendant's ongoing performance, and the distastefulness of ordering what amounts to involuntary servitude. Here, for instance, if the court grants an order compelling the carpenter to do the work at the contracted-for price and in the contracted-for time period, the court may have to make constant decisions about whether the carpenter is keeping up to the schedule and doing the work according to specifications, so that the court risks becoming enmeshed in burdensome project details, which the court probably will conclude is not a sensible use of judicial resources. Also, the court may have to imprison the carpenter if he doesn't perform, a consequence that seems somewhat like slavery.

(A) is wrong because the requirements for laches have not been satisfied here. It is true that if a plaintiff who is seeking equitable relief unjustifiably "sleeps on his rights," the defense of laches may preclude recovery. But here, there seem to be two reasons why laches would not apply: (1) we are told that the homeowner made a "reasonable and *prolonged* effort" to find a substitute, suggesting that the homeowner spent most or all of the one-year gap between repudiation and suit in reasonable efforts to mitigate, making the gap not unjustifiable; and (2) there is no evidence that the carpenter has been prejudiced by the delay, a usual requirement for laches.

(C) is wrong as a statement of law: when a plaintiff suffers from the defendant's anticipatory repudiation, all standard contract remedies are typically available to him, even though the time for performance has not yet arrived. So a decree of specific performance may be issued, though typically the decree would not require performance until the contractually-specified time for it.

(D) is wrong as a statement of law. It is true that a decree of specific performance, like other equitable relief, will not be granted where damages would provide an adequate remedy. But the availability of nominal damages alone will typically not be an adequate remedy, and that is certainly the case here, where the homeowner's actual damages will be more than nominal.

II. EXPECTATION DAMAGES

A. Formula for calculating

1. Breaching supplier of services

Question 38: A homeowner and a contractor entered into a contract for the construction of a home for the price of $300,000. The contractor was to earn a profit of $10,000 for the job. After the contractor had spent $45,000 on labor and materials, including $5,000 on oak flooring not yet installed, the homeowner informed the contractor that the homeowner had lost his job and could not pay for any services. The homeowner told the contractor to stop working immediately. The reasonable market value of the labor and materials provided by the contractor at that point, including the oak flooring, was $40,000. The contractor used the $5,000 worth of oak flooring on another job.

In an action by the contractor against the homeowner for damages, which of the following would be the largest amount of damages recoverable by the contractor?

(A) $40,000, the reasonable value of the services the contractor had provided.

(B) $40,000, the contractor's construction costs.

(C) $50,000, the contractor's construction costs of $45,000 plus the $10,000 profit minus the $5,000 saved by reusing the oak flooring on another job.

(D) $55,000, the contractor's construction costs of $45,000 plus the $10,000 profit.

[QA026]

Answer 38: Choice **(C)** is correct. $50,000 represents the contractor's expectation measure of recovery and gives the contractor the benefit of the bargain — this amount would place the contractor in the position he would have been in but for the breach. It is also the greatest amount the contractor is able to recover. The general expectation formula permits the contractor to recover $50,000 and can be computed as follows:

General expectation formula = Loss In Value + Other Loss – Cost Avoided – Loss Avoided:

LIV = the difference between the performance the nonbreaching party should have received under the contract and what was actually received, if anything, in this case, $300,000 less $0.

OL = consequential and incidental damages, if any, in this case, $0.

CA = the additional costs the nonbreaching party can avoid by rightfully discontinuing performance under the contract as a result of the other party's breach, in this case, $290,000 less $45,000. (Full performance would have cost the contractor $290,000, since he would have made $10,000 on a $300,000-revenue contract. But the contractor has already incurred $45,000 of this $290,000, leaving $245,000.)

LA = the beneficial effects of the breach due to the nonbreaching party's ability to salvage or reallocate resources that otherwise would have been devoted to performing under the contract, in this case, $5,000 (the oak flooring that can be reused).

So $300,000 + $0 – $245,000 – $5,000 = $50,000.

Rest. 2d, § 347; Farnsworth, § 12.9.

(A) is wrong, because it does not put the contractor in the position he would have been in had the contract been fulfilled. The $40,000 figure is an attempt to calculate the contractor's *restitution* recovery, measured by the benefit conferred on the owner. See Rest. 2d, § 371. That measure would yield the smallest amount of recovery, since it would not allow the contractor to recover damages related to the benefit of the bargain. "Innocent" (i.e., non-breaching) plaintiffs like the contractor usually have the option of suing for restitution damages where this would produce a higher recovery than the expectation measure, but restitution wouldn't produce a higher recovery here. Furthermore, the $40,000 amount is incorrect even as a restitution amount, since it fails to deduct the $5,000 worth of oak flooring the contractor used on another job (making the real benefit conferred on the owner $35,000).

(B) is wrong because it, too (like the measure in (A)) fails to put the contractor in the position he would have been in had the contract been fulfilled. $40,000 represents the contractor's *reliance* measure of recovery; that measure fails to take into account the contractor's benefit of the bargain, i.e., the profit the contractor anticipated making on the project. Reliance damages would consist of the contractor's unreimbursed expenses for labor and materials, $45,000, less the salvage value of the oak flooring, $5,000, which indeed equals $40,000, as this choice suggests. Cf. Rest. 2d, § 349. But nothing in this scenario would cause the contractor to seek damages based on the reliance principle and forgo his (larger) expectation measure of recovery. Rest. 2d, §§ 349, 347.

(D) is wrong because it's too generous to the contractor. A $55,000 damages recovery will place the contractor in a better position than he would have been in but for the breach, because it fails to take into account the "loss avoided" (see the discussion of Choice (C)) — the beneficial effects to the contractor from the breach, due to the contractor's ability to salvage or reallocate resources that otherwise would have been devoted to performing under the contract. Here the loss avoided is the $5,000 worth of oak flooring that the contractor used on another job.

B. "Reasonable certainty"

1. Profits from a new business

a. Not rule of law

i. Shift in law

Question 39: Swatter, a baseball star, contracted with the Municipal Symphony Orchestra. Inc., to perform for $5,000 at a children's concert as narrator of "Peter and the Wolf" Shortly before the concert, Swatter became embroiled in a highly publicized controversy over whether he had cursed and assaulted a baseball fan. The orchestra canceled the contract out of concern that attendance might be adversely affected by Swatter's appearance.

Swatter sued the orchestra for breach of contract. His business agent testified without contradiction that the cancellation had resulted in Swatter's not getting other contracts for performances and endorsements.

The trial court instructed the jury, in part, as follows: "If you find for the plaintiff, you may award damages for losses which at the time of contracting could reasonably have been foreseen by the defendant as a probable result of its breach. However, the law does not permit recovery for the loss of prospective profits of a new business caused by breach of contract."

On Swatter's appeal from a jury verdict for Swatter, and judgment thereon, awarding damages only for the $5,000 fee promised by the orchestra, the judgment will probably be

(A) affirmed, because the trial court stated the law correctly.

(B) affirmed, because the issue of damages for breach of contract was solely a jury question.

(C) reversed, because the test for limiting damages is what the breaching party could reasonably have foreseen at the time of the breach.

(D) reversed, because under the prevailing modern view, lost profits of a new business are recoverable if they are established with reasonable certainty.

[Q1007]

Answer 39: Choice **(D)** is correct. While it is true that any item of damages must be proved with reasonable certainty in order to be recovered, there is no fixed rule of law that prospective profits from a new business may not be recovered in a breach of contract action. Since the judge's instructions prevented the jury from even considering the possibility that some elements of Swatter's lost performance and endorsement income might be proven with reasonable certainty, the instruction was incorrect and not harmless. (For instance, Swatter might have been able to show that he got a certain amount of performance or endorsement revenue each year prior to Orchestra's cancellation, and that this dropped to $0 in the following year without any other explanation; such proof, if made, would likely have satisfied the requirement of reasonable certainty.)

(A) is wrong because the instruction was incorrect, for the reason discussed in Choice (D) above.

(B) is wrong as a matter of law — although the jury computes the damages, the judge can and must instruct the jury on the legal principles applicable to that computation (although here, the judge did so incorrectly).

(C) is wrong because, while it is true that contract damages are generally limited to those which the defendant could reasonably have foreseen, there is an additional requirement that each item of damages be proved with reasonable certainty, and this choice does not contain that important additional limitation.

C. Breaching seller of property

Question 40: On April 1, Owner and Buyer signed a writing in which Owner, "in consideration of $100 to be paid to Owner by Buyer," offered Buyer the right to purchase Greenacre for $100,000 within 30 days. The writing further provided, "This offer will become effective as an option only if and when the $100 consideration is in fact paid." On April 20, Owner, having received no payment or other communication from Buyer, sold and conveyed Greenacre to Citizen for $120,000. On April 21, Owner received a letter from Buyer enclosing a cashier's check for $100 payable to Owner and stating, "I am hereby exercising my option to purchase Greenacre and am prepared to close whenever you're ready." Owner explained that he had already sold the property to Citizen. Buyer brought suit against Owner for breach of contract.

Assume that Buyer prevails in the breach of contract suit against Owner. Which of the following is Buyer entitled to recover?

(A) Nominal damages only, because the remedy of specific performance was not available to Buyer.

(B) The fair market value, if any, of an assignable option to purchase Greenacre for $100,000.

(C) $20,000, plus the amount, if any, by which the fair market value of Greenacre on the date of Owner's breach exceeded $120,000.

(D) The amount, if any, by which the fair market value of Greenacre on the date of Owner's breach exceeded $100,000.

[Q3130]

Answer 40: Choice **(D)** is correct, because it correctly reflects the standard measure of damages for breach: expectation damages. In awarding expectation damages, the court attempts to put the plaintiff in the position she would have been in had the contract been performed by the defendant. Normally, this means that the plaintiff is awarded the profits she would have made had the contract been performed. That's the case here. Choice (D) best states this principle: in giving Buyer "the amount, if any, by which the fair market value of Greenacre on the date of [the] breach exceeded [the contract price]," the court will be giving Buyer the "benefit of her bargain," i.e., the profit she would have been able to make immediately by reselling the property.

(A) is wrong because nominal damages — which are a small sum that is fixed without regard to the amount of harm — are awarded only when a right of action for breach exists but no harm has been done or is provable. Here, Buyer has suffered provable harm (the contract-market differential). The fact that an equitable remedy (injunction) isn't available doesn't mean that Buyer didn't suffer provable harm, and doesn't prevent Buyer from collecting expectation damages.

(B) is wrong because the value of an assignable option would not be a measure of Buyer's expectation interest in this case. When Buyer sent the $100, she was exercising the option, and thus binding herself to purchase the property. Prior to that moment, it's possible that the measure of damages *would* be the value of the option (less the $100 price to "buy" that option). But once Buyer exercised by sending the $100, the option was no longer significant — there was a contract fully binding on both sides, and the usual measure of damages for a buyer whose seller breaches the contract of sale (benefit of the bargain) applied.

(C) is wrong because it incorrectly implies that the market value on the day of the sale to Citizen was at least $120,000. If the sale price to Citizen were the definitive proof of the market value of the property, this choice might be an accurate formulation. But that sale price is not legally dispositive, merely *evidence* of the fair market value. For instance, the sale to Citizen might have been at a price that the court finds to be greater than the actual market value on that day. In that event, guaranteeing Buyer a minimum recovery of $20,000 would be legally incorrect. (True, it seems unlikely that anyone would pay greater than the then "fair market value" on the day of sale. But the point is that the legal standard is "fair market value less plaintiff's contract price," not "the lesser of (1) the price paid by the third party minus the plaintiff's contract price or (2) the fair market value minus the plaintiff's contract price.")

III. SUITS IN QUASI-CONTRACT

A. Breaching plaintiff

1. Construction cases

a. Lesser of "cost to owner" and "change in value to owner"

Question 41: In a single writing, a painter contracted with a farmer to paint three identical barns on the farmer's rural estate for $2,000 each. The contract provided for the farmer's payment of $6,000 upon the painter's completion of the work on all three barns. The painter did not ask for any payment when the first barn was completely painted, but she demanded $4,000 after painting the second barn. The farmer rightfully refused the painter's demand for payment. The painter then immediately terminated the contract without painting the third barn. What is the painter entitled to recover from the farmer?

(A) Nothing, because payment was expressly conditioned on completion of all three barns.

(B) The painter's expenditures plus anticipated "profit" in painting the first two barns, up to a maximum recovery of $4,000.

(C) The reasonable value of the painter's services in painting the two barns, less the farmer's damages, if any, for the painter's failure to paint the third barn.

(D) The amount that the combined value of the two painted barns has been increased by the painter's work.

[Q3020]

Answer 41: Choice **(C)** is correct. Where a defaulting plaintiff has rendered some performance of value to the defendant, but has not substantially performed, the plaintiff may not recover "on the contract." But she may recover on a *quasi-contract* or *quantum meruit* ("as much as he deserved") theory — the court uses its equity-like powers to prevent unjust enrichment of the defendant. If the farmer didn't have to pay anything, he'd be unjustly enriched (at least with respect to the two painted barns, putting aside his damage from not getting the agreed-upon painting of the third barn) by the "value" to him of the painting of two barns. So the court would start by awarding the painter this value. But then, the farmer would be entitled to be made whole for the damages to him from not getting all three barns painted for the agreed-upon $6,000. So the court would compute how much it would now cost the farmer to get that single barn painted. If that cost would be $2,000 or less, the farmer's damages would be zero. But if it would cost more, then the difference would be deducted from the painter's quasi-contract "value of the services of painting two barns" recovery.

(A) is wrong because even though the painting of all three barns was an express condition of payment under the contract, the court can and would still award a quasi-contract recovery, as described above.

(B) is wrong because the painter is only entitled to a quasi-contract recovery, not to recover "on the contract." So any formula keyed to the painter's anticipated "profit" is irrelevant — it's the value to the defendant, not the profit that would have been made by the breaching plaintiff, that is the starting point. (Profits that would have been made by the plaintiff are relevant only where it's the defendant, not the plaintiff, who breached.)

(D) is wrong because this formula doesn't take into account the farmer's right to deduct damages for the painter's failure to paint the third barn. (The court might indeed use the increase in the value of the two painted barns as the measure of the "reasonable value" of the painter's services, but the court would deduct from this number the farmer's damages from the failure to paint the third barn.)

2. UCC gives partial restitution to breaching buyer

a. Exception for actual damages proved by seller

Question 42: Hydro-King. Inc., a high-volume, pleasure-boat retailer, entered into a written contract with Zuma, signed by both parties, to sell Zuma a power boat for $12,000. The manufacturer's price of the boat delivered to Hydro-King was $9,500. As the contract provided, Zuma paid Hydro-King $4,000 in advance and promised to pay the full balance upon delivery of the boat. The contract contained no provision for liquidated damages. Prior to the agreed delivery date, Zuma notified Hydro-King that he would be financially unable to conclude the purchase; and Hydro-King thereupon resold the same boat that Zuma had ordered to a third person for $12,000 cash.

If Zuma sues Hydro-King for restitution of the $4,000 advance payment, which of the following should the court decide?

(A) Zuma's claim should be denied, because, as the party in default, he is deemed to have lost any right to restitution of a benefit conferred on Hydro-King.

(B) Zuma's claim should be denied, because, but for his repudiation, Hydro-King would have made a profit on two boat-sales instead of one.

(C) Zuma's claim should be upheld in the amount of $4,000 minus the amount of Hydro-King's lost profit under its contract with Zuma.

(D) Zuma's claims should be upheld in the amount of $3,500 ($4,000 minus $500 as statutory damages under the UCC).

[Q1030]

Answer 42: Choice **(C)** is correct. The UCC controls. § 2-718 deals with a repudiating buyer's right to restitution of any deposit. § 2-718(2) states the general rule that if there is no liquidated damages clause in the contract (and there is none here), the seller must return all but 20% of the total contract price or $500, whichever amount is smaller. However, § 2-718(3) says that the buyer's right to restitution is subject "to offset to the extent that the seller establishes (a) a right to recover damages under the provisions of this Article other than [the liquidated damages provision]." So to the extent that Hydro-King can prove actual damages greater than $500, it need refund only the amount of the deposit less these greater actual damages. That's precisely the formulation listed in Choice (C). (We don't know what Hydro-King's lost profits actually will be, because we don't know whether it is a "lost volume" seller, or instead can only get fewer of the power boats in question than it has customers for, in which case it would not have suffered any actual lost profits. But whatever amount represents its actual lost profits, Hydro-King gets to keep that amount, as this choice specifies.)

(A) is wrong because it directly conflicts with § 2-718(2), which entitles even a defaulting buyer to restitution of his deposit less either the seller's actual damages or the lesser of 20% of the contract price and $500.

(B) is wrong for two reasons: (1) we don't actually know whether Hydro-King is indeed a "lost volume seller" as this choice suggests it is — if Hydro-King had more customers wanting to buy that particular model boat than it could get boats from the manufacturer, Hydro-King didn't lose a net sale; and (2) even if Hydro-King lost a net sale, its damages were only $2,500, so it can't keep the entire $4,000 as this choice asserts it can.

(D) is wrong because, while it correctly states the result that would occur under § 2-718(2) if Hydro-King couldn't prove any actual damages, it ignores the fact that Hydro-King can keep that part of the deposit representing its actual damages from the lost sale if this amount is greater than $500.

IV. LIQUIDATED DAMAGES

A. Reasonableness of amount

1. Modern view

a. Unexpectedly high damages

i. How tested on the MBE

Question 43: A sea captain owns an exceptionally seaworthy boat that she charters for sport fishing at a $500 daily rate. The fee includes the use of the boat with the sea captain as the captain, and one other crew member, as well as fishing tackle and bait. On May 1, a customer agreed with the captain that the customer would have the full-day use of the boat on May 15 for himself and his family for $500. The customer paid an advance deposit of $200 and signed an agreement that the deposit could be retained by the captain as liquidated damages in the event the customer canceled or failed to appear.

At the time of contracting, the captain told the customer to be at the dock at 5 a.m. on May 15. The customer and his family, however, did not show up on May 15 until noon. Meantime, the captain agreed at 10 a.m. to take a replacement customer and her family out fishing for the rest of the day. The replacement had happened to come by and inquire about the possibility of such an outing. In view of the late hour, the captain charged the replacement $400 and stayed out two hours beyond the customary return time. The original customer's failure to appear until noon was due to the fact that he had been trying to charter another boat across the bay at a lower rate and had gotten lost after he was unsuccessful in getting such a charter.

Which of the following is an accurate statement concerning the rights of the parties?

(A) The captain can retain the $200 paid by the customer, because it would be difficult for the captain to establish her actual damages and the sum appears to have been a reasonable forecast in light of anticipated loss of profit from the charter.

(B) The captain is entitled to retain only $50 (10% of the contract price) and must return $150 to the customer.

(C) The captain must return $100 to the customer in order to avoid her own unjust enrichment at the customer's expense.

(D) The captain must return $100 to the customer, because the liquidated-damage clause under the circumstances would operate as a penalty.

[Q2086]

Answer 43: Choice **(A)** is correct. Even in a court that has a relatively tough standard for the enforceability of litigated damages clauses, the court will enforce the clause if *both* of the following are true: (1) the forecast was a reasonable estimate of likely damages at the time the contract was entered into; and (2) the party seeking to enforce the clause has suffered actual damages that are hard to calculate accurately. Here, these two conditions are satisfied: (1) at the time the contract was made, the captain faced a real risk that the customer would fail to show up at the last minute, and that she would be unable to get another charter for that same day; therefore, a deposit of 40% of total contract price was a reasonable forecast of likely damages, especially since most of the captain's costs for a one-day charter are fixed (cost of boat) so that if she doesn't do the trip she recoups relatively little expense; (2) while the captain has collected $400 from the replacement as well as $200 from the customer, giving her a total for the day of $600 (i.e., $100 more than she would have gotten from the customer alone if the contract had been fulfilled), she had to stay out two hours beyond the customary return time, so some of her $100 "surplus" may have been due to this extra-long day rather than being a windfall; consequently, the captain's actual damages are indeed hard to calculate accurately after-the-fact.

(B) is wrong because it is a misstatement of law. In non-sales cases, there is no single formula that determines the outer bounds of permissible liquidated damages, as this choice suggests that there is. The examiners may have been trying to trick you into thinking of the formula applied in UCC cases, under which if the buyer of goods makes a deposit and then breaches (e.g., by canceling), and the contract does not contain a liquidated damages clause, the buyer gets back any part of his deposit in excess of "20% of the value of the total [contract price] or $500, whichever is smaller" if the seller does not establish actual damages. § 2-718(2)(b). Since this is a contract for the sale of services rather than goods, this provision does not apply (and the 10% amount in the choice doesn't match up with the UCC percentage anyway).

(C) is wrong because, while it arguably describes a treatment that puts the captain in the same position she would have been in had the contract been performed (she has collected $600 for the day from the combination of the customer and the replacement, versus $500 if the customer contract had been performed, so she arguably needs to give back $100), this choice ignores the liquidated damages clause. So long as the liquidated damages clause meets the rules for enforceability of such clauses, the fact that the clause gives the person trying to use it some slight benefit over the actual damage amount that a court might compute is irrelevant.

(D) is wrong because the liquidated damages clause here would not operate as a penalty. As long as such a clause at least meets the two-part test described in Choice (A), it by definition does not constitute a penalty. In other words, the "penalty" label is simply a shorthand method of stating that the clause doesn't pass the two-part test, which the clause here does pass.

V. DAMAGES IN SALES CONTRACTS

A. Where goods not accepted

1. Seller's damages for breach

a. Lost profits

i. "Lost volume" seller

Question 44: By the terms of a written contract signed by both parties on January 15, a computer retailer agreed to sell a specific ICB personal computer to a buyer for $3,000, and the buyer agreed to pick up and pay for the computer at the retailer's store on February 1. The buyer unjustifiably repudiated on February 1. Without notifying the buyer, the retailer subsequently sold at private sale the same specific computer to another buyer, who paid the same price ($3,000) in cash. The ICB is a popular product; the retailer can buy from the manufacturer more units than it can sell at retail.

If the retailer sues the buyer for breach of contract, the retailer will probably recover

(A) nothing, because it received a price on resale equal to the contract price that the buyer had agreed to pay.

(B) nothing, because the retailer failed to give the buyer proper notice of the retailer's intention to resell.

(C) the retailer's anticipated profit on the sale to the buyer plus incidental damages, if any, because the retailer lost that sale.

(D) $3,000 (the contract price), because the buyer intentionally breached the contract by repudiation.

[Q3009]

Answer 44: Choice **(C)** is correct. The retailer is a "lost volume" seller, that is, one who can obtain as many items from a supplier as she can sell. UCC § 2-708(2), which doesn't expressly mention lost-volume sellers but is designed for them, gives such sellers the profit that the seller would have made from full performance by the buyer, together with any incidental damages.

(A) is wrong because § 2-708(2) gives a lost-volume seller such as the retailer its lost profits regardless of the amount of the resale-contract differential. Indeed, the whole point of § 2-708(2) is to prevent a lost-volume seller from being limited to a $0 or very small resale-contract differential.

(B) is wrong because notice of intent to resell is not required where the recovery is on a lost-volume basis. When the seller elects the remedy of "cover" — i.e., the right to resell and collect the difference between the resale price and the (higher) contract price — and the resale is at a private sale, the seller *is* required to give the buyer "reasonable notification of his intention to resell." § 2-706(3). However, the retailer is *not* recovering on this resale/contract-price basis (since that basis would give him $0). Instead, he's recovering his lost profits as a lost-volume seller under § 2-708(2), and no advance notice is required for such a recovery.

(D) is wrong because the damages available to a lost volume seller are not the contract price. The retailer is entitled to its lost profits and any incidental damages suffered. Awarding the retailer the contract price would over-compensate it, since it has not had to bear the expense of buying the computer from the manufacturer.

CHAPTER 10

CONTRACTS INVOLVING MORE THAN TWO PARTIES

I. ASSIGNMENT

A. Assignee vs. obligor

Question 45: Under the terms of a written contract, a contractor agreed to construct for a homeowner a garage for $10,000. Nothing was said in the parties' negotiations or in the contract about progress payments during the course of the work. After completing 25% of the garage strictly according to the homeowner's specifications, the contractor assigned his rights under the contract to a banker as security for an $8,000 loan. The banker immediately notified the homeowner of the assignment. The contractor thereafter, without legal excuse, abandoned the job before it was half-complete. The contractor subsequently defaulted on the loan from the banker. The contractor has no assets. It will cost the homeowner at least $8,000 to get the garage finished by another builder.

If the banker sues the homeowner for $8,000, which of the following will the court decide?

(A) The banker wins, because the contractor-homeowner contract was in existence and the contractor was not in breach when the banker gave the homeowner notice of the assignment.

(B) The banker wins, because the banker as a secured creditor over the contractor is entitled to priority over the homeowner's unsecured claim against the contractor.

(C) The homeowner wins, because his right to recoupment on account of the contractor's breach is available against the banker as the contractor's assignee.

(D) The homeowner wins, because his claim against the contractor arose prior to the contractor's default on his loan from the banker.

[Q2032]

Answer 45: Choice **(C)** is correct. Generally, an assignee "stands in the shoes of his assignor." That is, the assignee generally takes subject to all defenses, set-offs, and counterclaims that the obligor could have asserted against the assignor. Here, therefore, the banker as assignee of the contractor's rights stands in the contractor's shoes, and is vulnerable to any counterclaim or defense to which the contractor would have been vulnerable if it was the contractor that was suing the homeowner. If the contractor had not made the assignment and had sued the homeowner for the $10,000 contract price (or any part of it), the homeowner could have raised the counterclaim or defense for damages for breach due to the contractor's abandonment, and used that counterclaim/defense as a set-off, i.e., to reduce any amount which the homeowner would otherwise owe. Consequently, the homeowner can make this same counterclaim or defense when sued by the banker as the contractor's assignee. (The homeowner could not achieve an affirmative recovery against the banker, but the homeowner isn't trying to do that here, just reduce the amount he owes the banker.)

(A) is wrong because it does not matter either that the contractor-homeowner contract was already in existence at the time of the notice of assignment or that the contractor was not yet in breach at that time. In a suit by the assignee against the obligor, the obligor can raise any defenses or counterclaims that it could have raised against the assignor, regardless of when those defenses or counterclaims came into existence. (If you selected this choice, you may be thinking that about the rules on *modification*, under which the giving of notice of assignment by assignee to obligor will deprive the obligor and assignor of the subsequent right to modify the contract if the assignor has fully performed.)

(B) is wrong because it states a completely fictitious rule of law. It is true that the homeowner's claim is unsecured and that the banker's is secured; this fact might prevent the homeowner from getting and collecting an *affirmative recovery* against the contractor (since the banker's secured claim would take priority over the homeowner's later-acquired judgment for the affirmative recovery). But what the homeowner cares about here is using its claim as a set-off (something that can reduce the banker's recovery against the homeowner), and the homeowner's claim is fully operative as a set-off even though the set-off claim is in a sense "unsecured."

(D) is wrong because, while it states the correct result, it gives the wrong reason. Whether or not the homeowner's claim against the contractor arose prior to the contractor's default on the loan from the banker, the homeowner gets to raise against the banker any defense he could use against the contractor (for reasons described in the discussion of Choice (C) above).

Question 46: On March 1, Mechanic agreed to repair Ohner's machine for $5,000, to be paid on completion of the work. On March 15, before the work was completed, Mechanic sent a letter to Ohner with a copy to Jones, telling Ohner to pay the $5,000 to Jones, who was one of Mechanic's creditors. Mechanic then completed the work.

Which of the following, if true, would best serve Ohner as a defense in an action brought against him by Jones for $5,000?

(A)   Jones was incapable of performing Mechanic's work.

(B)   Mechanic had not performed his work in a workmanlike manner.

(C)   On March 1, Mechanic had promised Ohner that he would not assign the contract.

(D)   Jones was not the intended beneficiary of the Ohner-Mechanic contract.

[Q4174]

Answer 46: Choice (B) is correct. An assignment of contractual rights is the transfer of that right to another. It requires assignor's intent to transfer, identification of the rights to be assigned, and assignee's acceptance (which is normally presumed if the assignment is beneficial). Under the contract here, Mechanic's *"right"* under the contract was to receive payment from Ohner. Thus, his letter to Jones and Ohner would serve to transfer the right to payment to Jones. This makes Jones the assignee, Mechanic the assignor, and Ohner the obligor. The result of the transfer is that Jones "stands in Mechanic's shoes" as to the right to payment. As a result, any defenses under the contract that Ohner could assert against Mechanic, he can assert against Jones. Thus, Mechanic's failure to perform under the contract would be a defense Ohner could successfully assert against Jones.

(A) is not the best response, because Jones's ability to do Mechanic's work is irrelevant to Jones's recovery. If you chose this response, you either confused an assignment of rights with a delegation of duties, or assumed that Mechanic assigned the *contract*, not just the right to payment, which would involve a presumption that the duties were delegated as well. Most "impersonal" duties can be delegated, and Mechanic's duty to repair the machine probably *could* be delegated, barring facts indicating that Ohner had a particular interest in receiving performance from Mechanic. Rest. of Contracts 2d § 318 (2). However, a delegation or an assignment is *not* valid where it materially increases the risk that Ohner will not receive return performance. Rest. of Contracts 2d § 317 (2). Where Jones can't perform the work, such a delegation would be invalid. However, since only an assignment of right to payment is involved here, A isn't the best response.

(C) is not the best response, because the prohibition against assignment would not be upheld. UCC § 9-406(d) provides that a party may assign its right to payment even though the contract under which payment is due prohibits assignment. Here, the proposed answer stipulates that Mechanic promised not to assign the contract. Nonetheless, applicable law would permit Mechanic to assign the right to collect Ohner's payment.

(D) is not the best response, because Jones's not being a third party beneficiary would *not* be determinative of his recovery. This choice suggests that the only way Jones can recover is as an intended beneficiary to the contract. While it's true that an intended beneficiary has enforceable rights under a contract, so does an assignee.

II. DELEGATION OF DUTIES

A. Delegatee's liability

1. Assignment of "the contract"

a. Delegator remains liable

Question 47: Gyro, an expert in lifting and emplacing equipment atop tall buildings, contracted in a signed writing to lift and emplace certain air-conditioning equipment atop Tower's building. The contract contained a clause providing for per diem damages if Gyro did not complete performance by a specified date, and a clause providing that "time is of the essence." Another clause provided that any subsequent agreement for extra work under the contract must be in writing and signed by both parties.

With ample time remaining under the contract for commencement and completion of his performance, Gyro notified Tower that he was selling his business to Copter, who was equally expert in lifting and emplacing equipment atop tall buildings, and that Copter had agreed to "take over the Gyro-Tower contract."

Tower orally agreed with Gyro to accept Copter's services. Copter performed on time but negligently installed the wrong air-conditioning equipment.

Will Tower succeed in an action against Gyro for damages for breach of contract?

(A) Yes, because Tower did not agree to release Gyro from liability under the Gyro-Tower contract.

(B) Yes, because Tower received no consideration for the substitution of Copter for Gyro.

(C) No, because by accepting the substitution of Copter for Gyro, Tower effected a novation, and Gyro was thereby discharged of his duties under the Gyro-Tower contract.

(D) No, because the liquidated-damage clause in the Gyro-Tower contract provided only for damages caused by delay in performance.

[Q1053]

Answer 47: Choice **(A)** is correct. The sale of the business by Gyro to Copter was both an assignment of rights under the Gyro-Tower contract and a delegation of duties under it. When a delegation occurs, the delegator (here, Gyro) remains liable to the obligee (here, Tower) unless the obligee *expressly releases* the delegator and agrees to look solely to the delegate (Copter); if this occurred it would be a "novation." The mere fact that the obligee agrees to the delegation does not by itself constitute a novation or release the delegator from liability. Here, therefore, although Tower agreed to the delegation (i.e., agreed to accept performance from Copter), he did not agree to a novation and therefore did not release Gyro.

(B) is wrong because: (1) an obligee's assent to a delegation does not require consideration; and (2) even though Tower validly assented to Copter's doing the work, this did not release Gyro from liability, for the reason explained in the analysis of Choice (A).

(C) is wrong because the mere fact that an obligee assents to a delegation does not effect a novation. Instead, a novation is deemed to occur only when the obligee expressly agrees to release the obligee and look solely to the delegate; there was therefore no novation here. (If there *had* been a novation, it would indeed have served to discharge Gyro, as this choice suggests.)

(D) is wrong because the fact that the liquidated-damages clause covered only delay damages does not mean that damages for other breaches (e.g., timely but non-conforming work) cannot be recovered. A liquidated damages clause that is restricted to a certain type of breach leaves common-law damages intact for other types of breach.

III. THIRD-PARTY BENEFICIARIES

A. When beneficiary may sue

1. Intended beneficiaries may sue

a. Intended beneficiary

i. Tie-breaker looks to whom the performance is rendered to

Question 48: Elda, the aged mother of Alice and Barry, both adults, wished to employ a live-in companion so that she might continue to live in her own home. Elda, however, had only enough income to pay one-half of the companion's $2,000 monthly salary. Learning of their mother's plight, Alice and Barry agreed with each other in a signed writing that on the last day of January and each succeeding month during their mother's lifetime, each would give Elda $500. Elda then hired the companion.

Alice and Barry made the agreed payments in January, February, and March. In April, however, Barry refused to make any payment and notified Alice and Elda that he would make no further payments.

Will Elda succeed in an action for $500 brought against Barry after April 30?

(A) Yes, because by making his first three payments, Barry confirmed his intent to contract.

(B) Yes, because Elda is an intended beneficiary of a contract between Alice and Barry.

(C) No, because a parent cannot sue her child for breach of a promise for support.

(D) No, because Alice and Barry intended their payments to Elda to be gifts.

[Q1064]

Answer 48: Choice **(B)** is correct. The issue is whether Elda was an intended beneficiary of the Alice-Barry contract; if she was, she can sue, and if she wasn't, she can't. It's pretty clear from the context that Alice (the promisee of Barry's promise) desired to help her mother; therefore, Elda is an intended beneficiary of Barry's promise even though Alice was also motivated by a desire not to pay for the companion entirely by herself. In other words, Alice's "mixed motives" don't disqualify Elda from being an intended beneficiary, as long as one of Alice's motives was to help Elda. The fact that performance by Barry (payment of $500 per month) was to be rendered directly to Elda, rather than to Alice, also pushes the classification toward a finding that Elda was an intended beneficiary.

(A) is wrong because Barry's making of the first three payments is irrelevant — from the conduct and motivation of the parties in making the contract, we know that Elda was an intended beneficiary (as discussed in Choice (B) above), so Elda would have been entitled to sue Barry for nonpayment even if he had not made any prior payments.

(C) is wrong because it ignores the significance of the three-party context. In a two-party scenario in which all that happens is that a child promises to pay for the parent's support, this promise may indeed be unenforceable for lack of consideration. But in a three-party case like this one, the law of third-party beneficiaries can change the result. Here, each of the children's promises supplies consideration for the other child's return promise; therefore, lack of consideration is not a problem even though Elda is not herself giving consideration.

(D) is wrong because, while it is true that Alice and Barry both intended their payments to be gifts, this fact does not prevent Elda from being an intended beneficiary, who therefore gets the right to sue either promisor for breach. The whole idea of a "donee beneficiary" (as opposed to a "creditor beneficiary") is that a person to whom the promisee intends to make a gift becomes an intended beneficiary (of the "donee" sub-category).

2. Incidental beneficiaries

a. Real estate neighbors

Question 49: A landowner was land-rich by inheritance but money-poor, having suffered severe losses on bad investments, but still owned several thousand acres of unencumbered timberland. He had a large family, and his normal, fixed personal expenses were high. Pressed for cash, he advertised a proposed sale of standing timber on a choice 2,000-acre tract. The only response was from a logging company, which operated a large, integrated construction enterprise. The logging company, after inspection of the advertised tract, offered a fair price for the timber rights in question, and the landowner accepted the offer. The 2,000-acre tract was an abundant wild-game habitat and had been used for many years, with the landowner's permission, by area hunters. The logging company's performance of the timber contract would destroy this habitat. Without legal excuse and over the landowner's strong objection, the logging company repudiated the contract before commencing performance. The landowner could not afford to hire a lawyer and take legal action, and made no attempt to assign any cause of action he might have had against the logging company.

If the logging company is sued for breach of the contract by the landowner's next-door neighbor, whose view of a nearby lake is obscured by the standing timber, the neighbor will probably

(A) lose, as only an incidental beneficiary, if any, of the logging company-landowner contract.

(B) lose, as a maintainer of nuisance litigation.

(C) prevail, as a third-party intended beneficiary of the logging company- landowner contract.

(D) prevail, as a surrogate for the landowner in view of his inability to enforce the contract.

[Q3083]

Answer 49: Choice **(A)** is correct. Incidental beneficiaries cannot enforce a contract if one of the original parties to it defaults. Since there will often be many people indirectly or even directly benefited by any given contractual performance, the term "incidental beneficiary" is used to describe those persons who would benefit by the performance but who were not intended by the original parties to be benefited. Here, the landowner's neighbor's rights under the landowner-logging company contract are those of an incidental beneficiary, at best — neither the landowner nor the logging company intended to confer any benefit (and certainly not the benefit of an improved view) upon the neighbor when they made the contract. Therefore, the neighbor cannot recover against the logging company for breach.

(B) is wrong because the fact that a suit is "nuisance litigation" will not be a ground on which the defendant to the suit can win. Instead, if the defendant wins "on the merits," the fact that the suit was so meritless as to have been a nuisance might be grounds for the original defendant to win a tort-like recovery from the original plaintiff in a second suit, brought by the original defendant for wrongful use of civil proceedings. So here, the fact that the neighbor was bringing a "nuisance litigation" would be irrelevant to whether the neighbor would win.

(C) is wrong because the neighbor was not an intended beneficiary. For a third-party to be an intended beneficiary, the circumstances must indicate that at least one of the original parties intended to give the beneficiary the benefit of the intended promise. Here, this is not so, for the reasons described in Choice (A) above.

(D) is wrong because no rights were transferred to the neighbor to allow him to sue as a surrogate. The neighbor cannot claim to be a surrogate standing in to enforce the landowner's rights under the contract unless he can show some relation to the contract. The facts state that the landowner has made no attempt to assign to his neighbor any cause of action he might have against the logging company; nor do the facts state any other legal relationship between the landowner and his neighbor that might be the basis for some sort of surrogacy.

B. Discharge or modification by the original parties

Question 50: On May 4, Mater and Nirvana Motors both signed a single document evidencing a contract for the sale by Nirvana to Mater, "as a wedding gift for Mater's son Gilbert," a new Mark XX

Rolls-Royce sedan, for $180,000 cash on delivery. On May 5, Mater handed Gilbert a photocopy of this document. In reliance on the prospective gift, Gilbert on May 20 sold his nearly new Cheetah (an expensive sports car) to a dealer at a "bargain" price of $50,000 and immediately informed Mater and Nirvana that he had done so.

On May 25, however, Mater and Nirvana Motors by mutual agreement rescinded in a signed writing "any and all agreements heretofore made between the undersigned parties for the sale-and-purchase of a new Mark XX Rolls-Royce sedan." Later that day, Nirvana sold for $190,000 cash to another buyer the only new Mark XX Rolls-Royce that it had in stock or could readily obtain elsewhere. On June 1, Gilbert tendered $180,000 in cash to Nirvana Motors and demanded delivery to him "within a reasonable time" of a new Mark XX Rolls-Royce sedan with all available equipment.

Nirvana rejected the tender and denied any obligation.

If Gilbert sues Nirvana for breach of contract, which of the following will the court probably decide?

(A) Gilbert wins, because his rights as an assignee for value of the May 4 Mater-Nirvana contract cannot be cut off by agreement between the original parties.

(B) Gilbert wins, because his rights as a third-party intended beneficiary became vested by his prejudicial reliance in selling his Cheetah on May 20.

(C) Nirvana wins, because Gilbert, if an intended beneficiary at all of the Mater-Nirvana contract, was only a donee beneficiary.

(D) Nirvana wins, because it reasonably and prejudicially relied on its contract of mutual rescission with Mater by selling the only readily available new Mark XX Rolls-Royce sedan to another buyer.

[Q1194]

Answer 50: Choice **(B)** is correct. Gilbert is an intended beneficiary of the Mater-Nirvana agreement, since Mater made it clear that her primary purpose in entering into the contract was to provide a wedding gift for Gilbert. The original parties' power to modify the contract without the beneficiary's consent terminates if the beneficiary, before she receives notification of the discharge or modification, does any of three things: (1) materially *changes her position in justifiable reliance* on the promise; (2) brings suit on it; or (3) manifests assent to it at the request of either of the original parties. Here, Gilbert did the first of these, by selling his old car at a discount, in justifiable reliance on the forthcoming gift. Once he did that, both Mater and Nirvana lost the ability to modify the contract without Gilbert's consent. Therefore, Gilbert has the right to sue the promisor, Nirvana, for breach.

(A) is wrong because Gilbert is not an "assignee for value" of the Mater-Nirvana contract, he's a third-party beneficiary of it. He's not an "assignee" at all (neither of the original parties assigned him any right), and he's certainly not an assignee "for value," since he didn't pay or give anything of value to either of the original parties.

(C) is wrong because, although Gilbert is indeed a donee beneficiary, that status did not prevent his rights from "vesting" when he changed position in reliance on the agreement. (Donee beneficiaries and creditor beneficiaries have the same rights regarding modifications by the original parties.)

(D) is wrong because Nirvana's reliance on the rescission is irrelevant. The promisor under a third-party beneficiary contract is expected to know the rules governing such contracts, and those rules include the rule that a beneficiary who detrimentally relies on the contract gets an immediate vesting.

Question 51: On March 1, Zeller orally agreed to sell his land, Homestead, to Byer for $46,000 to be paid on March 31. Byer orally agreed to pay $25,000 of the purchase price to Quincy in satisfaction of a debt which Zeller said he had promised to pay Quincy.

On March 10, Byer dictated the agreement to his secretary but omitted all reference to the payment of the $25,000 to Quincy. Neither Byer nor Zeller carefully read the writing before signing it on March 15. Neither raised any question concerning omission of the payment to Quincy.

In an action by Quincy against Byer for $25,000, which of the following, if proved, would best serve Byer as a defense?

(A) There was no consideration to support Zeller's antecedent promise to pay Quincy the $25,000.

(B) On March 5, before Quincy was aware of the oral agreement between Zeller and Byer, Zeller agreed with Byer not to pay any part of the purchase price to Quincy.

(C) Whatever action Quincy may have had against Zeller was barred by the statute of limitations prior to March 1.

(D) Before he instituted his action against Byer, Quincy had not notified either Byer or Zeller that he had accepted the Byer-Zeller arrangement for paying Quincy.

[Q4037]

Answer 51: Choice **(B)** is correct. An intended beneficiary to a contract only has enforceable rights under that contract when his rights "vest." Before the rights vest, the beneficiary can't stop the parties from modifying or rescinding the contract. Under the modern/Restatement view, a beneficiary's rights vest when any of these three events occurs: (1) the beneficiary manifests assent to the promise; (2) the beneficiary sues to enforce the promise; or (3) the beneficiary justifiably relies on the promise to his detriment. Thus, if Byer and Zeller eliminated the Quincy payment provision before Quincy even found out about the contract, Quincy couldn't possibly have either "manifested assent" (#1 above), "sued to enforce the promise" (#2) or "justifiably relie[d]" (#3). That meant that Quincy's rights could not yet have vested as of the moment the original two parties to the contract (Byer and Zeller) modified the contract, and not-yet-vested beneficiary rights may be rescinded or modified by the original parties at any time.

(A) is not the best response, because a promise by one of the original contracting parties to make payment to a third-party beneficiary does not need separate consideration from the beneficiary. The only consideration that's relevant under the Byer-Zeller contract is whether there was consideration to support the contract itself, and there was such — Byer received Zeller's promise to convey the property as consideration for his, Byer's, promise to make the $46,000 in total payments.

(C) is not the best response, because any time-bar of Quincy's right to sue Zeller is not relevant to *Byer's* duty to pay Quincy. As discussed in (A), there does not need to be separate consideration for one contracting party's promise to pay some of the contract price to a third party beneficiary. Therefore, Quincy can recover under the Byer-Zeller agreement if he was an intended beneficiary (or an assignee). Thus, it wouldn't matter if Zeller had an enforceable debt to Quincy or not – Zeller could be giving Quincy money as a gift and Quincy would *still* have enforceable rights. (The only significance of the debt is that it would make Quincy a *creditor* beneficiary instead of a *donee* beneficiary, but that distinction rarely matters today, and doesn't matter on these facts.)

(D) is not the best response, because Quincy's notifying the parties of his acceptance of the agreement wouldn't be relevant to his ability to prevail. An intended beneficiary can (as long as his rights haven't previously been cut off, by one of the events described in (B) above) sue the promisor without having first notified either of the two original parties that the beneficiary was "accepting." If Quincy had given such a notice, that would serve to "vest" his rights (it would be a "manifestation of assent"). But even absent such a manifestation, the bringing of suit would vest Quincy's rights, if the original parties hadn't modified or rescinded the rights first.

C. Defenses against the beneficiary

1. Promisor may invoke conditions to his duty

Question 52: Kabb, the owner of a fleet of taxis, contracted with Petrol, a dealer in petroleum products, for the purchase and sale of Kabb's total requirements of gasoline and oil for one year. As part of that agreement, Petrol also agreed with Kabb that for one year Petrol would place all his advertising with

Ada Artiste, Kabb's wife, who owned her own small advertising agency. When Artiste was informed of the Kabb-Petrol contract, she declined to accept an advertising account from the Detur-gid Soap Company because she could not handle both the Petrol and Deturgid accounts during the same year.

For this question only, assume the following facts. During the first month of the contract, Kabb purchased substantial amounts of his gasoline from a supplier other than Petrol, and Petrol thereupon notified Artiste that he would no longer place his advertising with her agency.

In an action against Petrol for breach of contract, Artiste probably will

(A) succeed, because she is a third-party beneficiary of the Kabb-Petrol contract.

(B) succeed, because Kabb was acting as Artiste's agent when he contracted with Petrol.

(C) not succeed, because the failure of a constructive condition precedent excused Petrol's duty to place his advertising with Artiste.

(D) not succeed, because Artiste did not provide any consideration to support Petrol's promise to place his advertising with her.

[Q2074]

Answer 52: Choice **(C)** is correct. It is true that Artiste was a third-party beneficiary of the Kabb-Petrol agreement. Therefore, if Petrol had breached the agreement by unjustifiably failing to place all of his advertising with Artiste, Artiste would have been able to recover against him for breach. However, when the original parties to an agreement each make a promise to the other, each party's substantial performance of his own promise is generally a constructive condition to the other party's obligation to perform any subsequent duties. Therefore, when Kabb failed to perform his obligations early in the contract by not purchasing all his gas from Petrol, this was not only a breach of the Kabb-Petrol agreement but also operated as the non-occurrence of a constructive condition to Petrol's subsequent duty to continue using Artiste as his sole source for advertising. Therefore, Petrol's notice to Artiste that he would not use her for any further advertising was neither an anticipatory repudiation nor a present breach, so that there is nothing for Artiste to recover on.

(A) is wrong because, although Artiste is in fact a third-party beneficiary of the Kabb-Petrol contract, this does not help her because Petrol committed no breach, for the reasons explained above.

(B) is wrong because even if Kabb is viewed as having been Artiste's agent when he obtained the promise from Petrol that Petrol would buy advertising exclusively from Artiste, this will not entitle Artiste to recover — Petrol's duty to Artiste was dependent upon Kabb's first not materially breaching any prior obligations to Petrol, and as described above Kabb *did* breach.

(D) is wrong because there *was* consideration for Petrol's promise to place all his advertising with Artiste. It's true that *Artiste* did not give consideration for this promise, but there is no rule that says that the beneficiary of a promise must be the one who supplies the consideration — a third-party can supply it. Here, Kabb, by promising to buy all his gas from Petrol, was supplying consideration for Petrol's return promise to place advertising with Artiste.

CHAPTER 11

IMPOSSIBILITY, IMPRACTICABILITY, AND FRUSTRATION

I. IMPOSSIBILITY OF PERFORMANCE

A. Three classes

1. Destruction of subject matter

a. Sale of goods

i. Destruction of identified goods

Question 53: On June 1, a seller agreed, in a writing signed by both the seller and the buyer, to sell an antique car to a buyer for $20,000. The car was at the time on display in a museum in a different city and was to be delivered to the buyer on August 1. On July 15, before the risk of loss had passed to the buyer, the car was destroyed by fire without fault of either party. Subsequent to the contract but before the fire, the car had increased in value to $30,000. The seller sued the buyer for the contract price of $20,000, and the buyer counterclaimed for $30,000.

Which of the following will the court conclude?

(A) Both claims fail.

(B) Only the seller's claim prevails.

(C) Only the buyer's claim prevails.

(D) Both claims prevail.

[QA020]

Answer 53: Choice **(A)** is correct. UCC § 2-613 provides that where goods that are "identified at the time the contract was made" are totally destroyed before the risk of their loss has passed to the buyer and without the fault of either party, the contract is "avoided," and each party is relieved of its respective obligation to perform. § 2-501 lists various ways that particular goods will be deemed "identified," one of which is that at the time of contract formation the parties agreed that what was being sold was a particular already-existing and identified item. Since the parties here agreed that what was being sold was the particular antique car on display in the museum, that car was deemed "identified" to the contract. Therefore, § 2-613 applied, and both parties' obligations were discharged by the total distraction of the car. Therefore, no claim under the contract could be asserted by either party.

(B), (C), and (D) are all wrong because (A) is correct — the total destruction of the car caused the contract to be discharged, and any claims asserted under it to be void. See the analysis of Choice (A) for more details.

2. Supervening illegality

Question 54: Mermaid owns an exceptionally seaworthy boat that she charters for sport fishing at a $500 daily rate. The fee includes the use of the boat with Mermaid as the captain, and one other crew member, as well as fishing tackle and bait. On May 1, Phinney agreed with Mermaid that Phinney would have the full-day use of the boat on May 15 for himself and his family for $500. Phinney paid an advance deposit of $200 and signed an agreement that the deposit could be retained by Mermaid as liquidated damages in the event Phinney canceled or failed to appear.

On May 15 at 1 a.m., the Coast Guard had issued offshore "heavy weather" warnings and prohibited all small vessels the size of Mermaid's from leaving the harbor. This prohibition remained in effect throughout the day. Phinney did not appear at all on May 15, because he had heard the weather warnings on his radio.

Which of the following is an accurate statement?

(A) The contract is discharged because of impossibility, and Phinney is entitled to return of his deposit.

(B) The contract is discharged because of mutual mistake concerning an essential feet, and Phinney is entitled to return of his deposit.

(C) The contract is not discharged, because its performance was possible in view of the exceptional seaworthiness of Mermaid's boat, and Phinney is not entitled to return of his deposit.

(D) The contract is not discharged, and Phinney is not entitled to return of his deposit, because the liquidated-damage clause in effect allocated the risk of bad weather to Phinney.

[Q2087]

Answer 54: Choice **(A)** is correct. The Coast Guard's prohibition had the force of law, so that prohibition constituted "supervening illegality," a form of impossibility. When the defense of impossibility applies, the court will normally cancel the contract and attempt to put the parties in the position they were in before the contract was made. Doing so in this case will require that Phinney get his deposit back.

(B) is wrong because "mutual mistake" is deemed to occur only when the parties are mistaken about some fact that exists at the time of the contract. Where some supervening event renders performance impossible, the case is treated as involving impossibility, not mutual mistake (although the legal effect is pretty much the same — the contract is canceled and the parties are restored to their pre-contract position to the extent possible).

(C) is wrong because the Coast Guard's prohibition made the performance impossible. Where a supervening rule of law would make it illegal for a party to perform, the fact that the party is physically capable of performing does not prevent the impossibility doctrine from applying. Therefore, the fact that the boat was extra seaworthy did not make performance possible.

(D) is wrong because the liquidated-damages clause did not allocate the risk of a supervening illegality to Phinney. Indeed, a liquidated damages clause normally does not allocate risk at all — it merely specifies what the amount of damages should be if, based on other contract provisions, a breach should occur. Here, there was no breach, so the liquidated-damages clause plays no role.

II. IMPRACTICABILITY

A. Modern view of impracticability

1. Allocation of risk by parties

a. Implicit allocation

i. Foreseeability and relative expertise

Question 55: For an agreed price of $20 million, a builder contracted with a developer to design and build on the developer's commercial plot a 15-story office building. In excavating for the foundation and underground utilities, the contractor encountered a massive layer of granite at a depth of 15 feet. By reasonable safety criteria, the building's foundation required a minimum excavation of 25 feet. When the contract was made, neither the developer nor the contractor was aware of the subsurface granite, for the presence of which neither party had hired a qualified expert to test.

Claiming accurately that removal of enough granite to permit the construction as planned would cost him an add itional $3 million and a probable net loss on the contract of $2 million, the contractor refused to proceed with the work unless the developer would promise to pay an additional $2.5 million for the completed building.

If the developer refuses and sues the contractor for breach of contract, which of the following will the court probably decide?

(A) The contractor is excused under the modern doctrine of supervening impossibility, which includes severe impracticability.

(B) The contractor is excused, because the contract is voidable on account of the parties' mutual mistake concerning an essential underlying fact.

(C) The developer prevails, because the contractor assumed the risk of encountering subsurface granite that was unknown to the developer.

(D) The developer prevails, unless subsurface granite was previously unknown anywhere in the vicinity of the developer's construction site.

[Q1172]

Answer 55: Choice **(C)** is correct. The doctrine of commercial impracticability can cover situations in which a pre-existing fact of which the parties were unaware at the time of contracting becomes known later, and renders performance impracticable. However, the impracticability defense will not apply where the party asserting it is found to have expressly or impliedly borne the risk of the event in question. Here, two facts strongly militate against the builder's being excused under the doctrine: (1) in any substantial excavation project, there is a very foreseeable risk of finding unexpectedly large rock deposits, and the more foreseeable the risk, the less likely it is to be excusable under the impracticability doctrine; and (2) the builder as a professional builder has more experience with the business risks involved in excavation than does a typical owner, so it makes economic sense to put the risk of an excavation-related surprise (or the burden of negotiating a clause dealing specifically with that risk) on the builder rather than on the owner.

(A) is wrong because, as described in the analysis of Choice (C), the doctrine of impracticability does not apply where the party seeking to use the doctrine is found to have impliedly borne the risk of the event in question, as the builder would be found to have done here.

(B) is wrong because, while mutual mistake might apply here just as impracticability might apply, the doctrine of mutual mistake will not apply where the party seeking to assert it would be found to have borne the risk of that type of mistake, and the builder would be found to have borne that risk here.

(D) is wrong because the builder would be found to have borne the risk of subsurface granite even if such granite was previously unknown in the vicinity of the construction site — as further explained in the analysis of Choice (C) above, a builder will normally be found to have borne the risk of unfavorable sub-surface conditions.

III. FRUSTRATION OF PURPOSE

A. Factors to be considered

1. Foreseeability

a. Allocation of risk

Question 56: On August 1, Geriatrics, Inc., operating a "lifetime care" home for the elderly, admitted Ohlster, who was 84 years old, for a trial period of two months. On September 25, Ohlster and Geriatrics entered into a written lifetime care contract with an effective commencement date of October 1. The full contract price was $20,000, which, as required by the terms of the contract, Ohlster prepaid to Geriatrics on September 25. Ohlster died of a heart attack on October 2.

In a restitutionary action, can the administratrix of Ohlster's estate, a surviving sister, recover on behalf of the estate either all or part of the $20,000 paid to Geriatrics on September 25?

(A) Yes, because Geriatrics would otherwise be unjustly enriched at Ohlster's expense.

(B) Yes, under the doctrine of frustration of purpose.

(C) No, because Ohlster's life span and the duration of Geriatrics' commitment to him was a risk assumed by both parties.

(D) No, but only if Geriatrics can show that between September 25 and Ohlster's death it rejected, because of its commitment to Ohlster, an application for lifetime care from another elderly person.

[Q1002]

Answer 56: Choice **(C)** is correct. The contract will be enforced as written (i.e., no restitutionary recovery) unless the estate can come up with a legal theory why it shouldn't be. The only plausible theory is frustration of purpose. But the frustration defense will not be recognized where the parties are found to have expressly or implicitly allocated the risk of the event in question. Here, a court would almost certainly conclude that given Ohlster's advanced age, he took the risk that he would die before obtaining substantial benefits from the contract, and Geriatrics took the opposite risk that he would live so long that the deal would be a very bad one for Geriatrics.

(A) is wrong because, although Geriatrics has clearly been "enriched," a court would be unlikely to hold that the enrichment was unjust, in view of the substantial risk that Geriatrics took that Ohlster would live a very long time.

(B) is wrong because the doctrine of frustration of purpose will not apply where the party seeking to use it is found to have impliedly borne the risk of the event in question, and the court will probably make such a finding here, as detailed in the discussion of Choice (C) above.

(D) is wrong because Geriatrics will win even if it cannot show that it rejected some other lifetime-care application on account of its deal with Ohlster — the contract will be enforced as written unless some defense applies, and no defense applies here.

IV. RESTITUTION AND RELIANCE WHERE THE PARTIES ARE DISCHARGED

A. Restitution

1. Time for measuring benefit

Question 57: A lawyer entered into a contract with a painter by the terms of which the painter was to paint the lawyer's office for $1,000 and was required to do all of the work over the following weekend so as to avoid disruption of the lawyer's business. The painter commenced work on Saturday morning, and had finished half the painting by the time he quit work for the day. That night, without the fault of either party, the office building was destroyed by fire.

Which of the following is an accurate statement?

(A) Both parties' contractual duties are discharged, and the painter can recover nothing from the lawyer.

(B) Both parties' contractual duties are discharged, but the painter can recover in quasi-contract from the lawyer.

(C) Only the painter's contractual duty is discharged, because the lawyer's performance (payment of the agreed price) is not impossible.

(D) Only the painter's contractual duty is discharged, and the painter can recover his reliance damages from the lawyer.

[Q1121]

Answer 57: Choice **(B)** is correct. First, since the continued existence of the office being painted was a major assumption on which the contract was based, the destruction of the office will cause both parties to be contractually discharged. Second, when contractual duties are discharged on account of impossibility, a party who has partly performed will generally be permitted to recover in quasi-contract for restitution, i.e., for the value of the benefit conferred on the other party. Therefore, the painter will be permitted to recover for the value of the painting that he had done as of the moment of the fire.

(A) is wrong because, as discussed in the analysis of Choice (B) above, a party who has partly performed by the time of the event causing the discharge is permitted to recover in quasi-contract for the value of his partial performance.

(C) is wrong because the lawyer's performance is discharged not because *it* is impossible, but because the performance which the lawyer was to receive in exchange for her own performance (a paint job) is impossible. When performance of one side of the agreed exchange is rendered impossible, the other side is discharged so as to prevent either side from being unjustly enriched.

(D) is wrong because: (1) both parties' contractual duties (not just the painter's) are discharged; and (2) the painter's damages would be measured by a restitution concept (value conferred on the lawyer just before the fire) rather than by a reliance concept.

Chapter 12

MISCELLANEOUS DEFENSES

I.   MISREPRESENTATION

A. Non-disclosure

1. Failure to correct other party's basic mistake

a. Possession of information by surreptitious and unfair means

Question 58: An heir, who knew nothing about horses, inherited a thoroughbred colt whose disagreeable behavior made him a pest around the barn. The heir sold the colt for $1,500 to an experienced racehorse-trainer who knew of the heir's ignorance about horses. At the time of sale, the heir said to the trainer, "I hate to say it, but this horse is bad-tempered and nothing special." Soon after the sale, the horse won three races and earned $400,000 for the trainer.

Which of the following additional facts, if established by the heir, would best support his chance of obtaining rescission of the sale to the trainer?

(A) The heir did not know until after the sale that the trainer was an experienced racehorse-trainer.

(B) At a pre-sale exercise session of which the trainer knew that the heir was not aware, the trainer clocked the horse in record-setting time, far surpassing any previous performance.

(C) The horse was the only thoroughbred that the heir owned, and the heir did not know how to evaluate young and untested racehorses.

(D) At the time of the sale, the heir was angry and upset over an incident in which the horse had reared and thrown a rider.

[Q2062]

Answer 58: Choice **(B)** is correct. Normally, even where one party knows that the other is making a mistake about a basic assumption, the former's non-disclosure of the relevant fact will not constitute a misrepresentation that the relevant fact does not exist. But the non-disclosure *will* constitute a misrepresentation that the mistaken fact does not exist — and will be grounds for rescission — if it amounts to a "failure to act in good faith and in accordance with reasonable standards of fair dealing." Rest. 2d, §161(b). Where the non-discloser learns of the true fact through improper or questionable means, the court is likely to find a failure to act in good faith. Here, since the horse was the heir's property at the time the trainer secretly timed it in the exercise session, the case is analogous to the Restatement's example of a mining company trespassing on the seller's property to gain mineral-deposit information; a court would therefore likely conclude that the trainer's timing session pushed the entire transaction into the bad-faith category.

(A) is wrong because the trainer's undisclosed experience as a trainer would not alter the general principle that one party's failure to disclose that the other party is making a mistake about a basic assumption does not constitute the sort of misrepresentation that would allow the "innocent" party to rescind. The test is whether the non-discloser's failure to correct the other's mistake constitutes bad faith, and a court would be unlikely to conclude that the non-discloser's failure to disclose his own credentials pushes the entire situation over into the bad-faith column.

(C) is wrong because the party with superior knowledge is normally not required to correct the other party's mistake about even a basic assumption where that assumption is due to the latter's lack of diligence or knowledge — "if the other [party] is indolent, inexperienced or ignorant, or if his judgment is bad or he lacks access to adequate information, his adversary is not generally expected to compensate for these deficiencies. A buyer of property, for example, is not ordinarily expected to disclose circumstances that make the property more valuable than the seller supposes." Rest. 2d, § 161, Comment d.

(D) is wrong because it cites a completely irrelevant fact. The trainer had no obligation to correct what he knew to be the heir's mistake as to a basic assumption, unless the failure to correct amounted to bad faith or a failure to follow reasonable standards of fair dealing. The fact that the mistaken party was angry does not push the more knowledgeable party's lack of disclosure into the bad-faith category, especially where (as here) there is nothing to indicate that the more-knowledgeable party even knew about the other's anger.

CRIMINAL LAW AND PROCEDURE

CRIMINAL LAW Q&A BY TOPIC

References to "LaFave" are to Wayne LaFave, *Principles of Criminal Law* (Thomson / West, 2003). References to "LaFave Criminal Law" are to Wayne LaFave, *Criminal Law* Hornbook (3d Ed., West, 2000). References to "M.P.C." are to the *Model Penal Code*.

CHAPTER 1
ACTUS REUS AND *MENS REA*

I. *ACTUS REUS*

A. Omissions

1. Existence of legal duty

a. Special relationship

Question 1: Kathy, a two-year-old, became ill with meningitis. Jim and Joan, her parents, were members of a group that believed fervently that if they prayed enough, God would not permit their child to die. Accordingly, they did not seek medical aid for Kathy and refused all offers of such aid. They prayed continuously. Kathy died of the illness within a week.

Jim and Joan are charged with murder in a common-law jurisdiction.

Their best defense to the charge is that

(A) they did not intend to kill or to harm Kathy.

(B) they were pursuing a constitutionally protected religious belief.

(C) Kathy's death was not proximately caused by their conduct.

(D) they neither premeditated nor deliberated.

[Q1094]

Answer 1: Choice **(C)** is **incorrect**. Even though Jim and Joan did not take any affirmative action that proximately contributed to Kathy's death, their failure to act did proximately cause the death. Since parents have a duty to act affirmatively to care for a minor child, their failure to act could expose them to criminal liability. And their failure to act would be deemed "conduct." (But they would not be liable for murder, since that requires a mental state going beyond mere negligence; therefore, the correct choice is (A).)

II. *MENS REA*

A. "Knowingly"

1. Knowledge of attendant circumstances

Question 2: Dart is charged with the statutory offense of "knowingly violating a regulation of the State Alcoholic Beverage Control Board" and specifically that he knowingly violated regulation number 345-90 issued by the State Alcoholic Beverage Control Board. That regulation prohibits the sale of alcoholic beverages to any person under the age of 18 and also prohibits the sale of any alcoholic beverage to a person over the age of 17 and under the age of 22 without the presentation of such person's driver's license or other identification showing the age of the purchaser to be 18 or older.

The evidence showed that Dart was a bartender in a tavern and sold a bottle of beer to a person who was 17 years old and that Dart did not ask for or see the purchaser's driver's license or any other identification.

Which of the following, if found by the jury, would be of the most help to Dart?

(A) The purchaser had a driver's license that falsely showed his age to be 21.

(B) Dart had never been told he was supposed to check identification of persons over 17 and under 22 before selling them alcohol.

(C) Dart did not know that the regulations classified beer as an alcoholic beverage.

(D) Dart mistakenly believed the purchaser to be 24 years old.

[Q2050]

Answer 2: Choice **(D)** is correct. Dart did not "knowingly" violate a regulation if he did not think that the requirements of the regulation were required to be applied in the situation he encountered. Dart believed the purchaser was 24 years old; therefore, he did not think that either of the provisions of the regulation applied: the prohibited sale to a purchaser under 18 and the requirement to check identification of a purchaser over the age of 17 and under the age of 22. The fact that his belief was mistaken is not relevant. (This scenario is different from the "ignorance of the law" scenario incorrectly asserted in choices (B) and (C). Here, defendant is mistaken about the underlying facts the existence of which trigger the law, not mistaken about what type of conduct the law prohibits. And a defendant who is mistaken about the underlying facts the existence of which make the conduct illegal won't be said to have "knowingly" violated the statute, according to the prevailing interpretation.)

(A) is wrong because, even though the purchaser had a false driver's license showing him to be 21, Dart never asked to see the license, and he was therefore in violation of the part of the regulation requiring that he do so (for purchasers over the age of 17 and under the age of 22). The fact that the purchaser was indeed of age and could purchase the beer does not affect a finding that Dart "knowingly" violated that part of the regulation.

(B) is wrong because it's argument based on the theory that ignorance of what conduct the law proscribes can be a defense. It can't — as a general principle, if the defendant intended to perform act X, and act X is proscribed by a valid statute, it's not a defense that the defendant didn't know that performing act X was against the law. In other words, the maxim "ignorance of the law is no excuse" is for the most part a true statement.

(C) is wrong for the same reason as (B) — it amounts to a defense based on defendant's ignorance that a particular act (selling beer to a minor) was against the law.

2. "Practically certain" standard for unintended effects

Question 3: A man decided to steal a car he saw parked on a hill. When he got in and started the engine, the car began rolling down the hill. The man quickly discovered that the car's brakes did not work. He crashed through the window of a store at the bottom of the hill.

The man was charged with larceny of the car and with the crime of knowingly damaging the store's property. At trial, the judge instructed the jury that if the jury found both that the man was guilty of larceny of the car and that the damage to the store was the result of that larceny, then it should also find him guilty of malicious damage of property.

The man was convicted on both counts. On appeal, he argued that the conviction for malicious damage of property should be reversed because the instruction was not a correct statement of the law.

Should the man's conviction be affirmed?

(A) Yes, because his intent to steal the car provides the necessary mental element.

(B) Yes, because he was committing a felony.

(C) No, because the instruction wrongly described the necessary mental state.

(D) No, because it would violate double jeopardy to convict the man of two crimes for a single act.

[QA092]

Answer 3: Choice **(C)** is correct. The man could be convicted only if he was found to have "knowingly damag[ed]" the store's property. For the man to have knowingly damaged the property, the jury would have to have found, beyond a reasonable doubt, that he either intended to damage the property, or knew that such damage was *practically certain* to result from his actions. See, e.g., Model Penal Code § 2.02(b)(i): "A person acts knowingly with respect to a material element of an offense when: ... (ii) if the element involves a result of his conduct, he is aware that it is practically certain that his conduct will cause such a result." Here, the judge's instructions are asserting that the man's mere act of stealing the car constitutes "knowingly damaging" the store's property as long as the damage resulted from the theft. For the instructions to be correct, they would have to require "concurrence" — that is, they would have to require that the guilty act and the guilty state of mind occurred at the same time. The guilty act here is the theft, which occurred at the moment the man started the engine and caused the car to make a small movement. So the guilty state of mind would have to be present at that same moment. At that start-the-engine-and-first-move-the-car moment, the man did not know that damage to the store was "practically certain" to occur, because the man had not yet even discovered that the brakes didn't work (and if the brakes *had* worked, the damage to the store wouldn't have occurred). So the requirement of concurrence wouldn't be satisfied. At the later moment when the man learned the brakes didn't work, he may now have known that damage to the store was practically certain to occur, but by that moment the larceny had already occurred, and it was too late for the requirement of concurrence to be satisfied.

(A) is wrong because it ignores the requirement that the man have "knowingly damaged" the store's property. To have knowingly damaged the store's property, the man would have had to know (at the time he stole the car by causing it to move) that damage to the store was practically certain to occur. And he didn't have that knowledge at that time, as is further described in Choice (C).

(B) is wrong because the man's commission of a felony is not enough to supply the intent necessary for the crime of knowingly damaging the store's property. To have "knowingly" damaged property, the man must have known, at the relevant time, that damage to the property was "practically certain" to occur. And the judge's instruction made the relevant time be the time at which the man committed larceny (since that's the time of the voluntary act, which is what has to have temporal concurrence with the guilty state of mind). As is further described in Choice (C), at the moment of larceny the man did not yet know that damage to the store's property was practically certain.

(D) is wrong because double jeopardy does not preclude conviction of two distinct crimes with separate legal elements. *Blockburger v. United States* (1932). If one of the two crimes was a *lesser included offense* of the other, then conviction of both would violate double jeopardy. But here, the elements are clearly different. For instance, the mental state needed here for larceny was an intent to steal the property of another (the car) by taking it away, whereas the mental state needed for malicious damage to the store's property was either intent to cause that damage, or knowledge that the damage was practically certain to occur. Therefore, neither crime is defined in a way that makes it a lesser included offense of the other, so double jeopardy doesn't apply.

B. Vicarious liability

1. Constitutionality

a. D has no control over offender

Question 4: Morten was the general manager and chief executive officer of the Woolen Company, a knitting mill. Morten delegated all operational decision making to Crouse, the supervising manager of the mill. The child labor laws in the jurisdiction provide, "It is a violation of the law for one to employ a person under the age of 17 years for full-time labor." Without Morten's knowledge, Crouse hired a number of 15- and 16-year-olds to work at the mill full time. He did not ask their ages and they did not disclose them. Crouse could have discovered their ages easily by asking for identification, but he did not do so because he was not aware of the law and believed that company policy was to hire young people. If the statute is interpreted to create strict liability and Morten is convicted of violating it. his contention that his conviction would violate the federal Constitution is

(A) correct, because it is a violation of due process to punish without a voluntary act.

(B) correct, because criminal liability is personal and the Woolen Company is the employer of the children, not Morten.

(C) incorrect, because regulatory offenses are not subject to due process limitations.

(D) incorrect, because he was in a position to exercise control over the hiring of employees for Woolen Company.

[Q1176]

Answer 4: Choice **(D)** is correct. Crouse was acting as Morten's agent in running Woolen Company. If a defendant principal had no control over whether the agent committed the crime, it might indeed be a violation of the defendant's due process rights for him to be convicted based on a vicarious-liability theory; but where the principal had control over the agent's conduct, vicarious liability does not pose a due process or other constitutional issue. Since Morten (the principal) had the ability to exercise control over how Crouse (the agent) ran the company, he may constitutionally be held responsible for the criminal acts Crouse performed within the scope of his agency.

(A) is wrong because due process allows punishment of an individual (call him "D") who has not committed a voluntary act in some circumstances. For instance, if D had the legal right and responsibility to supervise the behavior of another person (call him "A") and did not do so, it would not be a violation of due process for the state to impose vicarious criminal responsibility on D. Therefore, vicarious criminal liability of an employer or supervisor for failing to prevent the criminal acts of a worker in furtherance of the job does not violate due process.

(B) is incorrect because hiring the children was a criminal act on the part of Crouse. Therefore Morten, who was Crouse's supervisor and could have prevented him from doing such hiring, can be held criminally liable for Crouse's crimes that were committed within the scope of his employment.

(C) is wrong because due process limits *do* apply even to regulatory offenses. For example, some courts have found that imprisonment for unknowingly committing regulatory offenses can violate due process.

CHAPTER 2

JUSTIFICATION AND EXCUSE

I. DURESS

A. Not available for homicide

Question 5: Smith joined a neighborhood gang. At a gang meeting, as part of the initiation process, the leader ordered Smith to kill Hardy, a member of a rival gang. Smith refused, saying he no longer wanted to be part of the group. The leader, with the approval of the other members, told Smith that he had become too involved with the gang to quit and that they would kill him if he did not accomplish the murder of Hardy. The next day Smith shot Hardy to death while Hardy was sitting on his motorcycle outside a restaurant.

Smith is charged with first-degree murder. First-degree murder is defined in the jurisdiction as the intentional premeditated killing of another. Second-degree murder is all other murder at common law.

If Smith killed Hardy because of the threat to his own life, Smith should be found

(A) not guilty, because of the defense of duress.

(B) not guilty, because of the defense of necessity.

(C) guilty of first-degree murder.

(D) guilty of second-degree murder.

[Q1043]

Answer 5: Choice **(A)** is **incorrect**, and Choice **(C)** is **correct**. As to (A), what we care about now is whether the duress defense will work. It won't, for two reasons. First, duress is generally not allowed as a defense when the defendant is charged with the intentional killing of another — i.e. murder or voluntary manslaughter. Second, Smith was not in imminent danger when he killed Hardy, and duress only applies when the defendant believes that if he does not commit a criminal act he will suffer immediate or imminent death or serious bodily injury. The gang leader certainly made threats that Smith could reasonably believe would have resulted in his own death. However, there is no indication in the facts given that Smith was in fear of *imminent* death; at worst, Smith had fear of some future harm, which is insufficient to support a claim of duress.

(C) is **correct** — Smith should be convicted of first degree murder because he intentionally and with premeditation killed Hardy. From the facts given, it is clear that Smith intended to kill Hardy when he shot him. In addition, since Smith waited a full day between being told to kill Hardy and doing so, he had a reasonable amount of time to deliberate. If a defendant has a reasonable amount of time to think about the decision to kill, the homicide will be considered premeditated, supporting a conviction of murder in the first degree. (As discussed below in the analysis of choices (A) and (B), no defense applies to this situation.)

(B) is wrong for two reasons. First, necessity is generally not allowed as a defense when the defendant is charged with the intentional killing of another — i.e. murder or voluntary manslaughter. Second, the gang leader's threat was not the type of influence to which the defense of necessity applies. This question illustrates the distinction between the defenses of duress and necessity. Duress is available when the threat of harm comes from the threat or use of force by a third party. Necessity is available when the threat of harm is caused by non-human events — for example, sickness or weather. Since the gang leader is a person, rather than a force of nature, necessity is not a proper defense.

(D) is incorrect because, although Smith has met all the elements required for a conviction of second-degree murder, he would be more properly convicted of the more serious first-degree murder, as discussed in (C) above.

II. SELF-DEFENSE

A. Degree of force

1. Deadly force

a. Can't use deadly force to prevent non-serious harm

Question 6: Ralph and Sam were engaged in a heated discussion over the relative merits of their favorite professional football teams when Ralph said, "You have to be one of the dumbest persons around." Sam slapped Ralph. Ralph drew a knife and stabbed Sam in the stomach. Other persons then stepped in and stopped any further fighting. Despite the pleas of the other persons, Sam refused to go to a hospital or to seek medical treatment. About two hours later, he died as the result of a loss of blood. Ralph was charged with the murder of Sam. At trial, medical evidence established that if Sam had been taken to a hospital, he would have survived.

At the end of the case, Ralph moves for a judgment of acquittal or, in the alternative, for an instruction on the elements of voluntary manslaughter.

The court should

(A) grant the motion for acquittal.

(B) deny the motion for acquittal, but instruct on manslaughter because there is evidence of adequate provocation.

(C) deny both motions, because Ralph failed to retreat.

(D) deny both motions, because malice may be proved by the intentional use of a deadly weapon on a vital part of the body.

[Q2122]

Answer 6: Choice **(C)** is **incorrect**, because the issue of retreat would never even arise. Before the duty to retreat (in a jurisdiction imposing it) could ever make a difference, D would have to be entitled to use deadly force in self-defense. Here, Sam's slap neither caused Ralph serious bodily harm nor gave Ralph reason to fear serious bodily harm in the near future. Therefore, Ralph was not privileged to respond with deadly force. Since the duty to retreat (even if the jurisdiction imposes it) only makes a difference where defendant would otherwise be entitled to use deadly force, Ralph's loss of the motion of acquittal couldn't be due to his "fail[ure] to retreat." (It's not clear what the best answer is — all the other three choices were accepted by the examiners.)

B. Effect of mistake

1. Reasonable

Question 7: While walking home one evening, Harold, an off-duty police officer, was accosted by Jones, a stranger. Jones had been drinking and mistakenly thought Harold was a man who was having an affair with his wife. Intending to frighten Harold but not to harm him, Jones pulled out a knife, screamed obscenities, and told Harold he was going to kill him. Frightened and reasonably believing Jones was going to kill him and that using deadly force was his only salvation, Harold took out his service revolver and shot and killed Jones. Harold is charged with murder.

Harold's claim of self-defense should be

(A) sustained, because Harold reasonably believed Jones was planning to kill him and that deadly force was required.

(B) sustained, because the killing was in hot blood upon sufficient provocation.

(C) denied, because Jones did not in fact intend to harm Harold and Harold was incorrect in believing that he did.

(D) denied, because Harold was not defending his home and had an obligation to retreat or to repel with less than deadly force.

[Q1003]

Answer 7: Choice **(A)** is correct. Harold's claim of self-defense is valid because he reasonably believed that his life was in danger and that the use of deadly force was required to save his own life. Self-defense is a complete defense to a charge of murder. For the defense to be applicable, the defendant must believe that he had to use force to protect himself from the danger. The belief must meet both an objective and a subjective test: the defendant must actually believe that he was in danger (subjective) and that belief must be reasonable (objective). Here, we are told that Harold reasonably believed that Jones was going to kill him, so both the objective and subjective tests are satisfied.

Even if a claim of self-defense is valid, the court must still determine if the degree of force used was excessive. One may only use deadly force in self-defense if one reasonably believes that (1) the attack carries the threat of death or serious bodily harm, and (2) nothing less than deadly force is likely to repel the threat. Here, Harold's reasonable belief was that Jones intended to kill him, and Harold believed that deadly force would be his "only salvation," so these two requirements regarding deadly force are satisfied. The fact that Harold was mistaken (but reasonably so) on this point does not deprive him of the defense of self-defense, or of the right to use deadly force.

(B) is wrong because "provocation" is not an element of self-defense. Self-defense is a complete defense, which applies when a defendant uses a reasonable level of force in response to a reasonably feared threat. Provocation, on the other hand, is a partial defense which applies when a defendant uses force because something causes him to lose self-control. A defense based on provocation would not be used if the defendant was entitled, as Harold is here, to assert the complete defense of self-defense.

(C) is wrong because, when analyzing self-defense claims, it is the defendant's state of mind, not the victim's that is important. The issue is not whether Jones actually intended to harm Harold, but rather whether Harold was reasonable in his (admittedly mistaken) belief that James intended to attack.

(D) is wrong because the obligation to retreat is only triggered when the defendant believes that he may retreat to complete safety. Here, Harold believed that his "only salvation" was the use of deadly force, which indicates that he did not believe that retreat was possible. Even if Harold were mistaken in his belief, so long as that mistake was reasonable, he had no obligation to retreat. (Note: Only some states require that a defendant retreat before using deadly force in self-defense. And, by the way, retreat is *never* required before the use of *non-deadly* force in self-defense.)

III. ENTRAPMENT

A. "Predisposition" test

Question 8: Kingsley was prosecuted for selling cocaine to an undercover police agent. At his trial, he testified that he only sold the drugs to the agent, whom Kingsley knew as "Speedy," because Speedy had told him that he (Speedy) would be killed by fellow gang members unless he supplied them with cocaine. The prosecution did not cross-examine Kingsley. As rebuttal evidence, however, the prosecutor introduced records, over Kingsley's objection, showing that Kingsley had two prior convictions for narcotics-related offenses. The court instructed the jury concerning the defense of entrapment and added, also over Kingsley's objection but in accord with state law, that it should acquit on the ground of entrapment only if it found that the defendant had established the elements of the defense by a preponderance of the evidence. Kingsley was convicted.

On appeal, Kingsley's conviction should be

(A) reversed, because it was an error for the court to admit the evidence of his prior convictions as substantive evidence.

(B) reversed, because it was a violation of due process to impose on the defense a burden of persuasion concerning entrapment.

(C) reversed, for both of the above reasons.

(D) affirmed, because neither of the above reasons constitutes a ground for reversal.

[Q2194]

Answer 8: Choice **(D)** is correct. Neither of the reasons listed in (A) and (B) constitutes a ground for reversal.

(A) is wrong because where entrapment is at issue, the prosecution must prove that the defendant was disposed to commit the criminal act prior to first being approached by government agents. This may be done by showing the defendant's prior crimes that are related to or similar to the instant offense. (Generally, evidence of a person's other crimes or acts is inadmissible to show action in conformity with the person's character. FRE 404(b). However, such other-crimes evidence would be admissible here to show that a defense [entrapment] now being asserted lacks merit.)

(B) is wrong because entrapment is an affirmative defense. A defendant may constitutionally be required to bear both the burden of coming forward with some evidence as to an affirmative defense, and the burden of non-persuasion (by a preponderance of the evidence) as to such a defense.

(C) is wrong because neither of the reasons constitutes a ground for reversal, as explained in (A) and (B).

CHAPTER 3

ATTEMPT

I. IMPOSSIBILITY

A. Factual impossibility

1. Not accepted

a. Combined with accomplice liability

Question 9: A woman promised to pay $10,000 to a hit man if he would kill her neighbor in any manner that could not be traced to her. The hit man bought a gun and watched the neighbor's house for an opportunity to shoot him. One evening, unaware of the hit man's presence, the neighbor tripped as he was walking toward his house, falling and hitting his head against the front steps. Believing that the neighbor was unconscious, the hit man ran over to him and shot him twice in the chest.

When the woman learned of the neighbor's death, she paid the hit man $10,000. A medical examiner determined that the neighbor was already dead when the hit man shot him.

The crimes below are listed in descending order of seriousness.

What is the most serious crime for which the woman properly could be convicted?

(A) Murder.

(B) Attempted murder.

(C) Conspiracy.

(D) Solicitation.

[QA063]

Answer 9: Choice **(B)** is correct. Let's start with *murder*. One theory under which the woman might be guilty of murder would be on an accomplice theory, that she aided and abetted the hit man to commit murder — if he is substantively liable for murder, so is she as his accomplice. But the hit man is *not* guilty of murder, because, as a factual matter, he did not cause the neighbor's death. (You cannot cause the death of another by taking an action after the other is already dead.) Since the hit man is not guilty of murder, the woman can't be guilty of it either, on an accomplice theory. What about the woman's guilt of murder as a principal? Well, she can't be guilty of murder unless she played some causal role in bringing about the death; since the neighbor would have died in exactly the same way if the woman had not recruited the hit man, the woman was not a cause-in-fact of the death, and therefore cannot be liable for murder as a principal.

Now, what about *attempted murder*? The woman has certainly tried to bring about a murder, and has caused various acts to occur towards fulfillment of that objective (e.g., the hit man's lying in wait). So she is guilty of attempted murder unless some special doctrine helps her. The only doctrine that's even of remotely-plausible help to her here is the defense of *"factual impossibility"* — can either the woman or the hit man succeed with the argument that "It was impossible for us to kill the neighbor since he was already dead, making an attempted-murder conviction improper"? The answer is no: the factual impossibility defense is *rejected* by virtually every modern court. That is, where a defendant had an intent to commit crime X, and took actions that would have led to a completed crime X if external reality had been as the defendant mistakenly believed it to be, the fact that the defendant could never have succeeded in completing crime X because external reality made such success impossible does not constitute a defense. Clearly the hit man's actions and intent here were such that had the facts been as the hit man believed (i.e., the neighbor was only unconscious, not dead), the hit man would have been guilty of murder. Therefore, the hit man is guilty of attempted murder, and the factual impossibility defense won't work to save him. Since the woman urged the hit man to take the action he took, and since the woman, too, had an intent to kill, she is guilty of attempted murder on an accomplice theory. The factual impossibility defense doesn't work any better for her as an accomplice than it does for the hit man as a principal.

(A) is wrong because the woman cannot be guilty of murder, since the hit man did not in fact cause the neighbor's death. See Choice (B) for further analysis of why this is so.

(C) is wrong because the woman can be convicted of attempted murder, which the question tells us is a more serious crime than conspiracy. (But the woman can also be convicted of conspiracy to commit murder, since she agreed with another to try to bring about a murder.)

(D) is wrong because the woman can be convicted of attempted murder, which the question tells us is a more serious crime than solicitation. (But the woman can also be convicted of solicitation, since she tried to persuade another to commit a crime.)

b. Robbery cases where V is not intimidated

Question 10: Robert walked into a store that had a check-cashing service and tried to cash a $550 check which was payable to him. The attendant on duty refused to cash the check because Robert did not have two forms of identification, which the store's policies required. Robert, who had no money except for the check and who needed cash to pay for food and a place to sleep, became agitated. He put his hand into his pocket and growled, "Give me the money or I'll start shooting." The attendant, who knew Robert as a neighborhood character. did not believe that he was violent or had a gun. However, because the attendant felt sorry for Robert, he handed over the cash. Robert left the check on the counter and departed. The attendant picked up the check and found that Robert had failed to endorse it.

If Robert is guilty of any crime, he is most likely guilty of

(A) robbery.

(B) attempted robbery.

(C) theft by false pretenses.

(D) larceny by trick.

[Q2073]

Answer 10: Choice (B) is correct. For a defendant to be convicted of attempting a particular substantive crime, he must have had the intent to do acts which, if they had been carried out, would have resulted in the commission of that crime. Robert pretended to have a gun and threatened to shoot the attendant if he didn't hand over the money. The fact that Robert's threat was not real (because he didn't have a gun) or taken seriously by the attendant would not negate Robert's intent – to cause the attendant to be afraid and to cause him to hand over the money. Therefore, it is possible that he would be guilty of attempted robbery. Although this is not entirely clear from the circumstances of the case (he might be able to defend on the grounds that he wasn't trying to take "property of another" since he was giving equal value in the form of the check), of the choices given, this would be the most likely crime he would be guilty of if he were guilty of any crime.

(A) is wrong because property was not taken by using force or by putting the owner in fear. The elements of robbery are that (1) property is taken from the person or presence of the owner; and (2) the taking is accomplished by using force or putting the owner in fear. A threat of harm will suffice. It is not required that the victim be afraid, only that he be placed in apprehension of harm. However, since the attendant knew Robert as a neighborhood character and did not believe that he was violent or had a gun, he was not placed in apprehension of harm under these circumstances.

(C) is wrong because it is required that the person intend to defraud and that his misrepresentation cause the person to whom it was made to pass title to the property. The elements of the crime are: (1) a false representation (2) of a material present or past fact (3) which causes the person to whom it is made (4) to pass title to (5) his property to the misrepresenter who 6) knows that his representation is false, and intends to defraud. Robert pretended to have a gun and threatened to shoot. He did make a misrepresentation (that he had a gun), but he intended to make a transaction, where he would relinquish his check in return for getting money. The fact that he did not endorse the check is not proof of his intent to defraud because it might have been a careless mistake. Also, his misrepresentation did not cause the attendant to give him the cash – the attendant knew he didn't have a gun and merely felt sorry for him.

(D) is wrong because of the same reasons that Robert is not guilty of the crime of false pretenses, as discussed in the Choice C. Robert did not have the intent to defraud nor was the property turned over as a result of the fact that Robert pretended to have a gun and threatened to use it. Larceny by trick differs from false pretenses in that it requires only that possession has passed (not title) and also requires that the property be converted in some way as to deprive its owner of much of its utility. It does not apply in this situation.

B. "True legal" impossibility

1. Arson on the MBE

> **Question 11:** Arnold decided to destroy an old warehouse that he owned because the taxes on the structure exceeded the income that he could receive from it. He crept into the building in the middle of the night with a can of gasoline and a fuse and set the fuse timer for 30 minutes. He then left the building. The fuse failed to ignite, and the building was not harmed.
>
> Arson is defined in this jurisdiction as "The intentional burning of any building or structure of another, without the consent of the owner." Arnold believed, however, that burning one's own building was arson, having been so advised by his lawyer.
>
> Has Arnold committed attempted arson?
>
> (A) Yes, because factual impossibility is no defense.
>
> (B) Yes, because a mistake of law even on the advice of an attorney is no defense.
>
> (C) No, because his mistake negated a necessary mental state.
>
> (D) No, because even if his actions had every consequence he intended, they would not have constituted arson.

[Q1058]

Answer 11: Choice **(D)** is correct. Arnold is not guilty of attempted arson because, even if his actions had their desired result, a crime would not have been committed. This question involves the issue of legal impossibility, which applies when a defendant is mistaken about what type of conduct a statute prohibits. A defendant is not guilty of attempt when, had the attempt been successful, no crime would have been committed, regardless of whether the defendant in fact believed he was committing a crime. Although Arnold intended to burn the warehouse down, believing that doing so would be a crime, had everything gone as planned, he still wouldn't have committed arson because the statute specifies that an owner can't be guilty of burning of his own building.

(A) is wrong because Arnold's mistake was about the law, not about a fact. Factual impossibility arises when some fact, unknown to the defendant, makes it impossible to complete the crime that the defendant intended to commit. Factual impossibility is not accepted as a defense to attempt. For example, had Arnold believed the warehouse to belong to someone else while it in fact belonged to him, he would be guilty of attempted arson despite the fact that had he succeeded in burning the building, the completed act would not have been arson. In that example Arnold would be guilty of attempt because, had the facts been as he believed them to be, his actions would have been a crime. In the problem itself, Arnold was not mistaken about any material fact. He knew that he owned the warehouse and he knew that he was trying to burn it down. Therefore factual impossibility is not at issue.

(B) is wrong because, while it is true that mistake of law is not a defense, Arnold's mistake wouldn't help him in any event. This "defense" is tried (unsuccessfully) by those who have committed a criminal act, but believed their actions not to have been prohibited, as a means to show they lacked the *mens rea* to commit the crime. Arnold's situation is the opposite. He believed his act to be a crime when it was not prohibited by the statute. Therefore his mistake would not tend to negate the *mens rea* required for arson.

(C) is wrong because mental state is independent of any outside factual or legal circumstances. The mental state required for arson, as defined in the given statute, is intent to burn. Arnold certainly intended to burn the warehouse, so he possessed the required mental state to commit arson.

CHAPTER 4

CONSPIRACY

I.   PLURALITY

A. Inconsistent disposition

1. One is member of protected class

a. Modern / Model Penal Code "unilateral" view

Question 12: A foreign diplomat discovered that a small person could enter a jewelry store by crawling through an air vent. The diplomat became friendly with a woman in a bar who he believed was small enough to crawl through the air vent. Without telling her that he was a diplomat, he explained how she could get into the jewelry store. She agreed to help him burglarize the store. Someone overheard their conversation and reported it to the police. Shortly thereafter, the police arrested the diplomat and the woman. Both were charged with conspiracy to commit burglary.

Before trial, the diplomat moved to dismiss the charge against him on the ground that he was entitled to diplomatic immunity. The court granted his motion. The woman then moved to dismiss the conspiracy charge against her.

The jurisdiction has adopted the Model Penal Code version of conspiracy.

Should the woman's motion to dismiss the conspiracy charge against her be granted?

(A) No, because the diplomat's defense does not negate any element of the crime.

(B) No, because the woman was not aware of the diplomat's status.

(C) Yes, because a conspiracy requires two guilty participants.

(D) Yes, because but for the diplomat's conduct, no conspiracy would have occurred.

[QA058]

Answer 12: Choice **(A)** is correct. Model Penal Code § 5.03(1), by defining conspiracy as requiring agreement by the defendant but not by two or more persons, adopts a *"unilateral"* interpretation of conspiracy. Where the unilateral interpretation is applied, as long as one defendant meets all requirements for conspiracy (e.g., guilty mind plus agreement with another), that defendant may be convicted even though no other defendant could be convicted. (Furthermore, the woman might lose even in some jurisdictions that follow the common-law *bilateral* interpretation rather than the M.P.C.'s unilateral interpretation. That's because in many such jurisdictions, the fact that one co-conspirator has a special "personal" defense, like the diplomatic immunity here, does not prevent conviction of a co-conspirator who does not benefit from that defense. See Lafave Criminal Law, § 6.5(g).)

(B) is wrong because it cites an irrelevant fact. The woman would not be entitled to dismissal even if she knew of the diplomat's status, because the diplomat's capacity to be convicted of the crime would be irrelevant in a jurisdiction that adopted a unilateral view of conspiracy. And the M.P.C. adopts a unilateral view.

(C) is wrong because it misstates the M.P.C.'s definition of conspiracy. Section 5.03(1) of the M.P.C., which defines conspiracy, does not require that there be two guilty participants. All that the M.P.C. requires is that (1) there be two persons who appear to agree to pursue a criminal objective, and (2) the particular defendant being prosecuted have a guilty mind. So if X and Y appear to agree to a conspiratorial objective, the fact that Y has some personal defense (such as the diplomatic immunity here) does not prevent X from being convicted, as long as X meets all the requirements for conspiracy (e.g., a guilty mind, and absence of any personal defense).

(D) is wrong because the "but-for" factor that it cites is irrelevant. The woman can properly be convicted because, regardless of the diplomat's immunity, she agreed to commit a crime. *See* M.P.C. § 5.03(1). The fact that the diplomat's conduct was a but-for cause of the conspiracy is irrelevant. (If the diplomat had been acting as an agent of the government, and in order to get a conviction for the government had persuaded the woman to agree to a crime that she would not have agreed to without the diplomat's suggestion, then the woman might have a valid *entrapment* defense. But there is no suggestion in these facts that that's what happened here.)

II.   PUNISHMENT

A. Cumulative sentencing allowed

Question 13: Jackson and Brannick planned to break into a federal government office to steal food stamps. Jackson telephoned Crowley one night and asked whether Crowley wanted to buy some "hot" food stamps. Crowley, who understood that "hot" meant stolen, said, "Sure, bring them right over." Jackson and Brannick then successfully executed their scheme. That same night they delivered the food stamps to Crowley, who bought them for $500. Crowley did not ask when or by whom the stamps were stolen. All three were arrested. Jackson and Brannick entered guilty pleas in federal court to a charge of larceny in connection with the theft. Crowley was never charged with anything.

If Jackson and Brannick are charged with conspiracy to steal the stamps in the state court, they should, on the evidence stated, be found

(A) not guilty, because the charge of conspiracy is a lesser included offense in the charge of larceny.

(B) not guilty, because to charge them with conspiracy after their conviction of larceny would constitute double jeopardy.

(C) not guilty, because the state prosecution is barred by the prosecution in federal court.

(D) guilty, because they planned and conspired to steal the stamps.

[Q4003]

Answer 13: Choice **(D)** is **correct** and (A) is **incorrect** for the same reason: conspiracy is a distinct offense which is *not* merged into the crime which is the object of the conspiracy. A conspiracy requires an agreement between at least two people, an intent to enter into such an agreement, and the intent to achieve the agreement's unlawful objective (or, at common law, a lawful ultimate act to be done unlawfully). The conspiracy is complete once the agreement is entered into, at common law (the modern rule is to require an act in furtherance of the conspiracy); it does not encompass the ultimate act. If you chose this response, it could be because you confused conspiracy with *attempt*. Attempt *is* merged into the completed crime, so that the accused can only be convicted of attempt OR the completed offense, but not both. However, as stated, conspiracy is a separate and distinct offense, which doesn't merge into the completed crime.

(B) is wrong because it misstates the law, and arrives at an incorrect result: in fact, conspiracy is a separate and distinct offense from the crime which is the object of the conspiracy. Thus, being tried for it after pleading guilty to larceny would not be considered double jeopardy. Double jeopardy only attaches when two prosecutions meet two requirements: they must be based on the same conduct, AND proof of the facts needed for one must necessarily include proof of all facts needed for the other. Conspiracy focuses on the agreement aspect, and is complete once the agreement is made; larceny requires the actual larcenous taking of the stamps (without requiring any prior agreement between the participants).

(C) is wrong because it misstates the law. The facts in this problem suggest that the latter prosecution would not be barred. A state prosecution after a federal prosecution would be forbidden under two circumstances: Either due to double jeopardy, or a kind of collateral estoppel: the earlier, federal prosecution was resolved in defendant's favor due to a factual finding that would bar a later conviction in state court (e.g., an alibi was upheld). Neither of these exist under these facts. Larceny and conspiracy are two separate and distinct crimes, and the proof that would be necessary for them would be largely different. Double jeopardy would not attach to the federal larceny conviction (see the discussion of this point in Choice (B) above), and there is nothing under these facts to suggest that resolution of any factual issue precludes conviction in the later state prosecution.

CHAPTER 5

ACCOMPLICE LIABILITY AND SOLICITATION

I. ACCOMPLICES — THE ACT REQUIREMENT

A. Liability for aiding and abetting

1. Failure to intervene

Question 14: Bill and Chuck hated Vic and agreed to start a fight with Vic and, if the opportunity arose, to kill him. Bill and Chuck met Vic in the street outside a bar and began to push him around. Ray and Tom, who also hated Vic, stopped to watch. Ray threw Bill a knife. Tom, who made no move and said nothing, hoped that Bill would kill Vic with the knife. Chuck held Vic while Bill stabbed and killed him.

On a charge of murdering Vic, Tom is

(A) not guilty, because mere presence, coupled with silent approval and intent, is not sufficient.

(B) not guilty, because he did not tell Bill ahead of time that he hoped Bill would murder Vic.

(C) guilty, because he had a duty to stop the killing and made no attempt to do so.

(D) guilty, because he was present and approved of what occurred.

[Q4014]

Answer 14: Choice **(A)** is correct. Under these facts, Tom has done nothing to subject himself to liability. The most promising element for liability is the fact that he *hoped* Bill would kill Vic. However, even though he hoped that Bill would kill Vic, all that demonstrates is that Tom had a state of mind that, with nothing more, is not criminal. His failure to aid Vic would not subject him to liability because the law imposes no general duty to act affirmatively for the benefit of others, in the absence of some special pre-existing relationship between the defendant and the victim (e.g., defendant's negligence created the peril, or a special relationship mandates affirmative acts [parent and child, for instance]). Liability for murder would have required that Tom do *something* – either helping to plan Vic's murder, or aiding it in some other way – to make him liable under a conspiracy or accomplice theory. Under these facts, no such action exists.

(B) is wrong because although it arrives at the correct result, the reasoning it offers would not exonerate Tom. This choice suggests that Tom could only be liable if he told Bill ahead of time that he hoped Bill would murder Vic. This is both too narrow and too broad a statement of the applicable law. First, merely stating "I hope you kill Vic" might not be enough to make Tom liable, if he didn't plan the killing with Bill (conspiracy) or aid in any way (accomplice liability). (If the "I hope you kill..." statement amounted to active encouragement, and helped bring about the killing, that might be enough for accomplice liability; but a mere statement on a prior occasion, without any showing of a causal link to the actual killing, wouldn't be enough.) Second, prior encouragement isn't the only way Tom could be liable; had he encouraged Bill at the scene of the crime (e.g., by shouting "Kill him" at the pivotal moment), he would be liable for murder as an accomplice.

(C) is wrong because it arrives at an incorrect result, and misstates the law. As a general rule, an individual has no duty to act affirmatively for the benefit of others. Although certain relationships between the defendant and the one in peril change this (e.g., defendant's negligence created the peril, or a special relationship mandates affirmative acts [parent-child, for instance]), no such facts exist in this question. Since no duty to aid exists, and Tom did nothing to plan or aid in committing the killing, he cannot be liable for murder.

(D) is wrong because it arrives at an incorrect result, and misstates the law. In order to be found guilty of murder, Tom would have to undertake some type of activity – be it planning or aiding in the killing. Mere presence and tacit approval are insufficient for liability as a conspirator or as an accomplice. Presence is not sufficient for liability, since, as a general rule, the law imposes no duty to act affirmatively for the benefit of others. Even coupling presence with tacit approval is insufficient, since approval is a mere state of mind which, with nothing more, is not criminal.

II. GUILT OF THE PRINCIPAL

A. Conviction of principal for use of innocent agent

Question 15: Grace, while baby-sitting one night, noticed that Sam, who lived next door, had left his house but that the door did not close completely behind him. Grace said to Roy, the 11-year-old boy she was baby-sitting with, "Let's play a game. You go next door and see if you can find my portable television set, which I lent to Sam, and bring it over here." Grace knew that Sam had a portable television set and Grace planned to keep the set for herself. Roy thought the set belonged to Grace, went next door, found the television set, and carried it out the front door. At that moment, Sam returned home and discovered Roy in his front yard with the television set. Roy explained the "game" he and Grace were playing. Sam took back his television set and called the police.

Grace is

(A) not guilty of larceny or attempted larceny, because Roy did not commit any crime.

(B) not guilty of larceny but guilty of attempted larceny, because she never acquired possession of the television set.

(C) guilty of larceny as an accessory to Roy.

(D) guilty of larceny by the use of an innocent agent.

[Q3107]

Answer 15: Choice **(D)** is correct. Larceny is the: (1) taking, and (2) carrying away, of the (3) tangible property, (4) of another, (5) by trespass or without consent, (6) with the intent to steal it. Anyone who intentionally acts through an innocent agent is classified as a principal. Grace is guilty of larceny, even though she herself did not take television set. She knowingly created a mistake of fact in the mind of Roy, and intentionally induced him to commit acts satisfying the first five elements of the crime of larceny. Since Roy was an innocent agent who acted at the behest of Grace, Roy's acts will be ascribed to Grace as if she had done them herself. Grace herself satisfies the sixth requirement (intent to steal the item). Therefore, Grace is guilty of larceny.

(A) is wrong because as an innocent agent of Grace's, Roy's actions are imputed to Grace. It's true that Roy did not commit any crime. But as an innocent agent, his acts are ascribed to the principal. Therefore, his own innocence is irrelevant to whether Grace is guilty. See the analysis in Choice (D) above.

(B) is wrong because Grace's innocent agent acquired possession. When a person intentionally causes an innocent agent to perform an act, the agent's act is attributed to the principal. So once Roy took and carried away possession of the set, this act is ascribed to Grace as if she had done it herself. Therefore, it's not accurate to say, as this choice does, that Grace "never acquired possession."

(C) is wrong because Roy was not guilty of larceny, and Grace is a principal, not an accessory. A principal is one who with the requisite mental state, actually engages in the act or omission that causes the criminal result. An accessory is one who aids or counsels a principal in the completion of a crime. If Roy had been a principal, then Grace would probably have been an accessory. In this case, however, Grace is not guilty as an accessory, because she was the principal. Roy acted without criminal intent after being misled by Grace. Therefore (as explained more fully in the analysis of Choice (D) above), Roy was an innocent agent and Grace a principal in this crime.

CHAPTER 6
HOMICIDE AND OTHER CRIMES AGAINST THE PERSON

I. MURDER — GENERALLY

A. Intent-to-kill murder

1. Ill-will unnecessary

Question 16: Suffering from painful and terminal cancer, Willa persuaded Harold, her husband, to kill her to end her misery. As they reminisced about their life together and reaffirmed their love for each other, Harold tried to discourage Willa from giving up. Willa insisted, however, and finally Harold held a gun to her head and killed her.

The most serious degree of criminal homicide of which Harold can be legally convicted is

(A) no degree of criminal homicide.

(B) involuntary manslaughter.

(C) voluntary manslaughter.

(D) murder.

[Q2044]

Answer 16: Choice **(D)** is correct. Intent-to-kill murder requires that the defendant have the desire to bring about the death of another. Harold intended to kill Willa, held a gun to her head, and succeeded in killing her. He is guilty of murder. There is no exception in the doctrine of common-law murder for "mercy killings."

Choices (A), (B), and (C) are wrong for the reason that (D) is right — this is murder.

B. Intent-to-do-serious-bodily-injury murder

1. "Serious bodily injury" defined

Question 17: At a party for coworkers at Defendant's home, Victim accused Defendant of making advances toward his wife. Victim and his wife left the party. The next day at work, Defendant saw Victim and struck him on the head with a soft-drink bottle. Victim fell into a coma and died two weeks after the incident.

This jurisdiction defines aggravated assault as an assault with any weapon or dangerous implement and punishes it as a felony. It defines murder as the unlawful killing of a person with malice aforethought or in the course of an independent felony.

Defendant may be found guilty of murder

(A) only if the jury finds that Defendant intended to kill Victim.

(B) only if the jury finds that Defendant did not act in a rage provoked by Victim's accusations.

(C) if the jury finds that Defendant intended either to kill or to inflict serious bodily harm.

(D) if the jury finds that the killing occurred in the course of an aggravated assault.

[Q1101]

Answer 17: Choice **(C)** is correct. Defendant can be convicted of murder if he intended either to kill or inflict serious bodily harm when he hit Victim with the soft-drink bottle. Murder is the unlawful killing of another person with malice aforethought. "Malice aforethought" is a term of art that encompasses several mental states, including the intent to kill and the intent to cause serious bodily harm. Therefore, if the jury finds that Defendant intended either to kill Victim or to inflict serious bodily harm to Victim, then Defendant would have had the requisite *mens rea* to be found guilty of murder.

(A) is wrong because it is too restrictive. While it is true that intent to kill is one mental state that can support a murder conviction, it is not the only one. As discussed above, several other mental states are included in "malice aforethought." Since Choice (A) states that "Defendant may be found guilty of murder *only* if the jury finds that Defendant intended to kill Victim" it improperly omits the possibility of conviction based on a different mental state.

(B) is wrong because it is an incomplete statement of the "heat of passion" defense. A defendant who acted in the heat of passion when he killed may be entitled to have his crime reduced from murder to voluntary manslaughter. But "heat of passion" will result in a conviction of voluntary manslaughter rather than murder only if four conditions have been met: (1) The defendant acted in response to a provocation that would have caused a reasonable person to lose self-control (an objective test); (2) The defendant did, in fact, act while in the "heat of passion" (a subjective test); (3) There was no time between the provocation and the act for a reasonable person to "cool off" (objective); and (4) the defendant did not, in fact, "cool off" (subjective). Here, even if the jury were to accept that Defendant acted in a rage brought on by Victim's provocation, only the subjective elements would have been proven. Defendant would still have to show that Victim's accusations were enough to make a *reasonable person* lose his self control (unlikely) and that the full day that elapsed between the accusations and the attack was an insufficient amount of time for a *reasonable person* to cool off (very unlikely). Since Choice (B) omits the subjective elements of the partial defense, it is an incorrect statement of the law.

(D) is wrong because it is an inaccurate application of the felony-murder rule. The felony-murder rule states that if a defendant, in the process of committing certain dangerous felonies, kills another person, he is guilty of murder. The *mens rea* required to commit the underlying felony is used to supply the mental state required for murder. However, in order for the felony-murder rule to apply, the felony must be *independent* of the killing. In this case, Defendant's aggravated assault with the soft-drink bottle was a lesser included offense in the homicide, and can therefore not be used as the underlying felony for purposes of the felony-murder rule.

C. "Reckless indifference to value of human life" or "depraved heart" murder

1. MBE tip

Question 18: Phillips bought a new rifle and wanted to try it out by doing some target shooting. He went out into the country to an area where he had previously hunted. Much to his surprise, he noticed that the area beyond a clearing contained several newly constructed houses that had not been there before. Between the houses there was a small playground where several children were playing. Nevertheless, Phillips nailed a paper target to a tree and went to a point where the tree was between himself and the playground. He then fired several shots at the target. One of the shots missed the target and the tree and hit and killed one of the children in the playground.

Phillips was convicted of murder. He appealed, contending that the evidence was not sufficient to support a conviction of murder.

The appellate court should

(A) affirm the conviction, as the evidence is sufficient to support a conviction of murder.

(B) reverse the conviction and remand for a new trial, because the evidence is not sufficient for murder but will support a conviction of voluntary manslaughter.

(C) reverse the conviction and remand for a new trial, because the evidence is not sufficient for murder but will support a conviction of involuntary manslaughter.

(D) reverse the conviction and order the case dismissed, because the evidence is sufficient only for a finding of negligence and negligence alone cannot support a criminal conviction.

[Q2039]

Answer 18: Choice **(A)** is correct. A defendant is guilty of murder if he has acted with reckless indifference to the value of human life. (Cf. MPC § 201.2(1)(b).) Phillips deliberately shot in the direction of the playground. Although Phillips did not intend to shoot into the playground (he was aiming for the target), the fact that he put the target in between himself and the playground (where several children were playing) is enough to show that he had a reckless indifference to human life (sometimes called a "depraved heart.")

(B) is wrong because, in order to be guilty of voluntary manslaughter, it is required that the defendant either (1) acted in response to a provocation that would be sufficient to cause a reasonable person to lose his self-control; or (2) made an unreasonable mistake about the need for self-defense. The facts presented here don't fall within either of these scenarios.

(C) is wrong because Phillips' intent was more than just reckless. Shooting into the path of a small playground demonstrates an extreme indifference to the value of human life, which will suffice for murder (as further discussed in (A) above). Therefore, this choice's statement that the evidence is "not sufficient for murder" is incorrect.

(D) is wrong because it falsely asserts that the evidence supports only for a finding of negligence. In fact, as is explained in (A), the evidence supports a finding of extreme indifference to the value of human life, which will in turn support a murder conviction.

Question 19: Jack, a bank teller, was fired by Morgan, the president of the bank. Jack decided to take revenge against Morgan, but decided against attempting it personally, because he knew Morgan was protected around the clock by bank security guards. Jack knew that Chip had a violent temper and was very jealous. Jack falsely told Chip that Chip's wife, Elsie, was having an affair with Morgan. Enraged, Chip said, "What am I going to do?" Jack said. "If it were my wife, I'd just march into his office and blow his brains out." Chip grabbed a revolver and rushed to the bank. He walked into the bank, carrying the gun in his hand. One of the security guards, believing a holdup was about to occur, shot and killed Chip.

If charged with murder of Chip, Jack should be found

(A) guilty, based upon extreme recklessness.

(B) guilty, based upon transferred intent.

(C) not guilty, because he did not intend for Chip to be shot by the security guard.

(D) not guilty, because he did not shoot Chip and he was not acting in concert with the security guard.

[Q1115]

Answer 19: Choice **(A)** is correct. Jack should be found guilty of Chip's murder because he knowingly put Chip into a situation where Chip was very likely to be shot. Murder is the unlawful killing of another person with malice aforethought. "Malice aforethought" includes several mental states, including reckless indifference to the value of human life. Reckless indifference tends to be found in situations where the defendant was aware of a very high risk of death to the victim. Jack was so aware of the risk in this case that he was fearful to go after Morgan himself. Jack manifested reckless indifference to the value of Chip's life by sending Chip into the bank, gun in hand, knowing that the bank was staffed with armed security guards. Further, Jack's encouragement was the legal cause of Chip's death because the risk he created (getting shot by a security guard) was the actual means of death.

(B) is wrong because it is a misapplication of transferred intent. When a defendant intends a harmful result to one victim, but, while trying to affect that harm, causes similar harm to a different victim, the doctrine of transferred intent allows the intent to harm the intended victim to be transferred to the harming of the actual victim. However, transferred intent only applies when the actual result of an act only differs from the intended result in that a different victim was harmed. That is, the same action as intended causes the same type of harm as intended, but to a victim that was unintended. Here, Jack intended that Chip would fire a gun, killing Morgan. Thus, Jack's intent can only be transferred to a victim shot by Chip. Since it was the security guard who shot Chip, the act was fundamentally different from the one intended, so the doctrine of transferred intent will not apply.

(C) is wrong because intent is not always required to support a murder conviction. As discussed above, reckless disregard for the value of the victim's life is a sufficient mental state for murder. Although Jack did not intend for the security guard to shoot and kill Chip, he was certainly aware of the high risk that it would happen

(D) is wrong because Jack's creation of the very high risk to Chip's life is sufficient to find him guilty of murder. When the *mens rea* for murder is reckless indifference to the value of the victim's life, the defendant needs neither to personally kill the victim nor be an accomplice of the killer — so long as Jack created a situation in which he knew Chip would be at an unreasonably high risk of death, he can be convicted of murder.

Question 20: A statute in the jurisdiction defines murder in the first degree as knowingly killing another person after deliberation. Deliberation is defined as "cool reflection for any length of time no matter how brief." Murder in the second degree is defined as "all other murder at common law except felony-murder." Felony-murder is murder in the third degree. Manslaughter is defined by the common law.

At 2 a.m., Duncan held up an all-night liquor store using an assault rifle. During the holdup, two police cars with flashing lights drove up in front of the store. In order to create a situation where the police would hesitate to come into the store (and thus give Duncan a chance to escape out the back) Duncan fired several rounds through the front window of the store. Duncan then ran out the back but upon discovering another police car there, surrendered quietly. One of the shots he fired while in the store struck and killed a burglar who was stealing items from a closed store across the street.

The most serious degree of criminal homicide Duncan is guilty of is

(A) murder in the first degree.

(B) murder in the second degree.

(C) murder in the third degree.

(D) manslaughter.

[Q1182]

Answer 20: Choice **(B)** is correct. Duncan has committed murder in the second degree because he fired a gun toward an area where he knew others were located. Murder at common law is the unlawful killing of another with "malice aforethought," which includes, among other states of mind, a reckless indifference to the value of human life (sometimes called a "depraved heart"). Duncan, knowing that police officers were stationed outside the front of the store, fired several times through the front window. In doing so, he demonstrated a disregard for the lives of those standing outside since the gunfire created an obvious lethal risk to them. The fact that the person actually killed by one of the shots was unknown to Duncan is irrelevant since the "depraved heart" mental state does not require any particular victim to be in the defendant's mind at the time of his act.

(A) is wrong because Duncan lacked the required mental state to commit first degree murder. The statute that defines first degree murder in this jurisdiction requires that the defendant "knowingly" kill another person. "Knowingly" would be interpreted to require that the actor either intend a particular result, or be aware that his act will almost certainly cause that result. When Duncan fired his gun, he did not specifically intend either to hit or to kill anyone, or know with near-certainty that someone would be killed. Thus, it cannot be said that Duncan knowingly killed another, as required for first-degree murder.

(C) is wrong because felony murder is not the most serious degree of homicide of which Duncan is guilty. As discussed above, Duncan is guilty of murder in the second degree, which is a more serious crime than felony murder, which is defined here as murder in the third degree. Duncan is guilty of felony murder because, during the course of committing robbery (an independent, dangerous felony), Duncan caused the death of another.

(D) is wrong because, as discussed above, Duncan is guilty of the more serious crime of second degree murder. Duncan would be guilty of involuntary manslaughter because firing a gun toward a known group of people was grossly negligent to the risk of serious bodily harm or death to those standing outside.

2. Great recklessness required

a. Omission to act

Question 21: Trelawney worked at a day care center run by the Happy Faces Day Care Corporation. At the center, one of the young charges, Smith, often arrived with bruises and welts on his back and legs. A statute in the jurisdiction requires all day care workers to report to the police cases where there is probable cause to suspect child abuse and provides for immediate removal from the home of any suspected child abuse victims. Trelawney was not aware of this statute. Nevertheless, he did report Smith's condition to his supervisor, who advised him to keep quiet about it so the day care center would not get into trouble for defaming a parent. About two weeks after Trelawney first noticed Smith's condition, Smith was beaten to death by his father. Trelawney has been charged with murder in the death of Smith. The evidence at trial disclosed, in addition to the above, that the child had been the victim of beatings by the father for some time, and that these earlier beatings had been responsible for the marks that Trelawney had seen. Smith's mother had been aware of the beatings but had not stopped them because she was herself afraid of Smith's father.

Trelawney's best argument that he is NOT guilty of murder is

(A) he was not aware of the duty-to-report statute.

(B) he lacked the mental state necessary to the commission of the crime.

(C) his omission was not the proximate cause of death.

(D) the day care corporation, rather than Trelawney, was guilty of the omission, which was sanctioned by its supervisory-level agent.

[Q2128]

Answer 21: Choice **(B)** is correct. Violation of a statute might serve as a basis for a criminal conviction if the statute imposes upon the defendant a duty of care that the defendant has not met. The statute clearly imposed upon Trelawney the duty to report suspected child abuse. In order to be guilty of murder, it must be shown that a defendant had "malice aforethought." Malice aforethought includes various mental states: intent to kill, intent to do serious bodily injury, reckless indifference to human life, or intent to commit a felony. The only possible qualifying mental state here is reckless indifference to human life. But since Trelawney thought about the abuse issue, and brought the issue to his supervisor's attention, he's unlikely to be found to have manifested the required reckless indifference to the value of human life. In any event, that's his only plausible argument from among those listed.

(A) is wrong because ignorance of the duty to report is not an excuse. Criminal liability for omissions can arise where there is a statute imposing on the defendant a distinct duty to act. Here, the statute imposed a duty of care on day care workers to report to the police where there is probable cause to suspect child abuse. Generally, the fact that the defendant did not know that the law imputes a legal duty in a certain situation will not constitute a defense. Therefore, Trelawney's ignorance of the law is not a good argument to use in defending him from a murder charge.

(C) is wrong because Trelawney's omission *was* sufficiently related to Smith's death. It is required that the act (in this case, omission) and the harm were sufficiently related that the act is a proximate cause of the harm. Criminal law generally insists upon a substantially closer connection between the defendant's act and the ensuing harm, than that of tort law. An act is the proximate cause if it is "not too remote or accidental in its occurrence to have a [just] bearing on the actor's liability or on the gravity of his offense." M.P.C. § 2.03(2)(b). Since a report of the earlier abuse by Trelawney would likely have induced the state to remove Smith from exposure to his father, Trelawney's failure to report the beating by the father can easily be said to have proximately caused (i.e., been closely related to) the death of Smith at the hands of the father.

(D) is wrong because the statute imposes a duty on day care workers, regardless of what their superiors may have sanctioned. Any duty or criminal behavior attributable to the supervisor would not prevent conviction of Trelawney for violation of his duty.

II.   FELONY-MURDER

A. Causal relationship

1.   Robberies, burglaries and gunfights

a.   Victim or police officer kills bystander

i.   MBE tip

Question 22: Steve, in desperate need of money, decided to hold up a local convenience store. Determined not to harm anyone, he carried a toy gun that resembled a real gun. In the store, he pointed the toy gun at the clerk and demanded money. A customer who entered the store and saw the robbery in progress pulled his own gun and fired at Steve. The bullet missed Steve but struck and killed the clerk.

Steve was charged with felony murder.

His best argument for being found NOT guilty is that he

(A) did not intend to kill.

(B) did not commit the robbery because he never acquired any money from the clerk.

(C) did not intend to create any risk of harm.

(D) is not responsible for the acts of the customer.

[Q2122]

Answer 22: Choice **(D)** is correct. The felony-murder rule provides that if the defendant, while he is in the process of committing a felony (such as robbery), kills another (even accidentally), the killing is murder. However, if the killing that took place during commission of the felony was by an innocent party (the customer) and he killed an innocent party (the clerk), then a court may well hold that the robber would not be responsible for the shooting (though this is not at all certain).

(A) is wrong because, in a jurisdiction recognizing felony murder, it is not required that the defendant have the intent to kill, as long as he had the intent to commit a felony (in this case, robbery).

(B) is wrong because for felony-murder liability, it is not necessary that the defendant be successful in his commission of the felony, merely that the murder occurred in the process of an attempt to commit the felony.

(C) is wrong because where the defendant had the intent to commit one of the specified dangerous felonies that will support felony murder, that's the only intent the defendant needs to have. So the fact that the defendant didn't intend to "create any risk of harm" is irrelevant.

2. Arson

Question 23: Shore decided to destroy his dilapidated building in order to collect the insurance money. He hired Parsons to burn down the building. Parsons broke into the building and carefully searched it to make sure no one was inside. He failed, however, to see a vagrant asleep in an office closet. He started a fire. The building was destroyed and the vagrant died from burns a week later. Two days after the fire, Shore filed an insurance claim in which he stated that he had no information about the cause of the fire.

If Shore is guilty of felony-murder, it is because the vagrant's death occurred in connection with the felony of

(A) arson.

(B) fraud.

(C) conspiracy.

(D) burglary.

[Q1009]

Answer 23: Choice **(A)** is correct. If Shore is guilty of felony-murder, it will be because the vagrant's death occurred during the commission of arson. The felony-murder rule allows the intent to commit a felony to supply the *mens rea* required for murder when the felony is the proximate cause of the killing. The rule states that when a defendant commits a felony that is inherently dangerous, and in so doing causes the death of another, the killing is murder. A felony is considered inherently dangerous if death is a foreseeable result of the crime. Here, the underlying felony was arson, which is an inherently dangerous crime because it inherently carries with it the risk to human life. Shore is responsible for the results of the fire because, although he did not personally start the fire that resulted in the vagrant's death, he is guilty of arson as an accomplice since he hired Parsons to burn the building. Additionally, for the felony-murder rule to apply, the felony must be independent of the killing. This requirement is met here because the purpose of starting the fire was not to harm the vagrant, but only to destroy the building.

Choices (B) and (C) are wrong because neither fraud nor conspiracy is an inherently dangerous felony, and therefore cannot be the underlying felony for a felony-murder conviction.

(D) is wrong because Shore has not committed burglary. Burglary requires the unlawful breaking and entering of a building of another with the intent to commit a crime once inside. Although Parsons "broke" into the building, he did so with the consent of the building's owner. As a result, Parsons's presence in the building was lawful, despite his means of entry and intent to commit arson.

B. Accomplice liability of co-felons

1. "In furtherance" test

Question 24: Dawson was charged with felony murder because of his involvement in a bank robbery. The evidence at trial disclosed that Smith invited Dawson to go for a ride in his new car, and after a while asked Dawson to drive. As Smith and Dawson drove around town, Smith explained to Dawson that he planned to rob the bank and that he needed Dawson to drive the getaway car. Dawson agreed to drive to the bank and to wait outside while Smith went in to rob it. As they approached the bank, Dawson began to regret his agreement to help with the robbery. Once there, Smith got out of the car. As Smith went out of sight inside the bank, Dawson drove away and went home. Inside the bank, Smith killed a bank guard who tried to prevent him from leaving with the money. Smith ran outside and, finding that his car and Dawson were gone, ran down an alley. He was apprehended a few blocks away. Dawson later turned himself in after hearing on the radio that Smith had killed the guard.

The jurisdiction has a death penalty that applies to felony murder.

Consistent with the law and the Constitution, the jury may convict Dawson of

(A) felony murder and impose the death penalty.

(B) felony murder but not impose the death penalty.

(C) bank robbery only.

(D) no crime.

[Q2009]

Answer 24: Choice **(B)** is correct. The felony-murder rule provides that if the defendant, while he is in the process of committing a dangerous felony (such as robbery), kills another (even accidentally), the killing is murder. Dawson, by driving Smith to the bank, serving as lookout, and agreeing to drive the getaway car, was an accomplice to bank robbery. Once Dawson performed those "accomplice" services, in a way that contributed to Smith's carrying out the robbery, Dawson became substantively liable for robbery too. After that, any killing by Smith that could be said to be a "natural and probable" result of the felony will be attributable to Dawson under the felony murder doctrine.

With respect to the death penalty, the Supreme Court has held that the Eighth Amendment prohibits the use of the death penalty on a defendant "who does not kill himself, attempt to kill, or intend that a killing take place or that lethal force may be employed." *Enmund v. Florida* (1982). Therefore, the death penalty may not be imposed upon Dawson, who did not himself kill, attempt to kill or intend that a killing take place or that lethal force be used.

(A) is wrong because the death penalty may not be imposed under these circumstances, as discussed in the explanation of (B).

(C) is wrong because Dawson may be convicted of felony-murder due to the fact that he is responsible for his co-felon's killing of the bank guard that was committed in furtherance of the felony, as discussed in the explanation of (B).

(D) is wrong because (1) Dawson is guilty of bank robbery on an accomplice theory; and (2) he may be convicted of felony-murder, as discussed in the explanation of (B).

III.   RAPE

A. Rape defined

1. Without consent

a. Mistake no defense

Question 25: A statute provides: A person commits the crime of rape if he has sexual intercourse with a female, not his wife, without her consent.

Dunbar is charged with the rape of Sally. At trial, Sally testifies to facts sufficient for a jury to find that Dunbar had sexual intercourse with her, that she did not consent, and that the two were not married. Dunbar testifies in his own defense that he believed that Sally had consented to sexual intercourse and that she was his common-law wife.

At the conclusion of the case, the court instructed the jury that in order to find Dunbar guilty of rape, it must find beyond a reasonable doubt that he had sexual intercourse with Sally without her consent.

The court also instructed the jury that it should find the defendant not guilty if it found either that Sally was Dunbar's wife or that Dunbar reasonably believed that Sally had consented to the sexual intercourse, but that the burden of persuasion as to these issues was on the defendant.

The jury found Dunbar guilty, and Dunbar appealed, contending that the court's instructions on the issues of whether Sally was his wife and whether he reasonably believed she had consented violated his constitutional rights.

Dunbar's constitutional rights were

(A) violated by the instructions as to both issues.

(B) violated by the instruction as to whether Sally was his wife, but not violated by the instruction on belief as to consent.

(C) violated by the instruction on belief as to consent, but not violated by the instruction as to whether Sally was his wife.

(D) not violated by either part of the instructions.

[Q1168]

Answer 25: Choice **(B)** is correct. As a criminal defendant, the Due Process Clause guarantees that Dunbar carries no burden to prove or disprove any element of the crime of which he is charged. The prosecution carries the burden of persuasion as to every element of the crime. Dunbar only has a burden of persuasion as to any affirmative defense he may raise. Dunbar has been charged with rape, which in this jurisdiction (as at common law) is defined as a defendant's (1) having sexual intercourse with a female, (2) not his wife, (3) without her consent. This means that the prosecutor must prove each one of those elements and that Dunbar has no burden of persuasion as to any of them. The judge is required to give an instruction that does not unduly saddle Dunbar with any burden regarding any element of the crime. Let's examine each of the judge's instructions separately.

The judge's instruction that the jury should find Dunbar not guilty if it found that Sally was Dunbar's wife and that Dunbar carried the burden of persuasion on this issue violated Dunbar's constitutional rights. The issue of whether Sally was Dunbar's wife is an element of the crime, so Dunbar could never be required to bear the burden to prove or disprove it — it must be solely the prosecution's burden to prove that Sally was not Dunbar's wife. Therefore the judge's instruction improperly shifted the burden of persuasion on this issue from the prosecution to Dunbar, in violation of his due process rights.

The judge's instruction that the jury should find Dunbar not guilty if it found that Dunbar reasonably believed Sally had consented to the sexual intercourse, and that the burden was on Dunbar to persuade the jury of that fact did not violate Dunbar's constitutional rights. Dunbar's belief at the time is not an element of rape, so the prosecution does not have to prove that Dunbar knew Sally did not consent in order to convict him. (If this jurisdiction follows the majority rule, Dunbar's mistake about consent, even if reasonable, would be no defense to the charge of rape. In that case, the judge's instruction would be in error, but in a way that would be likely to cause a jury to acquit Dunbar, not convict him. Even if the defendant's reasonable belief as to consent was recognized by the jurisdiction as an affirmative defense, the defendant could constitutionally be required to bear the burden of producing evidence to support that defense, and the burden of persuasion by a preponderance of the evidence as to it.)

(A) and (C) are wrong because they incorrectly state that Dunbar's rights were violated by the instruction on reasonable belief.

(A) and (D) are wrong because they do not identify the erroneous instruction on whether Sally and Dunbar were married as a violation of Dunbar's constitutional rights.

IV. KIDNAPPING

A. Definition of kidnapping

1. Asportation

a. M.P.C. "substantial distance" rule

Question 26: A driver stopped at a red light in his home state. A stranger opened the passenger door, got in, and pointed a gun at the driver. The stranger then directed the driver to keep driving. They drove several miles, crossed into a neighboring state, and drove several more miles. When they reached a remote location, the stranger ordered the driver to pull over. The stranger then robbed the driver of his wallet and cash, and ordered him out of the car. The stranger drove off in the driver's car.

The stranger is charged with kidnapping in the neighboring state, which has adopted the Model Penal Code.

Could the stranger properly be convicted of kidnapping in the neighboring state?

(A) Yes, because the driver was transported under threat of force in the neighboring state.

(B) Yes, because the driver in effect paid ransom for his release.

(C) No, because any kidnapping took place in the driver's home state.

(D) No, because the restraint was incidental to the robbery.

[QA038]

Answer 26: Choice **(A)** is correct. First, notice that the question was carefully set up to involve two states: the victim's home state, and the neighboring state. The reason the examiners set it up this way is that they wanted to be able to ask you whether that part of the episode that involved transporting the victim into and within the neighboring state was part of the crime — for instance, if the crime of kidnapping was defined in such a way that the crime here was over as soon as the stranger got in the car and drove the first few miles with the victim, then there would be no kidnapping in the neighboring state, only in the home state. But the M.P.C. does not define kidnapping in such a narrow way. The M.P.C. (like nearly all states) defines kidnapping to require either transporting of the victim (usually called "asportation") or secret imprisonment of the victim. The M.P.C. then says that asportation occurs only if the defendant either (1) "removes" the victim from his "place of residence or business", or (2) moves the victim "a *substantial distance* from the vicinity where he is found." M.P.C. § 212.1. The Commentary says that the "substantial distance" requirement is designed to "preclude kidnapping convictions based on trivial changes of location having no bearing on the evil at hand" (e.g., a rapist who forces his victim a few steps into a parked car does not commit kidnapping).

Here, the stranger's act of forcing the driver to transport himself "several miles" to the state border, then several more miles, clearly meets the "substantial distance" requirement. And since the description of the crime makes it clear that the stranger wanted to abandon the driver in a secluded location, the transporting was not a "trivial change[] of location having no bearing on the evil at hand." So the part of the episode that occurred in the neighboring state was definitely part of the crime, under the definition of kidnapping in the M.P.C. (and indeed, under the definitions of virtually every state).

(B) is wrong because it reaches the correct conclusion by incorrect reasoning. First, it is hard to characterize the proceeds of the robbery as "ransom." But more importantly, the propriety of a kidnapping conviction does not turn on whether ransom was paid. The M.P.C. defines kidnapping to mean either the moving of a person "a substantial distance," or the "unlawful confine[ment]" of a person "for a substantial period in a place of isolation," so long as the moving or confinement is done with *any of a variety of purposes* (e.g., holding for ransom, holding as a hostage, facilitating commission of any felony or flight thereafter, inflicting any bodily injury, etc.). M.P.C. § 212.1. Here, the stranger carried out the "moving" ("asportation," as it's usually called) for the purpose of later committing robbery, a felony. So whether the driver did or did not pay ransom is irrelevant. (Indeed, kidnapping is like burglary, in the sense that as long as the defendant confines or transports with one of the forbidden purposes, the crime is complete as soon as the confinement or moving-a-substantial-distance occurs, even if the purpose is never fulfilled. So here, once a stranger had, say, transported the driver into the neighboring state, the crime was complete even if the stranger had then abandoned his plan of robbing the driver of his car and wallet.)

(C) is wrong because the stranger properly could be convicted of kidnapping in both states. The movement in the neighboring state was more than incidental to the robbery, and would constitute kidnapping there as well as in the driver's home state. That's especially true since the underlying felony of robbery — the "purpose" for which the transportation occurred — happened in the neighboring state. For more about why the crime is deemed to have occurred in both states, see analysis of Choice (A).

(D) is wrong because the restraint was not incidental to the robbery. It's true that the M.P.C. defines kidnapping in such a way that where a restraint and/or a transporting is for a brief time or distance, and is truly incidental to the "main" crime intended by the defendant, kidnapping will not be deemd to have occurred. So, for instance, a rapist who forces his victim into a parked car or dark alley does not commit kidnapping. M.P.C. § 212.1, Commentary. But here, the stranger caused the driver to be transported several miles to the state border, then another several miles, all for the purpose of getting him to a secluded location where the car could be stolen. Under these facts, the restraint (and the transporting) were *not* incidental to the robbery.

2. Confinement must be against V's will

Question 27: John asked Doris to spend a weekend with him at his apartment and promised her they would get married on the following Monday. Doris agreed and also promised John that she would not tell anyone of their plans. Unknown to Doris, John had no intention of marrying her. After Doris came to his apartment, John told Doris he was going for cigarettes. He called Doris's father and told him that he had his daughter and would kill her if he did not receive $100,000. John was arrested on Sunday afternoon when he went to pick up the $100,000. Doris was still at the apartment and knew nothing of John's attempt to get the money.

John is guilty of

(A) kidnapping.

(B) attempted kidnapping.

(C) kidnapping or attempted kidnapping but not both.

(D) neither kidnapping nor attempted kidnapping.

[Q1137]

Answer 27: Choice **(D)** is correct. John is guilty of neither kidnapping nor attempted kidnapping. Let's examine each crime separately.

John has not committed kidnapping because Doris was free to leave his apartment at any time. Kidnapping is the (1) unlawful confinement of another person, (2) accompanied by either the moving or secreting away of that person. Although John may have tricked Doris into spending the weekend at his apartment, he did nothing to confine her once she got there. Confinement occurs when the victim is either forced to remain where she does not wish to remain or compelled to go where she does not wish to be. Doris desired to be at John's apartment and could have left had she so chosen, so she was not confined. The lack of confinement negates the first element of kidnapping, so John has not committed the crime. (And the fact that Doris' presence was brought about by John's trickery about his intent to marry her won't matter — he hasn't confined her, and that's all that matters.)

John is not guilty of attempted kidnapping because he did not intend for his actions to confine Doris to his apartment. In order to find John guilty of attempt, the prosecution would have to show that John intended to commit each element of the crime. In this case, John didn't intent to confine, so he can't have attempt to kidnap.

Choices (A), (B), and (C) are all wrong because they each state that John is guilty of either kidnapping or attempted kidnapping, which cannot be true if there has been no confinement and no attempt to confine.

CHAPTER 7
THEFT CRIMES

I. LARCENY

A. Trespassory taking

1. Larceny by trick

a. Intent to steal required

Question 28: Smith asked Jones if he would loan him $500, promising to repay the amount within two weeks. Jones loaned him the $500. The next day Smith took the money to the race track and lost all of it betting on horse races. He then left town for six months. He has not repaid Jones.

Smith has committed

(A) both larceny by trick and obtaining money by false pretenses (although he can only be convicted of one offense).

(B) larceny by trick only.

(C) obtaining money by false pretenses only.

(D) neither larceny by trick nor obtaining money by false pretenses.

[Q2096]

Answer 28: Choice **(D)** is correct. What we care about most is whether this is larceny by trick. The fact pattern does not indicate that Smith had any intention other than the intent to repay the loan, when he asked to borrow money from Jones. Therefore, he did not intend to "steal" at the moment he received the money, which would be required for larceny by trick.

B. Personal property

1. No minimum value

Question 29: David entered the county museum at a time when it was open to the public, intending to steal a Picasso etching. Once inside, he took what he thought was the etching from an unlocked display case and concealed it under his coat. However, the etching was a photocopy of an original that had been loaned to another museum. A sign over the display case containing the photocopy said that similar photocopies were available free at the entrance. David did not see the sign.

Burglary in the jurisdiction is defined as "entering a building unlawfully with the intent to commit a crime."

David is guilty of

(A) burglary and larceny.

(B) burglary and attempted larceny.

(C) larceny.

(D) attempted larceny.

[Q1113]

Answer 29: Choice **(C)** is correct. What we care about here is that David has committed larceny. Larceny is the (1) trespassory (2) taking and (3) carrying away (4) of the personal property (5) of another with (6) the intent to steal. David's actions fulfill all of the elements: (1) he had no permission to take the document, (2) he took it, (3) and removed it from its case, (4) & (5) the document was property that didn't belong to him, and (6) he intended to steal it. David's mistaken belief that the photocopy was in fact a valuable Picasso original is irrelevant. The value of the item he stole would be relevant to the degree of larceny of which David is guilty, but the common law definition of larceny has no minimum value threshold. Also irrelevant is the fact that David could have lawfully obtained a duplicate for free — it's true that he could legally have taken one of the copies at the entrance, but he had no permission to take the copy in the display case.

(A) and **(B)** are **incorrect**. As defined in the given statute, burglary requires two elements: (1) entering a building unlawfully, (2) with the intent to commit a crime. It is indisputable that David intended to commit a crime once inside the museum since we are told that he entered "intending to steal a Picasso etching." However, David's entry wasn't unlawful. When he entered the museum, it was open to all members of the public, including David. The fact that a criminal purpose motivated his entry does not make that entry "unlawful." For the purposes of burglary, entry is only unlawful if the defendant entered a building, or remained in a building, in which he had no permission to be. Since David's entry to the museum was lawful, he has not committed burglary.

C. Intent to steal

1. Claim of right

a. Grievance not enough

Question 30: The defendant worked as the cashier in a restaurant. One night after the restaurant had closed, the defendant discovered that the amount of cash in the cash register did not match the cash register receipt tapes. He took the cash and the tapes, put them in a bag, gave them to the manager of the restaurant, and reported the discrepancy. The manager immediately accused him of taking money from the register and threatened to fire him if he did not make up the difference. The manager placed the bag in the office safe. Angered by what he considered to be an unjust accusation, the defendant waited until the manager left the room and then reached into the still open safe, took the bag containing the cash, and left.

The defendant is guilty of

(A) larceny.

(B) embezzlement.

(C) either larceny or embezzlement but not both.

(D) neither larceny nor embezzlement.

[Q2181]

Answer 30: Choice **(A)** is correct. Larceny is the (1) trespassory (2) taking and (3) carrying away of (4) personal property (5) of another (6) with intent to steal. The defendant took the restaurant's money from the safe with the intent to steal it, so he is guilty of larceny. The fact that the defendant felt (properly or not) aggrieved by the false accusation is irrelevant. If the defendant had had a genuine belief that he had a "claim of right" to money or property in the defendant's possession, and had taken the money in satisfaction of that claim, this might be a defense to larceny; but the defendant didn't have that belief here — he was just feeling aggrieved.

(B) is wrong because the defendant took the money from the office safe. Embezzlement is the (1) fraudulent (2) conversion of (3) the property (4) of another (5) by one who is already in lawful possession of it. The element missing here is the one requiring lawful possession. The defendant, as cashier, had lawful possession of the money while he was working the cash register and putting it into a bag in order to give it to the manager (so if he had taken it and carried it away with intent to steal at that point, it would have been embezzlement). But once the bag was put into the office safe, the defendant did not have lawful possession of it any more. Therefore, when he took it from the safe he could not be guilty of embezzlement.

(C) is wrong because the defendant is not guilty of embezzlement, as discussed in Choice (B). (Also, at common law, larceny and embezzlement are defined in mutually-exclusive ways, so it could not be the case that the prosecution had a choice of which crime to charge on any given state of facts.)

(D) is wrong because the defendant is guilty of larceny, as discussed in Choice (A).

II. BURGLARY

A. Breaking

1. No consent

Question 31: Sam told Horace, his neighbor, that he was going away for two weeks and asked Horace to keep an eye on his house. Horace agreed. Sam gave Horace a key to use to check on the house.

Horace decided to have a party in Sam's house. He invited a number of friends. One friend, Lewis, went into Sam's bedroom, took some of Sam's rings, and put them in his pocket.

Which of the following is true?

(A) Horace and Lewis are guilty of burglary.

(B) Horace is guilty of burglary and Lewis is guilty of larceny.

(C) Horace is guilty of trespass and Lewis is guilty of larceny.

(D) Lewis is guilty of larceny and Horace is not guilty of any crime.

[Q2102]

Answer 31: Choices **(A)** and **(B)** are **incorrect**, and Choice **(D)** is correct. What we care about here is whether either Horace or Sam committed burglary. The answer is that neither did. Burglary is the breaking and entering of the dwelling of another at night with intent to commit a felony. Breaking does not occur when one is invited into a house. Since Horace had a key to the premises and had permission to enter the house, there was no breaking. Furthermore, the facts do not indicate that Horace had the intention to commit a felony at the time he entered the premises (or at any time, for that matter); therefore, this requirement is not met either. As to Lewis, he was let into the premises by one who was authorized to be there (and presumably, who was authorized to let in others). Therefore, Lewis, too, did not "break." (Nor is there any indication that Lewis had the intent to commit a felony *at the time* he entered the premises — for all we know this intent might have been formed later, when he noticed the jewelry.) Therefore, Lewis is not guilty of burglary either.

Lewis is guilty of larceny because he took property belonging to another (Sam's rings) and "carried them away" (by putting them in his pocket); a jury could infer that he did this because he meant to steal them. Horace hasn't taken any property belonging to another or intended to; deciding to have a party in someone else's house, when one has the right to be in the house, is not any particular crime, theft or otherwise.

III. ARSON

A. Nature of offense

1. Act posing great risk of fire

a. Failure to take action

i. Failure to put out fire D started

Question 32: Defendant was upset because he was going to have to close his liquor store due to competition from a discount store in a new shopping mall nearby. In desperation, he decided to set fire to his store to collect the insurance. While looking through the basement for flammable material, he lit a match to read the label on a can. The match burned his finger and, in a reflex action, he dropped the match. It fell into a barrel and ignited some paper. Defendant made no effort to put out the fire but instead left the building. The fire spread and the store was destroyed by fire. Defendant was eventually arrested and indicted for arson.

Defendant is

(A) guilty, if he could have put out the fire before it spread and did not do so because he wanted the building destroyed.

(B) guilty, if he was negligent in starting the fire.

(C) not guilty, because even if he wanted to burn the building there was no concurrence between his *mens rea* and the act of starting the fire.

(D) not guilty, because his starting the fire was the result of a reflex action and not a voluntary act.

[Q2156]

Answer 32: Choice **(A)** is correct. Ordinarily, a defendant has no affirmative obligation to avoid harm, only an obligation to refrain from doing harm. But where a defendant brings about a risky situation, then he does have a duty to use reasonable efforts to avoid the harm. So once Defendant dropped the match (even if only reflexively), he had an affirmative obligation to stop the fire. When he didn't, and his mental state matched a state that will suffice for arson (intent to burn), he became guilty of arson.

(B) is wrong because mere negligence doesn't suffice for arson — it's a crime that requires either an intent to burn, or (in some states) recklessness with regard to the risk of burning.

(C) is incorrect, because there *was* concurrence. Even if Defendant behaved non-negligently in lighting a match in the first instance, and involuntarily in dropping it, once the fire started he had the obligation to make reasonable efforts to stop it, because he had caused the peril in the first place. Once he simultaneously failed to perform that duty to stop the peril and desired that the bad result defining the crime (burning) occur, he met the concurrence requirement.

(D) is wrong because, while Defendant may have started the fire reflexively, once he failed to put it out while under a duty to do so, this was a voluntary act.

CRIMINAL PROCEDURE Q&A BY TOPIC

References to "L&I" are to Lafave & Israel, *Criminal Procedure* Hornbook (2d Ed., West, 1992).

CHAPTER 1

ARREST; PROBABLE CAUSE; SEARCH WARRANTS

I. AREAS AND PEOPLE PROTECTED BY THE FOURTH AMENDMENT

A. Guests

1. Guest staying in hotel room

Question 33: A federal officer had probable cause to believe a woman had participated in a bank robbery. Two days after the robbery, the woman checked into a local hotel room. When the woman left for the evening, the hotel manager opened the hotel room door so the officer could enter the room and look inside. The officer did not find any of the stolen money but did see, lying open on the bed, the woman's diary. The diary contained an entry describing the woman's involvement in robbing the bank.

The woman was charged in federal court with bank robbery. She moved to suppress the diary.

Should the court suppress the diary?

(A) Yes, because the officer had no warrant.

(B) Yes, because admitting the diary would violate the woman's privilege against self-incrimination.

(C) No, because the hotel manager had actual authority to allow the officer into the hotel room.

(D) No, because the officer reasonably relied on the hotel manager's apparent authority to allow the officer into the hotel room.

[QA006]

Answer 33: Choice **(A)** is correct. The Fourth Amendment protects places as to which a person has a reasonable expectation of privacy. One of those places is a person's dwelling, even a temporary dwelling like a hotel room. See, e.g., *Minnesota v. Olson* (1990) (overnight social guest has reasonable expectation of privacy in the home in which she is staying); *Stoner v. California* (1964) (hotel guest is to be treated like any other tenant, and management may not consent to a search of the guest room prior to check-out). Before the police may enter a place as to which a suspect has a reasonable expectation of privacy, the police must (1) have probable cause to suspect a crime; and (2) have a search or arrest warrant, or benefit from some exception to the warrant requirement. Here, although requirement (1) (probable cause) was satisfied, the police did not have a search or arrest warrant, and there was nothing in the facts to suggest any exception to the warrant requirement. For example, although there is an exception to the warrant requirement for "exigent circumstances," no such circumstances were presented here, since the woman was out for the evening and thus did not pose an imminent threat to destroy evidence. (If the police were worried that she would destroy evidence as soon as she returned, they could have posted an officer outside the room to prevent her re-entry, while they sought a warrant.)

Nor did the permission from the hotel manager override the woman's right not to have her premises searched without a warrant, for the reasons described in the analysis of choices (C) and (D).

(B) is wrong because, although it reaches the right outcome, it does so on incorrect reasoning. The privilege against self-incrimination protects a person against being required by government to make an incriminating communication. Since the woman made the diary entries without being required to do so by government, the later seizure of that diary could not violate her privilege. (If she had been required by subpoena to *produce*, say, "any diary or other communication in which you discuss the alleged crime," then this probably *would* have violated her privilege, since it would in effect require her to communicate the information, "This is a diary that I wrote," a communication that would tend to incriminate her. But here, since the police seized the diary without requiring the woman to produce it or authenticate it, there is no self-incrimination problem.)

(C) is wrong because the hotel manager did not have actual authority to allow the officer into the hotel room. "Actual authority" is a concept of agency law: if the principal intentionally confers on the agent the right to do something, the agent is said to have actual authority to do that thing. So if the woman had indicated (either expressly or by implication) to the hotel management that it was OK for management to enter and search her room at any time, the management would have had actual authority to conduct its own search, and also authority to consent to the police search. In another context, suppose that D was an employee of X Corp. and had an office at corporate headquarters; if the understanding was that X Corp. had the right as owner of the office to search its contents at any time, then X Corp. would have had actual authority to permit the police to make such a search, and that permission would have overridden D's reasonable expectation of privacy in the office.

But here, hotel management had at most actual authority to enter for the *limited purposes* of cleaning, trash removal, and the like, not for the purpose of making a search of the guest's belongings. Therefore, the manager did not have actual authority to consent to the police search. See *Stoner v. California* (1964) (hotel guest is to be treated like any other tenant, and management may not consent to a search of the guest room prior to check-out).

(D) is wrong, because the hotel manager did not have apparent authority to allow the officer into the hotel room. "Apparent authority," like "actual authority," is a concept from agency law — if the principal puts the agent in such a position that the world reasonably infers that the agent has actual authority to do Act X, then the agent is deemed to have apparent authority to do X even though the agent does not have actual authority to do X.

Here, the defendant hotel guest (the principal) probably has, merely by checking into the room and not indicating otherwise, conferred on hotel management (the agent) apparent authority to enter for *limited purposes* like cleaning. But the guest has not conferred apparent authority on management to search the room, or to give consent to law enforcement to search the room — that's because renting a hotel room is not commonly understood to confer such authority on hotel management. Since hotel management did not have apparent authority to consent to the search, the police's reliance on what they thought was apparent authority was not reasonable, and therefore not effective. Consequently, the defendant's basic reasonable expectation of privacy in her temporary hotel dwelling prevailed, and was enough to make the warrantless entry a Fourth Amendment violation, as further described in Choice (A).

II.   THE "PLAIN VIEW" DOCTRINE

A. Aerial observation

Question 34: Police received an anonymous tip that Tusitala was growing marijuana in her backyard, which was surrounded by a 15-foot high, solid wooden fence. Officer Boa was unable to view the yard from the street, so he used a police helicopter to fly over Tusitala's house. Boa identified a large patch of marijuana plants growing right next to the house and used this observation to obtain a search warrant.

Tusitala is prosecuted for possession of marijuana and moves to suppress use of the marijuana in evidence.

The court should

(A) grant the motion, because the only purpose of Boa's flight was to observe the yard.

(B) grant the motion, because Tusitala had a reasonable expectation of privacy in the curtilage around her house and the police did not have a warrant.

(C) deny the motion, because a warrant is not required for a search of a residential yard.

(D) deny the motion, because Tusitala had no reasonable expectation of privacy from aerial observation.

[Q2110]

Answer 34: Choice **(D)** is correct. Where objects on private property can be seen from public places, observation by the police does not constitute a Fourth Amendment search. The fact that a police officer who obtains the "plain view" does so from a contorted or otherwise unusual position does not prevent the "plain view" doctrine from applying, assuming that the policeman is in a place where he has a prior right to be. *Harris v. U.S.* (1968). If the police use an aircraft to view the defendant's property from the air and the aircraft is in public, navigable, airspace, anything the police can see with the naked eye from that airspace falls within the "plain view" doctrine. Even a view taken by the police from a helicopter flying only 400 feet above the ground still fell within the "plain view" doctrine according to a five-Justice majority in *Florida v. Riley* (1989). Therefore, the search of Tusitala's yard from an aerial view was valid, and the subsequent issuance of a warrant to seize the marijuana observed in the search was valid.

(A) is wrong because the purpose of the flight was irrelevant, as long as the police officer was in a place where he had a prior right to be. There is nothing to indicate that the officer was not allowed to be in the airspace above Tusitala's property.

(B) is wrong because, although Tusitala had a reasonable expectation of privacy in his yard from ground-level observation due to his erection of a 15-foot high fence, this expectation of privacy did not extend to aerial observation, as explained in the discussion of (D).

(C) is wrong because if a person has a reasonable expectation of privacy in his yard, then a warrant would be required to enter it. In this case, ground-level observation of Tusitala's yard, which was enclosed by a 15-foot high fence, would require a warrant; by contrast, aerial observation of the yard would not require a warrant.

III. PROBABLE CAUSE GENERALLY

A. Only evidence heard by magistrate used

1. Perjured affidavit

a. Honest police error

Question 35: On October 22, a police officer submitted an application for a warrant to search 217 Elm Street for cocaine. In the application, the officer stated under oath that he believed there was cocaine at that location because of information supplied to him on the morning of October 22 by Susie Schultz. He described Schultz as a cocaine user who had previously supplied accurate information concerning the use of cocaine in the community and summarized what Schultz had told him as follows: the previous night, October 21, Schultz was in the defendant's house at 217 Elm Street. The defendant gave her cocaine. Schultz also saw three cellophane bags containing cocaine in the defendant's bedroom.

The warrant was issued and a search of 217 Elm Street was conducted on October 22. The search turned up a quantity of marijuana but no cocaine. The defendant was arrested and charged with possession of marijuana. The defendant moved to suppress the use of the marijuana as evidence, contending that Susie Schultz was not in 217 Elm Street on October 21 or at any other time.

If, after hearing evidence, the judge concludes that the statement in the application attributed to Susie Schultz is incorrect, the judge should grant the motion to suppress

(A) because the application contains a material statement that is false.

(B) because of the false statement and because no cocaine was found in the house.

(C) only if he also finds that Susie Schultz's statement was a deliberate lie.

(D) only if he also finds that the officer knew the statement was false.

[Q2117]

Answer 35: Choice **(D)** is correct. The exclusionary rule provides that evidence obtained by violating the defendant's constitutional rights may not be introduced by the prosecution, at least for purposes of providing direct proof of the defendant's guilt. The exclusionary rule does not bar evidence that was obtained by officers acting in reasonable reliance on a search warrant issued by a proper magistrate but ultimately found to be unsupported by probable cause. *U.S. v. Leon* (1984). This good-faith exception will not apply if the officer who prepared the affidavit on which the warrant is based knows that the information in it is false or recklessly disregards its truth or falsity. Therefore, the motion to suppress should be granted under these circumstances.

(A) is wrong because it is irrelevant that there was a false material statement in the application, as long as the police officers acted in reasonable reliance upon it. The informant was described as a cocaine user who had previously supplied accurate information concerning the use of cocaine in the community; she also supplied detailed information about how she came upon the information which she supplied to the police. It was reasonable for the police to rely on the warrant that was based on this information offered by this informant. And under *U.S. v. Leon, supra,* the evidence obtained by reasonable reliance on a search warrant is not excludible even though there was not in fact probable cause for issuance of the warrant. (See the analysis of Choice (D) above.)

(B) is wrong because not only is it irrelevant that there was a false statement in the application, but it is also irrelevant that no cocaine was found in the house, as long as the police officers acted in reasonable reliance upon the warrant. There was reasonable reliance on the warrant as explained in the discussion of Choice (A).

(C) is wrong because the nature of the false statement is irrelevant, as long as the police officers acted in reasonable reliance upon the warrant. There was reasonable reliance on the warrant, as explained in the discussion of Choice (A).

CHAPTER 2
WARRANTLESS ARRESTS AND SEARCHES

I.   SEARCH INCIDENT TO ARREST

A. Protective sweep

1.   Can't search too-small spaces

Question 36: The police had, over time, accumulated reliable information that a rock singer operated a large cocaine-distribution network, that he and his accomplices often resorted to violence, and that they kept a small arsenal of weapons in his home.

One day, the police received reliable information that a large brown suitcase with leather straps containing a supply of cocaine had been delivered to the singer's home and that it would be moved to a distribution point the next morning. The police obtained a valid search warrant to search for and seize the brown suitcase and the cocaine and went to the singer's house.

The police knocked on the singer's door and called out, "Police. Open up. We have a search warrant." After a few seconds with no response, the police forced the door open and entered. Hearing noises in the basement, the police ran down there and found the singer with a large brown suitcase with leather straps. They seized the suitcase and put handcuffs on the singer. A search of his person revealed a switchblade knife and a .45-caliber pistol.

The police then fanned out through the house, looking in every room and closet. They found no one else, but one officer found an Uzi automatic weapon in a box on a closet shelf in the singer's bedroom.

In addition to charges relating to the cocaine in the suitcase, the singer is charged with unlawful possession of weapons.

The singer moves pretrial to suppress the use as evidence of the Uzi automatic weapon. The singer's motion to suppress should be

(A) granted, because the search exceeded the scope needed to find out if other persons were present.

(B) granted, because once the object of the warrant—the brown suitcase—had been found and seized, no further search of the house is permitted.

(C) denied, because the police were lawfully in the bedroom and the weapon was immediately identifiable as being subject to seizure.

(D) denied, because the police were lawfully in the house and had probable cause to believe that weapons were in the house.

[Q3068]

Answer 36: Choice **(A)** is correct. Incident to a lawful arrest in an arrestee's home, the officers executing the warrant may conduct a "protective sweep" of all or part of the premises, if they have a "reasonable belief" that another person who might be dangerous to the officers may be present *in the areas swept. Maryland v. Buie* (1990). So here, the police had the right to search the house for accomplices. The Uzi, however, was found in a box on a closet shelf. Clearly the weapon was neither in plain sight nor in a place where a person could be found. Therefore, the protective-sweep exception doesn't apply. Since the search warrant covered only the brown suitcase (which the police had already seized), their search of the closet could not be justified on the grounds that they were executing the search warrant either.

(B) is wrong because the answer misstates the applicable law: the police had the right to search the house for accomplices. As is described in the analysis of Choice (A) above, the police had the right to check protectively for other persons. Therefore, this choice — since it says that no further search of the house was permitted once the suitcase was seized — is inconsistent with the officers' right to make the protective search (which may be made at any time that the police are still on the premises and are thus vulnerable to a sudden attack from someone who might be hiding).

(C) is wrong because the weapon was not in an area that could be searched. It's true that the police were lawfully in the bedroom (under their right to make a protective sweep — see Choice (A)). But while they were in the bedroom, the police were only permitted to look in places where a person might be hiding. They therefore weren't allowed to look in small boxes, as they did here.

(D) is wrong because, while the police knew that there might well be weapons in the house, they would have needed a warrant in order to look for such weapons at the top of the closet. There are two requirements that must be satisfied before a house may be searched for a particular item, unless there is some applicable exception: (1) probable cause to believe that the item will be found; and (2) a warrant to search for it. Here, since the facts tell us that the police had gotten reliable information that the singer and his accomplices "kept a small arsenal of weapons in [the singer's] home," requirement (1) was satisfied as to the weapons. But although the police procured a search warrant, that warrant did not cover the weapons, only the brown suitcase. Therefore, the fact that the police were already in the home, and the further fact that they had probable cause to believe that the weapons would or might be found, were not enough to permit them to look not either in the bedroom or in the closet. And while their need to make a "protective sweep" justified them in looking in the bedroom, this need did not, as described in the discussion of Choice (A), authorize them to search in a small box on a shelf, since no one could have been hiding there.

II. AUTOMOBILE SEARCHES

A. Two special exceptions

1. Field search for contraband

Question 37: Police received information from an undercover police officer that she had just seen two men (whom she described) in a red pickup truck selling marijuana to schoolchildren near the city's largest high school. A few minutes later, two police officers saw a pickup truck fitting the description a half block from the high school. The driver of the truck matched the description of one of the men described by the undercover officer.

The only passenger was a young woman who was in the back of the truck. The police saw her get out and stand at a nearby bus stop. They stopped the truck and searched the driver. In the pocket of the driver's jacket, the police found a small bottle of pills that they recognized as narcotics. They then broke open a locked toolbox attached to the flatbed of the truck and found a small sealed envelope inside. They opened it and found marijuana. They also found a quantity of cocaine in the glove compartment.

After completing their search of the driver and the truck, the police went over to the young woman and searched her purse. In her purse, they found a small quantity of heroin. Both the driver and the young woman were arrested and charged with unlawful possession of narcotics.

If the driver moves to suppress the use as evidence of the marijuana and cocaine found in the search of the truck, the court should

(A) grant the motion as to both the marijuana and the cocaine.

(B) grant the motion as to the marijuana but deny it as to the cocaine.

(C) deny the motion as to the marijuana but grant it as to the cocaine.

(D) deny the motion as to both the marijuana and the cocaine.

[Q1038]

Answer 37: Choice (D) is correct. The court should deny the driver's motion to suppress both types of evidence since the search that allowed the police to find the drugs was conducted properly. Generally, the Fourth Amendment requires that police have a warrant to search a person or location. There are many exceptions to this rule, several of which involve the searches of automobiles. In particular, the police could search the driver's car if they had probable cause to believe that it contained contraband or evidence of a crime. (*California v. Carney* (1985).) Since the officers who stopped the car were informed by another officer that, only a few minutes earlier, the occupants of the truck were observed selling marijuana, the arresting officers had a strong basis for a reasonable belief that the truck would contain drugs. Once we have determined that the search was allowed, we need to check whether the scope of the search was proper. When the police stop a vehicle and have probable cause to believe that contraband is contained in it, they may search any container that could possibly contain the object of the search. (*U.S. v. Ross* (1982).) Since the officers were searching driver's truck for evidence of a recent drug sale, the object of the search was marijuana, which can be stored in very small containers. Both the glove compartment of the truck and the toolbox in the flatbed were large enough to contain the drugs, so the police could lawfully search them without a warrant.

Choices (A), (B), and (C) are incorrect because they incorrectly conclude that the police improperly searched either the glove compartment or the toolbox.

III. CONSENT SEARCHES GENERALLY

A. D need not know he can refuse consent

1. Must be voluntary

a. Ignorance of police motive

Question 38: Larson was charged with the murder of a man who had been strangled and whose body was found in some woods near his home. Larson suffers from a neurological problem that makes it impossible for him to remember an occurrence for longer than 48 hours.

After Larson was charged, the police visited him and asked if they might search his home. Larson consented. The police found a diary written by Larson. An entry dated the same day as the victim's disappearance read, "Indescribable excitement. Why did no one ever tell me that killing gave such pleasure to the master?"

Larson was charged with murder. His attorney has moved to exclude the diary from evidence on the ground that its admission would violate Larson's privilege against self-incrimination. Counsel has also argued that Larson could not give informed consent to the search because more than 48 hours had passed since the making of the entry and hence he could not remember the existence of the incriminating entry at the time he gave his consent. There is no evidence that the police officers who secured Larson's consent to the search were aware of his memory impairment.

With regard to the diary, the court should

(A) admit it, because Larson's consent was not obtained by intentional police misconduct and Larson was not compelled to make the diary entry.

(B) admit it, pursuant to the good-faith exception to the exclusionary rule.

(C) exclude it, because Larson was not competent to consent to a search.

(D) exclude it, because use of the diary as evidence would violate Larson's privilege against self-incrimination.

[Q2006]

Answer 38: Choice **(A)** is correct. The police may make a constitutional warrantless search if they receive the consent of the individual whose premises, effects or person are to be searched. The police did not deceive Larson nor make any misrepresentations in order to obtain his consent. Nor did they compel him to make the diary entry, a requirement in order for him to claim that his Fifth Amendment privilege against self-incrimination was violated, as discussed more fully in the analysis of (D). Therefore, the diary should be admitted.

(B) is wrong because the "good faith" exception to the exclusionary rule does not apply in this context, nor is it even necessary to rely on an exception, since the search and seizure was valid. The exclusionary rule provides that evidence obtained by violating the defendant's constitutional rights may not be introduced by the prosecution, at least for purposes of providing direct proof of the defendant's guilt. The exclusionary rule does not bar evidence that was obtained by officers acting in reasonable reliance on a search warrant issued by a proper magistrate but ultimately found to be unsupported by probable cause ("good faith" exception). *U.S. v. Leon* (1984). There was no warrant issued in this case; therefore, the concept is misapplied here. In addition, the diary is admissible without reliance on an exception to the exclusionary rule, because of Larson's consent, as discussed in the explanation to (A).

(C) is wrong because Larson's disability did not affect his ability to understand the nature of his consent. It's true that Larson could not remember things that happened more than 48 hours previously, so that he did not remember making the diary entry. However, what is relevant is that he was fully competent to understand the consequences of his consent to a present search of his home. Therefore, the consent was valid.

(D) is wrong because the police did not compel the production of the diary, nor would evidence of a diary entry be considered "testimonial or communicative." The Fifth Amendment privilege against self-incrimination protects against compulsion to give "testimonial or communicative" evidence. Larson consented to the search without any compulsion on the part of the police. Additionally, Larson's earlier writing of the diary was not intended as a communication (the fact pattern does not indicate that it was intended to be anything other than a private writing meant to be read only by Larson) and would therefore not be covered under the privilege for that reason as well.

IV. INSPECTIONS AND WEAPONS SEARCHES

A. Searches in schools

1. Law enforcement agencies involved

Question 39: The police suspected that Yancey, a 16-year-old high school student, had committed a series of burglaries. Two officers went to Yancey's high school and asked the principal to call Yancey out of class and to search his backpack. While the officers waited, the principal took Yancey into the hall where she asked to look in his backpack. When Yancey refused, the principal grabbed it from him, injuring Yancey's shoulder in the process. In the backpack, she found jewelry that she turned over to the officers.

Yancey was charged with the burglaries, and moves to suppress the use of the jewelry.

The court should

(A) deny the motion on the ground that the search was incident to a lawful arrest.

(B) deny the motion on the ground that school searches are reasonable if conducted by school personnel on school grounds on the basis of reasonable suspicion.

(C) grant the motion on the ground that the search was conducted with excessive force.

(D) grant the motion on the ground that the search was conducted without probable cause or a warrant.

[Q2143]

Answer 39: Choice **(D)** is correct. School officials may search the person and property of a student without a warrant if there was "reasonable ground for suspecting that the search will turn up evidence that the student has violated or is violating either the law or the rules of the school." *New Jersey v. T.L.O.* (1985). However, this rule almost certainly doesn't apply where the school authorities are performing the search at the express request of the police. Consequently, the usual requirement of probable cause for a search, plus the requirement of a search warrant, apply if there is no other applicable exception to these requirements. There is no such exception to either of these requirements on these facts.

(A) is wrong because a search incident to an arrest must be made incident to a valid arrest, supported by probable cause. The facts do not offer a basis on which probable cause could have been found, only a vague reference that the police "suspected" Yancey. Additionally, the search here happened before the arrest; a valid search incident to an arrest occurs after the arrest has been made.

(B) is wrong because, while it's true that school officials may search the person and property of a student without a warrant if there was "reasonable ground for suspecting that the search will turn up evidence that the student has violated or is violating either the law or the rules of the school," (*N.J. v. T.L.O., supra*) this rule doesn't apply here. That's because the principal was acting at the specific behest of the police. Consequently, the search had to meet the same requirements as a police search (including satisfaction of the warrant requirement), and the "reasonableness" of the search wouldn't be enough to validate it.

(C) is wrong because there is no "excessive force" basis for excluding the fruits of a search.

CHAPTER 3

CONFESSIONS AND POLICE INTERROGATION

I. VOLUNTARINESS

A. Voluntariness generally

1. Must be police coercion

Question 40: Dan entered the police station and announced that he wanted to confess to a murder. The police advised Dan of the *Miranda* warnings, and Dan signed a written waiver. Dan described the murder in detail and pinpointed the location where a murder victim had been found a few weeks before. Later, a court-appointed psychiatrist determined that Dan was suffering from a serious mental illness that interfered with his ability to make rational choices and to understand his rights and that the psychosis had induced his confession.

Dan's confession is

(A) admissible, because there was no coercive police conduct in obtaining Dan's statement.

(B) admissible, because Dan was not in custody.

(C) inadmissible, because Dan's confession was a product of his mental illness and was therefore involuntary.

D) inadmissible, because under these circumstances, there was no valid waiver of Miranda warnings.

[Q1080]

Answer 40: Choice **(A)** is correct. Dan's confession is admissible because it was made voluntarily after he had validly waived his Fifth Amendment right against self-incrimination. A confession may only be introduced against a defendant if it meets two criteria. First, the defendant must have made the confession voluntarily. This hurdle is very easy to clear since a statement is considered "voluntary" unless there is evidence of police coercion. Nothing the police did in this situation forced Dan to confess, so his statement was voluntary. (As discussed in Choice (C) below, the Supreme Court has held that a suspect's mental illness, standing alone, will not result in a statement being considered involuntary.) Second, the confession must be made in accordance with the decision in *Miranda*, which requires that the suspect be given "*Miranda* warnings" and have validly waived them before he is questioned by law enforcement authorities. A waiver of the Fifth Amendment right against self-incrimination and the Sixth Amendment right to have counsel present at questioning is valid only if it is made "knowingly and intelligently." To meet this standard, the prosecution must show that (1) the suspect knew what his rights were when he waived them, and (2) he understood that he was giving up those rights. "Intelligence," for the purposes of waiver analysis, has nothing to do with whether the suspect was making a wise decision. Dan was given his *Miranda* warnings and signed a written waiver of his rights before confessing. Since there is no evidence that he was coerced into signing the waiver, the waiver was valid and the confession is admissible against him.

(B) is wrong because Dan was in custody when he confessed. A defendant is in custody when police action has restricted his "freedom of action in any significant way." The "reasonable suspect" test is used to determine if a defendant is in custody. The issue is whether a reasonable person in the suspect's position would believe that he would be allowed to leave. Dan had already walked into a police station and announced that he wanted to confess to murder. Since a reasonable person would believe that the police would not let him simply walk out of the station after making such an announcement, Dan was in custody at that point.

(C) is wrong because Dan's mental illness did not render either his confession or his waiver of his *Miranda* rights involuntary. The issue is not whether the decision to confess was rational, but rather whether it was made of Dan's free will. The Supreme Court has held that a mentally ill suspect's decision to confess and waive his *Miranda* rights, no matter how irrational, is voluntary absent police coercion. (*Colorado v. Connelly*, 479 U.S. 157 (1986).)

(D) is wrong because Dan's waiver of his *Miranda* rights was valid. As discussed above, a suspect's mental illness does not render his waiver invalid. Additionally, it should be noted that express, written waivers are almost always valid, absent some evidence of police trickery or coercion.

II. WHAT CONSTITUTES INTERROGATION

A. Volunteered statements

1. Voluntary custodial statements

Question 41: A grand jury indicted Alice on a charge of arson, and a valid warrant was issued for her arrest. Paul, a police officer, arrested Alice and informed her of what the warrant stated. However, hoping that Alice might say something incriminating, he did not give her *Miranda* warnings. He placed her in the back seat of his patrol car and was driving her to the police station when she said, "Look. I didn't mean to burn the building; it was an accident. I was just burning some papers in a wastebasket."

At the station, after being given *Miranda* warnings, Alice stated she wished to remain silent and made no other statements.

Alice moved to suppress the use of her statement to Paul as evidence on two grounds: first, that the statement was acquired without giving *Miranda* warnings, and second, that the police officer had deliberately elicited her incriminating statement after she was in custody.

As to Alice's motion to suppress, the court should

(A) deny the motion.

(B) grant the motion only on the basis of the first ground stated.

(C) grant the motion only on the basis of the second ground stated.

(D) grant the motion on either ground.

[Q1143]

Answer 41: Choice **(A)** is correct. The court should deny Alice's motion to suppress her statement because she wasn't being interrogated when she said it. Alice argues that her statement should be suppressed on two different grounds, so we should examine them separately.

First, Alice claims that because her statement was given before she had been read her *Miranda* warnings, it should not be admissible. Therefore, the question becomes, at what point must a police officer give a suspect *Miranda* warnings? *Miranda* only applies if three requirements have been met: (1) the defendant has been taken into custody, (2) the confession was given in response questioning, and (3) the interrogation was conducted by the police. If all three conditions are met, then any confession may not be admitted unless the police have informed the defendant that she had the right to remain silent, that anything she said could be used against her in a court of law, that she had the right to have an attorney present at questioning, and that if she could not afford an attorney, one would be appointed for her before questioning if she wished. In this case, Alice, having been arrested and put into a police car, was certainly in custody, since a defendant is considered in custody for *Miranda* purposes when a reasonable suspect in her position would not believe she was free to leave. But although Paul believed that Alice might say something incriminating while in the patrol car, he neither said nor did anything to her other than what was required to arrest her and take her into custody. Since, as discussed below, Paul did nothing that was reasonably likely to elicit an incriminating response from Alice, there was no "interrogation" that would trigger Alice's right to be read her *Miranda* warnings.

Second, Alice claims that Paul had deliberately elicited the incriminating statement she made while in the patrol car. The *Miranda* Court specifically said that "volunteered statements of any kind are not barred by the Fifth Amendment and their admissibility is not affected by our holding." The question now becomes what, if anything, did Paul do that would be considered an "interrogation," rendering Alice's statement non-voluntary? The Supreme Court has held that, in addition to direct questioning of a suspect, an interrogation has taken place whenever the police do anything that they should know is reasonably likely to elicit an incriminating response from the suspect. Here, Alice argues that arresting her for arson and putting her in the patrol car was enough to be the functional equivalent of questioning. However, that police conduct was insufficient to constitute interrogation without some further act by Paul, since "officers do not interrogate a suspect simply by hoping that he will incriminate himself." *Arizona v. Mauro* (1987).

Choices (B), (C), and (D) are wrong because they contradict the analysis given above.

B. Police allow situation to develop

1. Police set up situation

Question 42: The police suspected that Yancey, a 16-year-old high school student, had committed a series of burglaries. They arrested Yancey, took him to the station, and gave him Miranda warnings. Yancey asked to see a lawyer. The police called Yancey's parents to the station. When Yancey's parents arrived, the police asked them to speak with Yancey. They put them in a room and secretly recorded their conversation with a concealed electronic device. Yancey broke down and confessed to his parents that he had committed the burglaries.

Yancey was charged with the burglaries. Yancey moves to suppress the use of the statement Yancey made to his parents.

The best argument for excluding it would be

(A) Yancey was in custody at the time the statement was recorded.

(B) the police did not comply with Yancey's request for a lawyer.

(C) once Yancey had invoked his right to counsel, it was improper for the police to listen to any of his private conversations.

(D) the meeting between Yancey and his parents was arranged by the police to obtain an incriminating statement.

[Q2144]

Answer 42: Choice **(D)** is correct. Once Yancey asked for a lawyer, no "interrogation" could occur until the police provided one. Interrogation, for purposes of Miranda, occurs "whenever a person in custody is subjected to either express questioning or its functional equivalent...words or actions on the part of police that the police should know are reasonably likely to elicit an incriminating response from the suspect." *Rhode Island v. Innis* (1980). If the police conduct merely consists of arranging of a situation in which the police believe it likely that the defendant may volunteer an incriminating remark, there is no interrogation, because "officers do not interrogate a suspect simply by hoping that he will incriminate himself." *Arizona v. Mauro* (1987). However, if the arrangement involves sending in a trusted person to speak to the defendant alone and secretly recording the conversation, this would likely constitute interrogation. The police asked Yancey's parents to speak to him and then listened in secretly. This is a situation where the police should know it is reasonably likely that an incriminating remark will be elicited. Therefore, interrogation occurred and the statement should be suppressed because it was obtained in violation of Yancey's *Miranda* rights.

(A) is wrong because, regardless of the fact that Yancey was in custody at the time, it still needs to be established that Yancey was interrogated in order for the statement to be suppressed. This is the case, as discussed in the explanation to Choice (D).

(B) is wrong because the police don't have to provide a lawyer as long as the suspect is not interrogated. The essence of the warning about an attorney is not that a suspect has an automatic right to have the police provide him with a lawyer while they hold him in custody – all the police must do is to choose between providing a lawyer or questioning, so they are always free to defer their questioning until some later date if they can't (or don't want to) provide a lawyer. Therefore, the fact that a lawyer was not procured is not significant by itself. It is significant because, despite the fact that a lawyer was not procured, Yancey was subject to interrogation, as explained in the discussion of Choice D.

(C) is wrong because it is not true that the police may not listen to any of Yancey's private conversations. The argument for exclusion of the statement is based on the fact that Yancey's *Miranda* rights were violated because he was in custody and was subjected to interrogation despite his request for an attorney. The police were permitted to eavesdrop on Yancey's conversations while he was in custody, as long as the statements he made were not in response to interrogation (or the equivalent of interrogation) by them.

CHAPTER 4

LINEUPS AND OTHER PRE-TRIAL IDENTIFICATION PROCEDURES

I. THE PRIVILEGE AGAINST SELF-INCRIMINATION

A. General rule

1. Other procedures

Question 43: A defendant was lawfully arrested without a warrant for bank robbery. He was not given *Miranda* warnings, but was immediately taken to a police station where he and five other men were placed in a lineup to be viewed by the bank teller. Each man was required to say the words spoken by the bank robber: "Give me all your money. I've got a gun." After all the men in the lineup spoke those words, the teller identified the defendant as the robber.

The defendant subsequently moved to suppress the testimony of the teller, claiming the lineup violated his privilege against self-incrimination. At a suppression hearing, the teller testified that she had not gotten a good look at the robber's face, because the robber had been wearing a hat pulled down over most of his face, but that she was certain the defendant was the robber because she had recognized his voice at the lineup.

Should the defendant's motion be granted?

(A) No, because being required to speak at the lineup, while compelled, was not testimonial or communicative.

(B) No, because testimony of a witness based on firsthand observation is not subject to exclusion as the fruit of the poisonous tree.

(C) Yes, because the defendant was compelled to speak at the lineup, and this compelled speech led to the witness's identification testimony.

(D) Yes, because the defendant was never informed that he could refuse to make a statement and that any statement could be used as evidence against him.

[QA002]

Answer 43: Choice **(A)** is correct. The privilege against self-incrimination extends only to compelled "testimonial" communications. Compulsory physical-identification procedures, like being forced to give fingerprints, blood samples, voice prints, and the like, have been held not to be "testimonial," because the accused is not being asked to make statements that have communicative value. See, e.g., *United States v. Hubbell* (2000): "[t]hus, even though the act may provide incriminating evidence, a criminal suspect may be compelled . . . to make a recording of his voice." So here, the defendant could properly be required to utter the words spoken by the bank robber, since those words were being used merely to help the victim identify which of the men in the lineup was the robber, not for the communicative value of the words being spoken.

(B) is wrong because it is both overbroad and not applicable to these facts. Why is it overly broad? There is some testimony based on first-hand observation that *is* subject to exclusion as the fruit of the poisonous tree: if a law enforcement officer gets the opportunity to make a first-hand observation as the direct result of police illegality, then his testimony based on that observation will be excludable as fruit of the poisonous tree. So, for instance, if the officer breaks into D's house without a warrant and without probable cause, and while there secretly listens to D making a confession of crime to D's wife, the officer would not be permitted to testify to what he heard, because his first-hand observation is the fruit of the poisonous tree (the illegal break-in).

Nor is the statement in this choice applicable to these facts — since the teller's testimony here is based on the teller's own first-hand observation, and the teller got that observation without any improper law-enforcement procedures, the principle stated in this choice would not apply even if it was an accurate statement of the law.

(C) is wrong for the same reason that (A) is right: The privilege against self-incrimination extends only to compelled "testimonial" communications, and being compelled to supply a voice sample or other form of physical identification is not testimonial.

(D) is wrong because *Miranda* did not apply to these facts. *Miranda* warnings are designed to protect the suspect's ability to exercise his privilege against self-incrimination. The need to supply *Miranda* warnings is therefore triggered only when the suspect is being subjected to custodial "interrogation," meaning that the suspect in custody is being asked questions in an attempt to elicit communications. When the defendant here was asked to repeat the words from the holdup, he was not being asked to communicate or give " testimonial"-type information, but rather, to supply a form of physical identification. Therefore, *Miranda* warnings were not required.

Question 44: Devlin was charged with murder. Several witnesses testified that the crime was committed by a person of Devlin's general description who walked with a severe limp. Devlin in fact walks with a severe limp. He objected to a prosecution request that the court order him to walk across the courtroom in order to display his limp to the jury to assist it in determining whether Devlin was the person that the witnesses had seen.

Devlin's objection will most likely be

(A) sustained, because the order sought by the prosecution would violate Devlin's privilege against self-incrimination.

(B) sustained, because the order sought by the prosecution would constitute an illegal search and seizure.

(C) denied, because the order sought by the prosecution is a legitimate part of a proper courtroom identification process.

(D) denied, because a criminal defendant has no legitimate expectation of privacy.

[Q2093]

Answer 44: Choice **(C)** is correct. The Fifth Amendment protects only against the compulsion of "communications" or "testimony" (privilege against self-incrimination) and not against "compulsion which makes a suspect or accused the source of 'real or physical evidence'." *Schmerber v. California* (1966). In *U.S. v. Wade* (1967), the Court said that the privilege did not apply to a defendant forced to appear in a lineup and to speak for identification. Similarly, the displaying of a defendant's limp would not be covered by the privilege because it is a legitimate part of a proper courtroom identification process.

(A) is wrong because, as described in the explanation of Choice (C), the privilege against self-incrimination would not apply to these facts.

(B) is wrong because no search or seizure has been conducted under circumstances where the defendant is being asked to do something as part of a proper courtroom identification process.

(D) is wrong because every person has a legitimate expectation of privacy, regardless of one's status as a criminal defendant. In addition, this situation is not one where there has been an invasion of a person's legitimate expectation of privacy — Devlin is not in a place where he has the reasonable expectation of privacy (the courtroom), nor is his affliction a private matter (since it is readily apparent when he walks).

FORMAL PROCEEDINGS

I. GRAND JURY PROCEEDINGS

A. Self-incrimination and immunity

Question 45: A state grand jury investigating a murder learned that the key suspect might have kept a diary. The grand jury issued a subpoena duces tecum requiring the suspect to produce any diary. The subpoena made clear that the grand jury was seeking only the diary and not any testimony from the suspect. The suspect refused to produce the diary, citing the privilege against self-incrimination.

Under what circumstances, if any, could the grand jury compel production of the diary over the suspect's Fifth Amendment privilege?

(A) It may compel production without granting immunity because the suspect was not compelled to write a diary.

(B) It may compel production only if the suspect is granted use and derivative use immunity from the act of production.

(C) It may compel production only if the suspect is granted transactional immunity.

(D) It may not compel production of a private diary under any circumstances.

[QA097]

Answer 45: Choice **(B)** is correct. The confusing thing about this question is that at first glance, the Fifth Amendment privilege against self-incrimination doesn't seem to play any role at all. What the privilege protects against is government's compelling a person to make a testimonial communication, and it's hard to see what testimonial communication is being compelled here. After all, the government didn't compel the suspect to keep a diary (if he indeed kept one). But the Fifth Amendment has *also* been held to protect against orders compelling a person to *produce* (i.e., deliver to the government) a document or other thing, if the act of production would have testimonial significance by, say, *authenticating* the document or thing. So here, the government, by issuing the subpoena, is in effect saying to the suspect, "If you have kept a diary, give us that diary, and we'll know from the fact that you gave it to us that you are conceding that it is indeed something you wrote." So the suspect's mere act of complying with the subpoena would amount to implied testimony that the diary was written by him.

Because of the above analysis, the government may compel production only if it gives the suspect some sort of immunity against the testimonial consequences of being required to produce the diary. Of the two sorts of immunity — transactional and use — mere use immunity, the narrower of the two, suffices for Fifth Amendment purposes. So here, as this choice indicates, the government would have to give "use and derivative use immunity from the act of production"; what this means is that the diary would be admissible, but only as long as the government had some other, wholly-independent, way to prove to the jury that this was a diary kept by the suspect. For instance, the prosecution might have a friend or relative of the suspect testify that she saw the suspect keep a diary with a cover that matches this one, and/or that the witness now recognizes the handwriting as belonging to the suspect — that way, the government would not be relying in any way on the suspect's act of turning over this particular diary in order to show that the diary was kept by the suspect.

(A) is wrong because it ignores the problem that if the suspect complies by producing his diary, this mere act of production will itself tend to authenticate the diary, and thus be implicitly testimonial. See Choice (B) for more about this problem.

(C) is wrong because use immunity is enough to protect against violations of the Fifth Amendment. It's true that transactional immunity (which in this case would mean that the suspect would not be prosecuted for any crime described in the diary) would also suffice to avoid the Fifth Amendment problem. But that sort of immunity is overkill — it's more than the Constitution requires. As is further explained in Choice (B), the less-broad "use immunity" would be enough. Use immunity in this case would mean that the government must prove the diary's authenticity (i.e., that it was written by the suspect) by means wholly unconnected to the fact that the suspect produced it in response to the subpoena.

(D) is wrong because the suspect's limited privilege against self-incrimination here (the privilege not to have his act of producing the diary in response to the subpoena be used as proof of the diary's authenticity) is adequately protected by either use immunity or transactional immunity. See the analysis in Choice (B) for more about this. So the government *can* compel the production of this private diary.

B. No right to have attorney present in grand jury room

Question 46: A federal grand jury was investigating drug trafficking in the jurisdiction. It subpoenaed a witness to testify, and the prosecutor advised the witness that he had a Fifth Amendment privilege not to testify if he so chose. The witness asked that his counsel be allowed to advise him inside the grand jury room, but the prosecutor refused to allow the attorney inside. The witness, after speaking with his attorney outside the grand jury room, decided to testify and ended up making self-incriminating statements.

The witness subsequently was indicted for drug crimes. The indictment was based on the witness's grand jury testimony and on evidence seized in an unconstitutional search of the witness's home.

The witness moved to dismiss the indictment.

Should the court dismiss the indictment?

(A) Yes, because the witness was denied his constitutional right to advice of counsel.

(B) Yes, because the indictment was based upon illegally seized evidence.

(C) No, because the witness waived his constitutional rights by testifying.

(D) No, because the witness had no right to counsel inside the grand jury room and the illegally seized evidence did not affect the validity of the indictment.

[QA023]

Answer 46: Choice **(D)** is correct. First, a grand jury witness does not have a constitutional right to counsel inside a grand jury room. *U.S. v. Mandujano* (1976). Second, the Fourth Amendment exclusionary rule does not apply to the presentation of evidence before a federal grand jury. Therefore, such a grand jury can properly issue an indictment based on illegally-obtained evidence. *U.S. v. Calandra* (1974).

(A) is wrong because a grand jury witness does not have a constitutional right to counsel inside a grand jury room. And that is true even if the lawyer is "retained" rather than court-appointed. *U.S. v. Mandujano* (1976). (By the way, it's not even clear that the prosecutor was constitutionally required to let the witness leave the grand jury room to consult his lawyer, as the prosecutor did here.)

(B) is wrong because the Fourth Amendment exclusionary rule does not apply to the presentation of evidence before a federal grand jury. See the discussion of this issue in the analysis of Choice (D).

(C) is wrong because although it reaches the right outcome, it does so on reasoning that is less good than the reasoning in Choice (D). It's certainly the case that the witness indeed had a Fifth Amendment right to decline to testify, and that the witness waived that right by testifying voluntarily after learning that he had the right. (His having consulted with his lawyer outside the jury room further reinforces the idea that he voluntarily waived his right not to testify.) But this waiver does not really explain why the court will refuse to dismiss the indictment. That's because the indictment was based not only on the testimony but also on the evidence from the unconstitutional search, and even unconstitutionally-obtained evidence can be considered by a grand jury in reaching its decision to indict. (See Choice (D) for more about this.) In other words, even if the witness had not waived his right not to testify, the indictment would likely have been issued anyway, and properly so. Therefore, any waiver by the witness is not the best explanation of why the court refused to dismiss the indictment.

C. Use of illegally obtained evidence

1. MBE tip

Question 47: Suspecting that Scott had slain his wife, police detectives persuaded one of Scott's employees to remove a drinking glass from Scott's office so that it could be used for fingerprint comparisons with a knife found near the body. The fingerprints matched. The prosecutor announced that he would present comparisons and evidence to the grand jury. Scott's lawyer immediately filed a motion to suppress the evidence of the fingerprint comparisons to bar its consideration by the grand jury, contending that the evidence was illegally acquired.

The motion should be

(A) granted, because, if there was no probable cause, the grand jury should not consider the evidence.

(B) granted, because the employee was acting as a police agent and his seizure of the glass without a warrant was unconstitutional.

(C) denied, because motions based on the exclusionary rule are premature in grand jury proceedings.

(D) denied, because the glass was removed from Scott's possession by a private citizen and not a police officer.

[Q1067]

Answer 47: Choice **(C)** is correct. A grand jury may hear and use *any* piece of evidence regardless of its admissibility, including hearsay and illegally-obtained evidence. Therefore, there are no grounds to seek the suppression of any particular piece of evidence by a grand jury, and the filing of a motion to suppress before the grand jury proceeding was premature.

(A) is wrong because it misstates the law and does not address the relevant issue. During its deliberations, the grand jury may review *all* evidence available to it to determine whether there is sufficient evidence to justify a trial. In particular, the fact that the police's seizure of the glass may have been illegal (which it would have been if the police had not had probable cause and/or had not gotten a search warrant) would not matter, because even illegally-seized evidence may be considered by the grand jury, as discussed in Choice (C) above.

(B) is wrong because even if the seizure was unconstitutional, the grand jury was entitled to consider the evidence. By the way, on the underlying merits it probably *is* the case that: (1) the employee was acting as a police agent (he was doing what they requested him to do); (2) Scott probably had a reasonable expectation privacy in the glass located in his office (at least if it was his private office, rather than a part of the office space that he shared with employees); and (3) whether or not the police had probable cause to suspect Scott, they were required to get a search warrant before seizing an item as to which he had a reasonable expectation of privacy. But none of this matters here, because even if the seizure was a violation of Scott's Fourth Amendment rights, the grand jury was still entitled to consider the seized item, as described in the discussion of Choice (C) above.

(D) is wrong because it arrives at the correct result, but for the wrong reason. The reason the motion should be denied is because it was filed at the wrong time. Whether or not the employee was considered a private citizen when he obtained the drinking glass will become relevant only when a motion is properly made at a later point. (However, it is likely that in a pre-*trial* suppression hearing, a court would conclude that the employee *was* acting as a government agent, in which case the evidence would be inadmissible at trial since it was obtained without a search warrant, and its seizure therefore violated Scott's Fourth Amendment rights.)

II. THE TRIAL

A. Burden of proof in criminal cases

1. General rules of allocation

a. Elements

i. "Beyond a reasonable doubt" standard

Question 48: A state statute provides as follows: "In all criminal cases, whenever the Constitution permits, the burden of proof as to a defense claimed by the defendant shall rest on the defendant, and the magnitude of the burden shall be as great as the Constitution permits."

The same state defines the crime of forcible rape as follows: "Forcible rape consists of sexual penetration inflicted on an unconsenting person by means of force or violence. Consent of the victim is a complete defense to a charge of rape."

At a defendant's trial for forcible rape, he testified that the alleged victim had consented to having sexual intercourse with him.

How should the trial judge instruct the jury regarding the issue of consent?

(A) The burden of proving that the victim consented, by a preponderance of the evidence, rests on the defendant.

(B) The burden of proving that the victim consented, by clear and convincing evidence, rests on the defendant.

(C) The burden of proving that the victim consented, by proof beyond a reasonable doubt, rests on the defendant.

(D) The burden of proving that the victim did not consent, by proof beyond a reasonable doubt, rests on the prosecution.

[QA012]

Answer 48: Choice **(D)** is correct. The state statute includes lack of consent as an element of the offense. (We know that because the statute defines forcible rape as penetration inflicted on an "unconsenting person.") Therefore, constitutional due process requires the state to prove that element (and *every* element) of the crime beyond a reasonable doubt. *Patterson v. New York* (1977). What makes this question mildly confusing is that the statute also says "Consent of the victim is a complete defense to a charge of rape" — this might lead you to believe that the victim's consent is an affirmative defense. (The defendant may be constitutionally required to bear both the burden of production and the burden of persuasion with respect to an affirmative defense.) But once the state defined lack of consent as an element of the crime, as it did here, the state was no longer free to classify lack of consent as an affirmative defense, if the consequence of that classification was to impose on the defendant either the burden of coming forward with some evidence of lack of consent, or the burden of persuading the jury that the victim consented.

(A), (B), and (C) are all wrong because they are inconsistent with the principle — correctly expressed in (D) — that the prosecution bears the burden of proving lack of consent because the crime is defined so as to make lack of consent an element rather than an affirmative defense.

B. Motion for directed verdict

1. Standard

a. Not enough for dismissal

Question 49: State Y employs the Model Penal Code or American Law Institute test for insanity, and requires the state to prove sanity, when it is in issue, beyond a reasonable doubt. At Askew's trial for murder, he pleaded insanity. The state put on an expert psychiatrist who had examined Askew. He testified that, in his opinion, Askew was sane at the time of the murder. Askew's attorney did not introduce expert testimony on the question of sanity. Rather, he presented lay witnesses who testified that, in their opinion, Askew was insane at the time of the murder. At the end of the trial, each side moves for a directed verdict on the question of sanity.

Which of the following correctly describes the judge's situation?

(A) She may grant a directed verdict for the defense if she believes that the jury could not find the prosecution to have proved sanity beyond a reasonable doubt.

(B) She may grant a directed verdict for the prosecution if she believes that Askew's witnesses on the insanity question are not believable.

(C) She may not grant a directed verdict for the defense, because the state had expert testimony and the defense only lay witnesses.

(D) She may grant a directed verdict for the prosecution if she is convinced by their experts that Askew was sane beyond a reasonable doubt.

[Q2127]

Answer 49: Choice **(A)** is correct. When an insanity defense is raised, if the case is tried before a jury, the jury will have the task of deciding the merits of the defendant's insanity defense, just as it will decide the other factual issues in the case. Here, where the state must prove sanity beyond a reasonable doubt, a verdict should be granted for the defense if and only if the judge believes that a reasonable jury could not find the prosecution to have proved sanity beyond a reasonable doubt.

(B) is wrong because the judge's determination of the credibility of the witnesses is not relevant. It is up to the jury to determine the credibility of the witnesses and to decide the factual issue of sanity. In fact, granting a directed verdict for the prosecution on any element of the case would deprive defendant of his constitutional Sixth Amendment right to a jury trial.

(C) is wrong because the jury need not weigh an expert witness's testimony more heavily than that of a lay witness. The jury is always free to disregard or disbelieve any witness's evaluation of the defendant's condition.

(D) is wrong because the determination is made by the jury. In order to grant a directed verdict in favor of the prosecution, it is not necessary that the judge be convinced that Askew was sane, only that a jury could be convinced of Askew's sanity (beyond a reasonable doubt).

C. D's Confrontation Clause rights

1. Confession implicating someone else, used during joint trial

Question 50: Smith and Penn were charged with murder. Each gave a confession to the police that implicated both of them. Smith later retracted her confession, claiming that it was coerced.

Smith and Penn were tried together. The prosecutor offered both confessions into evidence. Smith and Penn objected. After a hearing, the trial judge found that both confessions were voluntary and admitted both into evidence. Smith testified at trial. She denied any involvement in the crime and claimed that her confession was false and the result of coercion. Both defendants were convicted.

On appeal, Smith contends her conviction should be reversed because of the admission into evidence of Penn's confession.

Smith's contention is

(A correct, unless Penn testified at trial.

(B) correct, whether or not Penn testified at trial.

(C) incorrect, because Smith testified in her own behalf.

(D) incorrect, because Smith's own confession was properly admitted into evidence.

[Q2060]

Answer 50: Choice **(A)** is correct. The Sixth Amendment gives any criminal defendant "the right…to be confronted with the witnesses against him." The Confrontation Clause has two main components (1) the right to compulsory process; and (2) the right to cross examine hostile witnesses. The Confrontation Clause prevents, in some circumstances, the use of one person's out-of-court confession against another. The Supreme Court has held that *A*'s Confrontation Clause rights are violated if the confession of *B*, his non-testifying co-defendant, naming *A* as a co-participant in the crime, is introduced at their joint trial. This is true even if the jury is instructed to consider the confession only against *B*, not *A*. *Bruton v. U.S.* (1968). The *Bruton* principle applies where the defendant who allegedly confessed declines to take the stand. If the confessor takes the stand and denies having made the confession – and perhaps even if he takes the stand and acknowledges the confession, but then opens himself up to the other defendant's cross-examination about it – there is probably no Confrontation Clause problem. Therefore, if and only if Penn testified at trial, Smith's appeal would be denied because his Confrontation Clause rights would not have been denied.

(B) is wrong because whether or not Smith's Confrontation Clause rights were denied does depend upon whether or not Penn testified. If Penn testified, then Smith's rights would not have been violated, as discussed in the explanation of Choice (A).

(C) is wrong because whether or not *Smith* testified is irrelevant. Smith's Confrontation Clause rights give him the right to cross examine hostile witnesses. Therefore, it is relevant whether or not *Penn* testifies, as he is a hostile witness that Smith has a right to cross examine.

(D) is wrong because the fact that Smith's confession was properly admitted has no bearing on whether his Confrontation Clause rights have been violated by admission of a co-defendant's confession. He is afforded the right to cross examine hostile witnesses, a right which has been denied to him in these circumstances.

III. DOUBLE JEOPARDY

A. Overlapping offenses

1. Lesser included offense tried first

a. Felony-murder scenario on MBE

Question 51: Donald was arrested in Marilyn's apartment after her neighbors had reported sounds of a struggle and the police had arrived to find Donald bent over Marilyn's prostrate body. Marilyn was rushed to the hospital where she lapsed into a coma. Despite the explanation that he was trying to revive Marilyn after she suddenly collapsed, Donald was charged with attempted rape and assault after a neighbor informed the police that she had heard Marilyn sobbing, "No, please no, let me alone."

At trial, the forensic evidence was inconclusive. The jury acquitted Donald of attempted rape but convicted him of assault. While he was serving his sentence for assault, Marilyn, who had never recovered from the coma, died. Donald was then indicted and tried on a charge of felony murder. In this common-law jurisdiction, there is no statute that prevents a prosecutor from proceeding in this manner, but Donald argued that a second trial for felony murder after his original thai for attempted rape and assault would violate the double jeopardy clause.

His claim is

(A) correct, because he was acquitted of the attempted rape charge.

(B) correct, because he was convicted of the assault charge.

(C) incorrect, because Marilyn had not died at the time of the first trial and he was not placed in jeopardy for murder.

(D) incorrect, because he was convicted of the assault charge.

[Q2091]

Answer 51: Choice **(A)** is correct. When a person is tried for offense *A*, then whether he is convicted or acquitted, the double jeopardy clause prevents him from being later tried of an offense B of which offense *A* was a lesser-included offense. So Donald can base his double jeopardy claim on, and only on, an offense that was a lesser-included-offense within the felony-murder charge. Courts and legislatures generally restrict application of the felony-murder doctrine to certain dangerous felonies. The doctrine does apply to rape (a crime of which Donald was acquitted), but generally does not apply to assault (a crime of which Donald was convicted). So the acquittal on the rape charge triggers double jeopardy, but the conviction on the assault charge does not.

(B) and (D) are wrong because generally, the felony-murder doctrine does not apply to assault. Therefore, the assault charge could not be a lesser-included-offense within the felony-murder charge, making the assault charge irrelevant for double jeopardy purposes.

(C) is wrong because it overlooks the fact that an acquittal on lesser-included-offense A will block a trial for greater-offense-B. Therefore, even though Donald couldn't have yet been prosecuted for felony-murder at the time his rape trial started (because Marilyn was still alive), the rape trial invoked Donald's double jeopardy rights. (If Donald had been *convicted* at the rape trial, the fact that the felony-murder charge couldn't have been tried yet would negate his double jeopardy claim; but given that the rape trial led to his acquittal, the fact that the felony-murder charge couldn't have been tried when the rape trial started probably *won't* negate Donald's use of double jeopardy.)

EVIDENCE

EVIDENCE Q&A BY TOPIC

All answers assume that the Federal Rules of Evidence ("FRE") are in force as to all issues. "ACN" refers to "Advisory Committee Notes" to a particular Federal Rule of Evidence. "M&K" refers to Mueller & Kirkpatrick, *Evidence* Hornbook (Aspen, 3d Ed., 2003).

CHAPTER 1
BASIC CONCEPTS

I. CONDITIONS FOR ADMITTING EVIDENCE

A. Relevant

1. Definition

Question 1: In a prosecution for aggravated battery, a police officer testified that when he arrested the defendant, he took a knife from the defendant and delivered it to the medical examiner. The medical examiner testified that the knife blade was consistent with the victim's wound but admitted on cross-examination that any number of other knives could also have caused the wound.

Should the judge grant a motion to strike the medical examiner's testimony?

(A) No, because the probative worth of this evidence is for the jury to assess.

(B) Yes, because in light of the medical examiner's admission, his testimony has insufficient probative value.

(C) Yes, because the medical examiner could not state the probability that the wound was caused by the defendant's knife.

(D) Yes, because the probative value is substantially outweighed by the danger of unfair prejudice.

[QA074]

Answer 1: Choice **(A)** is correct. This evidence has some probative value, because it links the knife in defendant's possession to the type of knife that could have caused the victim's wound. The evidence is not very strong, because other knives could also have caused the wound. But how much weight to give to the evidence is a decision for the jury. FRE 401 requires only that evidence have "any tendency to make the existence of any fact that is of consequence to the determination of the action more probable or less probable than it would be without the evidence." Thus to be relevant, evidence need only have *some* probative value in establishing a fact. The Advisory Committee's Note to Rule 401 quotes the famous statement "A brick is not a wall," making the point that evidence is admissible even if it is only a single brick that is a part of a large wall of evidence establishing a party's case.

(B) is wrong because evidence meets the relevancy requirement of FRE 401 if it has "any tendency to make the existence of any fact that is of consequence to the determination of the action more probable or less probable than it would be without the evidence." The medical examiner's testimony meets this minimal standard of probativity. And it is probative of a material fact — whether this knife was the crime weapon.

(C) is wrong because no statement of probability is required for admissibility. The medical examiner's testimony does not have to establish that defendant's knife caused the wound by any particular standard of proof, such as beyond a reasonable doubt, by clear and convincing evidence, or by a preponderance of the evidence — it's up to the jury to assess the value of the evidence in determining guilt. The testimony only needs to have some unspecified-but-minimal probative value to be admissible. That's shown by FRE 401, under which evidence is deemed to have probative value, and to be admissible (assuming it doesn't violate some other specific prohibition), if it has "any tendency to make the existence of any fact that is of consequence to the determination of the action more probable or less probable than it would be without the evidence."

(D) is wrong because it mischaracterizes the evidence here. It's true that FRE 403 requires a weighing of probative value against unfair prejudice, as this choice suggests. That rule establishes what might be described as a presumption of admissibility: evidence meeting Rule 401's definition of relevance is admissible unless its probative value is "*substantially* outweighed" by the danger of unfair prejudice. Here, the medical examiner's testimony does not appear to pose *any* significant degree of unfair prejudice, let alone enough to "substantially outweigh" the probative value of that testimony.

Question 2: A defendant's house was destroyed by fire and she was charged with arson. To prove that the defendant had a motive to burn down her house, the government offered evidence that the defendant had fully insured the house and its contents.

Should the court admit this evidence?

(A) No, because the probative value of the evidence of insurance upon the issue of whether the defendant intentionally burned her house down is substantially outweighed by the dangers of unfair prejudice and confusion of the jury.

(B) No, because evidence of insurance is not admissible upon the issue of whether the insured acted wrongfully.

(C) Yes, because evidence of insurance on the house has a tendency to show that the defendant had a motive to burn down the house.

(D) Yes, because any conduct of a party to the case is admissible when offered against the party.

[QA018]

Answer 2: Choice **(C)** is correct. This is a relevance problem. The main issue is whether the evidence meets the general relevance standard of FRE 401. Under that rule, evidence need only have "any tendency to make the existence of a fact that is of consequence to the determination of the action more probable or less probable than it would be without the evidence." Thus, evidence that has only the slightest probative value can be admitted under this rule. While evidence that the property is insured is not conclusive that the defendant committed arson (many people fully insure their houses), it is relevant to the issue of whether the defendant would have had a financial incentive or motive to commit the arson — the defendant might be able to generate cash more quickly by burning down the house and collecting insurance proceeds than by attempting to sell the house. This evidence meets the minimal probativity standard of FRE 401. (There is a special rule concerning the admissibility of evidence of insurance, but that rule doesn't bar the evidence here; see the discussion of Choice (B) for more about this.)

(A) is wrong because although the probative value of this evidence on the issue of whether defendant intentionally burned her house down is not particularly strong, it is somewhat probative of the issue of possible motive, so it meets the easy-to-satisfy probativity standard of FRE 401 (quoted in the discussion of Choice (C) above). FRE 403 provides that relevant evidence should be admitted unless its probative value is "substantially outweighed" by the dangers of unfair prejudice, confusion, or waste of time. Here, the evidence of insurance is probably not unfairly prejudicial at all (in the sense that it does not have an undue tendency to produce decision on an improper basis such as emotion); in any event, whatever small prejudicial tendency the evidence might have is certainly not enough to "substantially outweigh" the probative value of the evidence.

(B) is wrong because, although it is true that FRE 411 bars evidence of insurance to establish that the insured acted negligently or otherwise wrongfully, such evidence is admissible for *other purposes*, and proof of motive is such a purpose. (In this respect, Rule 411 is similar to Rule 404(b), under which evidence of past conduct cannot be admitted to prove a propensity to engage in such conduct but can be admitted for other purposes, such as to prove motive.)

(D) is wrong because there is no such broad rule that any conduct of a party may be admitted against that party.

2. Exclusion

Question 3: Deeb was charged with stealing furs from a van. At trial, Wallace testified she saw Deeb take the furs.

The jurisdiction in which Deeb is being tried does not allow in evidence lie detector results. On cross-examination by Deeb's attorney. Wallace was asked, "The light was too dim to identify Deeb, wasn't it?" She responded. "I'm sure enough that it was Deeb that I passed a lie detector test administered by the police." Deeb's attorney immediately objects and moves to strike.

The trial court should

(A) grant the motion, because the question was leading.

(B) grant the motion, because the probative value of the unresponsive testimony is substantially outweighed by the danger of unfair prejudice.

(C) deny the motion, because it is proper rehabilitation of an impeached witness.

(D) deny the motion, because Deeb's attorney "opened the door" by asking the question.

[Q1031]

Answer 3: Choice **(B)** is correct. FRE 403 provides: "Although relevant, evidence may be excluded if its probative value is substantially outweighed by the danger of unfair prejudice..." The fact pattern tells us that the jurisdiction excludes evidence of lie detector results, indicating that the jurisdiction questions the reliability of the test and considers evidence of the test results to be of low probative value. "Unfair" prejudice...means "an undue tendency to suggest decision on an improper basis..." Advisory Committee Note to FRE 403. It is reasonable to assume that some members of a jury may regard the results of a lie detector test as more scientific than they actually are, and consequently give the test too much weight. Therefore, in this jurisdiction, the danger of unfair prejudice would substantially outweigh the (low) probative value of the lie detector test.

(A) is wrong because, although the motion would be granted, it would not be for the stated reason. Leading questions are generally permissible on cross examination. FRE 611(c).

(C) is wrong because, even apart from the FRE 403 problem discussed in Choice (B), the reasoning supporting this answer mischaracterizes the concept of "rehabilitation." Once a witness has been impeached, rehabilitation is brought out through separate testimony that is offered by counsel representing the party who is a proponent of the impeached witness's testimony. It is incorrect to characterize the witness's own response to opposing counsel's "impeaching" question as "rehabilitation" of that witness's credibility.

(D) is wrong because (1) the motion would be granted for the reason discussed in Choice (B); and (2) the reasoning supporting this answer misapplies the concept of "opening the door." A topic which is otherwise off-limits to an opposing party is considered "opened for questioning" once it has been introduced by the other party — the rationale is that if the topic has been "opened" by one party it would be unfair to prohibit the opposing party from addressing it. In this case, the question "The light was too dim to identify Deeb, wasn't it?" is not even arguably related to the topic of Wallace's passing a lie detector test, so there is no unfairness in not allowing Wallace to talk about the lie detector test.

B. Offering testimonial evidence

1. Testimony by trial judge

Question 4: A defendant was charged with murder. While walking down the hallway during a recess in the defendant's trial, the judge overheard the defendant say to his attorney, "So what if I did it? There's not enough proof to convict." Upon the judge's reporting the incident to counsel, the prosecutor called the judge as a witness in the trial.

Is the judge's testimony regarding the defendant's statement admissible?

(A) Yes, as the statement of a party-opponent.

(B) Yes, because the defendant's statement, although otherwise privileged, was made without reasonable efforts to preserve confidentiality.

(C) No, because the statement was a privileged attorney-client communication.

(D) No, because a judge may never testify in a trial over which he or she is presiding.

[QA015]

Answer 4: Choice **(D)** is correct. Although the judge is being asked to recount an out-of-court statement made by a party that is offered against that party, admissibility here does not turn on the hearsay rule. Regardless of whether the evidence is admissible under the hearsay rule, FRE 605 provides that a "judge presiding at the trial may not testify in that trial as a witness." Thus, the judge cannot offer any testimony of any kind, no matter how probative and important his testimony.

(A) is wrong because even though the statement is the admission of a party-opponent and would be otherwise admissible non-hearsay under Rule FRE 801(d)(2)(A), FRE 605 says that the presiding judge cannot be called as a witness to testify about anything.

(B) is wrong because, although it is true that reasonable efforts were not made by the defendant and his attorney to preserve confidentiality, this means only that the communication was not privileged — it does not mean the statement is necessarily admissible. The problem here is that under FRE 605, the statement cannot be proven through the testimony of the presiding judge because that rule bars the presiding judge from offering any testimony of any kind. The defendant's lack of efforts to preserve confidentiality mean that the statement probably *would* be admissible if someone other than the presiding judge had heard it and been asked to testify about it.

(C) is wrong because, although it reaches the right outcome, it uses incorrect reasoning. The statement would *not* be privileged. That's because reasonable efforts were not made by the defendant and his attorney to preserve confidentiality, since the statement was made in a hallway open to the public in a voice loud enough to be overheard.

C. Making and responding to objections

1. Hearing outside of presence of jury

Question 5: A defendant was on trial for burglary. The prosecutor called the arresting officer to testify that shortly after the arrest the defendant had orally admitted her guilt to him. Before the officer testified, the defendant objected that no *Miranda* warning had been given, and she requested a hearing outside the presence of the jury to hear evidence on that issue.

How should the court proceed?

(A) The court should grant the request, because the hearing on the admissibility of the confession must be conducted outside the presence of the jury.

(B) The court may grant or deny the request, because the court has discretion whether to conduct preliminary hearings in the presence of the jury.

(C) The court should deny the request and rule the confession inadmissible, because only signed confessions are permitted in criminal cases.

(D) The court should deny the request and rule the confession admissible, because it is the statement of a party-opponent.

[QA010]

Answer 5: Choice **(A)** is correct. The admissibility of the officer's testimony turns on two issues: (1) whether a *Miranda* warning had to be given to the defendant before his confession can be admitted; and (2) whether the judge's determination of the first issue must be preceded by a hearing conducted in front of or outside the hearing of the jury. With respect to the first question, *Miranda* warnings must be given before a confession made by a person under arrest can be admitted. Since the defendant contends that no *Miranda* warnings were given, she is entitled to a hearing on the issue. The rule resolving the second question is contained in the first sentence of FRE 104(c), which says that "Hearings on the admissibility of confessions shall *in all cases* be conducted outside of the hearing of the jury." (Note that this provision goes on to say that hearings on all *other* preliminary matters shall be conducted outside the presence of the jury *only* when either justice requires or when a criminal defendant is a witness and requests a hearing outside of the jury's presence.) Thus under FRE 104(c), the hearing must be conducted outside the presence of the jury.

(B) is wrong because FRE 104(c) mandates that the admissibility of confessions "shall" be conducted out of the hearing of the jury. So the trial court has no discretion in this matter.

(C) is wrong because oral confessions, like signed written confessions, are admissible in criminal cases, assuming that any required *Miranda* warnings were given.

(D) is wrong because it ignores the effect of *Miranda*. It's true that a confession of a criminal defendant is an out-of-court statement made by a party-opponent, which makes it non-hearsay under FRE 801(d)(2)(A) and thus admissible — as a matter of evidence law — to prove the truth of the matter asserted within that statement. But the rules of evidence cannot alter the *constitutional* requirement that *Miranda* warnings must be given before a confession made by a person under arrest is admissible.

CHAPTER 2

CIRCUMSTANTIAL PROOF: SPECIAL PROBLEMS

I. CHARACTER EVIDENCE

A. Character is essential element of case

1. Other aspects of other-crimes evidence

a. Rule 403 balancing

Question 6: Decker, charged with armed robbery of a store, denied that he was the person who had robbed the store.

In presenting the state's ease, the prosecutor seeks to introduce evidence that Decker had robbed two other stores in the past year.

This evidence is

(A) admissible, to prove a pertinent trait of Decker's character and Decker's action in conformity therewith.

(B) admissible, to prove Decker's intent and identity.

(C) inadmissible, because character must be proved by reputation or opinion and may not be proved by specific acts.

(D) inadmissible, because its probative value is substantially outweighed by the danger of unfair prejudice.

[Q1062]

Answer 6: Choice **(D)** is correct. Although evidence of Decker's previous two robberies may arguably be relevant as to whether Decker robbed the store in the present case, its probative value is low and dwarfed by the prejudicial value of the evidence. FRE 403 says that "Although relevant, evidence may be excluded if its probative value is substantially outweighed by the danger of unfair prejudice…" "Unfair" prejudice means "an undue tendency to suggest decision on an improper basis..." ACN to FRE 403. The probative value of the evidence is pretty low, since the other acts don't bear very strongly on whether Decker is the robber in the present case (there's no indication that the m.o.'s are all that similar, for instance — see Choice (B) below). Conversely, there's a large risk that if the evidence were admitted, some members of the jury would likely regard it as more probative than it actually is, and consequently give the evidence too much weight.

(A) is wrong because the general rule is that "evidence of a person's character or a trait of character is not admissible for the purpose of proving action in conformity therewith on a particular occasion." FRE 404(a). There are some exceptions, but none applies here. This choice asserts a rule — admissibility of character-trait evidence to prove action in conformity with the trait on the present occasion — that is the exact opposite of the real rule of 404(a).

(B) is wrong for two reasons. First, the previous robberies are probably not sufficiently probative of Decker's identity or his intent (the latter isn't even an issue in this case). It's true that evidence of other acts may be admissible for purposes other than to show action in conformity with a person's character, and that two of these acceptable purposes are to prove identity and intent. FRE 404(b). But generally, when other acts are offered to prove identity, the prosecution's theory is that the other acts by the accused are so similar in method to the crime charged that all bear his "signature" (thus justifying the inference that if the defendant committed the prior acts, he also must have committed the present one). Here, the other robberies aren't similar enough to meet this "signature" standard.

Secondly, this evidence poses an extremely high risk of prejudice, far outweighing its limited probative value, and is thus excludible under FRE 403 (see the discussion of Choice (D) above).

(C) is wrong because (1) it at least slightly misstates the law; and (2) more importantly, it gives an explanation that is inapplicable here. While it's true that in general, character or a trait of character must be proved by reputation or opinion evidence, not specific-acts evidence (FRE 405(a)), there are some scenarios in which specific-acts evidence *is* admissible (e.g., where a character trait is an "essential element of a charge, claim or defense" — see FRE 405(b)). But the bigger problem is that what the prosecution is offering here is not, strictly speaking, character evidence — the prosecution is not offering the evidence to show that Decker has a character or tendency to commit robbery; rather, it's trying to qualify for one or more of the "other purposes than character" exceptions mentioned by 404(b), e.g. identity.

II. METHODS OF PROVING CHARACTER: REPUTATION, OPINION, AND PROOF OF SPECIFIC ACTS

A. FRE

1. D's good-character evidence

a. Rebuttal

Question 7: The defendant was charged with the crime of assaulting the victim. He admitted striking the victim, but claimed to have acted in self-defense when he was attacked by the victim, who was drunk and belligerent after a football game.

The defendant offered testimony of defendant's employer that he had known and employed the defendant for twelve years and knew the defendant's reputation among the people with whom he lived and worked to be that of a peaceful, law-abiding, nonviolent person. The trial judge admitted this testimony.

On cross-examination of the employer, the state's attorney asked the employer if he had heard that the defendant often engaged in fights and brawls. The trial judge should rule the question

(A) admissible, because evidence of the defendant's previous fights and brawls may be used to prove his guilt.

(B) admissible, because it tests the employer's knowledge of the defendant's reputation.

(C) inadmissible, because it seeks to put into evidence separate, unrelated offenses.

(D) inadmissible, because no specific time or incidents are specified and inquired about.

[Q4026]

Answer 7: Choice **(B)** is correct. The evidence will be admissible to impeach the employer as a reputation witness. The problem here is that the evidence the prosecutor is seeking is character evidence. Choice (B) offers a way to overcome this problem. Under these facts, the employer is testifying as a reputation witness on the defendant's behalf; that is, he's testifying that the defendant is known as a peaceful, nonviolent person. This evidence is admissible under FRE 404(1), which allows an accused to offer evidence of his own "pertinent trait of character." Then, FRE 405(a) says that where evidence of a "trait of character of a person is admissible" (which the evidence here is, as described in the prior sentence), "On cross-examination, inquiry is allowable into relevant specific instances of conduct." So once the employer gave the testimony favorable to the defendant about the defendant's peaceable reputation, the prosecution was entitled to make "inquiry ... into relevant specific instances of conduct." The specific instances being inquired about (frequent engaging in fights and brawls) are "relevant," because if the employer didn't know about these instances, his testimony about the defendant's reputation for peaceability would be of questionable accuracy. (If the employer didn't know these true facts, is he really knowledgeable about the defendant's reputation on this subject?)

(A) is wrong because it is unduly broad. Since the defendant offered favorable reputation evidence of his peaceability as he was permitted to do under 404(a)(1), the prosecution was permitted to rebut that evidence. The rebuttal evidence was in fact substantively admissible to prove that the defendant was not peaceable, and therefore probably wasn't acting in self-defense. However, this choice suggests that independent (extrinsic) evidence of the fights would have been admissible. In fact, only questioning of the defendant's character witness (the employer) was permissible, on account of FRE 405(a) — the prosecution couldn't have introduced extrinsic proof of the defendant's previous fights (e.g., by testimony from a different witness who observed them), and his choice falsely implies that such evidence could have been admitted.

(C) is wrong because it fails to identify that the evidence can be brought out on the cross of the employer, as further discussed in Choice (B).

(D) is wrong because, while impeachment of a reputation witness with specific instances is possible, the specific instances need not be identified as precisely as (D) suggests. Under FRE 404(a) a reputation witness (of which the employer is one) may be questioned about specific instances bearing on the reputation, since *not* knowing such information reflects on the witness's *competence* to testify as to the person's reputation in the community. However, the testimony here is specific enough to constitute specific acts; it clearly does not amount to opinion or reputation testimony.

III. SETTLEMENTS AND PLEA BARGAINS

A. Settlements

Question 8: Carr, a driver, ran into and injured Pedersen, a pedestrian. Pedersen has sued Carr, alleging that Carr, while drunk, struck Pedersen who was in a duly marked crosswalk. Pedersen's counsel wishes to prove that after the accident Carr went to Pedersen and offered $1,000 to settle Pedersen's claim.

The trial judge should rule this evidence

(A) admissible as an admission of a party.

(B) admissible as an admission to show Carr's liability, provided the court gives a cautionary instruction that the statement should not be considered as bearing on the issue of damages.

(C) inadmissible since it is not relevant either to the question of liability or the question of damages.

(D) inadmissible because even though it is relevant and an admission, the policy of the law is to encourage settlement negotiations.

[Q4029]

Answer 8: Choice **(D)** is correct. This choice correctly characterizes the statement as relevant and an admission, and correctly concludes that the evidence will be inadmissible due to public policy considerations. What's being proffered is a settlement offer by Carr. But under FRE 408, admissions in conjunction with settlement negotiations are inadmissible to prove negligence, liability, or a claim's value. That's the case here.

(A) is wrong because FRE 408 says that statements in conjunction with settlement offers are inadmissible to prove negligence, liability, or a claim's value. So even though Carr's statement would otherwise be admissible as an admission by a party-opponent, the special rule of FRE 408 makes it inadmissible.

(B) is wrong because a limiting instruction would not make the evidence here admissible. FRE 408 makes the statement inadmissible as a statement in connection with a settlement negotiation, and that's true if it's offered to prove liability, not just if it's offered to prove damages. So the limiting instruction wouldn't get around the FRE 408 problem.

(C) is wrong because it misstates the facts – the settlement offer *is* relevant. The settlement offer could be taken to mean that Carr acknowledges his own guilt. Thus, it's relevant to the issue of fault. The problem is that the evidence is barred by the special settlement-offers rule of FRE 408, not that it fails to be relevant to any issue in the case.

CHAPTER 3

EXAMINATION AND IMPEACHMENT OF WITNESSES

I. IMPEACHMENT BY PRIOR BAD ACTS

A. Federal Rule

1. May bring out on cross

a. Applies to any witness

Question 9: In an automobile negligence action by Popkin against Dwyer, Juilliard testified for Popkin. Dwyer later called Watts, who testified that Juilliard's reputation for truthfulness was bad.

On cross-examination of Watts, Popkin's counsel asks, "Isn't it a fact that when you bought your new car last year, you made a false affidavit to escape paying the sales tax?"

This question is

(A) proper, because it will indicate Watts's standard of judgment as to reputation for truthfulness.

(B) proper, because it bears on Watts's credibility.

(C) improper, because character cannot be proved by specific instances of conduct.

(D) improper, because one cannot impeach an impeaching witness.

[Q2010]

Answer 9: Choice **(B)** is correct. A witness's credibility may be impeached by evidence of specific instances conduct reflecting on his truthfulness, but only by the cross-examiner's making "inquiry" into those specific instances during the cross-examination of that witness. FRE 608(b). Since Watts is on the stand and being cross-examined, the question about his prior act of dishonesty meets these requirements (it's probative of his general truthfulness, and what Popkin's counsel is doing is merely making "inquiry" into the act). The fact that Watts is a witness called solely to give impeachment testimony, as opposed to substantive or occurrence-type testimony, doesn't matter — *any* witness may be impeached by inquiry into specific past conduct of the witness that is probative of untruthfulness.

(A) is wrong because Watts is not being asked about the reputation testimony, but is instead being impeached on account of his own bad acts. So what Watts' standard is for judging reputation is not what the question is about.

(C) is wrong because there is an exception to the general rule that, for the purpose of attacking a witness's character for truthfulness, specific instances of conduct may not be proved by extrinsic evidence. The judge may, in her discretion, allow such evidence if it is brought out through cross examination of the witness whose credibility is being attacked and if the bad acts are probative of truthfulness or untruthfulness. FRE 608(b). Watts is being cross-examined with evidence of his falsifying an affidavit to avoid paying sales tax on the sale of a new car. The act is probative of untruthfulness and is being brought out on cross-examination. Therefore, the question is proper even though it involves a specific instance of the witness's past conduct.

(D) is wrong because it states a non-existent rule: there is no rule against "impeaching an impeaching witness."

II.   IMPEACHMENT BY PRIOR INCONSISTENT STATEMENT

A.   General rule

Question 10: Davidson and Smythe were charged with burglary of a warehouse. They were tried separately. At Davidson's trial, Smythe testified that he saw Davidson commit the burglary. While Smythe is still subject to recall as a witness, Davidson calls Smythe's cellmate, Walton, to testify that Smythe said, "I broke into the warehouse alone because Davidson was too drunk to help."

This evidence of Smythe's statement is

(A) admissible as a declaration against penal interest.

(B) admissible as a prior inconsistent statement.

(C) inadmissible, because it is hearsay not within any exception.

(D) inadmissible, because the statement is not clearly corroborated.

[Q1148]

Answer 10: Choice **(B)** is correct. Under FRE 613(b), when a witness testifies at trial, evidence of his prior inconsistent statement is admissible to impeach his credibility (if a foundation is laid either before or after the impeachment where the witness has an opportunity to explain or deny the statement and where the opposite party has the opportunity to interrogate the witness). Since Smythe is "still subject to recall as a witness," the foundation can be laid. In addition, some types of prior inconsistent statements are not barred by the hearsay rule and may be admitted as substantive proof of the matters contained in the statement — i.e., those made in an earlier trial or proceeding, where the declarant spoke under oath and subject to perjury penalties. FRE 801(d)(1). Since Smythe's statement was not under oath, it may not be admitted substantively. Therefore, the statement is admissible as a prior inconsistent statement, but only for impeachment purposes. (Note that this answer is correct because Smythe is a non-party in this action. If Smythe were on trial here, his prior statement would be admissible for substantive purposes, as an admission.)

(A) is wrong because the declarant is available. Under FRE 804(b)(3), the requirements for the declaration-against-interest exception are: (1) the declaration must be against the declarant's pecuniary or proprietary interest when made; (2) the declarant must be unavailable; and (3) the declarant must have had first-hand knowledge of the facts asserted in the declaration. The fact pattern indicates that Smythe is still subject to recall as a witness when Walton is testifying about Smythe's prior statement, so he is available.

(C) is wrong because, although it is correct in identifying the statement as hearsay not within any exception, it does not recognize that the statement would still be admissible for impeachment purposes.

(D) is wrong because the statement is admissible, and the requirement of corroboration does not apply in the context of a prior inconsistent statement, but rather, to the hearsay exception of the declaration against interest. FRE 804(b)(3), which provides for the hearsay exception of declaration against interest, states, "a statement tending to expose the declarant to criminal liability and offered to exculpate the accused is not admissible unless corroborating circumstances clearly indicate the trustworthiness of the statement." This is the source of the language in (D), but it does not apply here. If the declarant was unavailable and the exception was applied, then corroboration *would* be required.

B. Special rules from FRE 613

1. "Extrinsic evidence," and the "explain or deny" and "interrogate" rules

Question 11: Perez sued Dawson for damages arising out of an automobile collision. At trial, Perez called Minter, an eyewitness to the collision. Perez expected Minter to testify that she had observed Dawson's automobile for five seconds prior to the collision and estimated Dawson's speed at the time of the collision to have been 50 miles per hour. Instead, Minter testified that she estimated Dawson's speed to have been 25 miles per hour.

Without finally excusing Minter as a witness, Perez then called Wallingford, a police officer, to testify that Minter had told him during his investigation at the accident scene that Dawson "was doing at least 50."

Wallingford's testimony is

(A) admissible as a present sense impression.

(B) admissible to impeach Minter.

(C) inadmissible, because Perez may not impeach his own witness.

(D) inadmissible, because it is hearsay not within any exception.

[Q1034]

Answer 11: Choice **(B)** is correct. Under FRE 613(b), when a witness testifies at trial, extrinsic evidence of his prior inconsistent statement is admissible to impeach his credibility, so long as the subsequently witness has an opportunity to explain or deny the statement and the opposite party has the opportunity to interrogate the witness about it. Wallingford's testimony as to Minter's statement at the accident scene — "the driver (defendant) was doing at least 50" — is inconsistent with Minter's previous testimony at trial that the defendant's speed was 25 miles per hour. The fact pattern indicates that Minter was not excused as a witness and that therefore there exists the opportunity for him to explain or deny the statement and to be interrogated on it by the opposite party (Dawson).

(A) is wrong because the statement was not made close enough to the time of the accident. FRE 803(1) provides for the hearsay exception of a present sense impression, defined as a statement "describing or explaining an event or condition made *while the declarant was perceiving* the event or condition, or *immediately thereafter.*" Minter's statement was made to the police officer during the investigation of the accident scene so it was not made immediately after viewing the collision.

(C) is wrong because "the credibility of a witness may be attacked by any party, including the party calling the witness." FRE 607.

(D) is wrong because what Minter said to the Officer is not hearsay. The out-of-court statement at issue is Minter's statement to the officer, "Dawson was doing at least 50." But the statement is not being offered to prove that Dawson really was doing at least 50 — it's merely being used to cast doubt on the credibility of Minter's in-court statement that Dawson was doing 25. If the statement to the officer *were* being offered as substantive evidence, i.e., to prove that Dawson really was "doing at least 50," then it *would* be inadmissible hearsay.

Chapter 4

HEARSAY

I. DEFINITION

A. Definition

1. Hearsay may be by the present witness

a. Statement about what declarant previously said

Question 12: Pawn sued Dalton for injuries received when she fell down a stairway in Dalton's apartment building. Pawn, a guest in the building, alleged that she caught the heel of her shoe in a tear in the stair carpet. Pawn calls Witt, a tenant, to testify that Young, another tenant, had said to him a week before Pawn's fall: "When I paid my rent this morning, I told the manager he had better fix that torn carpet."

Young's statement, reported by Witt, is

(A) admissible, to prove that the carpet was defective.

(B) admissible, to prove that Dalton had notice of the defect.

(C) admissible, to prove both that the carpet was defective and that Dalton had notice of the defect.

(D) inadmissible, because it is hearsay not within any exception.

[Q2082]

Answer 12: Choice **(D)** is correct. Young's statement, "I told the manager he had better fix that torn carpet," is an "out-of-court statement" being offered to "prove the truth of the matter asserted," that Young told the manager about the needed repair and that, therefore, the manager knew of the ripped carpet. In other words, Young's out-of court-statement "I told the manager X" is being offered to show that Young, the declarant, indeed told the manager X. So the statement is inadmissible hearsay if offered for that purpose. FRE 801. (Notice that this would be hearsay whether or not X was itself true.) And there is no other plausible purpose for which it is being offered on these facts.

(A) is wrong because the statement is inadmissible to prove that the carpet was defective, because it is hearsay not within any exception, as discussed in Choice (D). The statement can't tend to prove that the carpet was defective unless the trier first believes that Young made the statement about a defect to the manager; so the statement "Young told me he had told the manager X" would be offered to prove that Young indeed told the manager X, and that would be an offer to prove the truth of the matter asserted.

(B) is wrong because the statement is inadmissible hearsay, as explained in the discussion of (D). Young's statement "I told the manager thus-and-such" is being offered to prove that Young, the declarant, indeed told the manager thus-and-such. So even if the statement is not being offered to prove that Young's statement to the manager was true (and instead offered to merely prove "notice" to the manager of a fact that might or might not be true), Young's statement to Witt that Young had previously made the statement to the manager is inadmissible hearsay.

(C) is wrong because, as discussed in (D), the statement is inadmissible for both these purposes.

II. SPECIAL ISSUES

A. "Truth of matter asserted"

1. Verbal acts

Question 13: In a suit based on a will, inheritance of $1 million depended upon whether the wife had survived her husband when both died in the crash of a small airplane. An applicable statute provided that, for purposes of distributing an estate after a common disaster, there was a rebuttable presumption that neither spouse had survived the other. A witness was called to testify that as she approached the plane she heard what she thought was a woman's voice saying, "I'm dying," although by the time the two occupants were removed from the wreckage they were both dead.

Is the witness's testimony admissible?

(A) No, because the matter is governed by the presumption that neither spouse survived the other.

(B) No, because the witness's testimony is too speculative to support a finding.

(C) Yes, because the hearsay rule does not apply to statements by decedents in actions to determine rights under a will.

(D) Yes, because it is relevant and not otherwise prohibited.

[QA001]

Answer 13: Choice **(D)** is correct. The witness is testifying as to what she heard someone say outside of the courtroom. But this is not hearsay, because although the witness is recounting an out-of-court statement, that statement is not being offered to prove the truth of the matter asserted therein, i.e., that the declarant was, in fact, dying. Rather, the statement is being offered to prove that only that it was made, because that fact has independent legal significance. As such it is classified as a verbal act, i.e., an operative fact that gives rise to legal consequences. Thus, the statement does not constitute hearsay as defined by FRE 801(c) and, therefore, is not barred by FRE 802. And it is relevant as it helps establish that the wife survived the husband.

(A) is wrong because under the majority common law "bursting bubble" rule, which is followed by FRE 301, a presumption disappears when sufficient counterproof is offered about the presumed fact. Here the testimony of the witness, although not conclusive, is sufficient to rebut the presumption that neither spouse survived the other and to support a jury finding that the wife outlived the husband. Therefore, the presumption is no longer controlling, and the witness's testimony is admissible. In any event, regardless of how (or even whether) the bursting bubble rule applies, the witness's testimony would be admissible — in all jurisdictions, the party who does not benefit from a presumption is always entitled to submit otherwise-competent evidence rebutting the existence of the presumed fact.

(B) is wrong because the testimony is not "too speculative." A witness need not be absolutely certain of matters about which the witness testifies. Here the testimony is based on the perception and memory of a lay witness, and thus satisfies the FRE 701 standard that the testimony be "(a) rationally based on the perception of the witness, and (b) helpful to a clear understanding of the witness's testimony or the determination of a fact in issue."

(C) is wrong because it presumes that the statement is hearsay, But the statement is not hearsay under FRE 801(c), because it is not being offered to prove the truth of the matter asserted. Instead, the statement is an operative fact being offered to prove that the woman was alive at the time she made the statement; so the mere existence of the statement (regardless of its "truth value") is relevant on the issue of whether the speaker survived her husband, even if by only a few minutes.

CHAPTER 5

HEARSAY EXCEPTIONS AND EXCLUSIONS

I. ADMISSIONS

A. Personal admissions

1.   Question may not say "admission"

Question 14: A defendant was on trial for perjury for having falsely testified in an earlier civil case that he knew nothing about a business fraud. In the perjury trial, the defendant again testified that he knew nothing about the business fraud. In rebuttal, the prosecutor called a witness to testify that after the civil trial was over, the defendant admitted to the witness privately that he had known about the fraud.

Is the witness's testimony in the perjury trial admissible?

(A) Yes, but only to impeach the defendant's testimony.

(B) Yes, both to impeach the defendant's testimony and as substantive evidence of the perjury.

(C) No, because it is hearsay not within any exception.

(D) No, because it relates to the business fraud and not to the commission of perjury.

[QA076]

Answer 14: Choice **(B)** is correct. First, let's consider the statement's admissibility as substantive evidence of the perjury. The witness is testifying about an out-of-court statement. If the statement is offered to prove the truth of its contents, i.e., that the declarant knew about the fraud, this would meet the hearsay definition of FRE 801(c). But the declarant is the defendant in this case, and the declarant's statement is being offered against him. Consequently, the statement is a party admission and, therefore, FRE 801(d)(2)(A) says that it is deemed not hearsay. Since it is not hearsay, it is admissible to prove the truth of its contents (i.e., as substantive evidence of the perjury).

The statement is also admissible to impeach the declarant's testimony, since it is a prior statement that is inconsistent with the declarant/defendant's testimony at the present (perjury) trial. Rule 613, which deals with prior inconsistent statements, makes them generally admissible for impeachment, subject to some exceptions that are not relevant here. In fact, where, as here, the prior inconsistent statement was made by one who is a party opponent in the present proceeding, Rule 613(b) allows use of "extrinsic evidence" (which is what the prosecutor's witness's statement is) of the prior inconsistent statement even if the maker of the prior statement (here, the defendant) is not given an opportunity to "explain or deny" the prior statement.

(A) is wrong because although the testimony is certainly admissible to impeach the defendant's testimony, it can *also* be used substantively as an admission by a party-opponent under FRE 801(d)(2)(A), as the analysis of Choice (B) demonstrates.

(C) is wrong because under FRE 801(d)(2)(A), a statement of a party-opponent that is offered against that party is deemed to be not hearsay.

(D) is wrong because although the statement made to the witness does relate to the prior business fraud, it also relates to the present perjury charge. That's because the prior statement demonstrates that the defendant in fact *did* know about the fraud, despite his testimony in two trials that he did not know of it. Thus the statement is relevant to prove that the defendant's trial testimony was knowingly false and hence constituted perjury.

Question 15: The defendant was prosecuted for homicide. He testified that he shot in self-defense. In rebuttal, a police officer testified that he came to the scene in response to a telephone call from the defendant. The officer offers to testify that he asked, "What is the problem here, sir?" and the defendant replied. "I was cleaning my gun and it went off accidentally."

The offered testimony is

(A) admissible, as an excited utterance.

(B) admissible, to impeach the defendant and as evidence that he did not act in self-defense.

(C) inadmissible, because of the defendant's privilege against self-incrimination.

(D) inadmissible, because it tends to exculpate without corroboration.

[Q1049]

Answer 15: Choice **(B)** is correct. First, let's consider whether it's admissible substantively, i.e., to prove that the defendant did not act in self-defense. The police officer's testimony that the defendant had told him, "I was cleaning my gun and it went off accidentally," is an "out-of-court statement" offered to "prove the truth of the matter asserted," so it would on its face be hearsay if it's being used as evidence that the defendant did not act in self-defense. However, admissions of a party-opponent are treated as non-hearsay statements and are admissible under FRE 801(d)(2)(A). Next, once a statement is available substantively because it's non-hearsay (or falls within a hearsay exception), it can also be used for impeachment purposes. (A separate provision, FRE 613(b), allows for impeachment by a prior inconsistent statement, but use of this provision is necessary only when the witness is a non-party — if the witness that is the target of impeachment is a party, as here, then it's simpler to use FRE 801(d)(2)(A) to get the statement in for both impeachment and substantive purposes.)

(A) is wrong because the fact that a statement is an excited utterance matters only if the statement is hearsay. As described in Choice (B), under the FRE admissions by a party opponent are hearsay "exclusions" — i.e., non-hearsay — so the statement was never hearsay in the first place, and does not need a hearsay exception in order to be admitted. Furthermore, it's doubtful that the defendant' statement would qualify as an excited utterance even if offered by rather than against him (so that the statement was not a non-hearsay party-admission). FRE 803(2) defines the excited-utterance hearsay exception this way: "a statement relating to a startling event or condition made *while the declarant was under the stress of excitement* caused by the event or condition." Here, there's no affirmative indication that the statement was being uttered under the stress of excitement from the shooting (though we don't know for sure).

(C) is wrong because application of the Fifth Amendment privilege of self-incrimination that "no person...shall be compelled in any criminal case to be a witness against himself..." applies only where there is some element of compulsion that brought about (or threatens to bring about) the statement. So statements at a trial or other proceeding (e.g., a grand jury hearing or deposition) where the defendant is required to testify are covered. Similarly, statements made in response to custodial interrogation are covered if the *Miranda* warnings weren't given, because *Miranda* is a method of preventing Fifth Amendment violations. But the defendant' out-of-court statement here did not fall into either of these two categories. In particular, it is not covered by the *Miranda* anti-self-incrimination policy, because the defendant was not in custody at the time he made the statement, and no other element of compulsion was present. (Also, even a statement by a defendant that was given in custody in violation of *Miranda* may be used to impeach the defendant's contrary trial testimony; *Harris v. N.Y.* (1971).)

(D) is wrong because the principle cited does not apply in the context of admissions, but rather, to the declaration-against-interest hearsay exception. FRE 804(b)(3), which provides for that exception, says that "a statement tending to expose the declarant to criminal liability and offered to exculpate the accused is not admissible unless corroborating circumstances clearly indicate the trustworthiness of the statement." But the quoted language applies where *A* inculpates himself and simultaneously exculpates *B*, the accused — here, where the defendant is trying to exculpate himself, neither the general declaration-against-interest exception nor the corroborating-circumstances exception to it applies.

II.   SPONTANEOUS, EXCITED, OR CONTEMPORANEOUS UTTERANCES (INCLUDING STATEMENTS ABOUT PHYSICAL OR MENTAL CONDITION)

A. Statements made for purposes of medical diagnosis or treatment

1. **Cause:** The statement may include references to the ***cause*** of the bodily condition.

> **Question 16:** A plaintiff sued a ladder manufacturer for injuries he suffered to his neck and back when a rung of the ladder on which he was standing gave way. When the plaintiff's back and neck continued to be very sore after more than two weeks, his treating physician sent him to an orthopedist for an evaluation. Though the orthopedist did not treat the plaintiff, he diagnosed an acute cervical strain. At trial, the plaintiff called the orthopedist to testify that in response to the orthopedist's inquiry about how the plaintiff had injured his back, the plaintiff told him, "I was standing near the top of a 15-foot ladder when I abruptly fell, landing hard on my back, after which the ladder toppled onto my neck."

Should the statement be admitted?

(A) Yes, because the plaintiff is present and can be cross-examined about it.

(B) Yes, because it was made for the purpose of medical diagnosis or treatment.

(C) No, because it was not made to a treating physician.

(D) No, because it relates to the inception or the cause of the injury rather than the plaintiff's physical condition.

[QA040]

Answer 16: Choice **(B)** is correct. The witness orthopedist is testifying about an out-of-court statement to prove the truth of the contents of that statement. So the statement meets the definition of hearsay under FRE 801(c). (Although the declarant was a party to the case, the statement is being offered by that party, so is not a party admission within FRE 801(d)(2)(A).) But this hearsay statement fits within the exception codified at FRE 803(4) for statements made for the purpose of medical diagnosis that describe "medical history, or past or present symptoms, pain, or sensations, or the *inception or general character of the cause or external source thereof*" when pertinent to diagnosis or treatment. Both of these requirements are met: the plaintiff's statement relates to the cause of his injury, and the cause of his injury is relevant to the orthopedist's diagnosis. Moreover, Rule 803(4) allows not only statements made to treating physicians, but also statements made to other doctors for evaluation or diagnosis. So the fact that the orthopedist never treated the plaintiff doesn't affect admissibility of the statement. And, by the way, this exception applies regardless of whether or not the declarant is unavailable to testify at trial.

(A) is wrong because the choice gives an incorrect reason for the correct outcome. The statement is an admissible statement for purposes of medical diagnosis or treatment under FRE 803(4). While it is true that the plaintiff is present and presumably could be cross-examined about the statement, this exception to the hearsay rule does not depend on the declarant's being present — the statement would be admissible even if the plaintiff were not present to testify or be cross-examined.

(C) is wrong because FRE 803(4) does not require that the statement be made to a treating physician — the Rule also admits statements made to a non-treating doctor for purposes of diagnosis. The Rule is specifically designed to admit statements such as this, where an injured party is seeking a diagnosis and opinion from a medical specialist.

(D) is wrong because FRE 803(4) expressly permits the introduction of statements concerning the cause of injury when that information is pertinent to diagnosis or treatment. Thus it is admissible under FRE 803(4). (If the statement related to *fault* — e.g., "I fell when D tripped over the base of the ladder" — then the part of the statement relating to fault would likely *not* be covered by the 803(4) exception.)

a. **Does not cover fault**

Question 17: In a civil action for personal injury, Payne alleges that he was beaten up by Dabney during an altercation in a crowded bar. Dabney's defense is that he was not the person who hit Payne. To corroborate his testimony about the cause of his injuries, Payne seeks to introduce, through the hospital records custodian, a notation in a regular medical record made by an emergency room doctor at the hospital where Payne was treated for his injuries. The notation is: "Patient says he was attacked by Dabney."

The notation is

A) inadmissible, unless the doctor who made the record is present at trial and available for cross-examination.

(B) inadmissible as hearsay not within any exception.

(C) admissible as hearsay within the exception for records of regularly conducted activity.

(D) admissible as a statement made for the purpose of medical diagnosis or treatment.

[Q1139]

Answer 17: Choice **(D)** is **incorrect**. The statement does not fall under the purpose-of-medical-diagnosis-or-treatment exception because the identification of the attacker was not pertinent to the diagnosis or treatment of Payne's injuries. Under FRE 803(4), statements for purposes of medical diagnosis or treatment describing pain or "the inception or general character of the cause or external source thereof" are admissible if *"reasonably pertinent to diagnosis or treatment."* Payne's statements to his doctor that he was attacked and how he was attacked might well be admissible under FRE 803(4) on the theory that they were "reasonably pertinent to diagnosis or treatment." However, a statement identifying his attacker will not help in treatment or diagnosis in any way, and is therefore inadmissible under this exception. (The answer is (B), hearsay not within any exception.)

B. Declaration of present mental, emotional, or physical condition

1. State of mind directly in issue

Question 18: In a prosecution of Dale for murdering Vera, Dale testified that the killing had occurred in self defense when Vera tried to shoot him. In rebuttal, the prosecution seeks to call Walter, Vera's father, to testify that the day before the killing, Vera told Walter that she loved Dale so much she could never hurt him.

Walter's testimony is

(A) admissible within the hearsay exception for statements of the declarant's then existing state of mind.

(B) admissible, because Vera is unavailable as a witness.

(C) inadmissible as hearsay not within any exception.

(D) inadmissible, because Vera's character is not an issue.

[Q1171]

Answer 18: Choice **(A)** is correct. When the mental state of a declarant is directly at issue in a case, statements of the declarant's then existing state of mind are admissible under FRE 803(3) to prove the declarant's mental state pre-dating or post-dating the statement. Here, Vera's statement, that she loved Dale and she could never hurt him, is being offered to prove the truth of the matter asserted, that she could not hurt him, and that therefore, the next day, it is unlikely that she would have been the first aggressor in the encounter with Dale. This evidence would counter Dale's claim that he acted in self-defense.

(B) is wrong because the declarant's availability is immaterial when a statement is being offered under the exception for a then existing state of mind under FRE 803(3).

(C) is wrong because the statement is admissible under the then existing state of mind hearsay exception provided by FRE 803(3), as explained in the discussion of Choice A.

(D) is wrong because (1) the statement is admissible and (2) it does not reflect on Vera's "character," but rather, her state of mind, as further discussed in (A).

2. Proof of subsequent event

Question 19: Prine sued Dover for an assault that occurred March 5 in California. To support his defense that he was in Utah on that date, Dover identifies and seeks to introduce a letter he wrote to his sister a week before the assault in which he stated that he would see her in Utah on March 5.

The letter is

(A) admissible, within the state of mind exception to the hearsay rule.

(B) admissible, as a prior consistent statement to support Dover's credibility as a witness.

(C) inadmissible, because it lacks sufficient probative value.

(D) inadmissible, because it is a statement of belief to prove the fact believed.

[Q2192]

Answer 19: Choice **(A)** is correct. A statement is admissible to prove that a plan, design, or intention of the declarant was in fact carried out by the declarant, under the hearsay exception for a statement concerning a declarant's present mental, emotional or physical condition. FRE 803(3). That provision allows for the introduction of a statement showing that the declarant had the intent to take a certain action, in order to prove that the declarant did in fact eventually take that action where whether that act took place is an issue in the case. Here, Dover's stated intention to meet his sister in Utah on March 5 is admissible to prove that he in fact was in Utah on March 5; therefore, it is evidence that he did not commit an assault in California on that same day.

(B) is wrong because the general rule is that evidence offered to bolster the character of a witness is not admissible. Under FRE 801(d)(1)(b), a statement consistent with the declarant's testimony may only be "offered to rebut an express or implied charge against the declarant of recent fabrication or improper influence or motive." The fact pattern does not indicate that those circumstances occurred here.

(C) is wrong because the letter is admissible and it, in fact, has sufficient probative value. It makes the factual proposition that Dover was not in California on March 5 more likely than it would be without the evidence.

(D) is wrong because the letter is admissible and the concept stated does not apply. It's true that FRE 803(3) provides for an exception for the declarant's then existing mental, emotional or physical condition, "but not including a statement of memory or belief to prove the fact remembered or believed unless it relates to the...declarant's will." But, here, the letter is not a statement of belief about past actions or events. It is a stated intention to do something in the future, as explained in the discussion of (A).

3. Need for inference

Question 20: Daggett was prosecuted for murder of Vales, whose body was found one morning in the street near Daggett's house. The state calls Witt, a neighbor, to testify that during the night before the body was found he heard Daggett's wife scream, "You killed him! You killed him!"

Witt's testimony is

(A) admissible as a report of a statement of belief.

(B) admissible as a report of an excited utterance.

(C) inadmissible, because it reports a privileged spousal communication.

(D) inadmissible on spousal immunity grounds, but only if the wife objects.

[Q1106]

Answer 20: Choice **(B)** is correct. The wife's statement is hearsay, an "out-of-court statement" offered to "prove the truth of the matter asserted" — that Daggett was the killer. FRE 801. FRE 803(2) provides for the excited utterance exception to the hearsay rule – "a statement relating to a startling event or condition made while the declarant was under the stress of excitement caused by the event or condition." The screamed exclamation, "You killed him! You killed him!" would qualify — the fact that there was a scream strongly suggests that Daggett's wife was responding to some event that (1) startled her, (2) convinced her that her husband had been killed (the event), and (3) induced her to make the statement (showing causation between the startling event, and the statement).

(A) is wrong because it relies on a concept that doesn't exist. There is no hearsay exception provided for a "statement of belief." Indeed, FRE 803(3) indicates just the contrary, since it gives a hearsay exception for "A statement of the declarant's then existing state of mind ... but *not* including a statement of memory or belief to prove the fact remembered or believed[.]"

(C) is wrong because the evidence would not be barred by the confidential spousal communications privilege. If the wife thought her husband was dead, she could not have been intending to communicate with him (barring communications with the other world, which are presumably not protected by the privilege).

(D) is wrong because the evidence is not barred by the adverse testimony privilege. The privilege applies only to testimony against the spouse of the declarant. So there are two problems here: (1) the husband (the declarant's spouse) is not on trial; and (2) this out-of-court startled exclamation would not be deemed to be "testimonial" for purposes of the adverse-testimony privilege, even if it were used by the prosecution against the husband.

III. PAST RECOLLECTION RECORDED

A. Exception under the FRE

1. Four requirements

Question 21: A plaintiff sued a defendant for wrongful death arising out of a traffic collision between the plaintiff's decedent and the defendant. At trial, the investigating traffic officer authenticated a tape recording of her shift-end dictation of comments used in preparing the written report of her factual findings. She testified that the tape recording was accurate when made and that she currently had no clear memory of the details of the investigation.

Is the tape recording admissible as evidence?

(A) Yes, under the past recollection recorded exception to the hearsay rule.

(B) Yes, under the public records exception to the hearsay rule.

(C) No, because it is hearsay and is a police report being offered against the defendant in a wrongful death case.

(D) No, because the police report itself is the best evidence.

[QA048]

Answer 21: Choice **(A)** is correct. The tape recording is evidence of an oral out-of-court statement that is being offered to prove the truth of the contents of that statement. Thus it is hearsay under FRE 801(c). But it also satisfies the requirements of FRE 803(5), the past recollection recorded exception to the hearsay rule. Under that rule, a record is admissible "concerning a matter about which a witness once had knowledge but now has insufficient recollection to enable the witness to testify fully and accurately, shown to have been made or adopted by the witness when the matter was fresh in the witness's memory and to reflect that knowledge correctly[.]" So here all four requirements of FRE 803(5) are met: (1) we know that the "witness once had knowledge" requirement is satisfied because we're told that she was the investigating officer, and was dictating an account of what she had learned first-hand; (2) we know she "now has insufficient recollection to enable [her] to testify fully and accurately" because we're explicitly told in the facts that she "currently ha[s] no clear memory of the details"; (3) we know that she "made [the record] when the matter was fresh in [her] memory" from the fact that she made the tape recording at the end of the very shift in which she learned the underlying facts to which the recording pertained; and (4) we know the record "reflects [the witness's] knowledge correctly" because the facts tell us that the witness "testified that the tape recording was accurate when made." Accordingly, under FRE 803(5), the recording is admissible evidence (in the sense that it can be played for the jury, although not taken into the jury room as an exhibit).

(B) is wrong because although the officer's formal written report would qualify as a public record under FRE 803(8), the informal dictated comments she made to help her prepare the report would not. To be admissible under 803(8), the material must fall within one of clauses (A), (B), or (C) of 803(8). Let's see why none of these clauses applies:

Clause (A) of 803(8) covers reports of "the activities of the [public] office or agency." The clause is interpreted to refer to records of the internal activities of the agency, not to its inquiries into events occurring in the outside world. So the recording here does not qualify, since it's not about the police department, but about real-world non-police activities.

Clause (B) of 803(8) covers "matters observed pursuant to duty imposed by law as to which matters there was a duty to report, excluding, however, in criminal cases matters observed by police officers and other law enforcement personnel[.]" (B) is generally interpreted to cover only material that is "more concrete and simple than interpretive or evaluative" (see M&K, § 8.50, p. 862), so it would not apply to the dictated notes here, which clearly have an evaluative component. (Who caused the accident, which the officer didn't personally witness?)

Clause (C) of 803(8) covers "factual findings resulting from an investigation made pursuant to authority granted by law[.]" ((C) goes on to say that such findings may be used only "in civil actions and proceedings and against the Government in criminal cases"; since this is a civil action, this limit does not bar the use here.) But (C) by its terms covers "factual *findings*," and the preliminary, informal tape-recording here would not be construed to have produced such "factual findings" (a phrase that has the connotation of final and formal conclusions), especially given that the traffic officer knew that she would later use her recording in order to prepare her eventual "written report of her factual findings." (The written report is a document that *would* satisfy clause (C).)

So none of the three clauses of 803(8) applies.

(C) is wrong because although the tape recording is hearsay, it fits the hearsay exception of FRE 803(5) as a past recollection recorded. This choice's reference to a "police report being offered against the defendant in a wrongful death case" is an attempt to trick you into thinking that the prohibition in 803(8), clause (C), applies. As is covered in more detail in the analysis of Choice (B) above, 803(8)'s public-records hearsay exception says, in clause (C), that "factual findings resulting from an investigation made pursuant to authority granted by law" are admissible only in civil actions and against the government in criminal cases, not against the accused in a criminal case. And there is some (though weak) authority that where factual findings by law enforcement officials are prohibited by 803(8) clause (C) (i.e., where the findings are proposed to be used by the government against the accused), not only can't Rule 803(8) be used, but neither can other exceptions, like past recollection recorded. But even in a court following this minority authority, the 803(8), clause (C) prohibition wouldn't apply here, since the prohibition doesn't apply to any civil case, even one involving wrongful death.

(D) is wrong because the tape recording was made prior to the written report and was used as a basis for the written report. The recording is not being offered to prove the content of the written report, so its admission does not violate the best evidence/original document rule of FRE 1002. (If the officer gave courtroom testimony that the previous day, she had listened to the recording and here is what it said, then this testimony *would* violate the original document rule of FRE 1002, because the recording itself would have to be offered as the best evidence of what the recording's contents were.)

IV. RECORDS OF REGULARLY CONDUCTED ACTIVITY (a/k/a "BUSINESS RECORDS")

A. Person supplying info

1. Consumer complaints or reports

Question 22: Plaza Hotel sued Plaza House Hotel for infringement of its trade name. To establish a likelihood of name confusion, Plaintiff Plaza Hotel offers a series of memoranda which it had asked its employees to prepare at the end of each day listing instances during the day in which telephone callers, cab drivers, customers, and others had confused the two names.

The memoranda should be

(A) excluded, because they are more unfairly prejudicial and confusing than probative.

(B) excluded, because they are hearsay not within any exception.

(C) admitted, because they are records of regularly conducted business activity.

(D) admitted, because they are past recollection recorded.

[Q2200]

Answer 22: Choice **(C)** is **incorrect**. The series of memoranda are "out-of-court statements" offered to "prove the truth of the matter asserted," that the name confusion actually occurred. FRE 803(6) provides for the business record hearsay exception if the entries (a) are made in the routine of a business; (b) are made by, or from information transmitted by, a person with personal knowledge of the matter recorded, who is acting pursuant to a business duty to make the report or record (or whose statement meets some other hearsay exception); (c) are made "at or near the time" of the matter recorded; and (d) are not untrustworthy due to sources, methods or circumstances. There are two reasons why the memos here don't qualify: (1) requirement (b) is not met, because the consumers who are making the "I'm confused" statements aren't acting pursuant to any business duty, and their statements don't fall within any other hearsay exception; and (2) requirement (d) is not met, because the circumstances (anticipation of litigation), and the Hotel's strong self-interest, make the records untrustworthy. (The **correct** answer is (B) — this is hearsay not within any exception.)

V. PUBLIC RECORDS AND REPORTS

A. Public records and reports

1. Federal Rule

a. Matters observed under duty

Question 23: A plaintiff sued his insurance company for the full loss of his banquet hall by fire. The insurance company defended under a provision of the policy limiting liability to 50 percent if "flammable materials not essential to the operation of the business were stored on the premises and caused a fire." The insurance company called the keeper of the city fire inspection records to identify a report prepared and filed by the fire marshal as required by law, indicating that shortly before the fire, the fire marshal had cited the plaintiff for storing gasoline at the banquet hall.

Is the report admissible?

(A) No, because it is hearsay not within any exception.

(B) No, because the proceeding is civil, rather than criminal.

(C) Yes, as a public record describing matters observed as to which there was a duty to report.

(D) Yes, as a record of regularly conducted activity, provided the fire marshal is unavailable.

[QA061]

Answer 23: Choice **(C)** is correct. The report is an out-of-court written statement offered to prove the truth of its contents, so it meets the hearsay definition of FRE 801(c). Nevertheless, it is admissible because it falls within the hearsay exception for "public records and reports" codified at FRE 803(8). Under Clause (B) of this rule, a report made by a public official or agency concerning "matters observed pursuant to duty imposed by law as to which matters there was a duty to report" is admissible, "unless the sources of information or other circumstances indicate lack of trustworthiness." All of the requirements embedded in Clause (B) are met: (1) The fire marshal is a public official; (2) we know that the report concerned a matter that the marshal "observed," since the fact that he issued the citation indicates that he observed gasoline being stored in the banquet hall; and (3) we know that the report concerned something "as to which there was a duty to report," because the facts tell us that the report was prepared and filed "as required by law." As to the "lack of trustworthiness" proviso, there is no suggestion of any reason to believe that the report's contents are untrustworthy. Thus, the report meets the requirements of the FRE 803(8) public records exception to the hearsay rule, making it admissible.

(A) is wrong because this report is admissible as a public record under FRE 803(8). See the analysis of Choice (C) for why this is so.

(B) is wrong because the fact that this is a civil case does not make the report inadmissible. Public records are admissible in both civil and criminal cases. In fact, they are more broadly admissible in civil cases than in criminal cases, because law enforcement reports are generally not admissible against criminal defendants. See the analysis of Choice (C) for why the report here is admissible as a public record.

(D) is wrong because it incorrectly states how the regularly-conducted-activity exception works. This choice is correct in suggesting that the hearsay exception for records of regularly conducted activity contained in FRE 803(6) (commonly called the "business records" exception) would likely apply to this report. But the choice is incorrect in stating that the exception will apply only if the fire marshall is unavailable to testify. The 803(6) business-records exception, like all the exceptions contained in FRE 803, does not require a showing of the unavailability of the declarant (here, the fire marshal).

VI. DECLARATIONS AGAINST INTEREST

A. Generally

1. Text of Federal Rule

Question 24: The defendant, a man, has been charged with murdering the victim. The defendant defends on the grounds that the murder was really committed by a particular woman, who has since died. The defendant offers a properly authenticated photocopy of a transcript of a deposition in a civil suit brought against the woman by the victim's family for the victim's death, in which the woman said, "Yes, I killed him because I hated him." The civil suit was brought because the woman was known to have quarreled with and disliked the victim. Upon proper objection by the prosecution, the statement should be

(A) admitted as a declaration against interest.

(B) admitted as former testimony by a person now unavailable.

(C) inadmissible as hearsay not within any exception.

(D) inadmissible, because the original rather than a photocopy must be offered.

[Q6001]

Answer 24: Choice **(A)** is correct. First, this is hearsay: the declarant's statement "I killed him" is being offered to show that she did indeed kill him. But FRE 804(b)(3) (one of the declarant-unavailable exceptions) gives a hearsay exception for a statement by a now-unavailable witness which "was at the time of its making so far contrary to the declarant's pecuniary or proprietary interest, or so far tended to subject the declarant to civil or criminal liability . . . that a reasonable person in the declarant's position would not have made the statement unless believing it to be true." The woman's statement in the deposition qualifies, since: (1) her subsequent death of course makes her unavailable; (2) the statement, viewed as of the time she made it, potentially subjected her to such civil and criminal liability that she would be unlikely to have made it unless she believed it was true. 804(b)(3) adds a further requirement, that a statement "tending to expose the declarant to criminal liability and offered to exculpate the accused is not admissible unless corroborating circumstances clearly indicate the trustworthiness of the statement." Here, the fact that the woman was known to have quarreled with and disliked the victim, and the fact that the victim's family chose to bring civil suit against the woman, supply the required corroborating circumstances to indicate the statement's trustworthiness.

(B) is wrong because, although there is indeed an exception for former testimony given under oath at a trial or other proceeding, the exception applies only if "the party against whom the testimony is now offered . . . had an opportunity and similar motive to develop the testimony by direct, cross, or redirect examination." See FRE 804(b)(1). Since the "party against whom the testimony is now offered" is the government, the statement could qualify only if the government had the opportunity and similar motive to "develop" (i.e., undermine) the woman's testimony in the earlier civil suit; since the prosecution was not part of that suit, this requirement was not satisfied.

(C) is wrong because, while the statement is indeed hearsay, the declaration-against-interest exception applies, as described in Choice (A) above.

(D) is wrong because, although the Best Evidence Rule does indeed sometimes require an original, FRE 1003 says that "a duplicate is admissible to the same extent as an original unless (1) a genuine issue is raised as to the authenticity of the original or (2) in the circumstances it would be unfair to admit to duplicate in lieu of the original." There is no indication on these facts that either of these problems is present.

Question 25: Pamela sued Driver for damages for the death of Pamela's husband Ronald, resulting from an automobile collision. At trial, Driver calls Ronald's doctor to testify that the day before his death, Ronald, in great pain, said, "It was my own fault; there's nobody to blame but me."

The doctor's testimony should be admitted as

(A) a statement against interest.

(B) a dying declaration.

(C) a statement of Ronald's then existing state of mind.

(D) an excited utterance.

[Q2183]

Answer 25: Choice **(A)** is correct. There are three requirements for the declaration-against-interest exception to the hearsay rule: (1) the declarant must be unavailable; (2) the declaration must have been against the declarant's pecuniary or proprietary interest when made; and (3) the circumstances must be such that declarant would not have made the statement unless he believed it to be true. All of these requirements are fulfilled regarding the statement made by the now-deceased Ronald: (1) he's dead and thus unavailable; (2) he exposed himself to tort liability by acknowledging responsibility for the accident; and (3) there is no apparent reason why he'd acknowledge responsibility if he didn't think he was in fact at fault.

CHAPTER 6

PRIVILEGES

I. THE ATTORNEY-CLIENT PRIVILEGE

A. Generally

1. Client

Question 26: Pace sues Def Company for injuries suffered when Pace's car collided with Def Company's truck. Def's general manager prepared a report of the accident at the request of the company's attorney in preparation for the trial, and delivered the report to the attorney. Pace demands that the report be produced.

Will production of the report be required?

(A) Yes, because business reports are not generally privileged.

(B) No, because it is privileged communication from the client to the attorney.

(C) No, because such reports contain hearsay.

(D) No, because such reports are self-serving.

[Q8044]

Answer 26: Choice **(B)** is correct. A communication is subject to attorney-client privilege if it is a communication from the client to the attorney, made in confidence, concerning legal representation. A corporation is subject to the same privilege as an individual, and the general manager would be within the scope of the privilege under the modern "performance of duties" test, under which the privilege extends to any employee's communication if it was within his duties, and it was offered to advance the legal interests of the corporation. So the communication here is within the attorney-client privilege. A companion "work product immunity," in force as a matter of common-law in nearly all jurisdictions, gives an immunity from discovery or other "production" for materials that would be inadmissible at trial due to the attorney-client privilege.

(A) is not the best response because it does not correctly characterize the facts and law. A communication of *any* kind, business report or not, is subject to attorney-client privilege if it is a communication from the client to the attorney, made in confidence, concerning legal representation. Here, the report fits this description — the general manager made the report about the accident, intended that it be read only by the attorney, and it was made in preparation for trial. And apart from admissibility at trial, the "work product immunity" for direct client-attorney communication prevents the client (Def Co.) from having to produce it in discovery.

(C) is not the best response because (1) because it ignores the central reason the report will be non-producible: it is covered by the work-product immunity; and (2) it falsely asserts that because the report is or might be inadmissible, it need not be produced. As to (1), what makes the report non-producible is the attorney-client privilege and companion "work product immunity," not the presence of hearsay. As to (2), even materials that would not be admissible at trial because they contain hearsay are producible in discovery, if they are reasonably likely to lead to discoverable evidence. (And it's not so clear that the report wouldn't be admissible if it were not for the attorney-client work-product immunity problem; for instance, the report and the statements in it might all be admissible as non-hearsay admissions by a party-opponent or its agents.)

(D) is wrong because the self-serving nature of the report won't prevent the opposite party (the adversary of the report's author) from offering it. If Def Co. were offering the report as a business record under FRE 803(6), the fact that the "source of information or the method or circumstances of preparation indicate lack of trustworthiness" (803(6)) would be fatal. But where the adversary of the preparer of the record or report is offering it, the report can come in as admission, as to which its self-serving nature wouldn't matter.

B. Professional relationship

1. Fee arrangements not covered by privilege

Question 27: A defendant was on trial for tax evasion. The IRS, seeking to establish the defendant's income by showing his expenditures, called on the defendant's attorney to produce records showing only how much the defendant had paid his attorney in fees.

Should the demand for the attorney's fee records be upheld?

(A) Yes, because it calls for relevant information not within the attorney-client privilege.

(B) Yes, because the attorney-client privilege cannot be invoked to conceal evidence of a crime.

(C) No, because the records are protected by the attorney-client privilege.

(D) No, because the records are protected by the attorney work-product doctrine.

[QA098]

Answer 27: Choice **(A)** is correct. The attorney-client privilege applies only to confidential communications made for the purpose of facilitating legal representation of the client. Courts have uniformly held that the details of fee arrangements, including the amount paid by the defendant in fees, are not communications made for the purpose of facilitating representation, and are therefore not covered by the privilege. See M&K, § 5.19, p. 356.

(B) is wrong because it gives an incorrect explanation of the correct outcome. The attorney-client privilege *can* be invoked even where it conceals evidence of a *past* crime. (The examiners are trying to make you think of the "crime or fraud" exception, by which communications are not covered by the privilege if they are made for the purpose of accomplishing or concealing a *future* crime or fraud.)

(C) is wrong because the attorney-client privilege applies only to confidential communications made for the purpose of facilitating legal representation of the client. The amount the defendant paid in legal fees does not qualify as such a communication, as is described in the analysis of Choice (A).

(D) is wrong because the work-product doctrine provides a qualified immunity for only those materials prepared by an attorney or client in anticipation of litigation, such as witness statements, investigative reports, or trial memoranda. Documents showing the amount a client has paid or will pay to his attorney for legal representation are not deemed to be prepared "in anticipation of litigation," so they are outside the protection of the work-product doctrine.

II. THE PRIVILEGE AGAINST SELF-INCRIMINATION

A. Negative inference allowed in civil cases

Question 28: A plaintiff sued an individual defendant for injuries suffered in a collision between the plaintiff's car and the defendant's truck while the defendant's employee was driving the truck. The plaintiff sought discovery of any accident report the employee might have made to the defendant, but the defendant responded that no such report existed. Before trial, the defendant moved to preclude the plaintiff from asking the defendant in the presence of the jury whether he destroyed such a report, because the defendant would then invoke his privilege against self-incrimination.

Should the court allow the plaintiff to ask the defendant about the destruction of the report?

(A) No, because a report that was prepared in anticipation of litigation is not subject to discovery.

(B) No, because no inference may properly be drawn from invocation of a legitimate privilege.

(C) Yes, because a party in a civil action may not invoke the privilege against self-incrimination.

(D) Yes, because the defendant's destruction of the report would serve as the basis of an inference adverse to the defendant.

[QA068]

Answer 28: Choice **(D)** is correct. If a party destroys evidence, it is proper for the jury to draw an inference that the evidence was adverse to that party. It's true that the Supreme Court has held that in a *criminal* case, neither the judge nor the prosecution can encourage a jury to draw an inference of guilt from a defendant's invocation of her privilege against self-incrimination; *Griffin v. California* (1965). But it's proper for the jury to draw an adverse inference in a *civil* case from a party's assertion of that privilege against self-incrimination. Thus, the court should allow the question to be asked, because it is proper regardless of how the defendant responds.

(A) is wrong because although it is true that a report prepared in anticipation of litigation may qualify as work product, the work-product immunity is not absolute. Documents that are work product are still subject to discovery upon a showing of substantial need and the inability to obtain the substantial equivalent of the materials by other means. Moreover, a claim of work-product immunity must be asserted before, and ruled on by, the court — a party cannot simply destroy the material and claim work-product protection. Finally, here the plaintiff would not be asking the defendant to produce the report for the jury to see; the plaintiff would only ask whether such a report had been destroyed.

(B) is wrong because although the Supreme Court has held that neither the judge nor the prosecution can encourage a jury to draw an inference of guilt from a defendant's invocation of her privilege against self-incrimination in a *criminal* case, *Griffin v. California*

(1965), it is proper for the jury to draw an adverse inference in a *civil* case from a party's assertion of the privilege against self-incrimination.

(C) is wrong because the privilege against self-incrimination may be asserted in both civil and criminal cases.

CHAPTER 7

REAL AND DEMONSTRATIVE EVIDENCE, INCLUDING WRITINGS

I. AUTHENTICATION

A. Authentication of writings and recordings

1. Signature or handwriting

a. Non-expert

Question 29: When a man entered a bank and presented a check for payment, the bank teller recognized the signature on the check as a forgery because the check was drawn on the account of a customer whose handwriting she knew. The bank teller called the police. Before the police arrived, the man picked up the check from the counter and left.

The man was charged with attempting to cash a forged check. At trial, the prosecutor called the bank teller to testify that the signature on the check was forged.

Is the bank teller's testimony admissible?

(A) Yes, because a bank teller is by occupation an expert on handwriting.

(B) Yes, because it is rationally based on the bank teller's perception and is helpful to the jury.

(C) No, because the bank teller was at fault in allowing loss of the original by failing to secure the check.

(D) No, because it is not possible for either the jury or an expert to compare the signature on the missing check with a signature established as genuine.

[QA085]

Answer 29: Choice **(B)** is correct. The witness teller, who has not been qualified as a handwriting expert, is offering her lay opinion as to the genuineness of the signature on the check. FRE 701 allows lay opinion testimony in general when it is "rationally based on the perception of the witness" *and* is "helpful to a clear understanding of the witness's testimony or the determination of a fact in issue". Additionally, FRE 901(b)(2) provides that the authenticity of a document can be established by "[n]onexpert opinion as to the genuineness of handwriting, based upon familiarity not acquired for purposes of the litigation." This requirement is met here, since the facts tell us that the witness/teller already, at the time of the episode, knew the signature of the bank customer on whose account the check was drawn. This knowledge made it possible for her to recognize the signature on the check as a forgery, and to testify with first-hand knowlege that the signature on the check presented was different from the signature of the owner of the account. Thus, the testimony is permitted.

(A) is wrong because there is nothing in the fact pattern to suggest that the bank teller is an expert on handwriting — merely working as a bank teller would not give a person such expertise.

(C) is wrong because it misstates the application of the original document rule. This choice is premised on a plausible idea: that because what's being proved is the contents of a writing (namely, the signature on a check), the original of that writing must be produced. FRE 1002's implementation of the original documents rule (a/k/a the Best Evidence Rule) indeed says that "To prove the contents of a writing ... the original writing ... is required, except as otherwise provided in these rules[.]" So if the original of the check had been available to the prosecution, the prosecution's failure to present that original, and to have the teller testify about the check's contents instead, would indeed have been a violation of FRE 1002. But FRE 1004(1) grants an exception to the original documents rule where "All originals are lost or have been destroyed, unless the proponent lost or destroyed them in bad faith." The proponent here is the prosecution (not the bank teller), so even if the teller had acted in bad faith in not securing the check, the FRE 1004(1) exception would still have applied. In any event, on the facts here, there is no evidence that the teller behaved in bad faith (or was even "at fault") by not securing the check before the defendant could grab it and run away with it.

(D) is wrong because having an expert (or even the jury members themselves) compare an exemplar established as genuine with the disputed signature is not the only way to establish whether a signature is forged or authentic. It's true that FRE 901(b)(3) permits authentication of a document via "comparison by the trier of fact or by expert witnesses with specimens which have been authenticated." However, this is not the only method authorized by FRE 901. FRE 901(b)(2) permits authentication by "[n]onexpert opinion as to the genuineness of handwriting, based upon familiarity not acquired for purposes of the litigation." The testimony here satisfies that method, since the teller got her familiarity with the real account-holder's signature in a way that pre-dated the litigation.

b. Exemplars

Question 30: Parker sues Dix for breach of a promise made in a letter allegedly written by Dix to Parker. Dix denies writing the letter.

Which of the following would NOT be a sufficient basis for admitting the letter into evidence?

(A) Testimony by Parker that she is familiar with Dix's signature and recognizes it on the letter.

(B) Comparison by the trier of fact of the letter with an admitted signature of Dix.

(C) Opinion testimony of a nonexpert witness based upon familiarity acquired in order to authenticate the signature.

(D) Evidence that the letter was written in response to one written by Parker to Dix.

[Q1162]

Answer 30: Choice **(C)** is correct (i.e., the choice is not an acceptable method of authentication). FRE 901(b)(2) allows "nonexpert opinion as to the genuineness of handwriting, based upon familiarity *not acquired for purposes of the litigation.*" The fact pattern indicates that the nonexpert acquired familiarity in order to authenticate the signature; therefore, this would not serve as a sufficient basis for admitting the letter into evidence.

(A) is wrong because a nonexpert who is already familiar with a signature may testify as to its genuineness as provided by FRE 901(b)(2) and discussed in the explanation to (C). It is irrelevant that the nonexpert is a party to the litigation.

(B) is wrong because handwriting may be authenticated by the use of exemplars, in which case it is up to the jury to compare the exemplar with the offered writing to determine its genuineness.

(D) is wrong because evidence that the letter (relying on its contents and other circumstances) was written as a reply to one already authenticated is a method of authentication falling under the category of "distinctive characteristics and the like." FRE 901(b)(4).

2. Phone conversation

a. Incoming calls

Question 31: In a narcotics conspiracy prosecution against Daly, the prosecutor offers in evidence a tape recording of a telephone call allegedly made by Daly. A lay witness is called to testify that the voice on the recording is Daly's. Her testimony to which of the following would be the LEAST sufficient basis for admitting the recording?

(A) She had heard the same voice on a similar tape recording identified to her by Daly's brother.

(B) She had heard Daly speak many times, but never over the telephone.

(C) She had, specifically for the purpose of preparing to testify, talked with Daly over the telephone at a time after the recording was made.

(D) She had been present with Daly when he engaged in the conversation in question but had heard only Daly's side of the conversation.

[Q8060]

Answer 31: Choice **(A)** is the best response, because under this alternative, the lay witness is not *personally familiar* with Daly's voice, and thus the recording wouldn't be admissible with this testimony alone. The rule is that a voice can be authenticated by any person who recognizes it. Under FRE 901(b)(5), "*Identification of a voice, whether heard firsthand or through mechanical or electronic transmission or recording, [can be accomplished] by opinion based upon hearing the voice at any time under any circumstances connecting it with the alleged speaker.*" Here, the only thing linking the lay witness and Daly's voice is an assurance by Daly's brother that a recorded voice was Daly's; the witness herself has no personal familiarity with it. (Thus, if Daly's brother were lying or mistaken, the lay witness's testimony would be useless.) Since (A) states the only basis on which the lay witness *couldn't* authenticate the tape, of these four choices, it's the best response.

(B) is wrong because the fact that the witness had never heard Daly speak over the telephone would be irrelevant. Under FRE 901(b)(5), "Identification of a voice, whether heard firsthand or through mechanical or electronic transmission or recording, [can be accomplished] by opinion based upon hearing the voice at any time under any circumstances connecting it with the alleged speaker." Here, the lay witness satisfies this requirement because she had heard the voice many times. The rule doesn't require that the witness be familiar with the voice in the form in which it must be authenticated (here, a tape recording).

(C) is wrong because the lay witness could authenticate the recording on this basis, since any person who recognizes a voice can authenticate it. FRE 901(b)(5) (quoted in full in (A) above) allows lay testimony identifying a voice based upon "hearing the voice *at any time under any circumstances.*" This language means that familiarity acquired in anticipation of litigation does not disqualify the witness. (This makes the situation different from handwriting, as to which 901(b)(2) allows lay testimony only if "based on familiarity not acquired for purposes of the litigation.")

(D) is wrong because it represents possibly the *best* basis on which the lay witness *could* authenticate the recording. Not only would she be able to recognize the voice, but she'd be familiar with the very conversation that was recorded. Nothing in 901(b)(5) would come close to ruling out an identification of the speaker on a tape as having been the person whose side of the taped conversation the witness heard in person.

II. THE "BEST EVIDENCE RULE" FOR RECORDED COMMUNICATIONS

A. Communications covered

1. Other "real" evidence not covered

Question 32: Poole sued Darrel for unlawfully using Poole's idea for an animal robot as a character in Darrel's science fiction movie. Darrel admitted that he had received a model of an animal robot from Poole, but he denied that it had any substantial similarity to the movie character. After the model had been returned to Poole, Poole destroyed it.

In order for Poole to testify to the appearance of the model, Poole

(A) must show that he did not destroy the model in bad faith.

(B) must give advance notice of his intent to introduce the oral testimony.

(C) must introduce a photograph of the model if one exists.

(D) need do none of the above, because the "best evidence rule" applies only to writings, recordings, and photographs.

[Q2012]

Answer 32: Choice **(D)** is correct. Under FRE 1002, the best evidence rule applies only to writings recordings, and photographs. Since the Best Evidence Rule doesn't apply to models, the original model need not be produced and Poole may testify to its appearance without adhering to any of the requirements laid out in Choices (A), (B), and (C).

III. SUMMARIES OF VOLUMINOUS WRITINGS

A. Summaries generally

Question 33: A lawyer worked steadily on a case for a client over five-year period, with the billing agreed to be on particular amount charge per hour worked. The lawyer kept regular timesheets showing, for any day on which he worked on the matter, how long he worked and which of various activities (phone calls, letter-writing, etc.) he performed on that day. In the lawyer's suit against the client for non-payment, the lawyer did not offer into evidence the actual timesheets. Instead, in preparation for trial, the lawyer used the timesheets to create a summary showing, for each week, how much time the lawyer spent on each of the activity types. Then, at trial, the lawyer offered these weekly summaries, together with his testimony about how he had prepared them. If the client properly objects, the judge should hold that the summaries are

(A) inadmissible for any purpose, because the underlying timesheets from which they were prepared were not offered into evidence.

(B) inadmissible as substantive evidence, but usable as non-admitted materials to refresh the lawyer's present recollection.

(C) admissible as substantive evidence of hours worked, if the underlying timesheets were made available to the client prior to trial.

(D) admissible as substantive evidence only if the underlying timesheets were lost through no fault of the lawyer.

[Q6002]

Answer 33: Choice **(C)** is correct. FRE 1006 says that "the contents of voluminous writings, recordings or photographs which cannot conveniently be examined in court may be presented in the form of a chart, summary, or calculation." The individual timesheets here meet the "voluminous writings" standard, since they would be almost daily over a five-year timeframe, a stack that would be hard for the judge or jury to examine in court. FRE 1006 also says that "the originals, or duplicates, shall be made available for examination or copying, or both, by other parties at reasonable time and place." So the fact that the underlying timesheets were made available to the client prior to trial, as specified in this choice, is a necessary condition for the summaries' admission under FRE 1006. By the way, the summaries: (1) become evidence (i.e., they're not just non-evidentiary testimonial aids); and (2) substitute for the underlying originals, which means that those originals must be independently admissible. Here, the underlying timesheets are hearsay, but they fall within FRE 803(6)'s business records exception.

(A) is wrong because the summary-of-voluminous-writings provision of FRE 1006 applies as described in Choice (C) above, and that provision does not require that the underlying writings being summarized be offered into evidence (although they may be).

(B) is wrong because, under FRE 1006, the summaries can come in as substantive evidence, as described in Choice (C) above.

(D) is wrong because the summaries can come in under FRE 1006 even if the underlying timesheets have not been lost. If you picked this choice, you may be thinking of FRE 1004(1), under which the B.E.R. can be satisfied by something other than the original writing or a duplicate thereof (e.g., a summary) if "all originals are lost or have been destroyed, unless the proponent lost or destroyed them in bad faith[.]" But FRE 1006 provides an independent means of getting summaries into evidence (one that does not depend on loss of originals), and that means 1006 is available here as discussed in Choice (C) above.

CHAPTER 8
OPINIONS, EXPERTS, AND SCIENTIFIC EVIDENCE

I. EXPERT WITNESSES

A. Basis for expert's opinion

1. Inadmissible evidence

a. Proponent and expert can't disclose

Question 34: Phillips purchased a suit of thermal underwear manufactured by Makorp from synthetic materials. While he was attempting to stamp out a fire, Phillips' thermal underwear caught fire and burned in a melting fashion up to his waist. He suffered a heart attack a half hour later. In a suit against Makorp, Phillips alleged that negligence and breach of warranty caused both the burn and the heart attack. Phillips testified to the foregoing.

Dr. Jones, a physician, having listened to Phillips' testimony, is called by Phillips and asked whether, assuming the truth of such testimony, Phillips' subsequent heart attack could have resulted from the burns. His opinion is

(A) admissible as a response to a hypothetical question.

(B) admissible because the physician's expertise enables him to judge the credibility of Phillips' testimony.

(C) inadmissible, because a hypothetical question may not be based on prior testimony.

(D) inadmissible, because an expert's opinion may not be based solely on information provided by lay persons.

[Q8079]

Answer 34: Choice **(A)** is the best response because it correctly identifies that the testimony here is admissible as a response to a hypothetical question. Expert testimony is appropriate where the court determines that "scientific, technical, or other specialized knowledge will assist the trier of fact to understand the evidence or to determine a fact in issue." FRE 702. Here, physician's testimony will address the causation issue — whether or not flaming underwear could cause a heart attack. Physician's status as an expert entitles him to offer opinion evidence that would be inadmissible coming from a lay witness, and to rely on information unavailable to a lay witness. The related issue is whether Physician may rely on the testimony presented at trial. The answer is yes: FRE 703 says that "The facts or data in the particular case upon which an expert bases an opinion ... may be those perceived by or *made known to the expert at* or before the hearing." So data supplied "at" the hearing — whether in the form of testimony of other witnesses or a hypothetical posed by the questioner (here, it's a combination of both) — may be the basis for the expert opinion.

(B) is wrong because Jones's status as a physician wouldn't give him expert status in determining credibility. As a threshold matter, credibility itself is not a "fact," and expert testimony is only available to assist the trier of fact to understand evidence or to determine a fact in issue. FRE 702. Beyond that, a physician's expertise gives him the ability to offer opinion testimony on medical matters; it's irrelevant to assessing the credibility of testimony, since one's status as a doctor doesn't make him a better judge of witness credibility than anyone else.

(C) is wrong because it states an incorrect rule. FRE 703 says that "The facts or data in the particular case upon which an expert bases an opinion ... may be those perceived by or *made known to the expert at* or before the hearing." This language allows the expert to offer an opinion based on the "data" included in a hypothetical question. And the hypothetical question for this purpose can be based on prior trial testimony and on the assumption that that prior testimony is truthful. (That's in fact a very common way for a proponent of expert testimony to proceed.)

(D) is wrong because it states an incorrect rule. An expert may base her opinion on "[t]he facts or data ... made known to the expert at or before the hearing." FRE 703. Neither this nor any other provision prevents the expert from basing her opinion solely on information provided by lay persons.

BURDENS OF PROOF, PRESUMPTIONS, AND OTHER PROCEDURAL ISSUES

I. PRESUMPTIONS

A. Effect of presumptions in federal civil cases

1. How this works

a. Instructions to jury

Question 35: In litigation on a federal claim, Plaintiff had the burden of proving that Defendant received a notice. Plaintiff relied on the presumption of receipt by offering evidence that timely notice was addressed to Defendant, properly stamped, and mailed. Defendant, on the other hand, testified that she never received the notice.

Which of the following is correct?

(A) The jury must find that the notice was received.

(B) The jury may find that the notice was received.

(C) The burden shifts to Defendant to persuade the jury of nonreceipt.

(D) The jury must find that the notice was not received, because the presumption has been rebutted and there is uncontradicted evidence of nonreceipt.

[Q1091]

Answer 35: Choice **(B)** is correct. Under FRE 301, once the opponent of the presumption comes up with enough evidence of the presumed fact's non-existence that a jury could reasonably find that the presumed fact does not exist, the presumption disappears from the case in the sense that there is no effect on the burden of persuasion. When this happens, the court may instruct the jury that it *may* infer the existence of the presumed fact from proof of the basic fact, but the jury is not required to so infer. In this case, Defendant's testimony, "I never got the notice," is enough to entitle a reasonable jury to find that the presumed fact (receipt) does not exist. Therefore, the presumption of receipt has disappeared and the plaintiff still has the burden of persuasion regarding the issue of receipt of the notice. But notwithstanding the disappearance of the presumption, the jury is still entitled to conclude that notice was received from proof of the basic fact that notice was given. Therefore, this choice is accurate in saying that the jury may infer, but is not required to infer, that the notice was received.

(A) is wrong because, as noted in the explanation of (B), once the presumption disappears from the case, the court may instruct the jury that it *may* infer the existence of the presumed fact from proof of the basic facts, but it is *not required* that the jury do so.

(C) is wrong because, as explained in (B), the presumption has no effect on the burden of persuasion; it "remains throughout the trial upon the party on whom it was originally cast" (FRE 301) which, in this case, is the plaintiff.

(D) is wrong because, as discussed in (B), the jury may infer the existence of the presumed fact from proof of the basic fact (i.e., jury may find that the notice was received) even though the presumption has disappeared from the case.

II. JUDGE-JURY ALLOCATION

A. Issues of fact

1. Technical exclusionary rule

a. Rules of evidence not binding

Question 36: In a prosecution of Drew for forgery, the defense objects to the testimony of West, a government expert, on the ground of inadequate qualifications. The government seeks to introduce a letter from the expert's former criminology professor, stating that West is generally acknowledged in his field as well qualified.

On the issue of the expert's qualifications, the letter may be considered by

(A) the jury, without regard to the hearsay rule.

(B) the judge, without regard to the hearsay rule.

(C) neither the judge nor the jury, because it is hearsay not within any exception.

(D) both the judge and the jury, because the letter is not offered for a hearsay purpose.

[Q2015]

Answer 36: Choice **(B)** is correct. Questions of whether a person is qualified to be a witness (whether expert or lay) are to be decided by the judge. In doing so, the judge may take into account inadmissible evidence (except with respect to privileges). FRE 104(a).

(A), (C), and (D) are wrong because each is inconsistent with the above explanation.

Question 37: In a prosecution of the defendant for murder, the government seeks to introduce a properly authenticated note written by the victim that reads: "[the defendant] did it." In laying the foundation for admitting the note as a dying declaration, the prosecution offered an affidavit from the attending physician that the victim knew she was about to die when she wrote the note.

The admissibility of the note as a dying declaration is

(A) a preliminary fact question for the judge, and the judge must not consider the affidavit.

(B) a preliminary fact question for the judge, and the judge may properly consider the affidavit.

(C) a question of weight and credibility for the jury, and the jury must not consider the affidavit.

(D) a question of weight and credibility for the jury, and the jury may properly consider the affidavit.

[Q1005]

Answer 37: Choice **(B)** is correct. Both parts of this answer are true. As to the first part, before a declaration can be found to be an admissible "dying declaration," some preliminary questions of fact must be answered. In particular, it must be determined whether the declarant was indeed aware of her impending death. Under the FRE, the jury decides issues like this, of conditional relevance, but it is the judge who makes the initial decision of admissibility, in determining whether a reasonable jury could find that the preliminary fact exists: "When the relevancy of evidence depends upon the fulfillment of a condition of fact, the court shall admit it upon, or subject to, the introduction of evidence sufficient to support a finding of the fulfillment of the condition." FRE 104(b). In other words, if the judge decides that there is enough evidence that a jury could reasonably find that there was an awareness of impending death, he will let the jury hear the declaration (even though he may personally believe that it is less likely than not that there was such awareness).

As to the second part, the judge's ability to consider the affidavit, FRE 104(a) says that "Preliminary questions concerning … the admissibility of evidence shall be determined by the court… In making its determination it is not bound by the rules of evidence except those with respect to privileges." The affidavit is relevant to the issue of whether the declarant was aware of her impending death. It's true that the affidavit is hearsay (it's an out-of-court statement offered to prove the truth of the matter asserted, i.e., that the victim knew or believed she was dying). And this hearsay does not fall within any exception. But under 104(a), the court may consider this inadmissible hearsay to make his preliminary ruling on the admissibility of the note.

(A) is wrong because, although it correctly states that the admissibility of the note is a preliminary fact question for the judge, it incorrectly states that the judge must not consider the affidavit. As described in the discussion of Choice (B) above, the judge may consider inadmissible hearsay when resolving a preliminary question about the admissibility of other evidence.

(C) is wrong because, although it is true that the jury must not consider the affidavit, the admissibility of the note is not a question for the jury. It will be up to the jury to determine what weight and credibility to give the evidence of the note once it has been admitted.

(D) is wrong because the jury cannot consider the affidavit (it is hearsay) and also because the admissibility of the note is not a question for the jury. It will be up to the jury to determine what weight and credibility to give the evidence of the note once it has been admitted.

CHAPTER 10

JUDICIAL NOTICE

I. ADJUDICATIVE FACTS

A. Must take if requested, and may take without a request

1. Discretionary notice

Question 38: In contract litigation between Pixley and Dill, a fact of consequence to the determination of the action is whether Pixley provided Dill with a required notice at Dill's branch office "in the state capital." Pixley introduced evidence that he gave notice at Dill's office in the city of Capitan. Although Capitan is the state's capital, Pixley failed to offer proof of that fact.

Which of the following statements is most clearly correct with respect to possible judicial notice of the fact that Capitan is the state's capital?

(A) The court may take judicial notice even though Pixley does not request it.

(B) The court may take judicial notice only if Pixley provides the court with an authenticated copy of the statute that designates Capitan as the capital.

(C) If the court takes judicial notice, the burden of persuasion on the issue of whether Capitan is the capital shifts to Dill.

(D) If the court takes judicial notice, it should instruct the jury that it may, but is not required to, accept as conclusive the fact that Capitan is the capital.

[Q2007]

Answer 38: Choice **(A)** is correct. First, the location of the state capital is a fact that is *"generally known"* within the relevant community. FRE 201(b). So the fact that Capitan is the capital is appropriate for judicial notice. Second, FRE 201(c) provides that "A court may take judicial notice, whether requested or not." So the court may take notice here without a request from either party.

(B) is wrong because judicial notice of an appropriate fact may be taken without submission of formal evidence that the fact is true.

(C) is wrong because, in a civil case, once there is judicial notice, the issue is decided and the jury does not weigh the evidence in order to come to its own conclusion. See FRE 201: the judge "shall instruct the jury to accept as conclusive any fact judicially noticed."

(D) is wrong because in a civil case the jury is required to accept as conclusive the judicially noticed fact, as discussed in (C).

REAL PROPERTY

REAL PROPERTY Q&A BY TOPIC

References to "Rest. 2d" are to the *Second Restatement of Property.*

CHAPTER 1
ADVERSE POSSESSION

I. "HOSTILE" POSSESSION

A. Boundary disputes

Question 1: Twenty-five years ago a seller conveyed Lot 1 to a buyer by a warranty deed. The seller at that time also executed and delivered an instrument in the proper form of a deed, purporting to convey Lot 2 to the buyer. The seller thought she had title to Lot 2 but did not; therefore, no title passed by virtue of the Lot 2 deed. Lot 2 consisted of three acres of brushland adjoining the west boundary of Lot 1. The buyer has occasionally hunted rabbits on Lot 2, but less often than annually. No one else came onto Lot 2 except occasional rabbit hunters.

Twenty years ago, the buyer planted a row of evergreens in the vicinity of the opposite (east) boundary of Lot 1 and erected a fence just beyond the evergreens to the east. In fact both the trees and the fence were placed on Lot 3, owned by a neighbor, which bordered the east boundary of Lot 1. The buyer was unsure of the exact boundary, and placed the trees and the fence in order to establish his rights up to the fence. The fence is located ten feet within Lot 3.

Now, the buyer has had his property surveyed and the title checked and has learned the facts.

The period of time to acquire title by adverse possession in the jurisdiction is 15 years.

The buyer consulted his lawyer, who properly advised that, in an appropriate action, the buyer would probably obtain title to

(A) Lot 2 but not to the ten-foot strip of Lot 3.

(B) the ten-foot strip of Lot 3 but not to Lot 1.

(C) both Lot 2 and the ten-foot strip of
Lot 3.

(D) neither Lot 2 nor the ten-foot strip of Lot 3.

[Q1063]

Answer 1: Choice **(B)** is correct. Courts generally hold that one who possesses an adjoining landowner's land, under the mistaken belief that he has only possessed up to the boundary of his own land, meets the requirement of "hostile" possession and can become an owner by adverse possession. This is especially likely where the possessor has both planted and fenced in the land in question, since such actions are very likely to bring home to the record owner that the possessor is asserting an adverse claim. So the buyer is highly likely to be found to have gained title to the 10-foot strip of Lot 3 by adverse possession. On the other hand, the buyer has not met the requirement for "continuous" possession of Lot 2. The requirement of "continuous" position does not mean that the possessor must be physically on the property 100% of the time. However, a court would almost certainly require more than the very occasional rabbit-hunting at issue here in order to conclude that the buyer had "continuously" occupied Lot 2.

(A), (C), and (D) are wrong because they are inconsistent with the above analysis.

II. CONTINUITY OF POSSESSION

A. Continuity of possession

1. Temporary or seasonal gaps in possession

Question 2: Brown owned Blackacre, a tract of undeveloped land. Blackacre abuts Whiteacre, a tract of land owned by Agency, the state's governmental energy agency At Whiteacre, Agency has operated a waste-to-electricity recycling facility for 12 years. Blackacre and Whiteacre are in a remote area and Whiteacre is the only developed parcel of real estate within a ten-mile radius. The boundary line between Blackacre and Whiteacre had never been surveyed or marked on the face of the earth.

During the past 12 years, some of the trucks bringing waste to the Agency facility have dumped their loads so that the piles of waste extend from Whiteacre onto a portion of Blackacre. However, prior to the four-week period during each calendar year when the Agency facility is closed for inspection and repairs, the waste piles are reduced to minimal levels so that during each of the four-week closures no waste was, in fact, piled on Blackacre. Neither Brown nor any representative of Agency knew the facts about the relation of the boundary line to the waste piles.

The time for acquiring title by adverse possession in the jurisdiction is ten years.

Last year, Brown died, and his son, Silas, succeeded him as the owner of Blackacre. Silas became aware of the facts, demanded that Agency stop using Blackacre for the piling of waste, and, when Agency refused his demand, brought an appropriate action to enjoin any such use of Blackacre in the future.

If Agency prevails in that action, it will be because

(A) the facts constitute adverse possession and title to the portion of Blackacre concerned has vested in Agency.

(B) Brown's failure to keep himself informed as to Agency's use of Blackacre and his failure to object constituted implied consent to the continuation of that use.

(C) the interest of the public in the conversion of waste to energy overrides any entitlement of Silas to equitable remedies.

(D) the power of eminent domain of the state makes the claim of Silas moot.

[Q2089]

Answer 2: Choice **(A)** is correct. Agency will win on an adverse possession claim if its possession was open, notorious, visible, hostile and continuous. The requirement of hostility would likely be deemed satisfied, because in a boundary dispute an owner who openly occupies the adjacent parcel under the mistaken belief it is his own is typically found to meet the hostility requirement. The only other requirement that is seriously in issue here is whether Agency's possession was "continuous," in the light of the annual four-week period in which there was no trespass. A court would likely hold that this brief respite each year did not prevent the possession from being continuous, because Agency was treating Blackacre exactly the same way it treated its own adjacent portion of Whiteacre — doing annual cleanup that happened to have the unanticipated effect of removing the trespass. It is not certain that a court would conclude that the continuity requirement was met, but adverse possession is the only one of the choices that would plausibly yield a victory for Agency.

(B) is wrong because the only way in which Brown could be found to have given an implied consent to Agency's use would be if Brown's silence was found to have created either a license or an easement. A license is by its nature a revocable right of use, so even if Brown's silence had created a license by implication, Brown or his successor would be entitled to revoke the license at will, and Silas's suit would constitute such a revocation. As for an easement, easements must generally satisfy the statute of frauds. It is true that an easement by "estoppel" can be created, but this occurs only when the owner of the servient tenement allows a use of his land while he knew or should have known that the user would change position in reliance; here there has been no meaningful reliance by Agency, so this theory would not work.

(C) is wrong because Agency can win only if it obtained legal title to the part of Blackacre in question, and not degree of "public interest" in waste-conversion could ever give Agency title to the property by operation of law.

(D) is wrong because it concerns the wrong area of law. Agency is not trying to obtain title to the relevant portion of Blackacre through eminent domain (i.e. it is not trying to obtain title by paying just compensation). Instead, it is acting under "color of title" as if it already owned the portion of Blackacre concerned. Hence, the problem calls for an adverse possession analysis, not an eminent domain analysis.

CHAPTER 2
FREEHOLD ESTATES

I. THE FEE SIMPLE

A. Fee simple defeasible

1. Determinable

a. Distinguish from restrictive covenant

Question 3: A grantor executed an instrument in the proper form of a warranty deed purporting to convey a tract of land to his church. The granting clause of the instrument ran to the church "and its successors forever, so long as the premises are used for church purposes." The church took possession of the land and used it as its site of worship for many years. Subsequently, the church wanted to relocate and entered into a valid written contract to sell the land to a buyer for a substantial price. The buyer wanted to use the land as a site for business activities and objected to the church's title. The contract contained no provision relating to the quality of title the church was bound to convey. There is no applicable statute. When the buyer refused to close, the church sued the buyer for specific performance and properly joined the grantor as a party.

Is the church likely to prevail?

(A) No, because the grantor's interest prevents the church's title from being marketable.

(B) No, because the quoted provision is a valid restrictive covenant.

C) Yes, because a charitable trust to support religion will attach to the proceeds of the sale.

D) Yes, because the grantor cannot derogate from his warranty to the church.

[Q7018]

Answer 3: Choice **(A)** is correct. The warranty deed conveyed a fee simple determinable title to the church, and the grantor retained the future interest (a possibility of reverter). Such a reverter becomes possessory immediately upon the occurrence of the limitation. A title is unmarketable when a reasonable person would not purchase it. This buyer plans to use the land as a site for business purposes, which would cause the limitation to occur and the title to be forfeited automatically to the grantor. That possibility is easily enough to render the title unmarketable.

(B) is incorrect. Although this answer correctly states that the church is unlikely to prevail, it misstates the legal basis for this conclusion. The quoted provision creates a fee simple determinable title in the church (because the title in this case will be automatically forfeited to the grantor if the land is not used for church purposes), not a restrictive covenant. A restrictive covenant involves a promise regarding the use of the land and is not the title itself (though the existence of a restrictive covenant barring non-church uses would, like the determinable fee here, be enough to render title unmarketable).

(C) is wrong because it cites an irrelevant fact. The "so long as ..." clause created a possibility of reverter, making the church's title unmarketable. The clause will not create a trust for the benefit of religion, as this choice asserts (and even if it did, that wouldn't prevent the possibility of reverter from operating to divest the buyer of title if he were forced to close on the sale).

(D) is wrong because it's gibberish. The choice seems to be asserted that the grantor can't have a possibility of reverter because such an interest would be inconsistent with the warranty deed that grantor gave. But that's flatly untrue — the warranty deed just asserts that whatever title grantor is conveying, he has (and in this case, he gave a lesser interest than he had, i.e., reserved a possibility of reverter to himself).

2. **Fee simple subject to condition subsequent**

   a. **Distinguishing fee simple subject to condition precedent**

   Question 4: A landowner owned land in fee simple. A small house on the land was occupied, with the landowner's oral permission, rent-free, by the landowner's son and the son's college classmate. The son was then 21 years old.

   The landowner, by properly executed instrument, conveyed the land to "my beloved son, his heirs and assigns, upon the condition precedent that he earn a college degree by the time he reaches the age of 30. If, for any reason, he does not meet this condition, then the land shall become the sole property of my beloved daughter, her heirs and assigns." At the time of the conveyance, the son and the classmate attended a college located several blocks from the land. Neither had earned a college degree.

   One week after the delivery of the deed to the son, the son recorded the deed and immediately told the classmate that he, the son, was going to begin charging the classmate rent since "I am now your landlord." There is no applicable statute.

   The son and the classmate did not reach agreement, and the son served the appropriate notice to terminate whatever tenancy the classmate had. The son then sought, in an appropriate action, to oust the classmate.

   Who should prevail?

   (A) The son, because the conveyance created a fee simple subject to divestment in the son.

(B) The son, because the landowner's conveyance terminated the classmate's tenancy.

(C) The classmate, because the landowner's permission to occupy preceded the land-owner's conveyance to the son.

(D) The classmate, because he is a tenant of the landowner, not of the son.

[Q1173]

Answer 4: Choice **(D)** is correct. The conveyance to the son was a gift of a fee simple subject to the condition precedent that the son get a college degree prior to turning 30. Until the son got the degree, the conveyance did not create any present possessory interest in him (and the possessory interest remained in the landowner, with an executory interest in the daughter ready to spring out of the landowner if the son turned 30 without getting the degree). Therefore, the classmate continued to be a tenant of the landowner, not of the son, with the result that the son did not have the right to terminate the classmate's tenancy or oust him.

(A) is wrong because the phrase "upon the condition precedent..." in the landowner-to-son conveyance made the gift a fee simple subject to a condition precedent, not a fee simple subject to divestment. (If the gift had read, "to my son and his heirs, but if my son turns 30 without having obtained a college degree, then to my daughter," then the son *would* indeed have had a fee simple subject to divestment, and the son would have won the case, making this choice correct.)

(B) is wrong because a conveyance by the owner will not normally terminate a tenancy, even where the conveyance is a transfer of a fee simple absolute or a fee simple subject to divestment; furthermore, in this case the conveyance was of a fee simple subject to a condition precedent, so it was even further from terminating the classmate's tenancy.

(C) is wrong because the fact that the permission to occupy was both oral and rent-free establishes that it was a tenancy at will (or else a license); therefore, it could be terminated at any time by either party acting unilaterally. Consequently, although this choice correctly states the result that the classmate wins, it does not correctly state the reason this is so.

II. THE LIFE ESTATE

A. Duties and powers of life tenant

1. Duties

a. No waste

i. Demolition and rebuilding

Question 5: Alice owned a commercial property, Eastgate, consisting of a one-story building rented to various retail stores and a very large parking lot. Two years ago, Alice died and left Eastgate to her nephew, Paul, for life, with remainder to her godson, Richard, his heirs and assigns. Paul was 30 years old and Richard was 20 years old when Alice died. The devise of Eastgate was made subject to any mortgage on Eastgate in effect at the time of Alice's death.

When Alice executed her will, the balance of the mortgage debt on Eastgate was less than $5,000. A year before her death, Alice suffered financial reverses; and in order to meet her debts, she had mortgaged Eastgate to secure a loan of $150,000. The entire principal of the mortgage remained outstanding when she died. As a result, the net annual income from Eastgate was reduced not only by real estate taxes and regular maintenance costs, but also by the substantial mortgage interest payments that were due each month.

Paul was very dissatisfied with the limited benefit that he was receiving from the life estate. When, earlier this year, Acme, Inc., proposed to purchase Eastgate, demolish the building, pay off the mortgage, and construct a 30-story office building, Paul was willing to accept Acme's offer. However, Richard adamantly refused the offer, even though Richard, as the remainderman, paid the principal portion of each monthly mortgage amortization payment. Richard was independently wealthy and wanted to convert Eastgate into a public park when he became entitled to possession.

When Acme realized that Richard would not change his mind, Acme modified its proposal to a purchase of the life estate of Paul. Acme was ready to go ahead with its building plans, relying upon a large life insurance policy on Paul's life to protect it against the economic risk of Paul's death. Paul's life expectancy was 45 years.

When Richard learned that Paul had agreed to Acme's modified proposal, Richard brought an appropriate action against them to enjoin their carrying it out.

There is no applicable statute.

The best argument for Richard is that

(A) Acme cannot purchase Paul's life estate, because life estates are not assignable.

(B) the proposed demolition of the building constitutes waste.

(C) Richard's payment of the mortgage principal has subrogated him to Paul's rights as a life tenant and bars Paul's assignment of the life estate without Richard's consent.

(D) continued existence of the one-story building is more in harmony with the ultimate use as a park than the proposed change in use.

[Q2179]

Answer 5: Choice **(B)** is correct. Ordinarily, a life tenant may not demolish a structure on the premises, even in order to build a bigger structure at his own expense that would render the future interest more valuable; such a demolition is classified as waste. Courts have recognized a narrow exception where changes in the character of the neighborhood have deprived the property in its present form of "reasonable productivity or usefulness," but this would probably not be found to have occurred here, since the structure is being used for retail stores and produces meaningful rent. (The problem is the substantial mortgage that eats up the rents, not the lack of any reasonably-productive use.) It is not certain that Richard would win with this argument (since Paul might succeed in establishing the no-reasonably-productive-use-in-present-form exception), but this is the only one of the four listed arguments that might plausibly produce a victory for Richard.

(A) is wrong because life estates are completely assignable, without the consent of the holder of the future interest; the assignee simply receives a life estate *per autre vie*.

(C) is wrong because Richard's payment of the mortgage principal does not change his rights; even without such payments he would be entitled to veto a demolition and replacement of the premises unless the narrow exception described in (B) applied.

(D) is wrong because the maintenance of "harmony" with the use envisioned by the future interest holder is not a relevant factor in the decision about whether the proposed use violates the latter's rights; the issue is whether the proposed use would or would not constitute "waste," and harmony with the future holder's desires is not part of the waste analysis.

b. Current operating expenses

i.   Taxes

Question 6: Ody, owner of Profitacre, executed an instrument in the proper form of a deed, purporting to convey Profitacre "to Leon for life, then to Ralph in fee simple." Leon, who is Ody's brother and Ralph's father, promptly began to manage Profitacre, which is valuable income-producing real estate. Leon collected all rents and paid all expenses, including real estate taxes. Ralph did not object, and this state of affairs continued for five years until 2007. In that year, Leon executed an instrument in the proper form of a deed, purporting to convey Profitacre to Mona. Ralph, no admirer of Mona, asserted his right to ownership of Profitacre. Mona asserted her ownership and said that if Ralph had any rights he was obligated to pay real estate taxes, even though Leon had been kind enough to pay them in the past. Income from Profitacre is ample to cover expenses, including real estate taxes.

In an appropriate action to determine the rights of the parties, the court should decide

(A) Leon's purported deed forfeited his life estate, so Ralph owns Profitacre in fee simple.

(B) Mona owns an estate for her life, is entitled to all income, and must pay real estate taxes; Ralph owns the remainder interest.

(C) Mona owns an estate for the life of Leon, is entitled to all income, and must pay real estate taxes; Ralph owns the remainder interest.

(D) Mona owns an estate for the life of Leon and is entitled to all income; Ralph owns the remainder interest, and must pay real estate taxes.

[Q2138]

Answer 6: Choice **(C)** is correct. When Leon, the life tenant, purported to convey the fee simple to Mona, this conveyance had the effect of conveying all of Leon's interest in the property, i.e., his life tenancy. Therefore, Mona had a life estate *per autre vie*, i.e., an estate for the life of Leon. Once Mona stepped into Leon's shoes as life tenant, she had the right to collect all income from the property, but also the obligation to pay all current operating expenses including real estate taxes. Ralph always had a remainder interest following Leon's life estate, and Ralph's interest was not changed in any way by Leon's conveyance of his own interest to Mona.

(A) is wrong because a life tenant's attempt to convey a fee simple does not cause the life estate to be forfeited; such a conveyance merely transfers to the grantee the entirety of the grantor's interest (i.e., the life tenancy).

(B) is wrong because what Mona received is precisely what Leon had, namely an estate for the life of Leon.

(D) is wrong because real estate taxes are the responsibility of the life tenant, not the remainderman.

c. Payment of mortgage

i. No personal obligation

Question 7: A testator owned in fee simple a farm of 300 acres. He died and by will duly admitted to probate devised the farm to his surviving widow, for life with remainder in fee simple to his three children, two daughters and a son. All three children survived the testator.

At the time of the testator's death, there existed a mortgage on the farm that the testator had given ten years before to secure a loan for the purchase of the farm. At his death, there remained unpaid $40,000 in principal, payable in installments of $4,000 per year for the next ten years. In addition, there was due interest at the rate of 10% per annum, payable annually with the installment of principal. The widow took possession and out of a gross income of $50,000 per year realized $25,000 net after paying all expenses and charges except the installment of principal and interest due on the mortgage.

The daughters wanted the three children, including the son, to each contribute one-third of the amounts needed to pay the mortgage installments. The son objected, contending that the widow should pay all of these amounts out of the profits she had made in operation of the farm. When foreclosure of the mortgage seemed imminent, the son sought legal advice.

If the son obtained sound advice relating to his rights, he was told that

(A) his only protection would lie in instituting an action for partition to compel the sale of the life estate of the widow and to obtain the value of the son's one-third interest in remainder.

(B) he could obtain appropriate relief to compel the widow personally to pay the sums due because the income is more than adequate to cover these amounts.

(C) he could be compelled personally to pay his share of the amounts due because discharge of the mortgage enhances the principal.

(D) he could not be held personally liable for any amount but that his share in remainder could be lost if the mortgage installments are not paid.

[Q1107]

Answer 7: Choice **(D)** is correct. The general rule about personal liability for mortgage payments as between present and future interests is that neither party has personal liability, except to the extent that party is receiving net operating income from the property. Since the son as remainderman gets no operating income from the property, he has no personal liability to make any mortgage payments. However, if neither he nor anyone else makes all required mortgage payments, the property will presumably be lost to foreclosure, in which case the son's remainder interest will be lost. Therefore, the son has the right (which he may well want to exercise), but not the obligation, to contribute his one-third share of whatever mortgage payments that the widow is unable or unwilling to make.

(A) is wrong because the holder of a future interest generally does not have the right to bring a partition action to compel the sale of the possessory estate (here, the widow's life estate).

(B) is wrong because it overstates the widow's obligation; the widow probably does have a personal obligation to pay her fairly-allocated share of the mortgage payments (based on the relative value of the widow's life estate versus the remainder), up to the amount of net income she's receiving, but this choice incorrectly suggests that she would be personally liable to pay the *entire* installments rather than just her share if the net income were large enough.

(C) is wrong because the son, as a remainderman, has no personal liability to make mortgage payments at all (since he is not getting any operating income out of which to pay them).

CHAPTER 3
FUTURE INTERESTS

I.   POSSIBILITY OF REVERTER; RIGHT OF RE-ENTRY

A.   Possibility of reverter and right of re-entry

1.   Possibility of reverter

a.   Conflict between will and inheritance

Question 8: Twenty years ago, a landowner who owned Blackacre, a one-acre tract of land, duly delivered a deed of Blackacre "to School District so long as it is used for school purposes." The deed was promptly and properly recorded. Five years ago, the landowner died, leaving Sonny as his only heir at law. The landowner left a duly probated will, by which he left "all my Estate" to his friend, who was a doctor.

Last month, School District closed its school on Blackacre and for valid consideration duly executed and delivered a quitclaim deed of Blackacre to a developer, who planned to use the land for commercial development. The developer has now brought an appropriate action to quiet title against the son, the doctor and School District.

The only applicable statute is a provision in the jurisdiction's probate code which provides that any property interest which is descendible is devisable.

In such action, the court should find that title is now in

(A) the developer.

(B) the son.

(C) the doctor.

(D) School District.

[Q1200]

Answer 8: Choice **(C)** is correct. When the landowner conveyed to School District, School District got a fee simple determinable (a fee simple that would automatically end if the property ever ceased to be used for school purposes). The landowner retained a possibility of reverter, which is what the grantor retains following a fee simple determinable, if the fee simple determinable doesn't specify what happens upon failure of the condition. In virtually all states, a possibility of reverter can be inherited under the intestacy statute (i.e., it is "descendible"). The probate provision here tells us that if the interest is descendible, it is also devisable (i.e., can be left by will). Since we know that the possibility of reverter is descendible, we therefore know that it is also devisable. Since the landowner left a will devising his entire estate to the doctor, the reverter will pass by devise (i.e., by the will), not by inheritance. That's because of the basic rule that where a particular item of property is covered by a valid bequest in a will, the item will pass by will rather than by intestacy. Therefore, the reverter goes to the doctor under the will.

(A) is wrong because once School District closed its school, its interest in Blackacre was automatically extinguished, and there was nothing left to pass to the developer via the quitclaim deed.

(B) is wrong because the son's status as heir (i.e., as taker under the intestacy statute) was irrelevant given that the reverter here was bequeathed under the will, and was therefore not available to be passed by inheritance.

(D) is wrong because once School District closed its school, its interest was automatically extinguished.

II. REMAINDERS

A. Contingent remainders

1. Condition precedent

Question 9: A testator owned a tract of land in fee simple. By will duly admitted to probate after his death, the testator devised the land to "any wife who survives me with remainder to such of my children as are living at her death."

The testator was survived by his widow and by three children, who were an accountant, a lawyer, and a doctor. Thereafter, the lawyer died and by will duly admitted to probate devised his entire estate to his friend. The accountant and the doctor were the lawyer's heirs at law.

Later the widow died. In an appropriate lawsuit to which the accountant, the doctor, and the friend are parties, title to the land is at issue.

In such lawsuit, judgment should be that title to the property is in

(A) the accountant, the doctor, and the friend, because the earliest vesting of remainders is favored and reference to the surviving wife's death should be construed as relating to time of taking possession.

(B) the accountant, the doctor, and the friend, because the provision requiring survival of children violates the Rule Against Perpetuities since the surviving wife might have been a person unborn at the time of writing of the will.

(C) the accountant and the doctor, because the lawyer's remainder must descend by intestacy and is not devisable.

(D) the accountant and the doctor, because the remainders were contingent upon surviving the life tenant.

[Q2187]

Answer 9: Choice **(D)** is correct. The terms of the bequest made it clear that only a child who survived the testator's wife would take. Each child had a contingent remainder as of the testator's death. When the lawyer died before his mother (the widow) died, the lawyer's contingent remainder was nullified without ever becoming vested, leaving nothing to pass to the lawyer's friend by devise. At the widow's death, the contingent remainders in the accountant and the doctor vested (and, simultaneously, became possessory).

(A) is wrong for the same reason (D) is right: the remainders were intended by the testator to be contingent unless and until the remaindermen survived the widow, at which time they would vest. So when the lawyer died, his contingent remainder was destroyed by his failing to have survived the widow, and he had no interest to pass to the friend.

(B) is wrong because under the common law approach to the Rule against Perpetuities, the time for evaluating a will is when the testator *dies*, *not* when the will was *executed*. At the time the testator died, his widow (and, indeed, his children as well) were necessarily already in existence, and could therefore serve as measuring lives. So there was no risk that the remainder to the testator's children would vest beyond "measuring lives plus 21 years," making the gift to those children valid contingent remainders.

(C) is wrong as a matter of law: some remainders can indeed descend by intestacy. *Example*: O bequeaths "to A for life, then to B." Assume B is living at O's death, but dies intestate before A, and with C as his heir at law. At B's death, the vested remainder in B passes by intestacy to C, and C will have a fee simple once B dies.

2. Unborn or unascertained

a. Remainder "to A and her heirs or assigns" is vested

Question 10: A grantor owned a tract of land in fee simple. By warranty deed he conveyed the land to his nephew for life "and from and after the death of my nephew to my niece, her heirs and assigns."

Subsequently the niece died, devising all of her estate to the niece's boyfriend. The niece was survived by a cousin, her sole heir-at-law.

Shortly thereafter the nephew died, survived by the grantor, the niece's boyfriend, and the niece's cousin.

Title to the land now is in

(A) the grantor, because the contingent remainder never vested and the grantor's reversion was entitled to possession immediately upon the nephew's death.

(B) the boyfriend, because the vested remainder in the niece was transmitted by her will.

(C) the cousin, because she is the niece's heir.

(D) either the grantor or the cousin, depending upon whether the destructibility of contingent remainders is recognized in the applicable jurisdiction.

[Q1151]

Answer 10: Choice **(B)** is correct. The remainder to "my niece, her heirs and assigns" was a remainder to the niece in fee simple. Since the niece was alive and identifiable at the time of the grantor's deed, the remainder to the niece was vested. A vested remainder can be left by will. Therefore, the remainder passed by the will to the boyfriend.

(A) is wrong because the remainder was never contingent, not even for an instant.

(C) is wrong because a vested remainder can be passed by will, and the will here devised the remainder to the boyfriend; therefore, the fact that the niece's cousin was the niece's heir at law is irrelevant.

(D) is wrong because the remainder here was vested, not contingent; therefore, the doctrine of destructibility of contingent remainders is irrelevant.

III. THE RULE AGAINST PERPETUITIES (RAP)

A. Applicability of Rule to various estates

1. Options to purchase land

a. Right of first refusal (RAP may apply)

Question 11: A grantor owned two tracts of land, one of 15 acres and another of five acres. The two tracts were a mile apart.

Fifteen years ago, the grantor conveyed the smaller tract to a grantee. The grantor retained the larger tract. The deed to the grantee contained, in addition to proper legal descriptions of both properties and identifications of the parties, the following:

I, the grantor, bind myself and my heirs and assigns that in the event that the larger tract that I now retain is ever offered for sale, I will notify the grantee and his heirs and assigns in writing, and the grantee and his heirs and assigns shall have the right to purchase the larger tract for its fair market value as determined by a board consisting of three qualified expert independent real estate appraisers.

With appropriate references to the other property and the parties, there followed a reciprocal provision that conferred upon the grantor and her heirs and assigns a similar right to purchase the smaller tract, purportedly binding the grantee and his heirs and assigns.

Ten years ago, a corporation acquired the larger tract from the grantor. At that time, the grantee had no interest in acquiring the larger tract and by an appropriate written document released any interest he or his heirs or assigns might have had in the larger tract.

Last year, the grantee died. The smaller tract passed by the grantee's will to his daughter. She has decided to sell the smaller tract. However, because she believes the corporation has been a very poor steward of the larger tract, she refuses to sell the smaller tract to the corporation even though she has offered it for sale in the local real estate market.

The corporation brought an appropriate action for specific performance after taking all of the necessary preliminary steps in its effort to exercise its rights to purchase the smaller tract.

The daughter asserted all possible defenses.

The common law Rule Against Perpetuities is unmodified in the jurisdiction.

If the court rules for the daughter, what is the reason?

(A) The provision setting out the right to purchase violates the Rule Against Perpetuities.

(B) The grantee's release 10 years ago operates as a waiver regarding any right to purchase that the corporation might have.

(C) The two tracts of land were not adjacent parcels of real estate, and thus the right to purchase is in gross and is therefore unenforceable.

(D) Noncompliance with a right to purchase gives rise to a claim for money damages, but not for specific performance.

[QA040]

Answer 11: Choice **(A)** is correct. Each of the original parties granted a reciprocal right of first refusal to the other and the other's heirs and assigns. A right of first refusal provides that if the owner ever decides to sell the property, the one holding the right of first refusal has the right to purchase it. A right of first refusal is therefore a conditional option to purchase, and it is analyzed for Rule Against Perpetuities (RAP) issues like other purchase options that are "in gross" (i.e., not associated with a lease). Courts are split as to whether to apply the RAP to rights of first refusal or other options in gross. We don't know here that the RAP will definitely be applied to such interests, but we do know that *if* it's applied, the daughter will win (and the question is asking what the reason will be if the daughter wins). Why will the daughter win? Because the RAP invalidates an interest unless it can be said with certainty at the time of creation that that interest will vest or fail to vest within 21 years. Here, the right of first refusal extended to the heirs and assigns of the original parties, so the decision to exercise the right *might* occur more than 21 years after a life in being at the time the right was granted. (For instance, the grantor's great-grandchild might try to exercise the right as against the grantee's great-grandchild.) The RAP in this jurisdiction is unmodified by statute — therefore, the right of first refusal is deemed void as of the time it was created, and the court will not wait to see whether anyone tries to exercise that right more than 21 years after a life in being. Consequently, the right is already invalid, even though only 15 years have passed since the right was created.

(B) is wrong because the fact that the grant*ee* chose not to exercise *his* right of first refusal has no effect on whether the grant*or* can exercise the reciprocal right of first refusal regarding the land originally owned by the grantee. That is, even if the grantee's decision not to exercise the right 10 years ago was a waiver of any subsequent right of first refusal on the part of the grantee or his heirs (which it almost certainly was), there would be no reason why that decision should act as a waiver by the grantor or her heirs as to the reciprocal right held by them.

(C) is wrong because it misstates the effect of the fact that the option is "in gross." An option "in gross" is an option that is not associated with a lease to the option-holder of the property to which the option applies. So the right of first refusal here is indeed an option in gross, as the choice suggests. But the choice is wrong for two reasons: (1) an option in gross is enforceable as long as the time period during which it can be enforced is not longer than the RAP period (i.e., not longer than lives in being plus 21 years); and (2) the fact that the parcels are not adjacent is irrelevant to the analysis. (That is, even if the two parcels *were* adjacent, the option would still be in gross because there is no lease.)

(D) is wrong because it misstates the remedies for breach of a right of first refusal. A holder of a purchase option is entitled to a decree of specific performance, under which the other party will be compelled to make the sale in return for the payment of the option's strike price. A right of first refusal is a conditional option to purchase. Once the condition is satisfied (by the other party's decision to sell), the holder of the option has the same right to a decree of specific performance as would the holder of an unconditional purchase option.

CHAPTER 4

CONCURRENT OWNERSHIP

I. JOINT TENANCY

A. Severance

1. Conveyance by one joint tenant

a. Most important on MBE

Question 12: By warranty deed, Marta conveyed Blackacre to Beth and Christine "as joint tenants with right of survivorship." Beth and Christine are not related. Beth conveyed all her interest to Eugenio by warranty deed and subsequently died intestate. Thereafter, Christine conveyed to Darin by warranty deed.

There is no applicable statute, and the jurisdiction recognizes the common-law joint tenancy.

Title to Blackacre is in

(A) Darin.

(B) Marta.

(C) Darin and Eugenio.

(D) Darin and the heirs of Beth.

[Q2001]

Answer 12: Choice **(C)** is correct. When Beth conveyed her interest to Eugenio, this act caused a severance, destroying the joint tenancy immediately and leaving Eugenio and Christine as tenants in common. When Christine conveyed her interest to Darin, he stepped into Christine's shoes, becoming a tenant in common with Eugenia.

Choices (A), (B), and (D) are wrong because they are inconsistent with the above analysis.

b. Motive irrelevant

Question 13: A brother and sister owned a large tract of land in fee simple as joint tenants with rights of survivorship. While the sister was on an extended safari in Kenya, the brother learned that there were very valuable coal deposits within the land, but he made no attempt to inform his sister. Thereupon, the brother conveyed his interest in the land to his wife, who immediately reconveyed that interest to the brother. The common-law joint tenancy is unmodified by statute.

Shortly thereafter, the brother was killed in an automobile accident. His will, which was duly probated, specifically devised his one-half interest in the property to his wife.

The sister then returned from Kenya and learned what had happened. The sister brought an appropriate action against the brother's wife, who claimed a one-half interest in the property, seeking a declaratory judgment that she, the sister, was the sole owner of the land.

In this action, who should prevail?

(A) The brother's wife, because the brother and sister were tenants in common at the time of the brother's death.

(B) The brother's wife, because the brother's will severed the joint tenancy.

(C) The sister, because the joint tenancy was reestablished by the brother's wife's reconveyance to the brother.

(D) The sister, because the brother breached his fiduciary duty as her joint tenant.

[Q1047]

Answer 13: Choice **(A)** is correct. When the brother conveyed his interest in the property to his wife, this conveyance acted as an immediate severance, transforming the joint tenancy into a tenancy in common between the wife and the sister. When the wife immediately reconveyed to the brother, the brother and sister were tenants in common. When the brother died, his interest as a tenant in common passed back to his wife, making her a tenant in common with the sister.

(B) is wrong because the joint tenancy was severed before the brother's will took effect (at the moment the brother conveyed to his wife).

(C) is wrong because once the joint tenancy was broken by the conveyance from the brother to his wife, it could only be reestablished by a new conveyance joined in by both tenants in common, i.e., the wife and the sister (or, later, the brother and sister).

(D) is wrong because a conveyance by either joint tenant severs the joint tenancy regardless of whether the conveying joint tenant had or breached any fiduciary obligation to the other.

2. Creditors of deceased joint tenant take nothing

Question 14: A brother and sister owned a parcel as joint tenants, upon which was situated a two-family house. The brother lived in one of the two apartments and rented the other apartment to a tenant. The brother got in a fight with the tenant and injured him. The tenant obtained and properly filed a judgment for $10,000 against the brother.

The statute in the jurisdiction reads: Any judgment properly filed shall, for ten years from filing, be a lien on the real property then owned or subsequently acquired by any person against whom the judgment is rendered.

The sister, who lived in a distant city, knew nothing of the tenant's judgment. Before the tenant took any further action, the brother died. The common-law joint tenancy is unmodified by statute.

The sister then learned the facts and brought an appropriate action against the tenant to quiet title to the land.

The court should hold that the tenant has

(A) a lien against the whole of the property, because he was a tenant of both the brother and the sister at the time of the judgment.

(B) a lien against the brother's undivided one-half interest in the land, because his judgment was filed prior to the brother's death.

(C) no lien, because the sister had no actual notice of the tenant's judgment until after the brother's death.

(D) no lien, because the brother's death terminated the interest to which the tenant's lien attached.

[Q1090]

Answer 14: Choice **(D)** is correct. Since the tenant's judgment was only against the brother, the tenant's judgment lien was only against the brother's real property, not the sister's real property. That real property consisted of the brother's joint tenancy interest. At the moment of the brother's death, that joint tenancy interest ceased to exist, and there was nothing left for the judgment lien to be a lien against.

(A) is wrong because the basis for the tenant's judgment (and thus for his judgment lien) was the brother's having injured him in the fight; since this had nothing to do with the tenant's having been a tenant of both brother and sister, it did not create any lien against the sister's interest in the property.

(B) is wrong because it inaccurately characterizes the brother's interest: it was a joint tenancy, not an "undivided one-half interest" (a phrase that would be used to describe a tenancy in common). Therefore, the fact that the judgment was filed while the brother was still alive is irrelevant, because the brother's joint tenancy ceased to exist at the moment he died.

(C) is wrong because it cites an irrelevant factor; even if the sister had had actual notice of the judgment while the brother was still alive, there would be no lien after the brother died for the reasons described in the discussion of (D).

II. TENANCY IN COMMON

A. Tenancy in common

1. Conveyance by one co-tenant

a. Grant of mortgage or judgment lien

Question 15: A mother owned a two-family apartment house on a small city lot not suitable for partition-in-kind. Upon the mother's death, her will devised the property to "my son and my daughter."

A week ago, a creditor of the son obtained a money judgment against the son, and properly filed the judgment in the county where the property is located. A statute in the jurisdiction provides: any judgment properly filed shall, for ten years from filing, be a lien on the real property then owned or subsequently acquired by any person against whom the judgment is rendered.

The son needed cash, but the daughter did not wish to sell the property. The son commenced a partition action against the daughter and the creditor.

Assume that the court properly ordered a partition by judicial sale.

After the sale, the creditor's judgment will be a lien on

(A) all of the property.

(B) only a one-half interest in the property.

(C) all of the proceeds of sale of the property.

(D) only the portion of the proceeds of sale due the son.

[Q1066]

Answer 15: Choice **(D)** is correct. The mother's will had the effect of giving the property to the son and the daughter as tenants in common, with a undivided one-half interest going to each. (A conveyance "to *A* and *B*," without further specification, creates a tenancy in common with equal shares.) At the time the creditor got his money judgment against the son, that judgment became a lien only against real property owned by the son, and the son's real property consisted of his undivided one-half interest. When the partition by judicial sale occurred, the son's interest in the property became sole ownership of one-half of the proceeds, and the creditor's lien became a lien solely on that share of the proceeds.

Choices (A), (B), and (C) are wrong because they are inconsistent with the above analysis.

CHAPTER 5

LANDLORD AND TENANT

I. TORT LIABILITY OF LANDLORD AND TENANT

A. Landlord's liability

1. Common law

a. Assignment of interest by L

Question 16: Les leased a barn to his neighbor, Tom, for a term of three years. Tom took possession of the barn and used it for his farming purposes. The lease made Les responsible for structural repairs to the barn, unless they were made necessary by actions of Tom.

One year later, Les conveyed the barn and its associated land to Lottie "subject to the lease to Tom." Tom paid the next month's rent to Lottie. The next day a portion of an exterior wall of the barn collapsed because of rot in the interior structure of the wall. The wall had appeared to be sound, but a competent engineer, on inspection, would have discovered its condition. Neither Lottie nor Tom had the barn inspected by an engineer. Tom was injured as a result of the collapse of the wall.

Les had known that the wall was dangerously weakened by rot and needed immediate repairs, but had not told Tom or Lottie. There is no applicable statute.

Tom brought an appropriate action against Les to recover damages for the injuries he sustained. Lottie was not a party.

Which of the following is the most appropriate comment concerning the outcome of this action?

(A) Tom should lose, because Lottie assumed all of Les's obligations by reason of Tom's attornment to her.

(B) Tom should recover, because there is privity between lessor and lessee and it cannot be broken unilaterally.

(C) Tom should recover, because Les knew of the danger but did not warn Tom.

(D) Tom should lose, because he failed to inspect the barn.

[Q2036]

Answer 16: Choice **(C)** is correct. A landlord generally does not have tort liability for accidents that arise out of a dangerous condition on the property. For example, a landlord has no duty to inspect the property to discover dangerous conditions. But the landlord does have liability if he *knows* of the danger, or is in possession of facts that would reasonably have led a person in his position to know of the danger, and the tenant does not know of the danger. Les met this requirement because the facts tell us that he had "known that the wall was dangerously weakened by rot and needed immediate repairs." When Les assigned to Lottie, Les remained liable until Lottie actually discovered the condition and had a reasonable opportunity to fix it. Since Lottie had only owned the property for one day before the accident, and had not learned of the condition, liability had not yet passed to Lottie, and thus remained with Les, at the moment of the accident.

(A) is wrong because, while Lottie took "subject to" the lease, she did not assume Les's obligations to Tom, and her receipt of a payment from Tom did not change this. By the rule discussed in the prior paragraph, Lottie would not become liable for the condition until she learned of it and had time to fix it (unless she expressly assumed liability for conditions not known to her, which didn't happen here).

(B) is wrong because a landlord is liable to the tenant for failing to disclose a known dangerous condition. That liability persists regardless of whether landlord and tenant remain in privity of estate (and ends only when the successor on the landlord side becomes liable, which could only have been when the successor learned of the condition and had a chance to fix it).

(D) is wrong because, where a landlord is actually aware of a dangerous condition, and the tenant is not aware, the landlord is liable regardless of whether the tenant could have (or even reasonably should have) inspected the premises. In other words, the tenant has no duty to inspect, at least in a scenario where the landlord has actual knowledge of the danger.

II. TRANSFER AND SALE BY LESSOR; ASSIGNMENT AND SUBLETTING BY LESSEE

A. Generally allowed

1. Distinguish assignment from sublease

a. Significance

i. Question might not say "sublease"

Question 17: A landlord leased an apartment to a tenant by written lease for two years ending on the last day of a recent month. The lease provided for $700 monthly rental. The tenant occupied the apartment and paid the rent for the first 15 months of the lease term, until he moved to a new job in another city. Without consulting the landlord, the tenant moved a friend into the apartment and signed an informal writing transferring to the friend his "lease rights" for the remaining nine months of the lease. The friend made the next four monthly $700 rental payments to the landlord. For the final five months of the lease term, no rent was paid by anyone, and the friend moved out with three months left on the lease term. The landlord was on an extended trip abroad, and did not learn of the default and the vacancy until last week. The landlord sued the tenant and the friend, jointly and severally, for $3,500 for the last five months' rent.

What is the likely outcome of the lawsuit?

(A) Both the tenant and the friend are liable for the full $3,500, because the tenant is liable on privity of contract and the friend is liable on privity of estate as assignee.

(B) The friend is liable for $1,400 on privity of estate, which lasted only until he vacated, and the tenant is liable for $2,100 on privity of contract and estate for the period after the friend vacated.

(C) The friend is liable for $3,500 on privity of estate and the tenant is not liable, because the landlord's failure to object to the friend's payment of rent relieved the tenant of liability.

(D) The tenant is liable for $3,500 on privity of contract and the friend is not liable, because a sublessee does not have personal liability to the original landlord.

[Q7004]

Answer 17: Choice **(A)** is correct. An assignment arises when a tenant transfers all or some of the leased premises to another for the remainder of the lease term, retaining no interest in the assigned premises. In this case, prior to the agreement with the friend, the tenant had privity of contract with the landlord because of the lease. The tenant also had privity of estate because the tenant was in possession of the apartment. Subsequently, an assignment arose when the tenant transferred the premises to the friend for the remainder of the lease term of nine months. The friend was then in privity of estate with the landlord as to all promises that run with the land, including the covenant to pay rent. (When the friend moved out, this did not end the privity of estate, because the friend did not assign to someone else, and simply abandoned the premises. See Rest. 2d (Landlord & Tenant), § 16.1, Illustr. 24.) The tenant was not released by the landlord, however, and thus remained liable on privity of contract.

(B) is incorrect, because the friend entered privity of estate with the landlord when he received the assignment, and this privity of estate remained with the friend until the end of the lease because the friend made no assignment. Therefore, the friend remained liable on privity of estate for the period after he vacated. Furthermore, because the landlord never released the tenant, the tenant remained liable for the full $3,500 on privity of contract.

(C) is incorrect, because the landlord never released the tenant, thereby keeping the tenant liable on privity of contract based on the original lease. (There was no express release, and a release would not be implied merely because the landlord accepted rent from the friend.)

(D) is incorrect, because this choice assumes that the friend was a sublessee, which he was not. A sublease arises when a tenant transfers the right of possession to all or some of the leased premises to another for a time less than the remaining time of the lease, or when the tenant retains some other interest in the premises. Here, the tenant transferred all the remaining time of the lease to the friend and retained no other interest. Accordingly, this was an assignment and not a sublease. As an assignee, the friend was in privity of estate with the landlord as to all promises that run with the land, including the covenant to pay rent.

B. Running of benefit and burden

1. Purchase options in leases

a. Split on exercise apart from lease

Question 18: Lanny, the owner of Whiteacre in fee simple, leased Whiteacre to Ten for a term of ten years by a properly executed written instrument. The lease was promptly and properly recorded. It contained an option for Ten to purchase Whiteacre by tendering $250,000 as purchase price any time "during the term of this lease." One year later, Ten, by a properly executed written instrument, purported to assign the option to Oscar, expressly retaining all of the remaining term of the lease. The instrument of assignment was promptly and properly recorded.

Two years later, Lanny contracted to sell Whiteacre to Jones and to convey a marketable title "subject to the rights of Ten under her lease." Jones refused to close because of the outstanding option assigned to Oscar.

Lanny brought an appropriate action against Jones for specific performance.

If judgment is rendered in favor of Lanny, it will be because the relevant jurisdiction has adopted a rule on a key issue as to which various state courts have split.

Which of the following identifies the determinative rule or doctrine upon which the split occurs, and states the position favorable to Lanny?

(A) In a contract to buy, any form of "subject to a lease" clause that fails to mention expressly an existing option means that the seller is agreeing to sell free and clear of any option originally included in the lease.

(B) Marketable title can be conveyed so long as any outstanding option not mentioned in the purchase contract has not yet been exercised.

(C) Options to purchase by lessees are subject to the Rule Against Perpetuities.

(D) Options to purchase contained in a lease cannot be assigned separately from the lease.

[Q2013]

Answer 18: Choice **(D)** is correct. Courts disagree about whether a purchase option embodied in a lease may be assigned independently of the lease. Since Lanny is arguing that his title is marketable, the position that purchase options cannot be assigned independently of the lease is favorable to Lanny (because that position, if upheld, would certainly mean that Oscar could not exercise the option, and might even mean that Ten had rendered the option invalid by purporting to assign it independently of the lease).

(A) is wrong because, even if the contract's "subject to a lease" language meant what this choice says it means (that Lanny is committing to sell free and clear of any option), Lanny would still lose: he would not in fact be able to sell free and clear of the purchase option now purportedly held by Oscar.

(B) is wrong because the existence of a purchase option renders title unmarketable, even though the option has not yet been exercised. (If the rule were otherwise, the buyer would be paying full dollar for property that might be "called away" from him by exercise of the option at any time, perhaps at a below-market price.)

(C) is wrong because: (1) purchase options embodied in leases are typically not subjected to the Rule against Perpetuities; and (2) even if the option here *were* subject to the Rule, the option would not thereby be rendered invalid (since the option must be exercised during the lease term, and the lease terms falls within "lives in being plus 21 years").

CHAPTER 6

EASEMENTS AND SERVITUDES

I. CREATION OF EASEMENTS

A. Easement by prescription

1. Adverse use

Question 19: Oxnard owned Goldacre, a tract of land, in fee simple. At a time when Goldacre was in the adverse possession of Amos, Eric obtained the oral permission of Oxnard to use as a road or driveway a portion of Goldacre to reach adjoining land, Twin Pines, which Eric owned in fee simple. Thereafter, during all times relevant to this problem, Eric used this road between Goldacre regularly for ingress and egress between Twin Pines and a public highway.

Amos quit possession of Goldacre before acquiring title by adverse possession. Without any further communication between Oxnard and Eric, Eric continued to use the road for a total period, from the time he first began to use it, sufficient to acquire an easement by prescription. Oxnard then blocked the road and refused to permit its continued use. Eric brought suit to determine his right to continue use of the road. Eric should

(A) win, because his use was adverse to Amos and once adverse it continued adverse until some affirmative showing of a change.

(B) win, because Eric made no attempt to renew permission after Amos quit possession of Goldacre.

(C) lose, because his use was with permission.

(D) lose, because there is no evidence that he continued adverse use for the required period after Amos quit possession.

[Q4015]

Answer 19: Choice **(C)** is correct, because it correctly identifies the reason Eric will lose: his use of Goldacre was not "adverse," i.e., non-permissive. The key facts here are that Eric had oral permission from Oxnard *originally* to use the road across Goldacre, and Amos quit possession of Goldacre before acquiring title by adverse possession. What does this mean? That Eric's use of Goldacre was never adverse to the interests of the landowner, and that Amos never had any enforceable rights to Goldacre. In order to gain an easement by prescription, one's use of another's property must be actual, open and notorious, continuous for the statutory period, exclusive, and hostile and adverse (non-permissive). Here, the facts specifically state that Eric had Oxnard's oral permission to use the road across Goldacre. The red herring here is the presence of Amos. However, Amos is merely in possession of Goldacre. The facts state that he quit possession before he acquired title to it. Thus, the elements of an easement by prescription would apply to Eric vis-a-vis Oxnard, *not* Eric vis-a-vis Amos.

(A) is wrong because it focuses on the wrong fact. Here, it doesn't matter if Eric's use is adverse to Amos, because Amos is not the landowner – *Oxnard* is. Eric's use is not adverse to Oxnard, because the facts state that Oxnard granted Eric oral permission to use the road across Goldacre. An easement by prescription requires use of another's property that is actual, open and notorious, continuous for the statutory period, exclusive, and hostile and adverse. "Hostile and adverse" means non-permissive in this context. Here, since Eric's use was with the permission of the landowner the entire time, his use was *never* adverse. Since A does not recognize this, it's not the best response.

(B) is wrong because it falsely suggests that Amos's quitting possession of Goldacre is relevant. It is not, because an easement by prescription is gained by adverse use against the *landowner,* not the *possessor.* Eric could only gain an easement by prescription if his use of Goldacre *as against Oxnard* was actual, open and notorious, continuous for the statutory period, exclusive, and non-permissive.

(D) is wrong because it focuses on a basically irrelevant fact. What matters is whether Eric had the requisite open and hostile use *as against the true owner*, Oxnard. If Eric hadn't originally gotten permission from Oxnard, his time of use of the driveway while Amos was in adverse possession of the overall tract would count against Oxnard. So the problem is not that Eric didn't use the driveway long enough once Amos left, it's that Eric's entire use of the driveway (even when Amos was there) wasn't adverse as against Oxnard.

II.   SCOPE OF EASEMENTS

A. Development of dominant estate

1.   Remedy for misuse is injunction or damages, not forfeiture

Question 20: A large tract of land was owned by a religious order. On the land, the order erected a large residential building where its members reside. The land is surrounded by rural residential properties and its only access to a public way is afforded by an easement over a strip of land 30 feet wide. The easement was granted to the order by deed from a neighbor, who owned one of the adjacent residential properties. The order built a driveway on the strip, and the easement was used for 20 years without incident or objection.

Last year, as permitted by the applicable zoning ordinance, the order constructed a 200-bed nursing home and a parking lot on their land, using all of the land that was available for such development. The nursing home was very successful, and on Sundays visitors to the nursing home overflowed the parking facilities on the land and parked all along the driveway from early in the morning through the evening hours. After two Sundays of the resulting congestion and inconvenience, the neighbor erected a barrier across the driveway on Sundays preventing any use of the driveway by anyone seeking access to the order's land. The order objected.

The neighbor brought an appropriate action to terminate the easement.

The most likely result in this action is that the court will hold for

(A) the neighbor, because the order excessively expanded the use of the dominant tenement.

(B) the neighbor, because the parking on the driveway exceeded the scope of the easement.

(C) the order, because expanded use of the easement does not terminate the easement.

(D) the order, because the neighbor's use of self help denies her the right to equitable relief.

[Q2021]

Answer 20: Choice **(C)** is correct. The expanded use of the easement here — especially the parking along the driveway at all hours — probably does represent excessive use going beyond the intended scope of the easement. However, a court would almost certainly limit the remedy to an injunction against further violations, or to damages for the two past violations, and would not order a forfeiture of the easement. That's because forfeitures are drastic remedies, and will be awarded in excessive-use situations only if no other remedy will be adequate, which would not be the case for the violations here.

(A) is wrong because, while the order has indeed probably excessively expanded their use of the easement, the court would not order the easement forfeited as a remedy, for the reasons stated above.

(B) is wrong for the same reason (A) is wrong.

(D) is wrong because a court would not grant the neighbor the extreme remedy of forfeiture whether or not she had used self-help.

III.   REPAIR AND MAINTENANCE OF EASEMENTS

A. Dominant owner has right to maintain

Question 21: Two adjacent, two-story, commercial buildings were owned by a landowner.

The first floors of both buildings were occupied by various retail establishments. The second floors were rented to various other tenants. Access to the second floor of each building was reached by a common stairway located entirely in Building 1. While the buildings were being used in this manner, the landowner sold Building 1 to an accountant by warranty deed which made no mention of any rights concerning the stairway. About two years later the landowner sold Building 2 to a lawyer. The stairway continued to be used by the occupants of both buildings. The stairway became unsafe as a consequence of regular wear and tear. The lawyer entered upon the accountant's building and began the work of repairing the stairway. The accountant demanded that the lawyer discontinue the repair work and vacate the accountant's building. When the lawyer refused, the accountant brought an action to enjoin the lawyer from continuing the work.

Judgment should be for

(A) the accountant, because the lawyer has no rights in the stairway.

(B) the accountant, because the lawyer's rights in the stairway do not extend beyond the normal life of the existing structure.

(C) the lawyer, because the lawyer has an easement in the stairway and an implied right to keep the stairway in repair.

(D) the lawyer, because the lawyer has a right to take whatever action is necessary to protect himself from possible tort liability to persons using the stairway.

[Q1029]

Answer 21: Choice **(C)** is correct. At the time of the conveyance by the landowner to the lawyer, the lawyer received an implied easement to use the stairs for access to Building 2. (The three requirements for an easement by implication were met here: (1) the land was "severed" from common ownership when the landowner kept Building 2 while selling Building 1; (2) the use of the stairway for access to Building 2 existed prior to this severance; and (3) the easement was and is reasonably necessary to enjoyment of Building 2.) The holder of the easement (the lawyer) therefore had an implied right to maintain the property used in the easement, given that the maintenance was compatible with the intended use of the easement and did not unreasonably interfere with the servient owner's (the accountant's) use of the servient estate.

(A) is wrong because the lawyer *does* have rights in the stairway, namely an implied easement.

(B) is wrong because the lawyer as easement holder has the right to maintain or repair the structure indefinitely, not just for the normal life of the original staircase.

(D) is wrong because it misstates the reason for the lawyer's repair right, which is that the lawyer has an implied easement; if the lawyer did not have an implied easement, he would probably not face tort liability for failing to correct the stairway danger on property belonging to another, at least if he asked the owner (the accountant) to do the work and the owner refused.

Question 22: Maria is the owner and possessor of Goodacre, on which there is a lumber yard. Maria conveyed to Reliable Electric Company the right to construct and use an overhead electric line across Goodacre to serve other properties. The conveyance was in writing, but the writing made no provision concerning the responsibility for repair or maintenance of the line. Reliable installed the poles and erected the electric line in a proper and workmanlike manner. Neither Maria nor Reliable took any steps toward the maintenance or repair of the line after it was built. Neither party complained to the other about any failure to repair. Because of the failure to repair or properly maintain the line, it fell to the ground during a storm. In doing so, it caused a fire in the lumber yard and did considerable damage. Maria sued Reliable Electric Company to recover for damages to the lumber yard. The decision should be for

(A) Maria, because the owner of an easement has a duty to so maintain the easement as to avoid unreasonable interference with the use of the servient tenement by its lawful possessor.

(B) Maria, because the owner of an easement is absolutely liable for any damage caused to the servient tenement by the exercise of the easement.

(C) Reliable Electric Company, because the possessor of the servient tenement has a duty to give the easement holder notice of defective conditions.

(D) Reliable Electric Company, because an easement holder's right to repair is a right for his own benefit, and is therefore inconsistent with any duty to repair for the benefit of another.

[Q4187]

Answer 22: Choice **(A)** is correct. Reliable has an expressly-created easement for constructing and using overhead electric lines. Since Reliable was given the right to use Maria's land, it's the "dominant" tenement holder (and Maria is the "servient" tenement holder, since it's her land that's burdened by the easement). The rule on maintaining easements is that the dominant tenement holder has both the *right* and the *duty* to use reasonable care to maintain the easement. Thus, Reliable would have the *right* to enter Maria's land and repair the line and poles, as necessary, and Maria could not object to this interference. However, Reliable also had the duty to use reasonable care to maintain the equipment so it did not pose an unreasonable danger to Maria's land, and the utility, by failing to maintain the line at all, did not fulfill that duty. As a result, Maria will be able to recover for damages to the lumber yard.

(B) is wrong because although it arrives at the correct result, it misstates the responsibility of the dominant tenement holder. There is no doctrine that states that an easement owner is strictly liable for damage caused to the servient tenement by the exercise of the easement. Instead, the dominant holder merely has the obligation to use reasonable care to maintain the easement in such a way that it does not damage the servient property. If the accident had happened without the lack of due care by Reliable (which is not the way it happened), Reliable would not be liable to Maria.

(C) is wrong because it misstates the duty of the servient tenement holder, and arrives at the wrong result. In general, the dominant holder has the obligation to use reasonable care to maintain the easement so that it does not pose unreasonable risk to the servient parcel. This obligation includes an obligation to inspect. So the mere fact that Maria didn't give notice of the problem doesn't save Reliable from liability. (Indeed, an electric utility ought to be able to recognize maintenance issues more easily than a non-utility customer.)

(D) is wrong because it fails to recognize Reliable Electric's duty to Maria. The holder of an easement has both the *right* and the *duty* to take reasonable steps to maintain the easement.

1. Limited right to contribution

Question 23: Beach owned a tract of land called Blackacre. An old road ran through Blackacre from the abutting public highway. The road had been used to haul wood from Blackacre. Without Beach's permission and with no initial right, Daniel, the owner of Whiteacre, which adjoined Blackacre, traveled over the old road for a period of 15 years to obtain access to Whiteacre, although Whiteacre abutted another public road. Occasionally, Daniel made repairs to the old road.

The period of time to acquire rights by prescription in the jurisdiction is ten years.

After the expiration of 15 years, Beach conveyed a portion of Blackacre to Carrol. The deed included the following clause: "together with the right to pass and repass at all times and for all purposes over the old road." Carrol built a house fronting on the old road. After the conveyance, Beach has used the road once or twice per year. Daniel almost never uses the road anymore.

The road was severely damaged by a spring flood, and Carrol made substantial repairs to the road. Carrol asked Daniel and Beach to contribute one-third each to the cost of repairing the flood damage. They both refused, and Carrol brought an appropriate action to compel contribution from Beach and Daniel.

In this action, Carrol will

(A) lose as to both defendants.

(B) win as to both defendants.

(C) win as to Beach, but lose as to Daniel.

(D) win as to Daniel, but lose as to Beach.

[Q2191]

Answer 23: Choice **(A)** is correct. Carrol is the owner of the dominant tenement (i.e., the owner of the easement), and Beach is the owner of the servient tenement. Beach, as the servient owner, has no obligation to contribute one-third of Carrol's repair expenditures. Beach may have *some* obligation of reimbursement, based on the intensity and frequency of his bridge use versus Carrol's, but certainly not a one-third-of-total-cost obligation, since Beach clearly does not represent one third of the total usage of the bridge. As to Daniel, he may well have obtained an easement by prescription. But even if he has done so, he, too, has no obligation to reimburse Carrol for one-third of the latter's expenditures, because Daniel, like Beach, rarely makes use of the bridge, and has at most an obligation to reimburse for his small pro rata share of total usage.

Choices (B), (C), and (D) are wrong because they are inconsistent with the above analysis.

IV. TRANSFER AND SUBDIVISION OF EASEMENTS

A. Transfer of benefit

1. Transfer of easements appurtenant

a. Deed to dominant parcel is silent

Question 24: Olwen owned 80 acres of land, fronting on a town road. Two years ago, Olwen sold to Buck the back 40 acres. The 40 acres sold to Buck did not adjoin any public road. Olwen's deed to Buck expressly granted a right-of-way over a specified strip of Olwen's retained 40 acres, so Buck could reach the town road. The deed was promptly and properly recorded.

Last year, Buck conveyed the back 40 acres to Sam. They had discussed the right-of-way over Olwen's land to the road, but Buck's deed to Sam made no mention of it. Sam began to use the right-of-way as Buck had, but Olwen sued to enjoin such use by Sam.

The court should decide for

(A) Sam, because he has an easement by implication.

(B) Sam, because the easement appurtenant passed to him as a result of Buck's deed to him.

(C) Olwen, because Buck's easement in gross was not transferable.

(D) Olwen, because Buck's deed failed expressly to transfer the right-of-way to Sam.

[Q2055]

Answer 24: Choice **(B)** is correct. What we have here is an easement appurtenant, because the easement is for the benefit of a particular parcel (the back 40 acres). An easement appurtenant passes to the new holder of the dominant tenement automatically, even if the deed to the dominant tenement does not mention the easement.

(A) is wrong, because the easement here is an express easement, not one by implication. Furthermore, even if the easement here *were* an easement by implication, it would automatically pass together with the dominant tenement.

(C) is wrong because the easement here is appurtenant, not in gross. That is, it is clear from the surrounding circumstances that the easement is being used to benefit a particular parcel (the back 40 acres), not to benefit Buck irrespective of Buck's ownership of those 40 acres. So while many courts indeed hold that an easement in gross is not transferable if the document creating it is silent on the issue, this principle won't apply to the facts here.

(D) is wrong because, as described in the answer to (B) above, an easement appurtenant will pass together with the dominant tenement, even if the deed conveying the dominant tenement does not mention the easement.

V. LICENSES

A. Definition

1. Oral agreement must produce a license, not an easement

Question 25: A landowner orally gave his neighbor permission to share the use of the private road on the landowner's land so that the neighbor could have more convenient access to the neighbor's land. Only the landowner maintained the road. After the neighbor had used the road on a daily basis for three years, the landowner conveyed his land to a grantee, who immediately notified the neighbor that the neighbor was not to use the road. The neighbor sued the grantee seeking a declaration that the neighbor had a right to continue to use the road.

Who is likely to prevail?

(A) The grantee, because an oral license is invalid.

(B) The grantee, because the neighbor had a license that the grantee could terminate at any time.

(C) The neighbor, because the grantee is estopped to terminate the neighbor's use of the road.

(D) The neighbor, because the neighbor's use of the road was open and notorious when the grantee purchased the land.

[Q7098]

Answer 25: Choice **(B)** is correct. A license is permission to use the land of another. It is ordinarily revocable, and is not subject to the Statute of Frauds. In this case, because the neighbor had the landowner's permission to use the road and did not expend any money, property, or labor pursuant to the agreement (i.e., the neighbor did substantially rely on the continued availability of the license), the neighbor had a license that was revocable — and effectively revoked — by the grantee.

(A) is incorrect because, while this option correctly states that the grantee will prevail, it misstates the reason why this is so. A license (unlike an easement) is not subject to the Statute of Frauds; it may be oral, written, or implied.

(C) is incorrect because for estoppel to apply to make a license (which is ordinarily revocable) irrevocable, the neighbor must have expended money, property, or labor pursuant to the agreement. In this case, the landowner alone maintained the road. The neighbor's use of the land by permission, without expense, was therefore a revocable license that was effectively revoked by the grantee.

(D) is incorrect. An open and notorious use of the road suggests a claim for an easement by prescription. However, the use was with permission, which prevents a prescriptive claim. (Also, the use was for just three years, making it extremely unlikely that the statutory period for adverse possession-type claims could have run.) Instead, the neighbor's use of the land was a license that was effectively revoked by the grantee.

VI. EQUITABLE SERVITUDES / RESTRICTIVE COVENANTS

A. Running of benefit and burden

1. Requirement of notice

a. Constructive

Question 26: In 2000, Oscar, owner of a 100-acre tract, prepared and duly recorded a subdivision plan called Happy Acres. The plan showed 100 one-acre lots, and said that these lots would be "single-family, no mobile homes allowed."

In 2001, Oscar sold 60 of the lots to individual purchasers. Each deed referred to the recorded plan and also contained the following clause: "No mobile homes shall be erected on any lot within Happy Acres." Sarah was one of the original purchasers from Oscar.

In 2006, Oscar sold the remaining 40 lots to Max by a deed which referred to the plan and contained the restriction relating to mobile homes. Max sold the 40 lots to individual purchasers, whose deeds from Max did not include the mobile-home restriction. One of those purchasers was Joe, who did not know of the no-mobile-homes restriction in any prior deeds within Happy Acres. Joe then placed a mobile home on his lot. Sarah now brings an action against Joe to force him to remove the mobile home. The result of this action will be in favor of

(A) Sarah, because the restrictive covenant in her deed runs with the land.

(B) Sarah, because the presence of the mobile home may adversely affect the market value of her land.

(C) Joe, because his deed did not contain the restrictive covenant.

(D) Joe, because he is not a direct but a remote grantee of Oscar.

[Q4033]

Answer 26: Choice (A) is correct. A restrictive covenant will normally run with the land, i.e., be enforceable by subsequent grantees of the benefitted parcels, and against subsequent grantees of the burdened parcels, if the original parties intended that it run. The existence of the filed subdivision plat with the restriction, and the fact that Oscar took the trouble to insert the restriction in all his deeds, establish that he and his grantees intended the burden and benefit of the restriction to run. Meanwhile, Joe, as a subsequent grantee, will only be bound by the restrictive covenant if he was on actual or constructive notice when he took. "Constructive" notice includes "record" notice. Here, Joe was on record notice of the restriction. That's true because although Joe's deed did not itself refer to the no-mobile-homes restriction, that restriction was present in a prior recording in his chain of title (the Oscar-Max deed). And a purchaser is deemed to be on record notice of any restrictions in his chain of title. Intuitively, this makes sense — Joe's lawyer could have and should have found the Oscar-to-Max deed, and noticed the restriction. (Or, the lawyer could have and should have noticed that the lot was part of a filed subdivision plat that contained the restriction.)

(B) is wrong because the fact it cites is irrelevant to the issues here. The mere fact that the presence of mobile homes would adversely affect the value of Sarah's land does not mean that Sarah has a legally cognizable right to forbid their presence. As a general principle, the owner of land may put the land to any lawful use he chooses, without regard to the impact on the market value of other, neighboring properties. Thus, even if (B) were true, it would not provide a sound basis for Sarah to prevail.

(C) is wrong because it does not correctly cite the rule on restrictive covenants (or "equitable servitudes," as they are also called). Restrictive covenants will bind subsequent purchasers of the land as long as the original parties intended that the agreement will run with the land, and the subsequent purchaser had actual or constructive notice of the restriction. Here, Joe had constructive notice (namely, record notice) of the restriction, as further explained in (A). Therefore, the fact that Joe's own deed did not contain the covenant is irrelevant.

(D) is wrong because as long as the restriction was intended to run with the land, the fact that the person sought to be bound is a remote grantee of the original, covenanting party – here, Oscar — is irrelevant. That's what the fact that the covenant or restriction "runs with the land" *means* — the restriction binds remote grantees who take with actual or constructive (including record) notice.

b. Check for notice

Question 27: Able, owner of Blackacre and Whiteacre, two adjoining parcels, conveyed Whiteacre to Baker and covenanted in the deed to Baker that when he, Able, sold Blackacre he would impose restrictive covenants to prohibit uses that would compete with the filling station that Baker intended to construct and operate on Whiteacre. The deed was not recorded.

Baker constructed and operated a filling station on Whiteacre and then conveyed Whiteacre to Dodd, who continued the filling station use. The deed did not refer to the restrictive covenant and was promptly and properly recorded.

Able then conveyed Blackacre to Egan, who knew about Able's covenant with Baker to impose a covenant prohibiting the filling station use but nonetheless completed the transaction when he noted that no such covenant was contained in Able's deed to him. Egan began to construct a filling station on Blackacre.

Dodd brought an appropriate action to enjoin Egan from using Blackacre for filling station purposes.

If Dodd prevails, it will be because

(A) Egan had actual knowledge of the covenant to impose restrictions.

(B) Egan is bound by the covenant because of the doctrine of negative reciprocal covenants.

(C) business-related restrictive covenants are favored in the law.

(D) Egan has constructive notice of the possibility of the covenant resulting from the circumstances.

[Q1165]

Answer 27: Choice **(A)** is correct. Dodd can win only if Egan is found to have been bound by Able's promise to Baker that Able would impose a restriction on Blackacre when he sold it. A subsequent purchaser of a use-restricted parcel can be bound by the restriction only if he had some sort of *notice* of the restriction at the time he took. Egan did not have *record* notice of the restriction because (1) the restriction was not contained in the Able-to-Egan deed by which Egan took Blackacre; and (2) even if the Able-to-Baker deed to Whiteacre was held to be within Egan's chain of title (which it wouldn't be), that wouldn't give Egan notice, because the Able-to-Baker deed was not recorded, so Egan couldn't have discovered the restriction by tracing back title to Whiteacre in the public records. Therefore, the only way Egan could have received the required notice (and thus lose) is if he had actual notice or some form of *constructive* notice not involving record notice. (A), by referring specifically to Egan's "actual knowledge" of the restriction, is the only choice that satisfies the notice-to-Egan requirement. And as we know from the statement of facts, Egan indeed had such actual knowledge.

(B) is wrong because, while the doctrine of negative reciprocal covenants might apply to restrict Whiteacre, Egan wouldn't be bound by that restriction if he didn't have some form of notice, and this choice does not refer to the notice problem.

(C) is wrong because, like (B), it fails to refer to the key point, notice to Egan.

(D) is wrong because, while Egan might indeed lose if he had constructive notice of the possibility of the restriction, such constructive notice was not present in the facts here: the mere fact that Able sold Whiteacre to Baker and that Baker put a filling station on the property would not suggest to a reasonable purchaser of the adjacent Blackacre parcel that Able would likely have restricted Blackacre by giving Baker a non-compete. (Otherwise any purchaser of a commercially-zoned parcel would have to check into the facts surrounding his seller's sale of any other nearby parcel, to make sure that the seller didn't give a non-compete, too large a burden on buyers to make sense.)

B. Developer's building plan

1. Plan filed without restriction

Question 28: A fee-simple landowner lawfully subdivided his land into 10 large lots. The recorded subdivision plan imposed no restrictions on any of the 10 lots. Within two months after recording the plan, the landowner conveyed Lot 1 to a buyer, by a deed that contained no restriction on the lot's use. There was then a lull in sales. Two years later, the real estate market in the state had generally improved and, during the next six months, the landowner sold and conveyed eight of the remaining nine lots. In each of the eight deeds of conveyance, the landowner included the following language: "It is a term and condition of this conveyance, which shall be a covenant running with the land for the benefit of each of the 10 lots [with an appropriate reference to the recorded subdivision plan], that for 15 years from the date of recording of the plan, no use shall be made of the premises herein conveyed except for single-family residential purposes." The buyer of Lot 1 had actual knowledge of what the landowner had done. The landowner included the quoted language in part because the zoning ordinance of the municipality had been amended a year earlier to permit professional offices in any residential zone. Shortly after the landowner's most recent sale, when he owned only one unsold lot, the buyer of Lot 1 constructed a one-story house on Lot 1 and then conveyed Lot 1 to a doctor. The deed to the doctor contained no reference to any restriction on the use of Lot 1. The doctor applied for an appropriate certificate of occupancy to enable her to use a part of the house on Lot 1 as a medical office. The landowner, on behalf of himself as the owner of the unsold lot, and on behalf of the other lot owners, sued to enjoin the doctor from carrying out her plans and to impose the quoted restriction on Lot 1.

Who is likely to prevail?

(A) The doctor, because Lot 1 was conveyed without the inclusion of the restrictive covenant in the deed to the first buyer and the subsequent deed to the doctor.

(B) The doctor, because zoning ordinances override private restrictive covenants as a matter of public policy.

(C) The landowner, because the doctor, as a successor in interest to the first buyer, is estopped to deny that Lot 1 remains subject to the zoning ordinance as it existed when Lot 1 was first conveyed by the landowner to the first buyer.

(D) The landowner, because with the first buyer's knowledge of the facts, Lot 1 became incorporated into a common scheme.

[Q7061]

Answer 28: Choice (A) is correct. To be binding, a restrictive covenant must be placed on property *at the time it is conveyed.* Here, neither the deed to the first buyer nor the deed to the doctor contains the restrictive covenant. The burden cannot be attached to Lot 1 at a later time by someone who has no interest in Lot 1, even if that person (here, the landowner) purports to be acting on behalf of the entire subdivision. Therefore, the doctor may proceed with her plan to use part of the property as a medical office.

(B) is incorrect, because although this option correctly concludes that the doctor will prevail, it misstates the reason why this is so. Zoning ordinances do not automatically override a private restrictive covenant. The stricter of either the zoning ordinance or the covenant will prevail. In this case, the doctor will prevail because the restrictive covenant was not in the deed to the first buyer of Lot 1, nor was it in the deed to the doctor.

(C) is incorrect. Public land use controls and private land use controls are separate issues. Zoning may be changed. In this case, the zoning was changed a year after the first buyer purchased Lot 1. The doctor's use of Lot 1 is governed by the zoning in existence during the time of the doctor's ownership, and the previous zoning of the property is irrelevant. The doctor may proceed with her plan to use part of the property as a medical office, because the restrictive covenant was not in the deed to the first buyer of Lot 1, nor was it in the deed to the doctor.

(D) is incorrect. To be binding, a restrictive covenant must be placed on property at the time when it is conveyed. The first buyer's learning of the covenant two years after he acquired it is irrelevant, and does not incorporate Lot 1 into the common scheme of the subdivision; nor does the actual knowledge of any subsequent buyer of Lot 1 (even knowledge acquired before he took) have any effect. A common-scheme argument might prevail as to subsequent purchasers of other lots in the subdivision who took from the landowner after the landowner had already burdened other parcels with the restriction. As to Lot 1, however, the doctor may proceed with her plan to use part of the property as a medical office, because the restrictive covenant was not in the deed to the first buyer, nor was it in the deed to the doctor.

VII. MODIFICATION AND TERMINATION OF COVENANTS AND SERVITUDES

A. Modification and termination generally

1. No expiration from passage of time

Question 29: A grantor owned in fee simple two adjoining lots, Lots 1 and 2. He conveyed in fee simple Lot 1 to an investor. The deed was in usual form of a warranty deed with the following provision inserted in the appropriate place:

"Grantor, for himself, his heirs and assigns, does covenant and agree that any reasonable expense incurred by grantee, his heirs and assigns, as the result of having to repair the retaining wall presently situated on Lot 1 at the common boundary with Lot 2, shall be reimbursed one-half the costs of repairs; and by this provision the parties intend a covenant running with the land."

The investor conveyed Lot 1 in fee simple to a housewife by warranty deed in usual and regular form. The deed omitted any reference to the retaining wall or any covenant. Fifty years after the grantor's conveyance to the investor, the housewife conveyed Lot 1 in fee simple to a student by warranty deed in usual form; this deed omitted any reference to the retaining wall or the covenant.

There is no statute that applies to any aspect of the problems presented except a recording act and a statute providing for acquisition of title after ten years of adverse possession.

All conveyances by deeds were for a consideration equal to fair market value.

The deed from the grantor to the investor was never recorded. All other deeds were promptly and properly recorded.

Lot 2 is now owned by the grantor's son, who took by intestate succession from the grantor, now dead.

The student expended $3,500 on the retaining wall. Then he obtained all of the original deeds in the chain from the grantor to him. Shortly thereafter, the student discovered the covenant in the grantor's deed to the investor. He demanded that the grantor's son pay $1,750, and when the son refused, the student instituted an appropriate action to recover that sum from the son. In such action, the son asserted all defenses available to him.

If judgment is for the grantor's son, it will be because

(A) the student is barred by adverse possession.

(B) the investor's deed from the grantor was never recorded.

(C) the student did not know about the covenant until after he had incurred the expenses and, hence, could not have relied on it.

(D) the student's expenditures were not proved to be reasonable and customary.

[Q2107]

Answer 29: Choice **(D)** is correct. When the grantor conveyed Lot 1 to the investor, the grantor burdened Lot 2 with the covenant to reimburse the owner of Lot 1 for wall-repair expenses. This covenant was enforceable, and ran with the land on both the burden and benefit side. Even though more than 50 years have passed, no event has occurred (e.g., change of circumstances rendering fulfillment of the covenant's purposes impossible) that would cause the covenant to be extinguished, and the mere passage of time does not suffice to end the covenant. The fact that the covenant ran with the land on the benefit side means that the student as present owner of the benefited lot gets to enforce the covenant; this running of the benefit side occurs even though the deed to conveying the benefited parcel to the student did not mention the covenant or the wall (since mention of the covenant in the deed to the benefited lot is simply not a requirement). The running of the covenant on the burden side means that the obligation of payment attached to the grantor's son's interest in Lot 2. Therefore, the only way the student can lose is if his expenditures were not reasonable and customary (in which case they would not be covered by the terms of the covenant, even though the covenant is still enforceable).

(A) is wrong because nothing occurred to cause the doctrine of adverse possession to affect title to the benefited lot (Lot 1) while that lot was held by either the investor, the housewife, or the student. For instance, no action by any owner of Lot 2 could even arguably have constituted the requisite hostile, notorious, open, and continuous possession of the wall so as to wipe out the covenant governing repairs.

(B) is wrong because the fact that the investor's deed from the grantor for Lot 1 was not recorded had no effect on anyone who ever had an interest in Lot 2. It's true that the grantor, by conveying Lot 1 to the investor, simultaneously created a covenant burdening Lot 2, which was an interest in Lot 2. But a grantee's failure to record under a recording act has no effect on the rights as between the original grantor and grantee; therefore, in a contest between the grantor and the investor, the investor's failure to record his covenant against Lot 2 would not prevent the investor from recovering reimbursement from the grantor while the grantor still owned Lot 2. The interesting question is whether the investor's failure to record can be taken advantage of by the grantor's son as the grantor's successor. In other words, is the grantor's son a "subsequent purchaser without notice" who can take advantage of the fact that the deed creating the covenant never appeared in his chain of title? The answer is that because recording acts invariably protect only "purchasers for value," and because the son took by intestate succession (and thus did not give value for his interest), the son is *not* a purchaser for value and thus *cannot* take advantage of the recording act. (If the son had purchased for value and without notice of the covenant, he *would* have been free of the covenant on account of the investor's failure to record.)

(C) is wrong because the owner of a parcel benefited by an affirmative covenant does not lose the benefit merely because he did not act in reliance on the covenant's existence.

CHAPTER 7

LAND SALE CONTRACTS, MORTGAGES, AND DEEDS

I. LAND SALE CONTRACTS

A. Statute of Frauds

1. Spot the issue

> **Question 30:** Ozzie owned and occupied Blackacre, which was a tract of land improved with a one-family house. His friend, Victor, orally offered Ozzie $50,000 for Blackacre, the fair market value, and Ozzie accepted. Because they were friends, they saw no need for attorneys or written contracts and shook hands on the deal. Victor paid Ozzie $5,000 down in cash and agreed to pay the balance of $45,000 at an agreed closing time and place.
>
> Before the closing, Victor inherited another home and asked Ozzie to return his $5,000. Ozzie refused, and, at the time set for the closing, Ozzie tendered a good deed to Victor and declared his intention to vacate Blackacre the next day. Ozzie demanded that Victor complete the purchase. Victor refused. The fair market value of Blackacre has remained $50,000.
>
> In an appropriate action brought by Ozzie against Victor for specific performance, if Ozzie loses, the most likely reason will be that
>
> (A) the agreement was oral.
>
> (B) keeping the $5,000 is Ozzie's exclusive remedy.

(C) Victor had a valid reason for not closing.

(D) Ozzie remained in possession on the day set for the closing.

[Q1189]

Answer 30: Choice **(A)** is correct. The Statute of Frauds applies to all contracts for the sale of land, or for the sale of an interest in land. Therefore, such a contract will not be enforced unless it is in writing. There are a few exceptions to this rule (e.g., where there has been part performance in reliance on an oral agreement), but none of those exceptions applies here.

(B) is wrong because it is not the case that the seller's exclusive remedy for breach is to keep the deposit; often, a court will order the buyer to specifically perform even where the seller has a deposit. (Furthermore, unless the parties have agreed that the deposit will be the exclusive measure, the seller will be entitled to recover her actual damages from the buyer's breach if these are greater than the deposit.)

(C) is wrong because the fact that Victor inherited a different home is not a valid reason for not closing; the doctrine of frustration of purpose occasionally applies to land-sale contracts, but would virtually never apply where the only event alleged to have frustrated the buyer's purpose is that he found or acquired other property he liked better.

(D) is wrong because Ozzie's anticipated one-day delay in vacating would not have been a material breach, unless the agreement or the circumstances indicated that time was of the essence. There's no indication that that happened here. Therefore, the one-day delay would not have deprived Ozzie of his otherwise-existing right to obtain specific performance.

B. Marketable title

1. Time for measuring marketability

a. Outstanding mortgage

Question 31: A landowner mortgaged the land to a bank to secure his preexisting obligation to the bank. The mortgage was promptly and properly recorded. The landowner and a buyer then entered into a valid written contract for the purchase and sale of the land, which provided for the transfer of "a marketable title, free of encumbrances." The contract did not expressly refer to the mortgage.

Shortly after entering into the contract, the buyer found another property that much better suited her needs and decided to try to avoid her contract with the landowner. When the buyer discovered the existence of the mortgage, she asserted that the title was encumbered and that she would not close. The landowner responded by offering to provide for payment and discharge of the mortgage at the closing from the proceeds of the closing. The buyer refused to go forward, and the landowner brought an appropriate action against her for specific performance.

If the court holds for the landowner in this action, it will most likely be because

(A) the mortgage is not entitled to priority because it was granted for preexisting obligations.

(B) the doctrine of equitable conversion supports the result.

(C) the landowner's arrangements for the payment of the mortgage fully satisfied the landowner's obligation to deliver marketable title.

(D) the existence of the mortgage was not the buyer's real reason for refusing to close.

[Q2081]

Answer 31: Choice **(C)** is correct. Unless the sale contract specifies otherwise, the seller's title is not required to be marketable until the date set for the closing. The fact that there is an outstanding mortgage on the property, therefore, does not entitle the buyer to cancel the contract, as long as the seller has the right and probable ability to pay off the mortgage at the closing.

(A) is wrong because the fact that the mortgage was granted for pre-existing obligations (as opposed, say, to being a purchase money mortgage) is irrelevant to the issue of whether the seller's title is marketable. For instance, if the seller were not paying off the mortgage at the closing, the mortgage would indeed be an encumbrance rendering title unmarketable, even though it was granted to secure the seller's pre-existing obligation to the mortgagee.

(B) is wrong because the doctrine of equitable conversion is used to pass the risk of loss to the buyer under a purchase contract, and has nothing to do with whether the seller's title is marketable.

(D) is wrong because a purchaser's "real reason" (i.e., motive) for refusing to close is irrelevant to whether the purchaser has the right to so refuse. For example, if the seller's title had been unmarketable, the buyer would have been entitled to refuse to close even though her real reason for refusing was something entirely unrelated to the quality of the seller's title.

Question 32: Venner, the owner of Greenacre, a tract of land, entered into an enforceable written agreement with Brier providing that Venner would sell Greenacre to Brier for an agreed price. At the place and time designated for the closing. Venner tendered an appropriate deed, but Brier responded that he had discovered a mortgage on Greenacre and would not complete the transaction, because Venner's title was not free of encumbrances, as the contract required. Venner said that it was his intent to pay the mortgage from the proceeds of the sale, and he offered to put the proceeds in escrow for that purpose with any agreeable, responsible escrowee. The balance due on the mortgage was substantially less than the contract purchase price. Brier refused Venner's proposal. Venner began an appropriate legal action against Brier for specific performance. There is no applicable statute in the jurisdiction where Greenacre is located.

Venner's best legal argument in support of his claim for relief is that

(A) as the seller of real estate, he had an implied right to use the contract proceeds to clear the title being conveyed.

(B) the lien of the mortgage shifts from Greenacre to the contract proceeds.

(C) under the doctrine of equitable conversion, title has already passed to Brier and the only issue is how the purchase price is to be allocated.

(D) no provision of the contract has been breached by Venner.

[Q4109]

Answer 32: Choice (A) is correct. This choice correctly identifies that Venner can use the sale proceeds to pay off the mortgage, and thus force Brier to honor the contract. Where, as is usually the case, the seller in a land-sale contract covenants to deliver the property free and clear of encumbrances, the presence of a mortgage would be an encumbrance rendering the title unmarketable. But you're told here that the proceeds will cover the mortgage. When that's the case, the seller has an implied right to use the proceeds of the sale to pay off the mortgage. When you think about it, this rule comports with what you'd expect to happen, since many homeowners, in real life, couldn't sell their home if this weren't the case.

(B) is wrong because it misstates the law. Although it's possible that the law of the jurisdiction may make the mortgage payable from the proceeds, and the mortgage agreement itself may insist on payoff if the property is conveyed, the "rule" stated in this choice wouldn't cause the mortgage to be removed from Greenacre — and that's the central problem here. Instead, the key is that the seller gets to use the sale proceeds to pay off the mortgage simultaneously with the closing of title.

(C) is wrong because the doctrine of equitable conversion would not apply to these facts. The doctrine of equitable conversion addresses the period between the signing of the land sale contract and the closing. Under the doctrine, the vendor has a personal property interest in the property, between the signing of the contract and the closing, in the form of the balance of the purchase price owed to him; the vendee is considered the beneficial owner of the property. The doctrine wouldn't help with the problem here, which is that Venner can't deliver marketable title unless he can remove the mortgage.

(D) is wrong because it states an insufficient ground on which Venner could prevail. Of course, his underlying argument must be that he hasn't breached the contract, because if he had, he wouldn't be entitled to specific performance. However, Choice (D), in and of itself, doesn't provide a rule allowing Venner to use the proceeds to pay off the mortgage, and enforce the contract. Only Choice (A) does this.

C. Remedies for failure to perform

1. Damages

a. Where no earnest money deposit

i. Consideration argument

Question 33: Able was the owner of Blackacre, an undeveloped city lot. Able and Baker executed a written document in which Able agreed to sell Blackacre to Baker and Baker agreed to buy Blackacre from Able for $200,000; the document did not provide for an earnest money down payment. Able recorded the document, as authorized by statute.

Able orally gave Baker permission to park his car on Blackacre without charge prior to the closing. Thereafter, Baker frequently parked his car on Blackacre.

Another property came on the market that Baker wanted more than Blackacre. Baker decided to try to escape any obligation to Able.

Baker had been told that contracts for the purchase and sale of real property require consideration and concluded that because he had made no earnest money down payment, he could refuse to close and not be liable. Baker notified Able of his intention not to close and, in fact, did refuse to close on the date set for the closing. Able brought an appropriate action to compel specific performance by Baker.

If Able wins, it will be because

(A) Baker's use of Blackacre for parking constitutes part performance.

(B) general contract rules regarding consideration apply to real estate contracts.

(C) the doctrine of equitable conversion applies.

(D) the document was recorded.

[Q2030]

Answer 33: Choice **(B)** is correct. It is likely, though not absolutely certain, that Abel will be able to obtain specific performance (the court will have to be satisfied that money damages would not give him an adequate remedy). But one thing that *is* certain is that Baker will fail with his lack-of-consideration argument, because the general contract principle that an exchange of promises meets the consideration requirement applies to real estate contracts. Able has made a promise (to convey in return for the purchase price), and Baker has made a return promise (to pay the purchase price in return for title), so standard consideration requirements are easily satisfied. The fact that there was no earnest money deposit is completely irrelevant to the consideration issue — an earnest money deposit is not required, and where present is merely a form of liquidated-damages clause.

(A) is wrong because the contract, since it is in writing and meets the consideration requirement, would be binding even if Baker had not parked on the property and therefore arguably partly performed. (If the contract had been oral, Baker's parking might supply him with an argument for application of the part-performance exception to the Statute of Frauds, but even here, he would probably lose because the parking was not really part "performance.")

(C) is wrong because equitable conversion, where applicable, vests "equitable title" in the vendee under a land sale contract (thus passing the risk of loss to the vendee), and neither equitable title nor risk of loss is at issue on these facts.

(D) is wrong because a vendor under a land sale contract can recover for breach (including specific performance if money damages would not be an adequate remedy) whether the contract was recorded or not — recording is merely relevant to the vendee's rights vis-a-vis later grantees from the vendor (by giving the world constructive notice of the pending transfer), not to the vendee's rights vis-a-vis the vendor.

2. **Specific performance**

a. **Breaching buyer**

Question 34: Adam entered into a valid written contract to sell Blackacre, a large tract of land, to Betsy. At that time, Blackacre was owned by Adam's father, Fred; Adam had no title to Blackacre and was not the agent of Fred.

After the contract was executed and before the scheduled closing date. Fred died intestate, leaving Adam as his sole heir. Shortly thereafter, Adam received an offer for Blackacre that was substantially higher than the purchase price in the contract with Betsy. Adam refused to close with Betsy although she was ready, willing, and able to close pursuant to the contract.

Betsy brought an appropriate action for specific performance against Adam.

In that action, Betsy should be awarded

(A) nothing, because Adam had no authority to enter into the contract with Betsy.

(B) nothing, because the doctrine of after-acquired title does not apply to executory contracts.

(C) judgment for specific performance, because Adam acquired title prior to the scheduled closing.

(D) judgment for specific performance, to prevent unjust enrichment of Adam.

[Q1071]

Answer 34: Choice **(C)** is correct. The purchaser under a land-sale contract will normally be entitled to a decree of specific performance if the seller is able but unwilling to perform. Here, the fact that Adam did not have title at the time he signed the contract is irrelevant; the contract called for him to make a conveyance at the scheduled closing date, and he is able to do that. The case therefore falls within the familiar principle that the time for measuring whether a seller has marketable title is the time for closing, not some earlier date.

(A) is wrong because the fact that Adam did not have authority to sell the land at the moment of signing is irrelevant; he has title by now (prior to the scheduled closing date), and that's all that matters for purposes of specific performance.

(B) is wrong because the doctrine of after-acquired title is not necessary for a decree of specific performance here; all that matters is that Adam has title by the time scheduled for performance.

(D) is wrong because specific performance is used for breach of contract where (as here) damages would be an inadequate remedy, and the concept of unjust enrichment is not needed or relevant to whether specific performance should be decreed.

3. Deposit

a. Reasonable estimate

Question 35: Three months ago, Bert agreed in writing to buy Sam's single-family residence, Liveacre, for $110,000. Bert paid Sam a $5,000 deposit to be applied to the purchase price. The contract stated that Sam had the right at his option to retain the deposit as liquidated damages in the event of Ben's default. The closing was to have taken place last week. Six weeks ago, Bert was notified by his employer that he was to be transferred to another job 1,000 miles away. Bert immediately notified Sam that he could not close, and therefore he demanded the return of his $5,000. Sam refused, waited until after the contract closing date, listed with a broker, and then conveyed Liveacre for $108,000 to Conner, a purchaser found by the real estate broker. Conner paid the full purchase price and immediately recorded his deed. Conner knew of the prior contract with Bert. In an appropriate action, Bert seeks to recover the $5,000 deposit from Sam.

The most probable result will be that Sam

(A) must return the $5,000 to Bert, because Sam can no longer carry out his contract with Bert.

(B) must return the $5,000 to Bert, because was legally justified in not completing the contract.

(C) must return $3,000 to Bert, because Sam's damages were only $2,000.

(D) may keep the $5,000 deposit, because Bert breached the contract.

[Q2023]

Answer 35: Choice **(D)** is correct. The contract provision concerning the deposit was a liquidated damages clause. In most courts, a liquidated damages clause is enforceable if it was a reasonable estimate (viewed *either* as of the time the contract was made or at the time of suit) of the damages that the seller would likely incur if the buyer breached. Here, an estimate, as of the time the contract was signed, that the seller would sustain $5,000 in damages if there was a breach on a $110,000 contract, seems reasonable. The fact that the seller ended up with a slightly smaller-than-predicted loss of $2,000 (not counting any incidental expenses to the seller from having to re-list the property or wait for a later sale) does not change the reasonableness of the time-of-contract estimate; in fact, the $5,000 estimate is probably also reasonable viewed as of the time of suit.

(A) is wrong because Sam's present ability to carry out his contract with Bert was caused by Bert's breach, and therefore does not nullify Sam's ability to rely on the liquidated damages clause.

(B) is wrong because Bert's need to transfer is not the sort of extraordinary event that would excuse Bert's nonperformance.

(C) is wrong because, as explained in (D), the liquidated damages clause will be enforced here, even though it differs from the seller's actual damages.

D. Equitable conversion

1. Risk of loss

Question 36: Landover, the owner in fee simple of Highacre, an apartment house property, entered into an enforceable written agreement with VanMeer to sell Highacre to VanMeer. The agreement provided that a good and marketable title was to be conveyed free and clear of all encumbrances. However, the agreement was silent as to the risk of fire prior to the closing, and there is no applicable statute in the state where the land is located. The premises were not insured. The day before the scheduled closing date, Highacre was wholly destroyed by fire. When VanMeer refused to close, Landover brought an action in specific performance. If Landover prevails, the most likely reason will be that

(A) the failure of VanMeer to insure his interest as the purchaser of Highacre precludes any relief for him.

(B) the remedy at law is inadequate in actions concerning real estate contracts and either party is entitled to specific performance.

(C) equity does not permit consideration of surrounding circumstances in actions concerning real estate contracts.

(D) the doctrine of equitable conversion applies.

[Q4152]

Answer 36: Choice **(D)** is correct. Under the doctrine of equitable conversion, the vendee is considered the beneficial owner of the property after the sales contract takes effect, leaving the vendor with a personal property interest in the property, in the form of the balance of the purchase price the vendee owes him. This common law doctrine is followed by most states. In a state following equitable conversion, the vendee is required to close, even though the structures on the property have been destroyed. (But the vendee gets the benefit of any insurance policy the vendor may have had on the structure.)

(A) is wrong because it relies on a fact which is irrelevant: VanMeer's failure to insure the property is not dispositive of Landover's ability to recover the purchase price. Whether VanMeer did or did not buy insurance (which he could have — he had an insurable interest as soon as he signed the contract), Landover would still be able to force a closing, if and only if the jurisdiction applies equitable conversion (see Choice (D) above).

(B) is wrong because although it is a correct statement of the law, it would be insufficient, under these facts, to result in a decision for Landover. (B) is correct in that, in general, remedies at law (e.g., damages) are inadequate in actions where real estate is involved, since real estate is "unique." In such situations, specific performance is an appropriate remedy. However, specific performance is an *equitable* remedy, meaning that equitable considerations will be taken into account to determine if it's appropriate. Choice (D) is just such a consideration – the doctrine of equitable conversion. Conversely, if the jurisdiction does not apply equitable conversion, Landover won't be able to force a closing even though his remedy at law is inadequate.

(C) is wrong because it misstates the law. Specific performance is an equitable remedy. Equitable remedies are granted by determining whether the remedy will be just in the circumstances. As a result, the circumstances surrounding the contract *are* considered.

II. MORTGAGES AND INSTALLMENT CONTRACTS

A. Nature of mortgage

1. Sale of mortgaged property

a. Assumption

i. Receipt of deed with assumption clause

Question 37: A man borrowed money from a bank and executed a promissory note for the amount secured by a mortgage on his residence. Several years later, the man sold his residence. As provided by the contract of sale, the deed to the buyer provided that the buyer agreed "to assume the existing mortgage debt" on the residence.

Subsequently, the buyer defaulted on the mortgage loan to the bank, and appropriate foreclosure proceedings were initiated. The foreclosure sale resulted in a deficiency.

There is no applicable statute.

Is the buyer liable for the deficiency?

(A) No, because even if the buyer assumed the mortgage, the seller is solely responsible for any deficiency.

(B) No, because the buyer did not sign a promissory note to the bank and therefore has no personal liability.

(C) Yes, because the buyer assumed the mortgage and therefore became personally liable for the mortgage loan and any deficiency.

(D) Yes, because the transfer of the mortgage debt to the buyer resulted in a novation of the original mortgage and loan and rendered the buyer solely responsible for any deficiency.

[QA016]

Answer 37: Choice **(C)** is correct. When a buyer assumes the seller's mortgage, the buyer becomes primarily liable for the mortgage debt. (The seller is secondarily liable, assuming there is no release.) The lender may therefore sue buyer for the deficiency when foreclosure sale is not sufficient to discharge the debt. (Contrast this to the situation where the buyer takes "subject to the mortgage." In that situation, the buyer would not be personally liable for the mortgage debt or for a deficiency judgment after foreclosure.) When a buyer knowingly receives a deed that recites that the buyer is assuming the mortgage and intends to be bound, assumption occurs even though the buyer has not signed the deed. (Here, where the buyer previously signed the contract, which called for assumption, it's even more clear that the buyer will be deemed to have assumed even though he never signed the deed.)

(A) is wrong because it misstates the law. When a buyer agrees to "assume" a mortgage, this language is always interpreted to mean that if the lender forecloses and is left with a deficiency judgment, the lender can recover that deficiency from the assuming buyer without first trying to recover it from the original borrower. In other words, the assuming buyer becomes "primarily liable" for the mortgage debt and for any deficiency after foreclosure sale.

(B) is wrong because it was not necessary for the buyer to sign a promissory note to be liable. Once the buyer assumed the mortgage, he became primarily liable on the mortgage and thus is liable for the deficiency. (And the fact that the buyer didn't sign the deed doesn't prevent him from being deemed to have assumed, as long as the buyer knew the deed contained an assumption provision; see Choice (C) for more about this.)

(D) gives the right result but the wrong rationale. The buyer's assumption of the mortgage is not the same as a novation. With a novation, the bank agrees to *substitute* the personal liability of the buyer for that of the original debtor and *releases* the original debtor. Nothing in the facts suggests the bank's involvement in the transaction at all, let alone its willingness to release the original borrower.

Question 38: Ashton owned Woodsedge, a tract used for commercial purposes, in fee simple and thereafter mortgaged it to First Bank. She signed a promissory note secured by a duly executed and recorded mortgage. There was no "due on sale" clause, that is, no provision that, upon sale, the whole balance then owing would become due and owing. Ashton conveyed Woodsedge to Beam "subject to a mortgage to First Bank, which the grantee assumes and agrees to pay." Beam conveyed Woodsedge to Carter "subject to an existing mortgage to First Bank." A copy of the note and the mortgage that secured it had been exhibited to each grantee.

After Carter made three timely payments, no further payments were made by any party. In fact, the real estate had depreciated to a point where it was worth less than the debt.

There is no applicable statute or regulation.

In an appropriate foreclosure action, First Bank joined Ashton, Beam, and Carter as defendants. At the foreclosure sale, although the fair market value for Woodsedge in its depreciated state was obtained, a deficiency resulted.

First Bank is entitled to collect a deficiency judgment against

(A) Ashton only.

(B) Ashton and Beam only.

(C) Beam and Carter only.

(D) Ashton, Beam, and Carter.

[Q2147]

Answer 38: Choice **(B)** is correct. Ashton is personally liable because she signed the original promissory note. Beam is personally liable because he assumed the mortgage by means of the document that conveyed to him (and the fact that Beam may not have signed the deed won't matter, as long as he was aware of the assumption language in the deed and intended to be bound by it.) First Bank can recover even though it was not a party to the Beam-to-Ashton promise, because First Bank would be found to be an intended beneficiary (and thus a third party beneficiary who may recover) of that promise. Carter is not personally liable, because a person who receives a conveyance stating that the transfer is "subject to" an outstanding mortgage does not, without more, assume (i.e., become personally liable for) the mortgage. Carter's lack of liability did not change by virtue of the fact that he made several timely payments; only an express promise of assumption by Carter (made either to Ashton, Beam or First Bank) could have rendered him personally liable.

(A), (C), and (D) are wrong to the extent that they are inconsistent with the above analysis.

2. Redemption of mortgage

a. Who has right

i. No redemption until entire mortgage paid off

Question 39: A brother and sister owned a property in fee simple as tenants in common, each owning an undivided one-half interest. The two joined in mortgaging the property to an investor by a properly recorded mortgage that contained a general warranty clause. The brother became disenchanted with land-owning and notified his sister that he would no longer contribute to the payment of installments due to the investor. After the mortgage was in default and the investor made demand for payment of the entire amount of principal and interest due, the sister tendered to the investor, and the investor deposited, a check for one-half of the amount due the investor. The sister then demanded a release of her undivided one-half interest. The investor refused to release any interest in the property. The sister promptly brought an action against the investor to quiet title to an undivided one-half interest in the property.

In such action, the sister should

(A) lose, because the investor's title had been warranted by an express provision of the mortgage.

(B) lose, because there was no redemption from the mortgage.

(C) win, because the sister is entitled to marshalling.

(D) win, because the cotenancy of the mortgagors was in common and not joint.

[Q3065]

Answer 39: Choice **(B)** is correct. The mortgage attached to the entire property, and payment of 1/2 the total amount therefore did not "free up" a 1/2 undivided interest. The investor as mortgagee has a lien on the *entire property.* That is, the investor received a security interest on the full property — and the concomitant right upon default to conduct a judicial sale of the full property to get her debt repaid — regardless of whether one party paid that party's full share. A.L.P. § 16.172. In other words, the investor is entitled to say, "Who paid what is between the two of you — I've got the right to have the whole property sold at foreclosure if any part of my loan is in default and the default is not wholly cured." That's what happened here. (The sister's remedy is a suit in contribution against the brother for 1/2 the amount she paid to the investor.)

(A) is wrong, because the investor did not have title to the property. A mortgage is a security interest in a property securing a loan. The fact that the mortgage instrument contained a clause in which the brother and sister warranted that they owned the property free of encumbrances (which is what the general warranty clause did) is irrelevant to the issue of whether the sister is entitled to quiet title.

(C) is wrong, because the equitable doctrine of marshaling does not apply to these facts. Marshalling is the ranking of assets in a certain order toward the payment of debts. The concept arises in equity, and means that where there are two creditors, with the senior one having two funds to satisfy his debt, that senior creditor must resort first to the fund which is not subject to demand of the junior creditor. The concept is misapplied to this fact pattern, because the doctrine would be one a second mortgagee invoked to protect his interest from the first mortgagee's foreclosure. Under these facts there is only one mortgage on the property, and as a party who joined with the brother in making the mortgage on the property, the sister would not be able to have her interest released.

(D) is wrong, because the sister would lose even if the cotenancy was joint. Joint tenancy differs from tenancy in common only with respect to the right of survivorship, which exists as to the former but not the latter. There is no difference in the legal analysis here between the joint-tenancy and tenancy-in-common scenarios.

3. Priorities (allocation of foreclosure proceeds)

a. Judgment lien creditor's status

i. Two-property scenario

Question 40: A businessman owned a hotel, subject to a mortgage securing a debt he owed to a bank. The businessman later acquired a nearby parking garage, financing a part of the purchase price by a loan from a financing company, secured by a mortgage on the parking garage. Two years thereafter, the businessman defaulted on the loan owed to the bank, which caused the full amount of that loan to become immediately due and payable. The bank decided not to foreclose the mortgage on the hotel at that time, but instead properly sued for the full amount of the defaulted loan. The bank obtained and properly filed a judgment for that amount. A statute of the jurisdiction provides: "Any judgment properly filed shall, for ten years from filing, be a lien on the real property then owned or subsequently acquired by any person against whom the judgment is rendered." There is no other applicable statute, except the statute providing for judicial foreclosure of mortgages, which places no restriction on deficiency judgments. Shortly thereafter, the bank brought an appropriate action for judicial foreclosure of its first mortgage on the hotel and of its judgment lien on the parking garage. The financing company was joined as a party defendant, and appropriately counterclaimed for foreclosure of its mortgage on the parking garage, which was also in default. All procedures were properly followed and the confirmed foreclosure sales resulted in the following: The net proceeds of the sale of the hotel to a third party were $200,000 less than the bank's mortgage balance. The net proceeds of the sale of the parking garage to a fourth party were $200,000 more than the financing company's mortgage balance.

How should the $200,000 surplus arising from the bid on the parking garage be distributed?

(A) It should be paid to the bank.

(B) It should be paid to the businessman.

(C) It should be paid to the financing company.

(D) It should be split equally between the bank and the financing company.

[Q7057]

Answer 40: Choice **(A)** is correct. The foreclosure sale of the bank's mortgage on the hotel was insufficient to pay the businessman's debt to the bank. The bank had received a judgment against the businessman for the entire amount of the defaulted loan. This lien was properly recorded and applied to all property owned by the businessman during the following ten-year time period, including the parking garage. After the financing company was paid in full from the funds generated by the foreclosure sale of its mortgage on the parking garage, the additional funds generated by that sale would be paid to the bank not as a deficiency judgment, but because of the unsatisfied amount of the prior money judgment.

(B) is incorrect. The judgment lien was properly filed against the businessman. Therefore, the garage was subject not only to the loan of the financing company, but also to the judgment lien as a second priority. The businessman would be entitled to surplus proceeds only if both liens had been fully paid.

(C) is incorrect. The foreclosure sale of the financing company's mortgage on the parking garage was sufficient to pay the businessman's debt to the financing company in full. The fact that the garage was sold for more money than was owed under the garage mortgage is irrelevant to the amount owed to the financing company — a mortgagee doesn't receive any part of the "surplus" after its mortgage has been paid in full.

(D) is incorrect for the same reason that (C) is incorrect.

III. DEEDS

A. Formalities

1.   Identification of parties

a.   Void if not satisfied

i.   Imprecise identification

Question 41: A landowner owned a valuable parcel of land located in York County. The landowner executed a document in the form of a warranty deed of the parcel, which was regular in all respects except that the only language designating the grantees in each of the granting and *habendum* clauses was: "The leaders of all the Protestant Churches in York County." The instrument was acknowledged as required by statute and promptly and properly recorded. The landowner told his lawyer, but no one else, that he had made the conveyance as he did because he abhorred sectarianism in the Protestant movement and because he thought that the leaders would devote the asset to lessening sectarianism.

The landowner died suddenly and unexpectedly a week later, leaving a will that bequeathed and devised his entire estate to his cousin. After probate of the will became final and the administration on the landowner's estate was closed, the cousin instituted an appropriate action to quiet title to the parcel and properly served as defendant each Protestant church situated in the county.

The only evidence introduced consisted of the chain of title under which the landowner held, the probated will, the recorded deed, the fact that no person knew about the deed except the landowner and his lawyer, and the conversation the landowner had with his lawyer described above.

In such action, judgment should be for

(A) the cousin, because there is inadequate identification of grantees in the deed.

(B) the cousin, because the state of the evidence would not support a finding of delivery of the deed.

(C) the defendants, because a deed is *prima facie* valid until rebutted.

(D) the defendants, because recording established delivery *prima facie* until rebutted.
[Q1132]

Answer 41: Choice (A) is correct. In order to be valid, a deed must identify the grantee(s) with reasonable precision. Here, the grantees are "the leaders of all the Protestant churches in York County." It may be possible to identify with acceptable confidence all Protestant churches in the county, but it is unlikely that the "leader" of each church can be identified, given the imprecision of the term "leader" in the context of a church (is it the minister, or is it the president of the congregation, or is it the entire board of directors of the organization?). Where a deed does not identify the grantee with acceptable precision, the deed will be treated as if it had never been made. That would mean that the landowner died still holding title, which passed to the cousin.

(B) is wrong because the fact that the deed was recorded furnishes a strong presumption that delivery occurred (i.e., that the grantor intended the deed to take effect immediately, which is all that "delivery" means).

(C) is wrong because, while it may be true that a deed is presumed valid, the lack of an acceptably-precise designation of grantees here would be sufficient to rebut the presumption of validity.

(D) is wrong because, while recording will indeed create a *prima facie* (but rebuttable) case that delivery occurred, the problem here is not delivery but imprecision in the designation of the grantees.

b. Deceased grantee

Question 42: A vendee entered into a valid written contract to purchase a large tract of land from a vendor for its fair market value of $50,000. The contract was assignable by the vendee. The vendee duly notified the vendor to convey title jointly to the vendee and "Charles," Charles being the vendee's friend whom the vendee had not seen for many years.

When the vendee learned that Charles would have to sign certain documents in connection with the closing, she prevailed upon her brother to attend the closing and pretend to be Charles. The vendee and her brother attended the closing, and the vendor executed an instrument in the proper form of a deed, purporting to convey the property to "[the vendee] and Charles, as tenants in common." The brother pretended that he was Charles, and he signed Charles's name to all the required documents. The vendee provided the entire $50,000 consideration for the transaction. The deed was promptly and properly recorded.

Unknown to the vendee or her brother, Charles had died several months before the closing. Charles's will, which was duly probated, devised "all my real estate to my nephew" and the residue of his estate to the vendee.

The vendee and the nephew have been unable to agree as to the status or disposition of the property. The nephew brought an appropriate action against the vendor and the vendee to quiet legal title to an undivided one-half interest in the property.

The court should hold that legal title to the property is vested

(A) all in the vendor.

(B) all in the vendee.

(C) one-half in the vendee and one-half in the vendor.

(D) one-half in the vendee and one-half in the nephew.

[Q2114]

Answer 42: Choice **(C)** is correct. Because Charles was dead at the time of the purported conveyance to the vendee and Charles as tenants in common, the deed's attempt to pass an interest to him was not effective (i.e., the deed was "void" as to him). Therefore, no interest passed through to his estate or via his estate to his nephew. The "Charles" portion of the tenancy in common therefore remained in the vendor. The deed was effective as to the vendee's interest, however, since she was correctly named and the deed was delivered to and accepted by her; therefore, she has the tenancy in common interest that the vendor intended to convey to her.

Choices (A), (B), and (D) are wrong because they are inconsistent with the above analysis.

B. Delivery of deed

1. Delivery to agent of grantee

Question 43: When a homeowner became ill, he properly executed a deed sufficient to convey his home to his nephew, who was then serving overseas in the military. Two persons signed as witnesses to qualify the deed for recordation under an applicable statute. The homeowner handed the deed to his nephew's friend and said, "I want [the nephew] to have my home. Please take this deed for him." Shortly thereafter, the nephew's friend learned that the home-owner's death was imminent. One day before the homeowner's death, the nephew's friend recorded the deed. The nephew returned home shortly after the homeowner's death. The nephew's friend brought him up to date, and he took possession of the home. The homeowner died intestate, leaving a daughter as his sole heir. She asserted ownership of his home. The nephew brought an appropriate action against her to determine title to the home. The law of the jurisdiction requires only two witnesses for a will to be properly executed.

If the court rules for the nephew and against the daughter, what is the most likely explanation?

(A) The deed was delivered when the homeowner handed it to the nephew's friend.

(B) The delivery of the deed was accomplished by the recording of the deed.

(C) The homeowner's death consummated a valid gift causa mortis to the nephew.

(D) The homeowner's properly executed deed was effective as a testamentary document.

[Q7070]

Answer 43: Choice **(A)** is correct. An inter vivos gift (i.e., one made during the giver's lifetime) may be made of real estate. The gift is deemed made when "delivery" occurs, accompanied by the requisite donative intent. Here, the homeowner had the requisite donative intent as shown by his words. Delivery occurred when the homeowner physically handed the deed to the nephew's friend as the agent of the nephew; this was delivery because it is clear from the homeowner's words that he intended the gift to take place immediately rather than at some future time. Acceptance is presumed if the gift is beneficial. Once delivery occurred, the homeowner could not recall the gift.

(B) is incorrect, because although the recording of a deed may create a presumption of delivery, here the delivery occurred prior to the recordation of the deed (at the moment the home-owner physically handed the deed to the nephew's friend as the agent of the nephew, with the intent to pass the title).

(C) is incorrect, because a gift causa mortis may only be made of personal property. In addition, the gift was not made in view of pending death from a stated peril (the facts only note that the homeowner was ill).

(D) is incorrect, because a testamentary document takes effect at the death of the testator and must have been executed with the requisite testamentary intent. Here, the homeowner wanted the nephew to have title immediately and thus delivered the deed to the nephew's friend; the homeowner did not want to postpone delivery until his death.

2. Not revocable

a. Testable

Question 44: Ogle owned Greenacre, a tract of land, in fee simple. Five years ago, he executed and delivered to Lilly an instrument in the proper form of a warranty deed that conveyed Greenacre to Lilly "for and during the term of her natural life." No other estate or interest or person taking an interest was mentioned. Lilly took possession of Greenacre and has remained in possession.

Fifteen months ago, Ogle died, leaving a will that has been duly admitted to probate. The will, *inter alia,* had the following provision:

"I devise Greenacre to Mina for her natural life and from and after Mina's death to Rex, his heirs and assigns, forever."

Administration of Ogle's estate has been completed. Mina claims the immediate right to possession of Greenacre. Rex also asserts a right to immediate possession.

In an appropriate lawsuit to which Lilly, Mina, and Rex are parties, who should be adjudged to have the right to immediate possession?

(A) Lilly, because no subsequent act of Ogle would affect her life estate.

(B) Mina, because Ogle's will was the final and definitive expression of his intent.

(C) Mina, because Lilly's estate terminated with the death of Ogle.

(D) Rex, because Lilly's estate terminated with Ogle's death and all that Ogle had was the right to transfer his reversion in fee simple.

[Q2092]

Answer 44: Choice **(A)** is correct. When Ogle delivered the deed to Lilly, she received a life estate, and nothing Ogle did thereafter could undo or modify that life estate. Therefore, the clause in Ogle's will leaving a life estate to Mina did not affect Lilly's life estate. (Instead, Mina got an executory life estate that would not start until Lilly's death.)

(B) is wrong because of the principle stated in Choice (A) above. (C) and (D) are wrong because of this same principle; notice that a grantor (here, Ogle) can create a life estate in the grantee, and the grantor's death does not act to terminate that life estate, as Choices (C) and (D) suggest that it would.

C. Covenants for title in warranty deed

1. Present vs. future covenants

a. Future covenants

i. List of future covenants

Question 45: Seller owned Blackacre, improved with an aging four-story warehouse. The warehouse was built to the lot lines on all four sides. On the street side, recessed loading docks permitted semi-trailers to be backed in. After the tractors were unhooked, the trailers extended into the street and occupied most of one lane of the street. Over the years, as trailers became larger, the blocking of the street became more severe. The municipality advised Seller that the loading docks could not continue to be used because the trailers blocked the street; it gave Seller 90 days to cease and desist.

During the 90 days, Seller sold and conveyed Blackacre by warranty deed for a substantial consideration to Buyer. The problem of the loading docks was not discussed in the negotiations.

Upon expiration of the 90 days, the municipality required Buyer to stop using the loading docks. This action substantially reduced the value of Blackacre.

Buyer brought an appropriate action against Seller seeking cancellation of the deed and return of all monies paid.

Such action should be based upon a claim of

(A) misrepresentation.

(B) breach of the covenant of warranty.

(C) failure of consideration.

(D) mutual mistake.

[Q2135]

Answer 45: Choice (B) is **incorrect**. The covenant of warranty protects the grantee only against an eviction or disturbance, due to absence of title or to an encumbrance. So the facts here fail to support a claim for breach of the warranty covenant in two respects: (1) the problem with using the loading docks was not a problem with title or an encumbrance (merely a problem that the existing use violated city rules), and (2) more fundamentally, Buyer has not been evicted or even threatened with eviction (he can stay on the property forever as long as he doesn't unload trailers in a way that blocks the street).

(The correct choice is (A). By concealing the fact that the present use is the subject of current enforcement proceedings, Seller is liable on a fraudulent misrepresentation theory.)

D. Undisclosed condition in house

1. Emerging trend of liability for failure to disclose material defect

Question 46: Able, who owned Blackacre, a residential lot improved with a dwelling, conveyed it for a valuable consideration to Baker. The dwelling had been constructed by a prior owner. Baker had inspected Blackacre prior to the purchase and discovered no defects. After moving in, Baker became aware that sewage seeped into the basement when the toilets were flushed. Able said that this defect had been present for years and that he had taken no steps to hide the facts from Baker. Baker paid for the necessary repairs and brought an appropriate action against Able to recover his cost of repair.

If Baker wins, it will be because

(A) Able failed to disclose a latent defect.

(B) Baker made a proper inspection.

(C) the situation constitutes a health hazard.

(D) Able breached the implied warranty of habitability and fitness for purpose.

[Q2120]

Answer 46: Choice **(A)** is correct. An increasing number of courts now impose liability on a home seller who is aware of a material defect and who fails to disclose it to a buyer, where the defect is a latent one that cannot easily be found by an inspection. It is by no means certain that a court would find for Baker on this ground, but of the four possibilities this is the only one that offers Baker even a plausible chance of success.

(B) is wrong because Baker's having made a proper inspection, by itself, would not be enough to ensure him a victory. For instance, if the defect had been a "patent" one (one that ought to have been discovered by a reasonable inspection), virtually no courts would impose liability.

(C) is wrong because, while the fact that the condition constitutes a health hazard is a factor making liability slightly more likely, the key factor leading to liability is that the defect was latent (not readily discoverable), a factor that this choice does not refer to at all.

(D) is wrong because courts virtually never hold that the seller of a "used" house built by someone else makes an implied warranty of habitability or fitness for particular purpose; since the facts tell us that a prior owner built the house, this rule precludes liability on warranty-of-habitability grounds.

CHAPTER **8**

RECORDING ACTS

I. WHAT INSTRUMENTS MUST BE RECORDED

A. What instruments must be recorded

1. Contract of sale

a. Testable

Question 47: Able was the owner of Greenacre, a large tract of land. Able entered into a binding written contract with Baker for the sale and purchase of Greenacre for $125,000. The contract required Able to convey marketable record title.

Baker decided to protect his interest and promptly and properly recorded the contract.

Thereafter, but before the date scheduled for the closing, Charlie obtained and properly filed a final judgment against Able in the amount of $1 million in a personal injury suit. A statute in the jurisdiction provides: "Any judgment properly filed shall, for ten years from filing, be a lien on the real property then owned or subsequently acquired by any person against whom the judgment is rendered."

The recording act of the jurisdiction authorizes recording of contracts and also provides: "No conveyance or mortgage of real property shall be good against subsequent purchasers for value and without notice unless the same be recorded according to law."

There are no other relevant statutory provisions.

At the closing, Baker declined to accept the title of Able on the ground that Charlie's judgment lien encumbered the title he would receive and rendered it unmarketable. Able brought an appropriate action against Baker for specific performance of the contract and joined Charlie as a party.

In this action, the judgment should be for

(A) Able, because in equity a purchaser takes free of judgment liens.

(B) Able, because the contract had been recorded.

(C) Baker, because Able cannot benefit from Baker's action in recording the contract.

(D) Baker, because the statute creating judgment liens takes precedence over the recording act.

[Q2104]

Answer 47: Choice **(B)** is correct. In most states, a land-sale contract is recordable, and the facts here tell us that this is so for the state in question (by telling us that Baker "properly recorded the contract"). Once the contract was recorded, it created an interest in land on the part of the vendee (namely, the right to buy on the stated terms) that was superior to any later-created interest in the property. Therefore, Baker's right to purchase was superior to the later-filed judgment lien obtained by Charlie. Consequently, Able would be deemed to have marketable title, because notwithstanding the judgment lien he was capable of conveying the property free and clear to Baker.

(A) is wrong because it states the right result, but for the wrong reason. A purchaser would not always take free of a judgment lien; for instance, a purchaser would not take free of a judgment lien that was filed before the purchase contract. It is only the fact that the sale contract was recorded before the judgment lien was filed that lets the purchaser here take free of the lien.

(C) is wrong because Able can indeed benefit from Baker's action in recording. The issue is whether Able can convey marketable title to Baker, and the fact that Baker recorded means that Able can do this; there is no rule that one party cannot benefit from the other's action in recording.

(D) is wrong because it is a misstatement of law. The statute creating judgment liens merely describes that a judgment lien is an interest in property; the statute does not say anything about priorities, a subject that is left to the recording act. Under the recording act, an early-filed interest in land (here, the vendee's rights under the sale contract) takes priority over a later-filed interest (here, the judgment lien).

II. WHO IS PROTECTED BY THE RECORDING ACT

A. Who is a bona fide purchaser (BFP)

Question 48: Devlin was the owner of a large subdivision. Parnell became interested in purchasing a lot but could not decide between Lot 40 and Lot 41. The price and fair market value of each of those two lots was $50,000. Parnell paid Devlin $50,000, which Devlin accepted, and Devlin delivered to Parnell a deed which was properly executed, complete, and ready for recording in every detail except that the space in the deed for the lot number was left blank. Devlin told Parnell to fill in either Lot 40 or Lot 41 according to his decision and then record the deed. Parnell visited the development the next day and completely changed his mind, selecting Lot 25. He filled in Lot 25 and duly recorded the deed. The price of Lot 25 and its fair market value was $75,000.

Before Devlin had time to learn of Parnell's actions, Parnell sold Lot 25 to Caruso for $60,000 by a duly and properly executed, delivered, and recorded warranty deed. Caruso knew that Devlin had put a price of $75,000 on Lot 25, but he knew no other facts regarding the Devlin-Parnell transaction. Caruso's attorney accurately reported Parnell's record title to be good, marketable, and free of encumbrances. Neither Caruso nor his attorney made any further investigation outside the record. Devlin brought an appropriate action against Caruso to recover title to Lot 25. If Devlin loses, the most likely basis for the judgment is that

(A) the Statute of Frauds prevents the introduction of any evidence of Devlin's and Parnell's agreement.

(B) recording of the deed from Devlin to Parnell precludes any question of its genuineness.

(C) as between Devlin and a bona fide purchaser, Devlin is estopped.

(D) the clean hands doctrine bars Devlin from relief.

[Q4062]

Answer 48: Choice **(C)** is correct. The goal of recording statutes is to protect subsequent bona fide purchasers and incumbrancers — those who pay value and take without notice of prior conveyances, in good faith. Here, Caruso is a bona fide purchaser, because he has no notice of any defects in the chain of title. The price he paid, $60,000, was a bargain compared to what Devlin asked previously, but this would not in and of itself negate his bona fide purchaser status, since it would still constitute "value" and would not, barring other facts, indicate something untoward was involved. Since the chain of title indicates that Parnell was conveying marketable title, Caruso was not obligated to look further. Choice (C) goes on to suggest that Devlin is "estopped" from denying the validity of the deed. An estoppel occurs, in facts like these, when one has done or omitted to do something, and is as a result forbidden from pleading or proving an otherwise-important fact. Here, Devlin's carelessness in allowing Parnell to fill in the deed will lead to his being bound by the resultant deed — he'll be "estopped" from denying its validity.

(A) is wrong because the Statute of Frauds would *not* prevent proof of Devlin's and Parnell's oral agreement. Devlin is trying to show that the deed he signed has the wrong lot number on it, due to Parnell's wrongdoing. That's not a contracts problem, and the Statute of Frauds applies only to contracts. Except for the estoppel problem (discussed in (C)), Devlin would be able to show that the deed as filed was not genuine (i.e., was a forgery as to the lot number). And that would be true even though Devlin's proof would consist of proof of an oral agreement. So the Statute of Frauds wouldn't be relevant.

(B) is wrong because it states an incorrect rule of law: Recording a deed does not preclude any question as to its genuineness. The mere act of recording would not, for instance, make a fraudulent deed genuine. The upshot, nonetheless, might be that, *despite* the fact a deed is incorrect, *the bona fide purchaser may still prevail,* on grounds of estoppel. But (B) states as a concrete rule that recording a deed means its genuineness cannot be questioned, and this is incorrect.

(D) is wrong because it misstates the facts: Devlin's hands are not "unclean." Under the equitable doctrine of "unclean hands," one who has acted "unconscionably," or in a morally reprehensible manner, cannot recover. Here, at most Devlin has behaved negligently; there is no basis on which to attach any bad faith to his behavior. If anything, he was gullible in trusting Parnell to fill in the blank in the deed as instructed; but the creation of the agency did not involve wrongdoing. If anyone, it's Parnell who's the wrongdoer.

B. The "gave value" requirement

1. Judgment creditors

a. Lien creditor loses

Question 49: A seller owned a piece of land in fee simple, as the land records showed, when he contracted to sell the land to a buyer. Two weeks later, the buyer paid the agreed price and received a warranty deed. A week thereafter, when neither the contract nor the deed had been recorded and while the seller remained in possession of the property, a creditor of the seller properly filed a money judgment against the seller. The creditor knew nothing of the buyer's interest.

A statute in the jurisdiction provides: "Any judgment properly filed shall, for ten years from filing, be a lien on the real property then owned or subsequently acquired by any person against whom the judgment is rendered."

The recording act of the jurisdiction provides: "No conveyance or mortgage of real property shall be good against subsequent purchasers for value and without notice unless the same be recorded according to law."

The creditor brought an appropriate action to enforce her lien against the property in the buyer's hands.

If the court decides for the buyer, it will most probably be because

(A) the doctrine of equitable conversion applies.

(B) the jurisdiction's recording act does not protect creditors.

(C) the seller's possession gave the creditor constructive notice of the buyer's interest.

(D) the buyer was a purchaser without notice.

[Q3123]

Answer 49: Choice **(B)** is correct. Where the language of the recording act is ambiguous about whether judgment creditors are covered (e.g., where, as here, "purchasers for value" are what are covered), most courts have interpreted the statute so as not to cover the judgment creditor. There is no guarantee that a court would interpret the statute in this anti-creditor way, but that's at least a possibility, and of the four choices this is the most likely explanation for an anti-creditor result. (Remember, you're not asked to say how the case will come out — you're merely asked to say what the most likely rationale will be *if* the case is decided for the buyer.)

Choice (A) is wrong because the doctrine of equitable conversion has nothing to do with any issue presented by this question. Equitable conversion, where the court chooses to apply it, makes a vendor under a land-sale agreement the "equitable seller," and the vendee the "equitable buyer." The main consequence of the doctrine's application is that risk of loss passes to the buyer upon the signing of the contract, even though the seller still holds the legal title.

Choice (C) is wrong, because the seller's possession would not suggest the seller had sold the property to the buyer. Under a recording statute like the one here, a subsequent bona fide purchaser (i.e., a person who gives valuable consideration and has no actual or constructive notice of the prior instrument) prevails over a prior grantee who failed to record. If the creditor was trying to become covered by the recording act, and *the buyer* had been in possession at the time the creditor filed her lien, the fact that the buyer (not the seller, who was the record owner) was in possession at the date of lien filing might have been enough to cause the buyer to lose, since this possession might have put her on inquiry notice that the seller was perhaps no longer the owner. But the fact that *the seller* was still in possession didn't put the buyer on notice of anything, so it's irrelevant on these facts.

Choice (D) is wrong, because recording acts protect the second, not the first, purchaser in certain circumstances. Here, it would be the creditor (who can argue that she "purchased" by filing her lien), not the buyer, who is trying to get the protection of the recording act. It is the person seeking the protection of the recording act (the second purchaser), not the person resisting application of the act (the first purchaser) who needs to be "without notice." So here, the notice status of the creditor might well matter (if the recording act otherwise applied to judgment lien creditors). But the notice status of the buyer, the first "purchaser," does not matter at all.

Question 50: Able conveyed Blackacre to Baker by a warranty deed. Baker recorded the deed four days later. After the conveyance but prior to Baker's recording of the deed, Smollett properly filed a judgment against Able.

The two pertinent statutes in the jurisdiction provide the following: 1) any judgment properly filed shall, for ten years from filing, be a lien on the real property then owned or subsequently acquired by any person against whom the judgment is rendered, and 2) no conveyance or mortgage of real property shall be good against subsequent purchasers for value and without notice unless the same be recorded according to law.

The recording act has no provision for a grace period.

Smollett joined both Able and Baker in an appropriate action to foreclose the judgment lien against Blackacre.

If Smollett is unsuccessful, it will be because

(A) Able's warranty of title to Baker defeats Smollett's claim.

(B) Smollett is not a purchaser for value.

(C) any deed is superior to a judgment lien.

(D) four days is not an unreasonable delay in recording a deed.

[Q2048]

Answer 50: Choice **(B)** is correct. Smollett could win only if he were protected by the recording act. This is so because without the recording act's protection, Smollet would have to lose since Baker received his conveyance before Smollett filed his lien (meaning that Able no longer had any interest in the property at the moment Smollett's judgment became a lien on Able's "property" by means of Smollett's filing). In most jurisdictions, if the recording act protects only "purchasers for value," a judgment creditor will not be deemed to be a "purchaser." So if Smollett were found not to be a purchaser, and therefore not to receive any protection from the recording act, he would lose. It is not certain that the recording act here would be interpreted so as to not protect lien creditors, but of the four choices, this is the only one that could plausibly yield a defeat for Smollett.

(A) is wrong because Able's warranty of title to Baker might help Baker in a suit against Able, but would not help Baker in a suit against Smollett. Where a party (here, Baker) doesn't record immediately (or within the applicable grace period if any), nothing in that party's deed can save her from losing to a subsequent purchaser for value who is protected by the recording act. (That's the purpose of recording acts — to protect subsequent purchasers for value, and to allow them to rely on the record as of the time of the subsequent purchase.)

(C) is wrong because it is a gross misstatement of law, especially the law of the jurisdiction in question here. The first statute cited in the question gives a filed judgment a lien against all real property then owned by the judgment debtor; so if the judgment had been filed before the conveyance to Baker, the judgment lien would indeed be superior to Baker's deed (which this choice says could never happen).

(D) is wrong because, when a recording act does not have a grace period, the purchaser takes the risk of a subsequent purchaser's gaining rights in the gap between the first conveyance and a recording of that conveyance, no matter how small this gap is. (If there *had* been a grace period of more than four days, this choice would have been a good explanation of why Smollett would lose.)

C. Recording first in a race or race-notice state

Question 51: A landowner owned a piece of land in fee simple of record on January 10. On that day, a bank loaned the landowner $50,000 and the landowner mortgaged the property to the bank as security for the loan. The mortgage was recorded on January 18.

The landowner conveyed the property to an investor for a valuable consideration on January 11. The bank did not know of this, nor did the investor know of the mortgage to the bank, until both discovered the facts on January 23, the day on which the investor recorded his deed from the landowner.

The recording act of the jurisdiction provides: "No unrecorded conveyance or mortgage of real property shall be good against subsequent purchasers for value without notice, who shall first record." There is no provision for a period of grace and there is no other relevant statutory provision.

The bank sued the investor to establish that its mortgage was good against the property.

The court should decide for

(A) the investor, because he paid valuable consideration without notice before the bank recorded her mortgage.

(B) the investor, because the bank's delay in recording means that she is estopped from asserting her priority in time.

(C) the bank, because the investor did not record his deed before the mortgage was recorded.

(D) the bank, because after the mortgage to it, the landowner's deed to the investor was necessarily subject to the mortgage.

[Q1054]

Answer 51: Choice **(C)** is correct. This is a race notice statute, since it says that it protects only "subsequent purchasers for value without notice, *who shall first record.*" Therefore, the investor could only obtain the protection of the recording statute if he recorded before the prior interest (the bank's mortgage) was recorded. Since the bank recorded on Jan. 18 and the investor on Jan. 23, the investor did not satisfy the record-first requirement. Therefore, the recording act does not apply, and the bank wins under the common-law principle that the first-in-time conveyance takes priority over the second conveyance.

(A) is wrong because, while the investor's paying valuable consideration and taking without notice prior to the bank's recording were *necessary* elements for him to be covered by the recording act, they were not *sufficient* elements — he was also required to record first.

(B) is wrong because there is no principle of estoppel by which a party who delays in recording loses the right to rely on the recording act; the only risk taken by the delaying party is that during the delay, a subsequent purchaser may meet the requirements for protection under the recording act.

(D) is wrong because it gives an incorrect explanation for the correct result: after the bank received its mortgage, it would still lose to a subsequent purchaser for value without notice who beat it to the recording office.

III. PURCHASER MUST TAKE "WITHOUT NOTICE"

A. Notice to subsequent claimants

1. Record notice

a. Imputed knowledge

i. Mortgage and note

Question 52: A landowner executed and delivered a promissory note and a mortgage securing the note to a mortgage company, which was named as payee in the note and as mortgagee in the mortgage. The note included a statement that the indebtedness evidenced by the note was "subject to the terms of a contract between the maker and the payee of the note executed on the same day" and that the note was "secured by a mortgage of even date." The mortgage was promptly and properly recorded. Subsequently, the mortgage company sold the landowner's note and mortgage to a bank and delivered to the bank a written assignment of the note and mortgage. The assignment was promptly and properly recorded. The mortgage company retained possession of both the note and the mortgage in order to act as collecting agent. Later, being short of funds, the mortgage company sold the note and mortgage to an investor at a substantial discount. The mortgage company executed a written assignment of the note and mortgage to the investor and delivered to him the note, the mortgage, and the assignment. The investor paid value for the assignment without actual knowledge of the prior assignment to the bank and promptly and properly recorded his assignment. The principal of the note was not then due, and there had been no default in payment of either interest or principal.

If the issue of ownership of the landowner's note and mortgage is subsequently raised in an appropriate action by the bank to foreclose, the court should hold that

(A) the investor owns both the note and the mortgage.

(B) the bank owns both the note and the mortgage.

(C) the investor owns the note and the bank owns the mortgage.

(D) the bank owns the note and the investor owns the mortgage.

[Q1123]

Answer 52: Choice **(B)** is correct. The bank was the first grantee of both the note and the mortgage, so the bank is the owner unless the recording act somehow gave the investor superior title. When the bank promptly recorded the assignment to it of the note and mortgage, the bank complied with all requirements of the recording act. Therefore, no later assignment by the mortgage company to the investor (or anyone else) could take priority, under the recording act, over the assignment to the bank. The fact that the investor paid value for his assignment, and without actual notice of the prior assignment to the bank, doesn't change any of this — the investor is deemed to be on notice of what a proper record search would have indicated, and here a search on the mortgage company in the records would have disclosed the prior assignment to the bank. Similarly, the fact that the mortgage company kept possession of the note and mortgage after assigning these to the bank makes no difference; the investor as second grantee cannot take priority over a prior conveyance that was properly recorded.

(A), (C), and (D) are wrong because they are inconsistent with the above analysis.

B. Purchaser from one without notice

1. Donee from person protected by act

Question 53: A grantor who owned a parcel conveyed it by quitclaim deed as a gift to a woman, who did not then record her deed. Later, the grantor conveyed the parcel by warranty deed to a man, who paid valuable consideration, knew nothing of the woman's claim, and promptly and properly recorded. Next, the woman recorded her deed. Then the man conveyed the parcel by quitclaim deed to his nephew as a gift. When the possible conflict with the woman was discovered, the nephew recorded his deed.

The parcel at all relevant times has been vacant unoccupied land.

The recording act of the jurisdiction provides:

"No unrecorded conveyance or mortgage of real property shall be good against subsequent purchasers for value without notice, who shall first record." No other statute is applicable.

The nephew has sued the woman to establish who owns the parcel.

The court will hold for

(A) the nephew, because the woman was a donee.

(B) the nephew, because the man's purchase cut off the woman's rights.

(C) the woman, because she recorded before the nephew.

(D) the woman, because the nephew was a subsequent donee.

[Q2163]

Answer 53: Choice **(B)** is correct. The man met all the requirements of the recording statute: he took for value, he took without notice of the prior conveyance, and he recorded before the prior conveyance was recorded. Once the man met those requirements, his interest cut off all rights of the prior grantee (the woman) who didn't record first. The man therefore had the ability to pass a valid title to his nephew, even though the nephew did not take for value, and even though the nephew was on record notice of the woman's claim at the time he took (since by then the woman had recorded).

(A) is wrong because it is not the woman's status as a donee that causes her to lose, it is the fact that she did not record before a subsequent BFP (the man) recorded. Remember that under recording acts, it is never significant whether the *first* grantee took for value; it only matters whether the *subsequent* grantee, who is trying to take advantage of the recording act, took for value.

(C) is wrong because the fact that the woman recorded before the nephew cannot save her; once a subsequent grantee (the man) took for value and without notice and then recorded first, a person downstream from that subsequent grantee (the nephew) wins against the original late-filing grantee regardless of whether the downstreamer took for value, took without notice, or recorded first.

(D) is wrong because the fact that the nephew did not give value doesn't matter; as with Choice (C), once the subsequent grantee (the man) got the protection of the recording act, it doesn't matter whether a person downstream from him gave value, recorded first, or took without notice.

2. Lender to person protected by act

Question 54: Five years ago, an investor who owned a vacant lot in a residential area borrowed $25,000 from a friend and gave the friend a note for $25,000 due in five years, secured by a mortgage on the lot. The friend neglected to record the mortgage. The fair market value of the lot was then $25,000.

Three years ago, the investor discovered that the friend had not recorded his mortgage and in consideration of $50,000 conveyed the lot to a buyer. The fair market value of the lot was then $50,000. The buyer knew nothing of the friend's mortgage. One month thereafter, the friend discovered the sale to the buyer, recorded his $25,000 mortgage, and notified the buyer that he held a $25,000 mortgage on the lot.

Two years ago, the buyer needed funds. Although she told her bank of the mortgage claimed by the investor's friend, the bank loaned her $15,000, and she gave the bank a note for $15,000 due in two years secured by a mortgage on the lot. The bank promptly and properly recorded the mortgage. At that time, the fair market value of the lot was $75,000.

The recording act of the jurisdiction provides: "No conveyance or mortgage of real property shall be good against subsequent purchasers for value and without notice unless the same be recorded according to law."

Both notes are now due and both the investor and the buyer have refused to pay. The lot is now worth only $50,000.

What are the rights of the investor's friend and the bank in the lot?

(A) Both mortgages are enforceable liens and the friend's has priority because it was first recorded.

(B) Both mortgages are enforceable liens, but the bank's has priority because the buyer was an innocent purchaser for value.

(C) Only the friend's mortgage is an enforceable lien, because the bank had actual and constructive notice of the investor's fraud.

(D) Only the bank's mortgage is an enforceable lien, because the buyer was an innocent purchaser for value.

[QA089]

Answer 54: Choice **(D)** is correct. This is a complicated fact pattern, but the essential information is that the buyer purchased the lot from the investor before the friend recorded his mortgage. Thus, (1) the buyer was a bona fide purchaser (BFP) for value and is protected by the recording statute; and (2) the bank who lent to the buyer is also protected despite the fact that the buyer knew of the prior mortgage when it lent.

The jurisdiction's recording act is a "notice" statute because it provides, "No conveyance or mortgage of real property shall be good against subsequent purchasers for value and without notice *unless same be recorded according to law.*" A notice statute protects only a subsequent taker who takes for value and without notice of the prior conveyance or mortgage. (Because this is a pure notice rather than race-notice statute, the subsequent taker doesn't have to have recorded before the prior grantee or mortgagee records.) Notice can be actual, record, or inquiry. The facts do not indicate that the buyer had actual notice of the friend's mortgage. Since the friend had not recorded the mortgage at the time buyer purchased the lot, the buyer did not have record notice. Finally, the property is a vacant lot; so even if the buyer had inspected the property, he would not have been put on inquiry notice of the friend's mortgage. Thus, the buyer is a BFP (i.e., he took without any kind of notice) and receives the protection of the recording act. Therefore, the friend's lien is unenforceable against the buyer (or against anyone who deals with him, as we'll see in a minute).

The bank's mortgage, on the other hand, *is* an enforceable lien against the property, because the buyer is a party to the mortgage and the bank promptly and properly recorded the mortgage. (Even if you did not know this, you would be able to pick the correct answer by eliminating the other three choices, which all rely on the friend's having an enforceable lien.) And the fact that the bank made its loan while having notice (both actual and record) of the prior mortgage to the friend does not prevent the bank's mortgage from being a valid first lien — that's because the buyer took free of the friend's mortgage for the reasons described above, and once the buyer had this free-and-clear title he was entitled to place a first mortgage on it (or re-sell it) regardless of the state of knowledge possessed by the new mortgagee (or new buyer). If the rule were otherwise, an innocent buyer would never be able to take out a first mortgage or re-sell, if the holder of a prior interest who didn't record promptly eventually recorded, as happened here.

(A) is wrong because, for the reasons explained in the analysis of Choice (D), the friend did not have an enforceable lien against the property. Thus, the fact that the friend recorded before the bank is irrelevant.

(B) is wrong because, for the reasons explained in the analysis of Choice (D), the friend did not have an enforceable lien against the property. This answer choice misstates the significance of the buyer's being an innocent purchaser for value. The buyer's BFP status protects him from the enforcement of the friend's lien; it does not affect the "priority" of the liens (since there is only one valid lien, the bank's).

(C) is wrong because, for the reasons explained in the analysis of Choice (D), the friend did not have an enforceable lien against the property. The friend recorded too late to prevent the buyer from being a BFP; so, the fact that the buyer later learned of the friend's mortgage is of no consequence — the buyer took free of the friend's mortgage. Once the buyer had this free-and-clear title, he was entitled to place a first mortgage on it (or sell it) regardless of the state of knowledge possessed by the new mortgagee (or new buyer).

Such a rule is necessary to protect the innocent buyer's financing and resale market. See the analysis of Choice (D) for more about this.

CHAPTER 9
RIGHTS INCIDENT TO LAND

I.   WATER RIGHTS

A. Drainage of surface waters

1.   When party wants to get rid of the water

Question 55: A rancher and a farmer own adjacent tracts of rural land. For the past nine years, the rancher has impounded on her land the water that resulted from rain and melting snow, much of which flowed from the farmer's land. The rancher uses the water in her livestock operation. Recently, the farmer increased the size of his farming operation and built a dam on his land near the boundary between the two tracts. Because of the dam, these waters no longer drain from the farmer's land onto the rancher's land. There is no applicable statute. The rancher sued the farmer to restrain him from interfering with the natural flow of the water onto her land.

Who is likely to prevail?

(A) The farmer, because he has the right to use all of the water impounded on his land.

(B) The farmer, because the rancher's past impoundment of water estops her from asserting the illegality of the farmer's dam.

(C) The rancher, because she has acquired riparian rights to use the water.

(D) The rancher, because the farmer is estopped to claim all of the surface water on his land.
[Q7052]

Answer 55: Choice **(A)** is correct. This water is diffuse surface water. Although there are three different views regarding the way an owner may *expel* such water if he doesn't want it, there is only one view about whether the owner may impound it if he does want it: the rule is that an owner such as the farmer may impound all such water, at least in the absence of any malice (and there is none here).

(B) is wrong because although this option correctly concludes that the farmer will prevail, it misstates the reason why this is so. At least in the absence of malice, either landowner may impound diffuse surface waters, and that would be true even if the other party hadn't also previously impounded (so that the doctrine of estoppel doesn't apply).

(C) is wrong because water from melting snows and rain is diffuse surface water. Riparian waters are waters with defined beds and banks, such as streams, rivers, and lakes, and a riparian owner is one whose land borders such waters. Here, the only water at issue is diffuse surface water, and the rule for such waters is as stated in the discussion of Choice (A).

(D) is wrong because as described above, either party may impound surface waters that are on his own land, and the doctrine of estoppel would not apply to change this general rule.

II. AIR RIGHTS

A. Other air-rights issues

1. Right to sunlight

Question 56: Pauline and Doris own adjacent parcels of land. On each of their parcels was a low-rise office building. The two office buildings were of the same height.

Last year Doris decided to demolish the low-rise office building on her parcel and to erect a new high-rise office building of substantially greater height on the parcel as permitted by the zoning and building ordinances. She secured all the governmental approvals necessary to pursue her project.

As Doris's new building was in the course of construction, Pauline realized that the shadows it would create would place her (Pauline's) building in such deep shade that the rent she could charge for space in her building would be substantially reduced.

Pauline brought an appropriate action against Doris to enjoin the construction in order to eliminate the shadow problem and for damages. Pauline presented uncontroverted evidence that her evaluation as to the impact of the shadow on the fair rental value of her building was correct. There is no statute or ordinance (other than the building and zoning ordinances) that is applicable to the issues before the court.

The court should

(A) grant to Pauline the requested injunction.

(B) award Pauline damages measured by the loss of rental value, but not an injunction.

(C) grant judgment for Doris, because she had secured all the necessary governmental approvals for the new building.

(D) grant judgment for Doris, because Pauline has no legal right to have sunshine continue to reach the windows of her building.

[Q2124]

Answer 56: Choice **(D)** is correct. A landowner has no legal right to have sunlight continue to reach her building. For example, it is not a nuisance for a one owner to block another owner's access to sunlight, even if the consequence of the blockage is to reduce the latter building's rental or market value.

Since Doris has done nothing wrong, both (A) and (B) are incorrect.

Although (C) states the right result, the fact that Doris secured all necessary government approvals is not dispositive; for instance, if the government-approved building built by Doris had released noxious odors that substantially impaired the value of Pauline's building, the fact that Doris had obtained all necessary permits would not be a defense to Pauline's nuisance suit.

Question 57: The plaintiff and the defendant own adjoining lots in the central portion of a city. Each of their lots had an office building. The defendant decided to raze the existing building on her lot and to erect a building of greater height. The defendant received all governmental approvals required to pursue her project. There is no applicable statute or ordinance (other than those dealing with various approvals for zoning, building, etc.).

The defendant constructed her new building without incident. However, when it was completed, the plaintiff discovered that the shadow created by the new higher building placed the plaintiff's building in such deep shade that her ability to lease space was diminished and that the rent she could charge and the occupancy rate were substantially lower. Assume that these facts are proved in an appropriate action the plaintiff instituted against the defendant for all and any relief available.

Which of the following is the most appropriate comment concerning this lawsuit?

(A) The plaintiff is entitled to a mandatory injunction requiring the defendant to restore conditions to those existing with the prior building insofar as the shadow is concerned.

(B) The court should award permanent damages, in lieu of an injunction, equal to the present value of all rents lost and loss on rents for the reasonable life of the building.

(C) The court should award damages for losses suffered to the date of trial and leave open recovery of future damages.

(D) Judgment should be for the defendant, because the plaintiff has no cause of action.
[Q1157]

Answer 57: Choice **(D)** is correct. A landowner has no legal right to have sunlight continue to reach her building. Therefore, it is not a nuisance or other violation for one owner to block another owner's access to sunlight, even if the consequence of the blockage is to reduce the latter building's rental or market value.

Since the defendant has done nothing wrong, (A), (B), and (C) are all incorrect.

TORTS

TORTS Q&A BY TOPIC

"Rest. 2d" refers to the *Second Restatement of Torts.*

CHAPTER 1

INTENTIONAL TORTS AGAINST THE PERSON

I. BATTERY

A. Intent

1. Intent to create apprehension of contact

a. Prank gone bad

Question 1: A golfer was annoyed that his caddie was joking about the golfer's bad last shot. The golfer swung his newly-purchased golf club in the direction of the caddie's head, intending to frighten the caddie but not to hit him. The caddie started to duck to avoid the blow. The golfer stopped his swing so that the club would not have hit the caddie, except that due to the club manufacturer's negligence the club head flew off and hit the caddie in the top of the head, seriously injuring him. The caddie will be able to recover for:

(A) assault but not battery.

(B) battery but not assault.

(C) assault and battery.

(D) neither battery nor assault.

[Q6008]

Answer 1: Choice **(C)** is correct. This is both assault and battery. Here, we're concerned just with battery. Battery occurs when the defendant, with the intention of causing either a harmful or offensive contact or an imminent apprehension of such a contact, causes a harmful contact with the plaintiff. Rest. 2d, §13. The golfer had the requisite intention to induce apprehension of an imminent harmful or offensive contact, even though the golfer did not in fact intend to make such a contact. Since a harmful contact with the caddie's person resulted, the required result for battery also occurred, so all elements of battery have been satisfied. The fact that the club manufacturer's negligence was a but-for cause of the harmful contact won't act as a superseding cause; in intentional torts (as opposed to negligence, for instance), an intervening act caused by negligence won't supersede unless it is totally bizarre and unforeseeable, and a clubhead flying off is unusual but not unforeseeable (especially in the case of a newly-purchased club). Cf. Rest. 2d, §16, Illustr. 2. Notice, by the way, that if what had resulted was merely an "offensive" but not harmful contact (e.g., a light tap on the caddie's head), this would not be enough for battery — whereas the intent for battery can be to create an apprehension of either a harmful or offensive contact, the result required for battery must be harmful, not merely offensive. See Rest. 2d, §13(b).

Choices (A), (B), and (D) are wrong because they are inconsistent with the above analysis.

Question 2: Peter and Donald were in the habit of playing practical jokes on each other on their respective birthdays. On Peter's birthday. Donald sent Peter a cake containing an ingredient that he knew had, in the past, made Peter very ill. After Peter had eaten a piece of the cake, he suffered severe stomach pains and had to be taken to the hospital by ambulance. On the way to the hospital, the ambulance driver suffered a heart attack, which caused the ambulance to swerve from the road and hit a tree. As a result of the collision, Peter suffered a broken leg.

In a suit by Peter against Donald to recover damages for Peter's broken leg, Peter will

(A) prevail, because Donald knew that the cake would be harmful or offensive to Peter.

(B) prevail, only if the ambulance driver was negligent.

(C) not prevail, because Donald could not reasonably be expected to foresee injury to Peter's leg.

(D) not prevail, because the ambulance driver's heart attack was a superseding cause of Peter's broken leg.

[Q1061]

Answer 2: Choice **(A)** is correct. Battery is the intentional infliction of a harmful or offensive bodily contact. Rest 2d §§ 13, 18. Once it is established that the defendant intended to commit a harmful or offensive touching and such a contact occurred, the defendant is liable for any consequences which ensue, even though he did not intend them, and in fact could not reasonably have foreseen them.

(B) is incorrect because the issue of proximate cause, not Driver's negligence, is determinative of Donald's liability. Donald is liable if his tortious conduct was the (or "a") proximate cause of Peter's injury, and that's true regardless of whether the ambulance driver was also negligent.

(C) is wrong because it is both legally and factually incorrect. Peter's suit would have to be either for battery or negligence, and in neither of these cases doesn't foreseeability supply a defense. In a suit for battery, the tortfeasor will be liable for virtually every result stemming directly or even somewhat indirectly from his conduct, however unlikely it might have seemed at the time of his act that this result would follow. Rest. 2d, § 435B. In a negligence suit, the defendant will be held liable only for those consequences that were at least somewhat foreseeable.

(D) is wrong because an accident in the ambulance on the way to the hospital that would cause Peter injury was not so unexpected that it would be a superseding cause. Only an intervening cause that is so unlikely as to be bizarre will be deemed "superseding." Negligence of rescue professionals and medical professionals is sufficiently foreseeable (even if unlikely) that it will almost never be deemed superseding.

2. D must intend contact

Question 3: Plaintiff, a jockey, was seriously injured in a race when another jockey, Daring, cut too sharply in front of her without adequate clearance. The two horses collided, causing Plaintiff to fall to the ground, sustaining injury. The State Racetrack Commission ruled that, by cutting in too sharply, Daring committed a foul in violation of racetrack rules requiring adequate clearance for crossing lanes. Plaintiff has brought an action against Daring for damages in which one count is based on battery.

Will Plaintiff prevail on the battery claim?

(A) Yes, if Daring was reckless in cutting across in front of Plaintiff's horse.

(B) Yes, because the State Racetrack Commission determined that Daring committed a foul in violation of rules applicable to racing.

(C) No, unless Daring intended to cause impermissible contact between the two horses or apprehension of such contact by Plaintiff.

(D) No, because Plaintiff assumed the risk of accidental injury inherent in riding as a jockey in a horse race.

[Q2066]

Answer 3: Choice **(C)** is correct. Battery is the intentional infliction of a harmful or offensive bodily contact. An assault is the intentional causing of an apprehension of harmful or offensive contact. The intent necessary for a battery is the intent to make contact with the plaintiff or the intent to commit an assault with a resulting accidental "harmful or offensive contact." A battery may be committed not only by a contact with the plaintiff's body, but also by contact with anything that is so closely identified with her body that contact with it is as offensive as contact with the body would be. Rest 2d §18, Comment c. Therefore, Plaintiff will not prevail on the battery claim unless Daring intended to cause either contact between the horses or apprehension of such by Plaintiff.

(A) is wrong because a reckless intent is not sufficient to be liable for battery. If Daring acted recklessly (i.e., in deliberate disregard of a high probability that the result would occur) this is a broader mental state than what is required in a case of battery — that the defendant must desire a certain outcome and also know with substantial certainty that the result will occur.

(B) is wrong because the fact that Daring violated the racing rule requiring adequate clearance for crossing lanes by itself does not show that he had the requisite intent to be liable for battery. Only if the intent as described in (C) was present, may Daring be liable for battery.

(D) is wrong because the doctrine of assumption of risk would not apply in this context, where the injury was intentional. A plaintiff is said to have assumed the risk of certain harm if he has voluntarily consented to take his chances that that harm will occur. Within the context of sports, if the risk of the sort of injury that occurred is inherent in the sport or activity, then the plaintiff will be blocked from recovering based on application of the doctrine. However, courts now hold that, in co-participant sports, although *ordinary carelessness* is inherent in the game, a defendant who *intentionally* injures a participant will be held liable and the doctrine will not apply.

3. Must intend contact with a "person"

Question 4: Peavey was walking peacefully along a public street when he encountered Dorwin, whom he had never seen before. Without provocation or warning, Dorwin picked up a rock and struck Peavey with it. It was later established that Dorwin was mentally ill and suffered recurrent hallucinations.

If Peavey asserts a claim against Dorwin based on battery, which of the following, if supported by evidence, will be Dorwin's best defense?

(A) Dorwin did not understand that his act was wrongful.

(B) Dorwin did not desire to cause harm to Peavey.

(C) Dorwin did not know that he was striking a person.

(D) Dorwin thought Peavey was about to attack him.

[Q2002]

Answer 4: Choice **(C)** is correct. Battery is the intentional infliction of a harmful or offensive bodily contact. Rest. 2d §13. An insane person is capable of forming the intent to do a harmful act, and the fact that the insanity may have been the cause of the intent is irrelevant. Rest. 2d § 895J. However, if Dorwin didn't know he was striking a person, then he in fact did not have the requisite intent to inflict a harmful or offensive bodily contact on Peavey. Therefore, this would be his best defense in Peavey's claim for battery.

(A) is wrong because it is irrelevant whether or not Dorwin understood that his act was wrongful; he only needed to intend to cause an offensive bodily contact in order to be liable for battery.

(B) is wrong because it is not required that Dorwin wished to cause harm to the plaintiff, only that he wished to inflict an offensive contact, i.e., one damaging to a "reasonable sense of dignity."

(D) is wrong because if Dorwin struck Peavey because he mistakenly and unreasonably thought Peavey was about to attack him, he still had the requisite intent to inflict an offensive bodily contact on Peavey. And although a reasonable mistake about the need for self-defense will be a defense to battery, an unreasonable mistake will not. Here, the facts indicate that if Dorwin believed Peavey was attacking him, that belief was based on Dorwin's hallucinations, which would make the mistake "unreasonable." (Courts apply an objective standard for reasonableness of mistake, i.e., a standard that does not take into account the defendant's particular mental peculiarities or defects.)

B. Extends to personal effects

1. Indirect contact

Question 5: A customer ordered some merchandise from a retail store. After a dispute about payment, the store turned the account over to a bill collector. The bill collector called at the customer's house at 7 p.m. on a summer evening while many of the customer's neighbors were seated on their porches. When the customer opened the door, the bill collector, who was standing just outside the door, raised an electrically amplified bullhorn to his mouth. In a voice that could be heard a block away, the bill collector called the customer a "deadbeat" and asked him when he intended to pay his bill to the store. The customer, greatly angered, slammed the door shut. The door struck the bullhorn and jammed it forcibly against the bill collector's face. As a consequence, the bill collector lost some of his front teeth.

If the bill collector asserts a claim of battery against the customer, will the bill collector prevail?

(A) Yes, because the customer had not first asked the bill collector to leave the property.

(B) Yes, if the customer knew that the door was substantially certain to strike the bullhorn.

(C) No, if the bill collector's conduct triggered the customer's response.

(D) No, because the bill collector was an intruder on the customer's property.

[Q4067]

Answer 5: Choice **(B)** is correct. A prima facie claim of battery includes proof that defendant intended to bring about a harmful or offensive contact with plaintiff's person. It's not clear from these facts that the customer intended to bring about a harmful or offensive contact with the bill collector's person. Intent can take one of two forms: either a desire that a certain result will come about, or the *substantial certainty* that it will, regardless of one's desire that it do so. Thus, if the customer knew that the door was substantially certain to hit the bullhorn, he could be said to have *intended* that the contact with the bullhorn happen even if he didn't desire that contact.

By the way, the customer need not have intended that the bullhorn in turn hit the bill collector's teeth or some other part of his body. The tort of battery occurs when the defendant intends to bring about, and in fact brings about, a harmful or offensive touching "of another's person." The "person" of another includes not only the other's body, but any item so connected with the body as to be regarded as part of the other's essence, such as clothing or something that the other person is holding. Certainly where the bill collector was not only holding the bullhorn but placing it near his lips, the customer's intent to create a contact that was merely with the bullhorn would suffice even if the customer did not intend the bullhorn to hit or harm the bill collector's mouth. (Also, the fact the contact was intended to be between the *door* and the bullhorn rather than between the customer's body and the bullhorn would not matter — as long as the customer intended to bring about a contact with the bill collector's "person," the fact that there was some intermediate object, the door, in between the customer and the bill collector's person wouldn't change things.)

(A) is wrong because this might have been battery even if the customer *had* first asked the bill collector to leave. This choice is referring to the defense of property, which requires a request to desist, unless it would be dangerous or futile, before physical force is used. The problem with applying this to these facts is that even if the customer *had* asked the bill collector to leave first, the physical force the customer used would be considered excessive and thus beyond the scope of his privilege making him liable for battery.

(C) is wrong because it does not offer a valid defense to battery. This option suggests that verbal provocation is a valid defense to battery. In fact, it's not. If the facts were different, and the bill collector's taunts had prompted the customer to *kill* him, the conduct may be enough to reduce murder to manslaughter (due to provocation), but that's criminal law. Instead, in tort law, provocation would have to rise to the level of justifying self defense to be a valid defense. And mere words — however offensive — cannot be a justification for what would otherwise be a battery.

(D) is wrong because the fact it offers is not determinative of the bill collector's recovery. This option suggests that the bill collector's trespasser status gave the customer the privilege to use the force he used. While there *is* a defense based on defense of property, there are two principal reasons it wouldn't apply here. First, a valid defense on this basis requires a request to desist, unless it would be dangerous or futile, before physical force is used. Under these facts there's no evidence of such a request. Second, the privilege would only entitle the customer to use *reasonable* force. Putting out a couple of teeth would exceed the scope of the customer's privilege, and constitute a battery (if the act were intentional).

II. ASSAULT

A. Imminence

Question 6: Pocket, a bank vice president, took substantial kickbacks to approve certain loans that later proved worthless. Upon learning of the kickbacks, Dudd, the bank's president, fired Pocket, telling him, "If you are not out of this bank in ten minutes, I will have the guards throw you out bodily." Pocket left at once.

If Pocket asserts a claim against Dudd based on assault, will Pocket prevail?

(A) No, because the guards never touched Pocket.

(B) No, because Dudd gave Pocket ten minutes to leave.

(C) Yes, if Dudd intended to cause Pocket severe emotional distress.

(D) Yes, because Dudd threatened Pocket with a harmful or offensive bodily contact.

[Q1135]

Answer 6: Choice **(B)** is correct. An assault is the intentional causing of an apprehension of harmful or offensive contact. It must appear to the plaintiff that the harm being threatened is imminent. Threats of future harm cannot constitute assaults, and the courts have taken a relatively strict view requiring a short period between the making of the threat and the time when, according to the threat, the harm will take place. Rest. 2d § 29, Comment c. A threatened harm ten minutes later would be considered a future harm, and not an assault.

(A) is wrong because an assault results in an apprehension of contact. It is not necessary that the plaintiff actually be touched.

(C) is wrong because the intent to cause severe emotional distress is not an element of the crime of assault. The question asks if the plaintiff would "prevail" in a claim for assault, and plaintiff would have been able to prevail (i.e., recover some damages) for impairment of his interest in "dignity," even without any showing of emotional distress, if the "imminence" requirement discussed in (B) had been satisfied.

(D) is wrong because, as discussed in the explanation of (B), threats of future harm are not actionable.

III. INTENTIONAL INFLICTION OF EMOTIONAL DISTRESS ("IIED")

A. "Extreme and outrageous"

Question 7: Poe ordered some merchandise from Store. When the merchandise was delivered, Poe decided that it was not what he had ordered, and he returned it for credit. Store refused to credit Poe's account, continued to bill him, and, after 90 days, turned the account over to Kane, a bill collector, for collection.

Kane called at Poe's house at 7 p.m. on a summer evening while many of Poe's neighbors were seated on their porches. When Poe opened the door, Kane, who was standing just outside the door, raised an electrically amplified bullhorn to his mouth. In a voice that could be heard a block away, Kane called Poe a "deadbeat" and asked him when he intended to pay his bill to Store. Poe, greatly angered, slammed the door shut. Poe's neighbors teased him on and off for several weeks about being a deadbeat, causing him severe embarrassment.

If Poe asserts a claim based on intentional infliction of emotional distress against Kane, will Poe prevail?

(A) Yes, because Kane's conduct was extreme and outrageous.

(B) Yes, because Kane was intruding on Poe's property.

(C) No, unless Poe suffered physical harm.

(D) No, if Poe still owed Store for the merchandise.

[Q4066]

Answer 7: Choice **(A)** is correct. An intentional infliction of emotional distress claim has four elements: (1) extreme and outrageous conduct of defendant; (2) defendant's intent to cause plaintiff to suffer emotional distress; (3) causation; and (4) severe distress on the plaintiff's part. Thus, the element Choice (A) states — the extreme and outrageous conduct — is the lynchpin of an emotional distress claim. In fact, where creditors are concerned, a pattern of abuse, hounding and extreme conduct can form the basis for an emotional distress claim, *even if* the plaintiff really owes the money! The conduct here — especially the use of the bullhorn to embarrass Poe in front of his neighbors — rises to the level of the required outrageousness.

(B) is wrong because, while Kane's invading Poe's property *might* contribute to the outrageousness of his conduct, it's not a necessary element. If Kane had gone up to Poe in a restaurant and undertaken the same behavior, it would have constituted emotional distress. Where creditors are concerned, severe abuse, hounding and otherwise-outrageous conduct will form the basis for an emotional distress claim (whereas garden-variety phone calls, even rude ones, won't).

(C) is wrong because, while plaintiff must show that he suffered severe emotional distress, the distress need not be accompanied by, or lead to, physical injury or bodily harm. For instance, plaintiff's embarrassment and humiliation, if severe enough, can constitute the requisite severe distress.

(D) is wrong because it's not relevant to Poe's claim. Even if Poe actually *did* owe the store money, this would not preclude his recovery on an emotional distress claim. If you chose this response, you may have been thinking of a defamation claim, where truth *is* a defense. Thus, if Poe actually owed money and Kane called him a "deadbeat" in the hearing of others, even if Poe proved special damages Kane would have a valid defense to defamation — Poe's actually being a deadbeat. However, the claim here is for emotional distress, and truth is not a defense to that tort.

B. Actual severe distress

1. Required element

Question 8: Dumont, a real estate developer, was trying to purchase land on which he intended to build a large commercial development. Perkins, an elderly widow, had rejected all of Dumont's offers to buy her ancestral home, where she had lived all her life and which was located in the middle of Dumont's planned development. Finally, Dumont offered her $250,000. He told her that it was his last offer and that if she rejected it, state law authorized him to have her property condemned.

Perkins then consulted her nephew, a law student, who researched the question and advised her that Dumont had no power of condemnation under state law. Perkins had been badly frightened by Dumont's threat, and was outraged when she learned that Dumont had lied to her.

If Perkins sues Dumont for damages for emotional distress, will she prevail?

(A) Yes, if Dumont's action was extreme and outrageous.

(B) Yes, because Perkins was frightened and outraged.

(C) No, if Perkins did not suffer emotional distress that was severe.

(D) No, if it was not Dumont's purpose to cause emotional distress.

[Q2125]

Answer 8: Choice **(C)** is correct. In order to prevail in a case of intentional infliction of emotional distress, the plaintiff must show that the defendant's conduct was extreme and outrageous and that she, in fact, suffered severe emotional distress. If Perkins did not suffer emotional distress that was severe, she will not prevail.

(A) is wrong because the plaintiff must not only show that the defendant's conduct was extreme and outrageous, but also that she, in fact, suffered severe emotional distress. The facts state that Perkins was badly frightened and outraged; however, this does not indicate that she suffered severe emotional distress. Therefore, Perkins is not certain to prevail merely by showing "extreme and outrageous" conduct, as this choice suggests.

(B) is wrong because, as discussed in the explanation of Choice (A), the fact that Perkins was frightened and outraged does not indicate that she suffered severe emotional distress, as required in a claim for intentional infliction of emotional distress.

(D) is wrong because the plaintiff is not required to show that the defendant's purpose was to cause emotional distress. The plaintiff may recover if she can show that the defendant either intended to cause severe emotional distress or acted recklessly with respect to the risk of plaintiff's emotional distress (i.e., in deliberate disregard of a high probability that the distress would occur).

2. Bodily harm not required

Question 9: Dayton operates a collection agency. He was trying to collect a $400 bill for medical services rendered to Pratt by Doctor.

Dayton went to Pratt's house and when Martina, Pratt's mother, answered the door, Dayton told Martina he was there to collect a bill owed by Pratt. Martina told Dayton that because of her illness, Pratt had been unemployed for six months, that she was still ill and unable to work, and that she would pay the bill as soon as she could.

Dayton, in a loud voice, demanded to see Pratt and said that if he did not receive payment immediately, he would file a criminal complaint charging her with fraud. Pratt, hearing the conversation, came to the door. Dayton, in a loud voice, repeated his demand for immediate payment and his threat to use criminal process.

If Pratt asserts a claim against Dayton, based on infliction of emotional distress, will Pratt prevail?

(A) Yes, if Pratt suffered severe emotional distress as a result of Dayton's conduct.

(B) Yes, unless the bill for medical services was valid and past due.

(C) No, unless Pratt suffered physical harm as a result of Dayton's conduct.

(D) No, if Dayton's conduct created no risk of physical harm to Pratt.

[Q1072]

Answer 9: Choice **(C)** is **incorrect**. (C) is incorrect because whether or not the plaintiff suffers physical harm is not determinative. As long as the conduct is extreme and outrageous, plaintiff is not required to show that she suffered physical harm in order to recover for intentional infliction of emotional distress.

Rather, the correct answer is **(A)**. In order to prevail in a case of intentional infliction of emotional distress, the plaintiff must show that the defendant's conduct was extreme and outrageous and that she, in fact, suffered severe emotional distress. The conduct must be "…so outrageous in character, and so extreme in degree, as to go beyond all possible bounds of decency, and to be regarded as atrocious, and utterly intolerable in a civilized community." Rest. 2d § 46, Comment d. In determining whether the defendant's conduct is sufficiently outrageous, the court will take into account the particular characteristics of the plaintiff and the relationship between him and the defendant. Pratt has been ill for six months and unable to work, apparently in a physically frail or mentally frail condition. As a bill collector, Dayton's conduct, repeatedly screaming at Pratt (even when she came to the door) and threatening to file criminal fraud charges against her, while aware of her poor state of health, would rise to the level of extreme and outrageous. Therefore, if Pratt suffered severe emotional distress, she would prevail.

(B) is wrong because Pratt would not prevail unless she showed that she suffered severe emotional distress as a result of Dayton's extreme and outrageous behavior, an element missing from this choice. In any case, it is irrelevant whether or not the $400 bill was indeed valid and past due, since Dayton's conduct would be deemed extreme and outrageous regardless of the validity of the debt.

(D) is wrong because whether or not the defendant's conduct created risk of physical harm is irrelevant in a case for intentional infliction of emotional distress. In order to prevail in a case of intentional infliction of emotional distress, the plaintiff must show that the defendant's conduct was extreme and outrageous and that she, in fact, suffered severe emotional distress.

C. Suits by public figures

Question 10: Doe, the governor of State, signed a death warrant for Rend, a convicted murderer. Able and Baker are active opponents of the death penalty. At a demonstration protesting the execution of Rend, Able and Baker carried large signs that stated, "Governor Doe, Murderer." Television station XYZ broadcast news coverage of the demonstration, including pictures of the signs carried by Able and Baker. If Doe asserts against XYZ a claim for damages for intentional infliction of emotional distress, will Doe prevail?

(A) Yes, if the broadcast showing the signs caused Doe to suffer severe emotional distress.

(B) Yes, because the assertion on the signs was extreme and outrageous.

(C) No, unless Doe suffered physical harm as a consequence of the emotional distress caused by the signs.

(D) No, because XYZ did not publish a false statement of fact with "actual malice."

[Q1023]

Answer 10: Choice **(D)** is correct in its emphasis on two distinct, and important, points. First is the issue of defendant's mental state. In the case of a *defamation* suit, the media defendant must have acted with knowledge of the statement's falsity or with reckless disregard of its truth ("actual malice"). *New York Times Co. v. Sulllivan* (1964).The Supreme Court has made the *New York Times* standard *also* application to actions against public figures for intentional infliction of emotional distress (IIED): the defendant must have acted with "actual malice" (i.e., with intent or reckless disregard) with respect to the accuracy of the statement. *Hustler Magazine v. Falwell* (1988). Second, in an IIED case involving a public figure, as in a defamation case, the defendant must have made a provably false statement of fact, as opposed, for instance, to a statement of opinion. Here, any reasonable reader of the sign who took into account the political context of its display (death-penalty protest) would have understood that Able and Baker were making statements of opinion, not provably-false statemens of fact. Therefore, XYZ couldn't be liable for either defamation or IIED for repeating those non-factually-false statements.

(A) is wrong because the plaintiff must show a provable false statement made with actual malice (not merely that plaintiff suffered severe emotional distress) as described in (D).

(B) is wrong because the plaintiff must show a provable false statement made with actual malice (not merely that defendant's conduct was extreme and outrageous) as described in (D).

(C) is wrong because whether or not the plaintiff suffers physical harm is not determinative. Most modern courts do not require physical harm — merely severe emotional distress — for claims of intentional infliction of emotional distress. In any event, plaintiff won't recover for the reasons described in (D).

CHAPTER 2
INTENTIONAL INTERFERENCE WITH PROPERTY

I. TRESPASS TO LAND

A. Intent

1. Involuntary entry onto land of another

Question 11: A car driven by Dan entered land owned by and in the possession of Peter, without Peter's permission.

Which, if any, of the following allegations, without additional facts, would provide a sufficient basis for a claim by Peter against Dan?

I.   Dan intentionally drove his car onto Peter's land.

II. Dan negligently drove his car onto Peter's land,

III. Dan's car damaged Peter's land.

(A) I only.

(B) III only.

(C) I, II, or III.

(D) Neither I, nor II, nor III.

[Q1074]

Answer 11: Choice **(A)** is correct, because it recognizes that only Choice I contains an allegation which by itself would provide the plaintiff with a sufficient basis for relief.

I. A trespass to land can occur when the defendant enters the plaintiff's land, or causes another person or an object to enter the plaintiff's land. If a defendant intentionally drives his car onto plaintiff's land, he has committed a trespass, and the plaintiff is entitled to nominal damages regardless of whether any harm has occurred. Rest. 2d §163. This answer choice contains an allegation that would provide the plaintiff with a sufficient basis for relief.

II. If the plaintiff relies on a negligence theory in a trespass case, he must prove not only that the defendant was in fact negligent, but also that he (the plaintiff) suffered actual damages. Rest. 2d §165. The facts do not indicate that the plaintiff suffered any harm; therefore, this answer choice does not contain an allegation that would provide the plaintiff with a sufficient basis for relief.

III. To be liable for trespass, entry on another's land must be intentional, negligent, or pursuant to the carrying out of an "abnormally dangerous activity." Rest. 2d §166. Although the facts do indicate that Dan's car damaged Peter's land, he would not be liable for trespass unless one of those three conditions applied. Therefore, the allegation by itself would not provide the plaintiff with a sufficient basis for relief.

2. Effect of mistake

Question 12: David built in his backyard a garage that encroached two feet across the property line onto property owned by his neighbor, Prudence. Thereafter, David sold his property to Drake. Prudence was unaware, prior to David's sale to Drake, of the encroachment of the garage onto her property. When she thereafter learned of the encroachment, she sued David for damages for trespass.

In this action, will Prudence prevail?

(A) No, unless David was aware of the encroachment when the garage was built.

(B) No, because David no longer owns or possesses the garage.

(C) Yes, because David knew where the garage was located, whether or not he knew where the property line was.

(D) Yes, unless Drake was aware of the encroachment when he purchased the property.

[Q2011]

Answer 12: Choice **(C)** is correct. A trespass to land can occur when the defendant enters the plaintiff's land, or causes another person or an object to enter the plaintiff's land. A "continuing trespass" is one where the object stays on the land. If a defendant intentionally enters onto the plaintiff's land, the plaintiff is entitled to nominal damages regardless of whether any harm has occurred. David built the garage, so his intentional actions caused an object to enter onto Prudence's land and constituted a continuing trespass. The fact that he may not have known where the property line was and so was unaware of the encroachment is irrelevant.

(A) is wrong because it implies that there is no liability for trespass if a defendant enters onto the land and is unaware that he is trespassing. If the defendant enters onto the plaintiff's land thinking that it is his own, or thinking erroneously that he is entitled to be there, he has still committed an intentional trespass.

(B) is wrong because David committed the tort and is liable for it regardless of whether or not he has current ownership of the trespassing object.

(D) is wrong because David committed an act that constituted trespass and he is liable for it. That's true even if the new owner knew of the encroachment — once David built the encroaching structure he had committed trespass (which was an ongoing tort as long as he owned the structure), and nothing that happened at or after the time of sale by David could retroactively change this fact.

II. CONVERSION

A. Forced sale

Question 13: Dower, an inexperienced driver, borrowed a car from Puder, a casual acquaintance, for the express purpose of driving it several blocks to the local drug store. Instead, Dower drove the car, which then was worth $12,000, 100 miles to Other City. While Dower was driving in Other City the next day, the car was hit by a negligently driven truck and sustained damage that will cost $3,000 to repair. If repaired, the car will be fully restored to its former condition.

If Puder asserts a claim against Dower based on conversion, Puder should recover a judgment for

(A) $12,000.

(B) $3,000.

(C) $3,000 plus damages for the loss of the use of the car during its repair.

(D) nothing, unless Dower was negligent and his negligence was a substantial cause of the collision.

[Q1154]

Answer 13: Choice **(A)** is correct. Conversion occurs when the defendant so substantially interferes with the plaintiff's possession or ownership of property that it is fair to require the defendant to pay the property's full value. Rest 2d § 222A. One must consider the extent and duration of the defendant's exercise of control over the object, the defendant's good faith, the harm done to the property, and the inconvenience and expense caused to the plaintiff. The defendant had permission to drive the plaintiff's car several blocks and instead drove 100 miles to Other City and continued to drive it in Other City the following day. There does not appear to be any good faith exhibited by the defendant. The car sustained $3,000 in damages (1/4 of its total value). Considering these facts, it is fair to require that the defendant pay the full value of the car as damages for conversion.

(B) and (C) are wrong because they incorrectly assert that plaintiff's recovery would provide for only for repair of the car and loss of use of the car (as in a claim of trespass to chattels). The suit here is for conversion, and in conversion plaintiff recovers the full value of the item (viewed as of the moment before the taking).

(D) is wrong because in a claim of conversion, the issue of who was at fault in damaging the plaintiff's property (once the defendant committed a substantial interference with it) is irrelevant. In other words, if the car was the subject of conversion, then the defendant is responsible to pay for its full value regardless of whether it was physically damaged (or by whom).

CHAPTER 3
DEFENSES TO INTENTIONAL TORTS

I. SELF-DEFENSE

A. Injury to third person

Question 14: In the course of a bank holdup, Robber fired a gun at Guard. Guard drew his revolver and returned the fire. One of the bullets fired by Guard ricocheted, striking Plaintiff.

If Plaintiff asserts a claim against Guard based upon battery, will Plaintiff prevail?

(A) Yes, unless Plaintiff was Robber's accomplice.

(B) Yes, under the doctrine of transferred intent.

(C) No, if Guard fired reasonably in his own defense.

(D) No, if Guard did not intend to shoot Plaintiff.

[Q1184]

Answer 14: Choice **(C)** is correct. In a situation where the defendant is entitled to use reasonable force in his self-defense, and does so, the fact that he injures an innocent bystander does not prevent the use of force from being privileged (as long as the defendant did not act negligently in choosing to shoot, and in how he shot). That's what this choice says.

(A) is wrong because Plaintiff will not prevail if the defendant's actions were privileged, which they would be if the defense of self-defense applied. And that's true regardless of whether Plaintiff was Robber's accomplice or was instead an innocent bystander (as discussed in the explanation of (C)).

(B) is wrong because Guard's actions may have been privileged, and if so, he will not be liable for battery despite application of the transferred intent doctrine. The doctrine of transferred intent provides that as long as the defendant held the necessary intent with respect to one person, he will be held to have committed an intentional tort against any other person who he happens to injure. Ordinarily this would mean that if Guard had the requisite intent to commit battery against Robber he would also be deemed to have had the requisite intent to commit battery against Plaintiff who was injured by accident. However, if Guard was acting in self-defense, his actions were privileged, in which case Plaintiff would not prevail, as discussed in the explanation of Choice (C).

(D) is wrong because it cites a fact that will not be dispositive. According to the transferred intent doctrine, as explained in the discussion of (B), Guard could be held liable for battery of Plaintiff even if he didn't intend to shoot Plaintiff, as long as he had the requisite intent to shoot Robber. (Instead, the outcome will depend on whether Guard qualifies for the defense of self-defense.)

II. DEFENSE OF OTHERS

A. General rule

1. Unreasonable mistake

Question 15: Karen was crossing Main Street at a crosswalk. John, who was on the sidewalk nearby, saw a speeding automobile heading in Karen's direction. John ran into the street and pushed Karen out of the path of the car. Karen fell to the ground and broke her leg.

In an action for battery brought by Karen against John, will Karen prevail?

(A) Yes, because John could have shouted a warning instead of pushing Karen out of the way.

(B) Yes, if Karen was not actually in danger and John should have realized it.

(C) No, because the driver of the car was responsible for Karen's injury.

(D) No, if John's intent was to save Karen, not to harm her.

[Q3014]

Answer 15: Choice **(B)** is correct. Since John has intentionally caused a harmful or offensive contact with another, he's liable for battery unless he has a defense. The only defense that plausibly applies here is "defense of others." That is, just as a person has the right to use self-defense to save himself from harm, he has that right with respect to another person who is threatened with harm (even a stranger, under the modern view). However, the defense-of-others defense, like the right of self-defense, requires that both the actor's belief that danger exists, and his belief that the proposed conduct is a good way to deal with the danger, be reasonable. If John should have realized that Karen was not in fact in danger, this requirement for the defense-of-others defense would not be satisfied.

(A) is wrong because the fact that an alternative method of dealing with the danger might have solved the problem does not automatically mean that John's method was unreasonable. As described in the analysis of Choice (B) above, John was entitled to the defense of defense-of-others unless either his choice of methods, or his belief in Karen's peril, was unreasonable. The mere fact that the alternative method of shouting a warning might have solved the problem doesn't mean that John's approach was unreasonable. (For one thing, pushing Karen to the ground merely threatened minor injury, whereas if she were hit she might well be killed or seriously injured. For another, John could reasonably have believed that Karen wouldn't hear his shout, that she wouldn't know that she was the one being shouted at, or that there wasn't time for her to react if she did hear.)

(C) is wrong because John might be jointly-and-severally liable with the driver. The speeding driver would clearly be *a* cause of the injury, and would therefore likely be jointly-and-severally liable with John if John was liable. But this fact wouldn't save John from liability, if John's choice of methods (or his belief in the danger) was unreasonable. Always remember that a given injury can have multiple causes, and can thus lead to multiple tortfeasors (even if they did not act in concert) being held jointly liable.

(D) is wrong because John's intent to save Karen wouldn't immunize him if his belief in the danger was unreasonable. As is discussed in the analysis of Choice (B), John only qualifies for the defense of defense-of-others if his belief in the existence of the danger, and his choice of methods, were reasonable.

III. NECESSITY

A. Private necessity

1. Actual damage

Question 16: Husband and Wife, walking on a country road, were frightened by a bull running loose on the road. They climbed over a fence to get onto the adjacent property, owned by Grower. After climbing over the fence, Husband and Wife damaged some of Grower's plants which were near the fence. The fence was posted with a large sign, "No Trespassing."

Grower saw Husband and Wife and came toward them with his large watchdog on a long leash. The dog rushed at Wife. Grower had intended only to frighten Husband and Wife, but the leash broke, and before Grower could restrain the dog, the dog bit Wife.

If Grower asserts a claim against Wife and Husband for damage to his plants, will Grower prevail?

(A) Yes, because Wife and Husband entered on his land without permission.

(B) Yes, because Grower had posted his property with a "No Trespassing" sign.

(C) No, because Wife and Husband were confronted by an emergency situation.

(D) No, because Grower used excessive force toward Wife and Husband.

[Q4119]

Answer 16: Choice **(A)** is correct. This choice correctly identifies the basis on which Husband and Wife will be liable: Although their entry was privileged, it was not authorized, so they'll be liable for any damage they cause. The charging bull created the necessity that created the privilege to enter Grower's land. However, private necessity is a *qualified* privilege, requiring that the entrant pay for any damage caused. While (A) does not explicitly mention necessity, it does identify the essential reason Husband and Wife will be liable, so it's the best response.

(B) is wrong because it's not relevant. Without a "No Trespassing" sign, Wife and Husband would still be liable as trespassers if their entry wasn't authorized or justified; and with it, they wouldn't be liable if their entry *was* authorized or justified. In fact, under these facts Husband and Wife were privileged to enter Grower's property due to necessity: They were escaping from a bull. The reason they'll be liable for the damage to the plants is because necessity is only a *qualified* privilege, meaning any loss caused must be compensated. The existence of a "No Trespassing" sign is thus irrelevant to Husband and Wife's liability.

(C) is wrong because, although it correctly characterizes the facts, it ignores the fact that Husband and Wife will be liable for the damage to the plants. Husband and Wife entered Grower's land under a privilege of private necessity: They were being chased by a bull. However, the defense of private necessity is a *qualified* one, requiring that any loss caused by compensated. If you chose this response, it could be that you confused private necessity with *public* necessity, which involves a threat to the public necessitating entry (e.g., burning down a house to stop the spread of a fire). Most courts hold that public necessity is an *absolute* defense, such that the entrant will *not* be liable for damage caused. However, that's not the case here — the threat is only to Husband and Wife. As a result, they'll be liable for the damaged plants.

(D) is wrong because it cites an irrelevant fact. Even if Husband and Wife have a viable assault claim against Grower (which is doubtful — he was probably using reasonable measures to protect his property, and was not negligent in failing to foresee that the leash might break), the assault claim wouldn't be a defense against Grower's claim for the damage to the plants. The damage to the plants had already occurred by the time the dog rushed at Wife, so the couple's liability for that damage must rise or fall without reference to the dog's later actions or Grower's role in enabling those actions.

CHAPTER 4
NEGLIGENCE GENERALLY

I. THE REASONABLE PERSON

A. Physical and mental characteristics

1. Children

Question 17: Dora, who was eight years old, went to the grocery store with her mother. Dora pushed the grocery cart while her mother put items into it. Dora's mother remained near Dora at all times. Peterson, another customer in the store, noticed Dora pushing the cart in a manner that caused Peterson no concern. A short time later, the cart Dora was pushing struck Peterson in the knee, inflicting serious injury.

If Peterson brings an action, based on negligence, against Dora, Dora's best argument in defense would be that

(A) Dora exercised care commensurate with her age, intelligence, and experience.

(B) Dora is not subject to tort liability.

(C) Dora was subject to parental supervision.

(D) Peterson assumed the risk that Dora might hit Peterson with the cart.

[Q1070]

Answer 17: Choice **(A)** is correct. Children are not held to the level of care which would be exercised by a reasonable adult. A child must merely conform to the conduct of a "reasonably careful person of the same age, intelligence, and experience." Rest. 3d (Liab. For Phys. Harm), § 10(a).

(B) is wrong because children are subject to liability for intentional torts and also for negligence. Dora is eight years old — capable of negligence, and subject to liability using the "reasonable person" standard discussed in (A). Traditionally, children under seven have been deemed incapable of negligence; under modern cases, only children under the age of five are usually deemed incapable of negligence. Rest. 3d (Liab. For Phys. Harm, § 10(b)). Children are also subject to liability for intentional torts if it can be proven that they had the requisite intent. So there is no principle by which an eight-year-old would get immunity from tort law, as this choice asserts.

(C) is wrong because a parent's duty to supervise her child is separate from the duty of the child to not cause intentional or negligent harm to others. The fact that Dora was supervised (or should have been supervised) would not relieve her of tort liability for her actions.

(D) is wrong because the assumption-of-risk doctrine would not apply in this context. Assumption of risk applies when a plaintiff has voluntarily consented to take his chances that harm will occur. A grocery store is not a dangerous place where one expects to get struck in the knee and suffer serious injury. Nor was Peterson alerted to a possible danger, because Dora was not pushing the cart in a manner that caused her concern.

B. Anticipating conduct of others

1. Negligence

a. Parental supervision

i. Direct liability

Question 18: An eight-year-old girl went to the grocery store with her mother. The girl pushed the grocery cart while her mother put items into it. The girl's mother remained near the girl at all times. The plaintiff, another customer in the store, noticed the girl pushing the cart in a manner that caused the plaintiff no concern. A short time later, the cart the girl was pushing struck the plaintiff in the knee, inflicting serious injury.

If the plaintiff brings an action, based on negligence, against the girl's mother, will the plaintiff prevail?

(A) Yes, if the girl was negligent.

(B) Yes, because the girl's mother is responsible for any harm caused by the girl.

(C) Yes, because the girl's mother assumed the risk of her child's actions.

(D) Yes, if the girl's mother did not adequately supervise the girl's actions.

[Q1069]

Answer 18: Choice **(D)** is correct. The issue is whether and when a parent has a duty to supervise a child. The Restatement says: "A parent is under a duty to exercise reasonable care so to control his minor child as to prevent it from intentionally harming others or from so conducting itself as to create an unreasonable risk of bodily harm to them, if the parent (a) knows or has reason to know that he has the ability to control his child, and (b) knows or should know of the necessity and opportunity for exercising such control." Rest. 2d § 316. Since the girl's mother was with her when she was pushing the cart in the supermarket the mother had the duty to control the girl's actions if they caused an unreasonable risk of harm to others.

(A) is wrong because the parent's duty is independent and is not affected by the fact that the child is or is not subject to liability for her own actions. Rest. 2d § 316, Comment c. So even if the child was negligent, the mother wouldn't be liable (e.g., vicariously liable) as long as the mother didn't fail to make reasonable supervision of the child.

(B) is wrong because it is too broad a statement. There is a duty to exercise reasonable care to prevent intentional harm or an unreasonable risk of harm if and only if "the parent (a) knows or has reason to know that he has the ability to control his child, and (b) knows or should know of the necessity and opportunity for exercising such control." Rest. 2d § 316. And a parent has no vicarious liable for her child's torts, whether that tort consists of negligence or an intentional tort.

(C) is wrong because it misapplies the assumption-of-risk concept. Assumption of risk applies when a plaintiff has voluntarily consented to take her chances that harm will occur and is therefore barred from recovery under traditional common law principles. Here, whether the mother was or wasn't tolerating a risk to a third person, the assumption-of-risk concept wouldn't apply to the mother's liability to the third person.

2. Criminal or intentionally tortious acts

a. Premises liability

Question 19: The plaintiff and a salesman, who were strangers to each other, were passengers sitting in adjoining seats on an airline flight. There were many empty seats on the aircraft.

During the flight, a flight attendant served the salesman nine drinks. As the salesman became more and more obviously intoxicated and attempted to engage the plaintiff in a conversation, the plaintiff chose to ignore the salesman. This angered the salesman, who suddenly struck the plaintiff in the face, giving her a black eye. If the plaintiff asserts a claim for damages against the airline based on negligence, the plaintiff will

(A) not recover, because a person is not required by law to come to the assistance of another who is imperiled by a third party.

(B) not recover, if the plaintiff could easily have moved to another seat.

(C) recover, because a common carrier is strictly liable for injuries suffered by a passenger while aboard the carrier.

(D) recover, if the flight attendants should have perceived the salesman's condition and acted to protect the plaintiff before the blow was struck.

[Q2129]

Answer 19: Choice **(D)** is correct. A business operator whose premises are open to third persons owes a duty of reasonable care to those on the premises to make reasonable efforts to control the behavior of others on the premises, so as to prevent them from causing bodily harm. Therefore, if the flight attendants should have perceived that the salesman posed an unreasonable risk of bodily harm to the plaintiff, and should have realized that they could or might be able to protect the plaintiff, the airline (the business operator) will be liable for negligence because its employees did not intervene. The defendant's employees (the flight attendants) seem to have had the power to intervene — even if only by cutting off the drinks, or moving either the plaintiff or the salesmen. Therefore, under the doctrine of respondeat superior, the airline would be vicariously liable for this failure to intervene if the attendants should have recognized the danger and acted to avoid it.

(A) is wrong because, while this choice correctly states the general rule, there is an exception where some special relationship exists between the defendant and the plaintiff, such as where the defendant operates business premises open to the public on which the plaintiff is present at the defendant's invitation (in which case the defendant owes a duty of care to make reasonable efforts to prevent harm to the plaintiff). This "business premises" exception applies here, as discussed in the explanation to Choice D.

(B) is wrong, because whether or not the plaintiff could have easily changed his seat does not change the fact that the flight attendants had a duty to act reasonably to protect him from foreseeable harm. The plaintiff's failure to change seats would have been at most comparative negligence, which would have reduced but not eliminated the plaintiff's recovery (so that plaintiff would still have "recovered," though not the full amount of his damages).

(C) is wrong because breach of the duty of reasonable care may result in negligence liability of a common carrier, but a common carrier is not strictly liable for injuries to its passengers, as this choice asserts.

C. MBE tip

1. Failure to supervise customers or others

Question 20: Dora, who was eight years old, went to the grocery store with her mother. Dora pushed the grocery cart while her mother put items into it. Dora's mother remained near Dora at all times. Peterson, another customer in the store, noticed Dora pushing the cart in a manner that caused Peterson no concern. A short time later, the cart Dora was pushing struck Peterson in the knee, inflicting serious injury. If Peterson brings an action, based on negligence, against the grocery store, the store's best defense will be that

(A) a store owes no duty to its customers to control the use of its shopping carts.

(B) a store owes no duty to its customers to control the conduct of other customers.

(C) any negligence of the store was not the proximate cause of Peterson's injury.

(D) a supervised child pushing a cart does not pose an unreasonable risk to other customers.

[Q1068]

Answer 20: Choice **(D)** is correct. Grocery store shoppers are invitees — members of the public who come onto land held open to them and who do so for the purpose for which the land is held open. Such people reasonably expect that the premises have been made safe for them, and the owner must exercise reasonable care for the safety of such people. Reasonable care by the owner may require that she exercise control over third persons on the premises. But the fact pattern indicates that Dora's mother was near her at all times and that the plaintiff herself was not concerned by Dora's pushing of the grocery cart. Under these circumstances, it does not appear that Dora posed an unreasonable risk to the grocery shoppers. Therefore, the store acted reasonably and should not be held responsible for her actions.

(A) is wrong because, as discussed in Choice (D), a store *does* owe a duty of reasonable care to provide for the safety of its invitees — this duty would likely include reasonable attempts to protect customers from various harms that might foreseeably result from shopping carts.

(B) is wrong because, as discussed in Choice (D), a store *does* owe a duty of reasonable care to provide for the safety of its invitees, and this might include trying to protect them from harm posed by other customers. For instance, had Dora been an unsupervised cart-pushing menace about whom customers had complained, then the store, under its duty of reasonable care, would have had to control her actions for the safety of its invitees. However, the store did not act unreasonably under the circumstances presented in the fact pattern, as discussed in the explanation of Choice D.

(C) is wrong because on the facts here, "lack of negligence" (Choice (D)) is more convincing than "lack of proximate" cause. If Dora had posed a foreseeable risk of injury to Peterson, while on the store's premises and using an instrument (the cart) belonging to the store, the store's failure to intervene *would* be a proximate cause of Peterson's injuries. (By using the phrase "<u>the</u> proximate cause" instead of "a proximate cause," this choice incorrectly suggests that there can be only one proximate cause. If the store negligently failed to supervise Dora or intervene to take the cart away from her, both the store's failure and Dora's conduct would be proximate causes.)

Question 21: Ohner owns the Acme Hotel. When the International Order of Badgers came to town for its convention, its members rented 400 of the 500 rooms, and the hotel opened its convention facilities to them. Badgers are a rowdy group, and during their convention they littered both the inside and the outside of the hotel with debris and bottles. The hotel manager knew that objects were being thrown out of the hotel windows. At his direction, hotel employees patrolled the hallways telling the guests to refrain from such conduct. Ohner was out of town and was not aware of the problems which were occurring. During the convention, as Smith walked past the Acme Hotel on the sidewalk, he was hit and injured by an ashtray thrown out of a window in the hotel. Smith sued Ohner for damages for his injuries.

Will Smith prevail in his claim against Ohner?

(A) Yes, because a property owner is strictly liable for acts on his premises if such acts cause harm to persons using the adjacent public sidewalks.

(B) Yes, if the person who threw the ashtray cannot be identified.

(C) No, because Ohner had no personal knowledge of the conduct of the hotel guests.

(D) No, if the trier of fact determines that the hotel employees had taken reasonable precautions to prevent such an injury.

[Q4063]

Answer 21: Choice **(D)** is correct. The most likely basis on which Ohner would be liable is vicarious liability for the negligence of his employees in failing to take reasonable precautions for the safety of passersby. The facts here tell you that hotel employees patrolled the hallways, telling the guests to refrain from destructive conduct (of the type which injured Smith). It's clear that the employees couldn't *stop* guests from misbehaving, so it's possible that such patrols would be considered reasonable precautions to prevent injuries like Smith's. Negligence requires *unreasonable* conduct, so if the employees were *reasonable* in their behavior, there could be no basis for negligence, and Ohner would not be liable.

(A) is not the best response, because it misstates the law, and arrives at an incorrect result. Without more, a property owner is *not* strictly liable for acts on his premises vis a vis *any* adjacent property, public or private. Instead, in order to be strictly liable, the owner (or his employees) will have to engage in some activity that involves strict liability — e.g., an ultrahazardous activity, like blasting.

(B) is wrong because it assumes the applicability of a doctrine that doesn't in fact apply to these facts. The examiners are probably trying to trick you into thinking that *res ipsa loquitur* applies — they are guessing that you'll remember that the doctrine originated in a case in which a barrel of flour fell from an upper-story window and injured a passerby. But *res ipsa* applies only where the accident is of a type that ordinarily would not occur without the negligence of the defendant. That, in turn, means that the doctrine usually doesn't apply where, even though we don't know exactly who was negligent, we have reason to believe that the tortfeasor was someone other than the defendant. Here, even if we don't know who threw the ashtray, it's likely that it was thrown by a Badger, and not by (or in the face of negligence by) a hotel employee. So *res ipsa* wouldn't apply, and the lack of precise identification of the thrower won't matter.

(C) is not the best response, because it turns on an irrelevant fact. If Ohner's employees were negligent within the scope of their employment and Smith was injured as a result, Ohner would be liable on the basis of respondeat superior *regardless* of whether he had personal knowledge of his guests' behavior.

II. *RES IPSA LOQUITUR*

A. P's failure to exclude other causes

1. Object falling from window in multi-tenant building

> **Question 22:** Landco owns and operates a 12-story apartment building containing 72 apartments, 70 of which are rented. Walker has brought an action against Landco alleging that while he was walking along a public sidewalk adjacent to Landco's apartment building a flower pot fell from above and struck him on the shoulder, causing extensive injuries. The action was to recover damages for those injuries.

If Walker proves the foregoing facts and offers no other evidence explaining the accident, will his claim survive a motion for directed verdict offered by the defense?

(A) Yes, because Walker was injured by an artificial condition of the premises while using an adjacent public way.

(B) Yes, because such an accident does not ordinarily happen in the absence of negligence.

(C) No, if Landco is in no better position than Walker to explain the accident.

(D) No, because there is no basis for a reasonable inference that Landco was negligent.

[Q1050]

Answer 22: Choice **(D)** is correct. Walker's only hope of prevailing would be res ipsa loquitur, since there's no direct proof of negligence by Landco or anyone for whose conduct Landco is responsible. The doctrine of res ipsa loquitur allows the plaintiff to point to the fact of the accident, and to create an inference that, even without a precise showing of how the defendant behaved, the defendant was probably negligent. The courts generally agree on four requirements before the doctrine may be applied: (1) there must be no direct evidence of the defendant's conduct; (2) the event must be of a kind which ordinarily does not occur except through negligence; (3) the instrument which caused the injury must have been, at the relevant time, in the exclusive control of the defendant; and (4) plaintiff must show that her injury was not due to her own action. It is questionable whether at least two of these requirements are fulfilled. Requirement (3) would require that the flower pot have been in the exclusive control of Landco, which is not the case (given that 70 or the 72 apartments have been rented to third persons for whose behavior Landco would not be vicariously liable). Requirement (2) would require proof that a flower pot usually does not fall without negligence, which is not true. Therefore, the doctrine of res ipsa loquitur could not be applied here.

(A) is wrong because: (1) a landowner is not strictly liable for injuries from an artificial condition to persons on an adjacent public way (only required to use reasonable care to prevent such injuries); and (2) there's no evidence here that Landco failed to use reasonable care in trying to prevent such accidents (since flowerpots on windowsills are not all that dangerous, and in any event there's no evidence that Landco even knew of the particular flowerpot, or had any practical right to have the pot taken off the sill by what was probably a tenant who was not under Landco's direct control).

(B) is wrong because, as discussed in (D), it is possible for a flower pot to fall and for it not to be due to negligence. Furthermore, even if the falling pot was due to someone's negligence, that someone was probably not Landco (since 70 of 72 apartments were rented to outsiders), and was not someone for whose acts Landco was vicariously responsible. (A landlord is not vicariously liable for torts committed by a tenant.) So the statement in this choice is both probably untrue as a factual matter, and legally irrelevant.

(C) is wrong because this factor wouldn't make a difference. It's true that some courts (though probably no longer a majority) will apply res ipsa only if plaintiff can show that a true explanation of the events is more readily accessible to the defendant than herself in order to apply res ipsa loquitur. But apart from this factor, plaintiff must show that the type of accident usually doesn't happen without someone's negligence, and that defendant was probably in exclusive control of the instrumentality that caused the accident. As is further discussed in (D), plaintiff can't meet either of these requirements.

B. Rebuttal evidence

1. Rebuttal shows some other explanation

a. Frequent on MBE

Question 23: Defendant left her car parked on the side of a hill. Two minutes later, the car rolled down the hill and struck and injured Plaintiff.

In Plaintiff's negligence action against Defendant, Plaintiff introduced into evidence the facts stated above, which are undisputed. Defendant testified that, when she parked her ear, she turned the front wheels into the curb and put on her emergency brakes, which were in good working order. She also introduced evidence that, in the weeks before this incident, juveniles had been seen tampering with cars in the neighborhood. The jury returned a verdict in favor of Defendant, and Plaintiff moved for a judgment notwithstanding the verdict.

Plaintiff's motion should be

(A) granted, because it is more likely than not that Defendant's negligent conduct was the legal cause of Plaintiff's injuries.

(B) granted, because the evidence does not support the verdict.

(C) denied, because, given Defendant's evidence, the jury was not required to draw an inference of negligence from the circumstances of the accident.

(D) denied, if Defendant was in no better position than Plaintiff to explain the accident.

[Q2047]

Answer 23: Choice **(C)** is correct. The doctrine of res ipsa loquitur allows the plaintiff to point to the fact of the accident, and to create an inference that, even without a precise showing of how the defendant behaved, the defendant was probably negligent. The consequence of the doctrine's application is that the plaintiff has met her burden of production. The defendant may counter with evidence that rebuts any or all of the elements required for res ipsa (e.g., by showing other possible causes not involving the defendant's negligence). It will then be up to the jury to decide whether the defendant's evidence is enough to negate the inference of negligence stemming from application of res ipsa. Here, the defendant provided enough evidence (proper use of the emergency brakes and evidence of juveniles tampering with cars in the neighborhood) that a jury was not required to infer negligence of the defendant from the fact that defendant parked her car and two minutes later it rolled down the hill.

(A) and (B) are wrong because, as discussed in the explanation of (C), there was enough evidence provided by the defendant to entitle a reasonable jury to conclude that it should not apply res ipsa, i.e., that it should not infer negligence. This fact will be dispositive, since the verdict-loser's motion for a JNOV should be granted only if there was not enough evidence to permit a reasonable jury to find for the verdict-winner.

(D) is wrong because it focuses on a factor that won't be dispositive. It's true that some courts (though probably no longer a majority) hold that in order for the plaintiff to benefit from res ipsa, plaintiff must show that a true explanation of the events is more readily accessible to the defendant than herself in order to apply res ipsa loquitur. But the court probably wouldn't apply this rule, and even if it did, plaintiff will lose because defendant came up with enough evidence that a reasonable jury could find that the inference of negligence by defendant was unjustified.

CHAPTER 5

ACTUAL AND PROXIMATE CAUSE

I. CAUSATION IN FACT

A. "But-for" test

1. Must be tied to D's negligence

a. Rescue scenarios

Question 24: Desmond fell while attempting to climb a mountain, and lay unconscious and critically injured on a ledge that was difficult to reach. Pearson, an experienced mountain climber, was himself seriously injured while trying to rescue Desmond. Pearson's rescue attempt failed, and Desmond died of his injuries before he could be reached.

Pearson brought an action against Desmond's estate for compensation for his injuries. In this jurisdiction, the traditional common-law rules relating to contributory negligence and assumption of risk remain in effect.

Will Pearson prevail in his action against Desmond's estate?

(A) Yes, if his rescue attempt was reasonable.

(B) Yes, because the law should not discourage attempts to assist persons in helpless peril.

(C) No, unless Desmond's peril arose from his own failure to exercise reasonable care.

(D) No, because Pearson's rescue attempt failed and therefore did not benefit Desmond.

[Q1100]

Answer 24: Choice **(C)** is correct. A rescuer who sustains injuries can recover from the rescuee, if the rescuee acted negligently in putting himself in the position of needing rescue. But if the rescuee did not act negligently (or any negligence did not contribute directly to the arising of the peril), then the rescuer would not be permitted to recover, even though the peril was the proximate cause and cause in fact of the harm to the rescuer.

(A) is wrong because, even if Pearson's rescue attempt was reasonable, if it was not in response to a danger caused by the defendant's negligence, then Pearson would not prevail in an action against defendant for his injuries.

(B) is wrong because, even if rescue attempts should be encouraged, if Pearson's rescue attempt was not in response to a danger caused by the defendant's negligence, then Pearson would not prevail in an action against defendant for his injuries.

(D) is wrong because, even though Desmond didn't benefit from the rescue attempt, he would still be liable to the rescuer if the rescue attempt was in response to Desmond's own negligence in putting himself in need of rescue.

II. PROXIMATE CAUSE — FORESEEABILITY

A. How tested on the MBE

Question 25: Doe negligently caused a fire in his house, and the house burned to the ground. As a result, the sun streamed into Peter's yard next door, which previously had been shaded by Doe's house. The sunshine destroyed some delicate and valuable trees in Peter's yard that could grow only in the shade. Peter has brought a negligence action against Doe for the loss of Peter's trees. Doe has moved to dismiss the complaint.

The best argument in support of this motion would be that

(A) Doe's negligence was not the active cause of the loss of Peter's trees.

(B) Doe's duty to avoid the risks created by a fire did not encompass the risk that sunshine would damage Peter's trees.

(C) the loss of the trees was not a natural and probable consequence of Doe's negligence.

(D) Peter suffered a purely economic loss, which is not compensable in a negligence action.

[Q2038]

Answer 25: Choice **(B)** is correct. Doe's liability extends to foreseeable damages from a fire. It was not foreseeable that a fire would damage trees by depriving them of the structure that was sustaining them by providing shade. Had the trees burned down, this *would* be a foreseeable consequence of the fire, but that was not the case here.

(A) is wrong because Doe's negligence did in fact cause the loss of the trees, albeit in an unexpected manner.

(C) is wrong because the loss of trees *is* a natural and probable consequence of a fire. The manner in which Peter's trees were lost was not foreseeable, however, which is why Choice (B) is the correct answer.

(D) is wrong because Peter suffered property damage, which is compensable in a negligence action. Examples of pure economic loss are loss of profits or wages. Property damage does not fall under this category.

III. PROXIMATE CAUSE — INTERVENING CAUSES

A. Foreseeable intervening causes

1. "Second collision" scenarios

Question 26: While driving at a speed in excess of the statutory limit, Dant negligently collided with another car, and the disabled vehicles blocked two of the highway's three northbound lanes. When Page approached the scene two minutes later, he slowed his car to see if he could help those involved in the collision. As he slowed, he was rear-ended by a vehicle driven by Thomas. Page, who sustained damage to his car and was seriously injured, brought an action against Dant to recover damages. The jurisdiction adheres to the traditional common-law rules pertaining to contributory negligence.

If Dant moves to dismiss the action for failure to state a claim upon which relief may be granted, should the motion be granted?

(A) Yes, because it was Thomas, not Dant, who collided with Page's car and caused Page's injuries.

(B) Yes, if Page could have safely passed the disabled vehicles in the traffic lane that remained open.

(C) No, because a jury could find that Page's injury arose from a risk that was a continuing consequence of Dant's negligence.

(D) No, because Dant was driving in excess of the statutory limit when he negligently caused the first accident.

[Q1131]

Answer 26: Choice **(C)** is correct. Dant's initial negligence brought about the condition in which lanes were blocked, and in which other drivers might slow down to rubberneck. The fact that other drivers might behave in this way (and that one of the slowing drivers might in turn cause a second accident) was relatively foreseeable. At the least, a reasonable jury *could* find (even if it need not find) that the causal connection between Dant's initial negligence and the second accident was not so far-fetched or attenuated that the second accident (and Thomas's negligence) should be regarded as a superseding cause. Remember, a second event must be very, very bizarre and hard to foresee before it will be deemed superseding.

(A) is wrong because, although Dant did not collide with Page's car, Dant's negligence proximately caused Page's injuries, as discussed in Choice C.

(B) is wrong because, even if Page could have safely passed the disabled vehicles, it is probably not the case that his not doing so would constitute contributory negligence. This jurisdiction adheres to the traditional common-law rules pertaining to contributory negligence, under which the plaintiff will be barred from recovering if he was contributorily negligent. Page's action in slowing down his car when he saw that an accident had blocked two lanes of traffic, and his intention to see if he could help, were probably reasonable under the circumstances. Therefore, he was not contributorily negligent.

(D) is wrong because it doesn't address the key factor. Dant was clearly negligent in causing the first accident — that's not disputed. The interesting question is whether the connection between the first accident and the second one involving Page was so attenuated that the second (or Page's negligence in bringing about the second) should be viewed as superseding. Since this choice doesn't refer to this key issue, it's not the best answer.

B. Responses to defendant's actions

1. Escape

Question 27: While Driver was taking a leisurely spring drive, he momentarily took his eyes off the road to look at some colorful trees in bloom. As a result, his car swerved a few feet off the roadway, directly toward Walker, who was standing on the shoulder of the road waiting for a chance to cross. When Walker saw the car bearing down on him, he jumped backwards, fell, and injured his knee.

Walker sued Driver for damages, and Driver moved for summary judgment. The foregoing facts are undisputed.

Driver's motion should be

(A) denied, because the record shows that Walker apprehended an imminent, harmful contact with Driver's car.

(B) denied, because a jury could find that Driver negligently caused Walker to suffer a legally compensable injury.

(C) granted, because the proximate cause of Walker's injury was his own voluntary act.

(D) granted, because it is not unreasonable for a person to be distracted momentarily.

[Q2164]

Answer 27: Choice **(B)** is correct. When *A* puts *B* in peril, it's typically quite foreseeable that *B* will try to escape the peril. Therefore, if *A* acted negligently in putting *B* in peril, *A* will be liable for injury to *B* that occurs during *B*'s foreseeable efforts to escape the peril. Here, it's completely foreseeable that one in Walker's position might jump backwards to escape the oncoming car, and thereby be injured. That's all that this choice is asserting.

(A) is wrong because Driver's actions were negligent and apprehension of an imminent harmful contact is the definition of an assault, an intentional tort.

(C) is wrong because, when *A* is put in peril by *B*'s negligence, *A*'s efforts to escape the peril — unless they are truly bizarre and unforeseeable — won't act as superseding causes. So while Walker's injury may have been due in part to his "voluntary act" of jumping backward, this certainly doesn't prevent Driver's negligence from also being a proximate cause of the injury. (Remember that there can be, and often are, multiple proximate causes for a given event.) Given that Walker's behavior in jumping wasn't even negligent, it's even less likely that his behavior would let Driver off the hook on proximate-cause grounds.

(D) is wrong because, although sometimes it, may not be unreasonable for a person to be distracted momentarily, in this case it was unreasonable. In assessing reasonableness, courts do a cost-benefit analysis. Here, a driver's looking at "colorful trees in bloom" during a "leisurely spring drive" is certainly not an event whose social value outweighs the major risk to others.

CHAPTER 6

JOINT TORTFEASORS

I. JOINT LIABILITY

A. Joint-and-several liability generally

1. Meshing with P's comparative negligence

Question 28: Jones, who was driving his car at night, stopped the car and went into a nearby tavern for a drink. He left the car standing at the side of the road, projecting three feet into the traffic lane. The lights were on and his friend, Peters, was asleep in the back seat. Peters awoke, discovered the situation, and went back to sleep. Before Jones returned, his car was hit by an automobile approaching from the rear and driven by Davis. Peters was injured.

Peters sued Davis and Jones jointly to recover the damages he suffered resulting from the accident. The jurisdiction has a pure comparative negligence rule and has abolished the defense of assumption of risk. In respect to other issues, the rules of the common law remain in effect.

Peters should recover

(A) nothing, if Peters was more negligent than either Davis or Jones.

(B) nothing, unless the total of Davis's and Jones's negligence was greater than Peters's.

(C) from Davis and Jones, jointly and severally, the amount of damages Peters suffered reduced by the percentage of the total negligence that is attributed to Peters.

(D) from Davis and Jones, severally, a percentage of Peters's damages equal to the percentage of fault attributed to each of the defendants.

[Q1196]

Answer 28: Choice **(C)** is correct. If more than one person is a proximate cause of the plaintiff's harm, and the harm is indivisible, then under the traditional common-law rule, each defendant is liable for the entire harm. Davis and Jones would be jointly and severally liable. In a pure comparative fault system, the plaintiff is allowed to recover even if his fault is greater than that of the defendant. The plaintiff's recovery is reduced by a proportion equal to the ratio between his own fault and the total fault contributing to the accident. Therefore, Peter's recovery would be the amount of damages suffered reduced by the percentage of the total negligence that is attributed to him. And Peter can recover that entire amount of "net" damages from either defendant.

(A) and (B) are wrong because in a pure comparative fault system, the plaintiff is allowed to recover even if the percentage of his fault is greater than that of either defendant or greater than the fault of both defendants combined.

(D) is wrong because the harm is indivisible; therefore, the defendants are jointly and severally liable (each defendant is liable for the entire harm).

II. CONTRIBUTION

A. Contribution generally

1. Amount

Question 29: While driving his car, Plaintiff sustained injuries in a three-car collision. Plaintiff sued the drivers of the other two cars, D-1 and D-2, and each defendant crossclaimed against the other for contribution. The jurisdiction has adopted a rule of pure comparative negligence and allows contribution based upon proportionate fault. The rule of joint-and-several liability has been retained.

The jury has found that Plaintiff sustained damages in the amount of $100,000, and apportioned the causal negligence of the parties as follows: Plaintiff 40%, D-1 30%, and D-2 30%.

How much, if anything, can Plaintiff collect from D-1, and how much, if anything, can D-1 then collect from D-2 in contribution?

(A) Nothing, and then D-1 can collect nothing from D-2.

(B) $30,000, and then D-1 can collect nothing from D-2.

(C) $40,000, and then D-1 can collect $10,000 from D-2.

(D) $60,000, and then D-1 can collect $30,000 from D-2.

[Q1088]

Answer 29: Choice **(D)** is correct. In a pure comparative negligence jurisdiction, the plaintiff is allowed to recover even if his fault is greater than that of the defendant. The plaintiff's recovery is reduced by a proportion equal to the ratio between his own negligence and the total negligence contributing to the accident. Under the rule of joint-and-several liability, if two defendants acted separately to produce an indivisible harm to the plaintiff, then each can be required to pay 100% of the plaintiff's damages. (Of course, plaintiff can recover only one satisfaction.) A defendant who is required to pay more than her fair share can recover the balance from the other. So here, the plaintiff can collect the full $60,000 (the total damage for which plaintiff himself is not responsible) from either defendant; the defendant who pays the whole $60,000 may in turn collect from the other that portion representing the overpayment. Since D-1 has paid $60,000 when his fair share was only $30,000, he can recover the $30,000 overpayment from D-2.

(A) is wrong because, in a pure comparative negligence jurisdiction, the plaintiff is allowed to recover even if he is at fault and even if his fault is greater than that of the defendant. (A) incorrectly supposes that the plaintiff will not be able to collect damages because of his own fault.

(B) is wrong because it does not allow for the plaintiff to collect the full amount of damages owed to him ($60,000) from one defendant (even though each defendant's proportional share of the damages is $30,000) as provided under the rule of joint-and-several liability. See discussion of Choice (D).

(C) is wrong because it limits plaintiff's recovery to the amount of his own negligence (40% of $100,000). In a pure comparative negligence jurisdiction, the plaintiff is allowed to recover even if his fault is greater than that of the defendant. The plaintiff's recovery is reduced by a proportion equal to the ratio between his own negligence and the total negligence contributing to the accident. (In this case the computation produces $100,000 reduced by 40%, or a net of $60,000.)

Question 30: The plaintiff sustained personal injuries in a three-car collision caused by the concurrent negligence of the three drivers, who consisted of the plaintiff, Donald, and Drew. In the plaintiff's action for damages against Donald and Drew, the jury apportioned the negligence 30% to the plaintiff, 30% to Donald, and 40% to Drew. The plaintiff's total damages were $100,000. Assume that a state statute provides for a system of pure comparative negligence, joint-and-several liability of concurrent tortfeasors, and contribution based upon proportionate fault.

If the plaintiff chooses to execute against Donald alone, she will be entitled to collect at most

(A) $70,000 from Donald, and then Donald will be entitled to collect $40,000 from Drew.

(B) $30,000 from Donald, and then Donald will be entitled to collect $10,000 from Drew.

(C) $30,000 from Donald, and then Donald will be entitled to collect nothing from Drew.

(D) nothing from Donald, because Donald's percentage of fault is not greater than that of the plaintiff.
[Q2195]

Answer 30: Choice (A) is correct. Under the rule of joint-and-several liability, if two or more defendants are joint tortfeasors, the plaintiff may sue and collect from either of them or all of them. In a comparative fault system, the plaintiff's recovery is reduced by a proportion equal to the ratio between his own fault and the total fault contributing to the accident. If the plaintiff's total damages were $100,000, her damages will be reduced by 30% (her percentage of fault) for a total of $70,000. Where the negligence has been apportioned between the two defendants (at 30% for Donald and 40% for Drew) yet they were joint tortfeasors, the plaintiff may collect the total amount of damages from one defendant and then that defendant may later seek reimbursement ("contribution") from the other defendant for his share of the damages award. So the plaintiff can collect $70,000 from Donald (i.e., the full percentage of fault represented by all parties other than plaintiff), but Donald will then be able to collect $40,000 from Drew for the latter's share of the damages.

(B) is wrong because it allows Donald to be liable for only his proportion of the damages, which is not the case in a jurisdiction applying joint-and-several liability. This choice also allows Donald to recover $10,000 from Drew; however, in the case that Donald paid only $30,000, he would not be entitled to contribution, since he is responsible for at least his percentage of fault ($30,000). In other words, a defendant bringing a third-party contribution action against another joint tortfeasor is entitled to contribution only if he pays more than his percentage of fault.

(C) is wrong because it allows for Donald to be liable for only his proportion of the damages, which is not the case in a jurisdiction applying joint-and-several liability.

(D) is wrong because, in a pure comparative fault system, the plaintiff is allowed to recover even if his fault is greater than that of the defendant (indeed, even if the plaintiff's fault is greater than that of all defendants put together).

III. INDEMNITY

A. Negligent vs. intentional tortfeasor

Question 31: David owned a shotgun that he used for hunting. David knew that his old friend, Mark, had become involved with a violent gang that recently had a shoot-out with a rival gang. David, who was going to a farm to hunt quail, placed his loaded shotgun on the back seat of his car. On his way to the farm, David picked up Mark to give him a ride to a friend's house. After dropping off Mark at the friend's house, David proceeded to the farm, where he discovered that his shotgun was missing from his car. Mark had taken the shotgun and, later in the day, Mark used it to shoot Paul, a member of the rival gang. Paul was severely injured.

Paul recovered a judgment for his damages against David, as well as Mark, on the ground that David was negligent in allowing Mark to obtain possession of the gun, and was therefore liable jointly and severally with Mark for Paul's damages. The jurisdiction has a statute that allows contribution based upon proportionate fault and adheres **to** the traditional common-law rules on indemnity.

If David fully satisfies the judgment, David then will have a right to recover from Mark

(A) indemnity for the full amount of the judgment, because Mark was an intentional tortfeasor.

(B) contribution only, based on comparative fault, because David himself was negligent.

(C) one-half of the amount of the judgment.

(D) nothing, because David's negligence was a substantial proximate cause of the shooting.

[Q2053]

Answer 31: Choice **(A)** is correct. If there is a great difference in the degree of culpability of the defendants, the court will shift the financial responsibility for a tort from the less-culpable to the more-culpable one, by the use of the doctrine of indemnity. In this case, where Mark was an intentional tortfeasor (causing severe injury with a gun) and David was merely a negligent one (in allowing Mark to obtain possession of the gun), David will have the right to indemnity, i.e., the right to recover from Mark the full amount of the judgment that David paid.

(B) is wrong because, as stated in (A), David will be indemnified for the full amount of damages he paid, because of the great difference in the degree of culpability of the defendants.

(C) is wrong because it incorrectly implies that the parties are equally culpable and it does not recognize that David will be indemnified for the full amount of damages because of the great difference in the degree of culpability of the defendants.

(D) is wrong because, despite the fact that David's negligence was a proximate cause of the injury, David will be indemnified by Mark for the full amount of damages.

CHAPTER 7
DUTY

I. EMOTIONAL DISTRESS

A. Emotional distress without physical impact

1. No bodily harm

a. Exceptions

i. Negligent handling of corpse

Question 32: Ann's three-year-old daughter, Janet, was killed in an automobile accident. At Ann's direction, Janet's body was taken to a mausoleum for interment. Normally, the mausoleum's vaults are permanently sealed with marble plates secured by "tamper-proof" screws. After Janet's body was placed in the mausoleum, however, only a fiberglass panel secured by caulking compound covered her vault. About a month later, Janet's body was discovered in a cemetery located near the mausoleum. It had apparently been left there by vandals who had taken it from the mausoleum.

As a result of this experience, Ann suffered great emotional distress.

If Ann sues the mausoleum for the damages arising from her emotional distress, will she prevail?

(A) No, because Ann experienced no threat to her own safety.

(B) No, unless the mausoleum's behavior was extreme and outrageous.

(C) Yes, if the mausoleum failed to use reasonable care to safeguard the bod.

(D) Yes, unless Ann suffered no physical harm as a consequence of her emotional distress.

[Q1177]

Answer 32: Choice **(C)** is correct. Most courts allow recovery for pure emotional distress, even if unaccompanied by bodily harm, where the defendant has negligently handled the corpse of the plaintiff's relative. This answer choice correctly applies this rule.

(A) is wrong because, although it is generally true that a plaintiff who does not suffer any physical impact or even threat to her own safety can't recover in negligence for emotional distress, there are exceptions. One exception is where the plaintiff has suffered emotional distress do to the defendant's mishandling of a corpse belonging to the plaintiff's close relative.

(B) is wrong because, although it is necessary to show that the defendant's behavior was extreme and outrageous in a suit for intentional infliction of emotional distress, this is not required to be proven in a case of negligent infliction of emotional distress. And by inference, what Ann is alleging here is negligent, not intentional, infliction of emotional distress.

(D) is wrong because a claim for negligent mishandling of a corpse is one of the few special situations where courts have allowed damages for pure emotional suffering despite the fact that the defendant has suffered no physical harm.

Question 33: John's father, Jeremiah, died in Hospital. Hospital maintains a morgue with refrigerated drawers a bit larger than a human body. Jeremiah's body was placed in such a drawer awaiting pickup by a mortician. Before the mortician called for the body, a Hospital orderly placed two opaque plastic bags in the drawer with Jeremiah's body. One bag contained Jeremiah's personal effects, and the other contained an amputated leg from some other Hospital patient. It is stipulated that Hospital was negligent to allow the amputated leg to get into Jeremiah's drawer. The mortician delivered the two opaque plastic bags to John, assuming both contained personal effects. John was shocked when he opened the bag containing the amputated leg. John sued Hospital to recover for his emotional distress. At the trial, John testified that the experience had been extremely upsetting, that he had had recurring nightmares about it, and that his family and business relationships had been adversely affected for a period of several months. He did not seek medical or psychiatric treatment for his emotional distress.

Who should prevail?

(A) John, because of the sensitivity people have regarding the care of the bodies of deceased relatives.

(B) John, because hospitals are strictly liable for mishandling dead bodies.

(C) Hospital, because John did not require medical or psychiatric treatment.

(D) Hospital, because John suffered no bodily harm.

[Q2103]

Answer 33: Choice **(A)** is correct. Most courts allow recovery for negligent infliction of emotional distress when there has been a negligent mishandling of a corpse. The fact pattern indicates that the Hospital was negligent in its care of the body. Where the facts are such that it can confidently be believed that there has been actual mental distress (i.e., where mental distress would be the normal human reaction), courts ignore the ban on recovery for purely mental harm in a claim for negligent infliction of emotional distress.

(B) is wrong because it misstates the law — neither hospitals nor any other class of defendant is strictly liable for mishandling dead bodies. What's special about dead bodies is that when they're *negligently* mishandled, a close relative of the body can recover for emotional distress that's not accompanied by bodily harm (something that is not usually the case in negligence actions).

(C) is wrong because, in the case of a claim for negligent mishandling of a corpse, it is not necessary that the plaintiff seek treatment for his distress. Where such mishandling occurs, courts are confident in inferring that a close relative of the corpse would indeed have suffered actual mental distress from the mishandling.

(D) is wrong because a claim for negligent mishandling of a corpse is a situation where courts have allowed damages for pure emotional suffering despite the fact that the defendant has suffered no physical harm.

b. The "at risk" plaintiff

i. Where P suffers bodily harm

Question 34: Palko is being treated by a physician for asbestosis, an abnormal chest condition that was caused by his on-the-job handling of materials containing asbestos. His physician has told him that the asbestosis is not presently cancerous, but that it considerably increases the risk that he will ultimately develop lung cancer.

Palko brought an action for damages, based on strict product liability, against the supplier of the materials that contained asbestos. The court in this jurisdiction has ruled against recovery of damages for negligently inflicted emotional distress in the absence of physical harm.

If the supplier is subject to liability to Palko for damages, should the award include damage for emotional distress he has suffered arising from his knowledge of the increased risk that he will develop lung cancer?

(A) No, because Palko's emotional distress did not cause his physical condition.

(B) No, unless the court in this jurisdiction recognizes a cause of action for an increased risk of cancer.

(C) Yes, because the supplier of a dangerous product is strictly liable for the harm it causes.

(D) Yes, because Palko's emotional distress arises from bodily harm caused by his exposure to asbestos.

[Q1036]

Answer 34: Choice **(D)** is correct. Palko is an at-risk plaintiff, one who by virtue of his exposure to a particular substance, has suffered an increased likelihood of a particular disease. Even in jurisdictions disallowing recovery for pure emotional distress (unaccompanied by bodily harm) for negligently-inflicted harm or harm caused by a defective product, a plaintiff may recover for emotional distress as an "add on" if the plaintiff has also suffered bodily harm. That's true here — Palko's asbestosis is bodily harm, so he can add recovery for emotional distress due to the increased cancer risk on top of it to his recovery from the already-existing (though perhaps minor) bodily harm from asbestosis.

(A) is wrong because, in a suit for negligent infliction of emotional distress, it is not required that the emotional distress be the cause of a physical condition; it is possible that physical harm can cause compensable emotional distress, as is the case here.

(B) is wrong as a matter of law. If plaintiff had not already suffered bodily harm (the abnormal chest condition called asbestosis), this choice would be correct — many courts don't recognize a cause of action for "increased risk of cancer" even against a tortfeasor who has brought about that increased risk. But where plaintiff has already been injured — and asbestosis is an injury, i.e., a form of bodily harm regardless of whether it later produces cancer — virtually all courts allow the injured plaintiff to "tack on" a recovery for emotional distress due to the injury. And distress at the knowledge of increased cancer risk is no different, for this purpose, from any other distress.

(C) is wrong because it misses the issue. True, a supplier of a defectively dangerous product is strictly liable for the "harm" it causes. But the key question is, what *is* the harm that's compensible? (D) is a better explanation of why plaintiff will recover from harm that might seem to be purely intangible.

II. PURE ECONOMIC LOSS

A. Traditional rule

1. Rationale

Question 35: Star, who played the lead role in a television soap opera, was seriously injured in an automobile accident caused by Danton's negligent driving. As a consequence of Star's injury, the television series was canceled, and Penn, a supporting actor, was laid off.

In an action against Danton, can Penn recover for his loss of income attributable to the accident?

(A) Yes, because Danton's negligence was the cause in fact of Penn's loss.

(B) Yes, unless Penn failed to take reasonable measures to mitigate his loss.

(C) No, unless Danton should have foreseen that by injuring Star he would cause harm to Penn.

(D) No, because Danton's liability does not extend to economic loss to Penn that arises solely from physical harm to Star.

[Q1169]

Answer 35: Choice **(D)** is correct. The general rule is that even if D negligently causes physical harm or property harm to *A*, D will not be liable for pure economic harm to *B*, where the latter harm stems from the harm to *A*. There is an exception if B was in the zone of physical danger. In many courts, there is a second exception if B watched physical harm to A, at least where B and A are close relatives. But here, neither exception applies. So the default rule applies: since Penn was never placed at physical risk, and didn't witness the physical risk or injury to Star, Penn can't recover for his pure economic loss. (The theory behind this principle is that such pure-economic-loss recovery were allowed, negligence liability would extend too far, and lawsuit costs would go through the roof.)

(A) and (B) are wrong, because neither recognizes the key issue, which is discussed in (D).

(C) is wrong because it cites an irrelevant factor. Even if Danton had been able to foresee that by injuring Star he would cause harm to Penn, Danton would still not be liable, because the harm to Penn here is purely economic. In other words, this choice, like (A) and (B), fails to deal with the key issue, liability for pure economic harm.

CHAPTER 8

OWNERS AND OCCUPIERS OF LAND

I. TRESPASSERS

A. General rule

Question 36: A bright nine-year-old child attended a day care center after school. The day care center was located near a man-made duck pond on the property of a corporation. During the winter, the pond was used for ice skating when conditions were suitable. At a time when the pond was only partially frozen, the child sneaked away from the center and walked out onto the ice covering the pond. The ice gave way, and the child fell into the cold water. He suffered shock and would have drowned had he not been rescued by a passerby. At the time of the incident, the pond was clearly marked with signs that stated, "THIN ICE - NO SKATING." When the child left the day care center, the center was staffed with a reasonable number of qualified personnel, and the center's employees were exercising reasonable care to ensure that the children in their charge did not leave the premises. The jurisdiction follows a rule of pure comparative negligence.

In a suit brought on the child's behalf against the corporation, who is likely to prevail?

(A) The child, because the corporation owes a duty to keep its premises free of dangerous conditions.

(B) The child, because the pond was an attractive nuisance.

(C) The corporation, because the danger of thin ice may reasonably be expected to be understood by a nine-year-old child.

(D) The corporation, because the day care center had a duty to keep the child off the ice.

[Q7093]

Answer 36: Choice **(C)** is correct. As a general rule, a landowner owes no duty to a trespasser to make her land safe. There are several exceptions, but none of those exceptions applies here. The exception that comes closest to applying is that an owner may have a duty of reasonable care to a trespassing child, if the owner has maintained an "attractive nuisance." But for reasons described in the analysis of Choice (B) below, this exception does not apply here.

(A) is wrong because the duty of a landowner to trespassers to keep the property free of dangerous artificial conditions exists only where the owner has reason to know that trespassers are in dangerous proximity to the condition and that they are unlikely to appreciate the risk. Even then, the duty is only to exercise reasonable care to warn trespassers of the danger, which was done here.

(B) is wrong because, while it is true that an owner may be liable to a trespasser if the owner has maintained an "attractive nuisance," the condition here was not an attractive nuisance. For a condition on land to be considered an attractive nuisance, there must be evidence that the possessor had reason to know that children were likely to trespass, as well as evidence that the plaintiff did not appreciate the risk involved. No such evidence is mentioned in the facts; for instance, there is no suggestion that children often stray from the day care center, and there is no reason to believe the child was not aware of the danger (since we're told he was a "bright nine-year-old" and that the danger was well-marked).

(D) is wrong because, while, this answer correctly states that the corporation will prevail, it misstates the legal basis for this conclusion. Even if the day care center had a duty to keep children from the ice, the corporation could also be liable if it was negligent. That is, if A is negligent as to a risk, the fact that B was also negligent as to the same risk is unlikely to save A from liability.

B. Exceptions to general rule

1. Discovered trespassers

Question 37: Prad entered Drug Store to make some purchases. As he was searching the aisles for various items, he noticed a display card containing automatic pencils. The display card was on a high shelf behind a cashier's counter Prad saw a sign on the counter that read, "No Admittance, Employees Only." Seeing no clerks in the vicinity to help him, Prad went behind the counter to get a pencil. A clerk then appeared behind the counter and asked whether she could help him. He said he just wanted a pencil and that he could reach the display card himself. The clerk said nothing further. While reaching for the display card, Prad stepped sideways into an open shaft and fell to the basement, ten feet below. The clerk knew of the presence of the open shaft, but assumed incorrectly that Prad had noticed it.

Prad sued Drug Store to recover damages for the injuries he sustained in the fall. The jurisdiction has adopted a rule of pure comparative negligence, and it follows traditional common-law rules governing the duties of a land possessor.

Will Prad recover a judgment against Drug Store?

(A) No, because Prad was a trespasser.

(B) No, unless Prad's injuries resulted from the defendant's willful or wanton misconduct.

(C) Yes, because the premises were defective with respect to a public invitee.

(D) Yes, if the clerk had reason to believe that Prad was unaware of the open shaft.

[Q1181]

Answer 37: Choice **(D)** is correct. Normally, a shopper in a store would be considered an invitee — a member of the public who comes onto land held open to him and who does so for the purpose for which the land is held open. Such people reasonably expect that the premises have been made safe for them. A visitor who is an invitee as to one part of the premises may become a trespasser if he goes beyond the part of the land held open to him. When Prad went behind the counter despite seeing the sign "No Admittance, Employees Only," he might be found to have been a trespasser. But even if that's true, when the clerk saw him in that position, he was a "discovered trespasser," and as such the store had an obligation to warn him of dangers known to it and likely unknown to Prad. Therefore, if the clerk had reason to believe that Prad was unaware of the open shaft (and given that the facts tell us the *clerk* knew about the open shaft), Drug Store will be liable for the clerk's failure to warn Prad of the danger.

(A) is wrong because Prad was a licensee when he was behind the cashier's counter, as explained in the discussion of Choice D.

(B) is wrong because liability arose from breach of the owner's duty to warn Prad of a danger that it should reasonably anticipate that Prad may not discover. Willful or wanton conduct is not required.

(C) is wrong because this is not a claim for strict liability. Premises are not "defective." Liability arises here, if at all, from negligence principles, not from strict liability. So the key issue is whether the clerk should have realized that Prad didn't know about the open shaft (as discussed in (D).

2. Children

a. Not usually the answer on the MBE

Question 38: Davis has a small trampoline in his backyard which, as he knows, is commonly used by neighbor children as well as his own. The trampoline is in good condition, is not defective in any way, and normally is surrounded by mats to prevent injury if a user should fall off. Prior to leaving with his family for the day, Davis leaned the trampoline up against the side of the house and placed the mats in the garage.

While the Davis family was away, Philip, aged 11, a new boy in the neighborhood, wandered into Davis's yard and saw the trampoline. Philip had not previously been aware of its presence, but, having frequently used a trampoline before, he decided to set it up, and started to jump. He lost his balance on one jump and took a hard fall on the bare ground, suffering a serious injury that would have been prevented by the mats.

An action has been brought against Davis on Philip's behalf to recover damages for the injuries Philip sustained from his fall. In this jurisdiction, the traditional common-law rules pertaining to contributory negligence have been replaced by a pure comparative negligence rule.

In his action against Davis, will Philip prevail?

(A) No, if children likely to be attracted by the trampoline would normally realize the risk of using it without mats.

(B) No, if Philip failed to exercise reasonable care commensurate with his age, intelligence, and experience.

(C) No, because Philip entered Davis's yard and used the trampoline without Davis's permission.

(D) No, because Philip did not know about the trampoline before entering Davis's yard and thus was not "lured" onto the premises.

[Q2151]

Answer 38: Choice **(A)** is correct. A trespassing child may sue for harm suffered from an injurious condition on the defendant's land. The only plausible basis for Philip to recover would be the special rule under which a landowner will be liable for an artificial condition that is highly dangerous to trespassing children. The requirements set forth in Rest. 2d, § 339 for such liability are that: (1) the place where the condition exists must be (as the owner knows) one on which children are likely to trespass; (2) there is, as the owner knows, an unreasonable risk of death or serious bodily harm to such children from the condition; (3) the children because of their youth do not discover the condition or don't known recognize the risk from it; (4) the utility of maintaining the condition is slight compared with the risks to the children involved; and (5) the owner fails to exercise reasonable care. Choice (A) correctly addresses requirement (3), that the child, because of his youth, either did not discover the condition or did not realize the danger posed by it.

(B) is wrong because, if Philip failed to exercise reasonable care, this would merely reduce his recovery, but not block it altogether. The facts indicate that the traditional common-law rules pertaining to contributory negligence (which would block recovery by a negligent plaintiff) have been replaced by a pure comparative negligence rule (where the plaintiff's recovery is reduced by a proportion equal to the ratio between his own fault and the total fault contributing to the accident). Therefore, if Philip was negligent, his recovery would be reduced, but not eliminated as this choice implies.

(C) is wrong because a duty is owed to child trespassers as long as certain requirements are met, as discussed in the explanation of Choice (A).

(D) is wrong because most modern courts reject the requirement that the child must have been attracted by the particular condition which ends up injuring him (the "attractive nuisance" doctrine).

II. LICENSEES

A. Social guests

Question 39: At the trial of an action against Grandmother on behalf of Patrick, the following evidence has been introduced. Grandson and his friend, Patrick, both aged eight, were visiting at Grandmother's house when, while exploring the premises, they discovered a hunting rifle in an unlocked gun cabinet. They removed it from the cabinet and were examining it when the rifle, while in Grandson's hands, somehow discharged. The bullet struck and injured Patrick. The gun cabinet was normally locked. Grandmother had opened it for dusting several days before the boys' visit, and had then forgotten to relock it. She was not aware that it was unlocked when the boys arrived.

If the defendant moves for a directed verdict in her favor at the end of the plaintiff's case, that motion should be

(A) granted, because Grandmother is not legally responsible for the acts of Grandson.

(B) granted, because Grandmother did not recall that the gun cabinet was unlocked.

(C) denied, because a firearm is an inherently dangerous instrumentality.

(D) denied, because a jury could find that Grandmother breached a duty of care she owed to Patrick.

[Q2140]

Answer 39: Choice **(D)** is correct. Patrick was a licensee, a person who has the owner's consent to be on the owner's property, but who does not have a business purpose for being there, or anything else entitling him to be there apart from the owner's consent. When the plaintiff is a licensee, the defendant does not have a "duty to inspect" for dangers. But if the defendant knows of a dangerous condition, the defendant has a duty to take reasonable precautions to make the premises safe. In this case, a reasonable jury could find that since Grandmother knew of the danger from guns, she had a duty to take reasonable care to keep the cabinet locked.

(A) is wrong because, even though there may not be a special duty arising from the Grandmother-Grandson relationship, a duty did arise for Grandmother, as owner of the premises and the gun cabinet, to use reasonable care in safeguarding the guns. She is therefore liable for the foreseeable consequences of her breach of this duty regardless of whether it was Grandson or some other child who got his hand on the gun.

(B) is wrong because if Grandma did not recall that the gun cabinet was unlocked, this is evidence of her unreasonable behavior. Reasonable care would require that an owner of a gun cabinet be extremely vigilant in making sure that the cabinet is locked, especially when there are young children exploring the premises.

(C) is wrong because it relies on an inappropriate concept. The concept of an "inherently dangerous instrumentality" might apply to strict product liability, or to strict liability for conducting an abnormally dangerous activity. But it would not apply to a negligence suit. In other words, plaintiff can't win unless defendant was negligent — it's not enough that defendant possessed an inherently dangerous instrumentality (if, indeed, a gun is such). Also, guns can themselves be locked (trigger guards), so the factual accuracy of this choice is questionable as well.

III. INVITEES

A. Duty of due care

1. Effect of warning

a. Torts by third persons

Question 40: Supermarket is in a section of town where there are sometimes street fights and where pedestrians are occasionally the victims of pickpockets and muggers. In recognition of the unusual number of robberies in the area, the supermarket posted signs in the store and in its parking lot that read:

> Warning: There are pickpockets and muggers at work in this part of the city. Supermarket is not responsible for the acts of criminals.

One evening, Lorner drove to Supermarket to see about a special on turkeys that Supermarket was advertising. She decided that the turkeys were too large and left the store without purchasing anything. In the parking lot, she was attacked by an unknown man who raped her and then ran away.

If Lorner sues Supermarket, the result should be for the

(A) plaintiff, if Supermarket failed to take reasonable steps to protect customers against criminal attack in its parking lot.

(B) plaintiff, because Supermarket is liable for harm to business invitees on its premises.

(C) defendant, if the warning signs were plainly visible to Lorner.

(D) defendant, because the rapist was the proximate cause of Lorner's injuries.

[Q2018]

Answer 40: Choice **(A)** is correct. Grocery store shoppers are invitees — members of the public who come onto land held open to them and who do so for the purpose for which the land is held open. Such people reasonably expect that the premises have been made safe for them, and the owner must exercise reasonable care for the safety of such people. Reasonable care by the owner will typically require that she attempt to exercise control over third persons on the premises. A storekeeper, for instance, will generally be required to take reasonable security measures to prevent attacks or thefts against her customers.

(B) is wrong because Supermarket is liable for harm caused to its invitee only if it has breached a duty of reasonable care to that invitee. (B) asserts a blanket rule of liability, and is therefore incorrect.

(C) is wrong because Supermarket's duty requires that it use reasonable efforts to control third persons on the premises. Issuing a warning does not necessarily satisfy this duty.

(D) is wrong because if Supermarket breached its duty in failing to protect Lorner against the rapist, it is liable for injuries inflicted by the rapist that were a foreseeable result of breach of that duty. Note that an event may have multiple proximate causes; so here, the fact that the rapist was a proximate cause of Lorner's injuries doesn't prevent Supermarket's negligence (in failing to use adequate security measures) from also being a proximate cause of those injuries.

CHAPTER 9

VICARIOUS LIABILITY

I. EMPLOYER-EMPLOYEE RELATIONSHIP

A. Torts by non-employees (e.g., guests and customers)

Question 41: Perkins and Morton were passengers sitting in adjoining seats on a flight on Delval Airline. There were many empty seats on the aircraft.

During the flight, a flight attendant served Morton nine drinks. As Morton became more and more obviously intoxicated and attempted to engage Perkins in a conversation, Perkins chose to ignore Morton. This angered Morton, who suddenly struck Perkins in the face, giving her a black eye.

If Perkins asserts a claim for damages against Delval Airline based on battery, she will

(A) prevail, because she suffered an intentionally inflicted harmful or offensive contact.

(B) prevail, if the flight attendant acted recklessly in continuing to serve liquor to Morton.

(C) not prevail, because Morton was not acting as an agent or employee of Delval Airline.

(D) not prevail, unless she can establish some permanent injury from the contact.

[Q2130]

Answer 41: Choice **(C)** is correct. The doctrine of vicarious liability provides that in some special relationships, such as that of employer-employee, the tortious act of an employee may be imputed to his employer. As a result, the latter will be held liable, even though its own conduct may have been completely blameless. In order for Delval Airline to be liable for the battery perpetrated by Morton, there would have to be such a relationship between Morton and the airline. Since as (C) correctly recites, Morton was not acting as an agent or employee of Delval, vicarious liability would not be applied.

(A) is wrong because the fact that Perkins suffered a battery by itself doesn't justify imposing liability on Delval for the battery.

(B) is wrong because the airline has not committed battery here. Battery is, of course, an intentional tort, so the airline can be liable for that intentional tort (as opposed to liable in negligence) only if the airline or someone for whom the airline is directly responsible had the requisite intent to commit a harmful or offensive contact. Since Morton wasn't the airline's agent or employee, this requirement of intent isn't satisfied. The fact that the airline may have been *reckless* in facilitating Morton's intentional tort won't be enough, because a reckless mental state on the part of the airline won't suffice for battery. (Whereas a business owner can be liable in *negligence* for failing to stop someone else's negligent or intentional tort, there's no comparable principle whereby a business owner becomes liable for intentional tort X merely for recklessly bringing about a third person's commission of X.)

(D) is wrong the because severity of the injury is irrelevant in determining Delval's liability for the conduct of another.

CHAPTER 10
STRICT LIABILITY

I.   ABNORMALLY DANGEROUS ACTIVITIES

A. Examples

1. Nuclear reactor

Question 42: As a result of an accident at the NPP nuclear power plant, a quantity of radioactive vapor escaped from the facility and two members of the public were exposed to excessive doses of radiation. According to qualified medical opinion, that exposure will double the chance that these two persons will ultimately develop cancer. However, any cancer that might be caused by this exposure will not be detectable for at least ten years. If the two exposed persons do develop cancer, it will not be possible to determine whether it was caused by this exposure or would have developed in any event.

If the exposed persons assert a claim for damages against NPP shortly after the escape of the radiation, which of the following questions will NOT present a substantial issue?

(A) Will the court recognize that the plaintiffs have suffered a present legal injury?

(B) Can the plaintiffs prove the amount of their damages?

(C) Can the plaintiffs prove that any harm they may suffer was caused by this exposure?

(D) Can the plaintiffs prevail without presenting evidence of specific negligence on the part of NPP?

[Q1102]

Answer 42: Choice **(D)** is correct. Operation of a nuclear power plant is an ultrahazardous activity. Therefore, NPP can be strictly liable for the accident without any proof by the exposed plaintiff that NPP behaved negligently.

(A) is incorrect because the question of whether doubling the risk of contracting cancer ten years into the future presents a substantial issue, that is, whether the plaintiff's have already suffered a present compensable legal injury.

(B) is incorrect because valuing the damages suffered by a plaintiff who is now healthy but is at an increased risk of contracting a deadly disease, raises the substantial issue of whether the damages are too speculative to calculate at the present time.

(C) is incorrect because causation is a real issue in the case. Plaintiffs ordinarily have the burden of proving harm. At present they have not contracted cancer and have suffered no present harm. So it's a real issue whether any cancer they suffer in the future (the "present value" of which they're trying to recover now) will have been caused by the radiation exposure.

2. Construction activities

Question 43: Innes worked as a secretary in an office in a building occupied partly by her employer and partly by Glass, a retail store. The two areas were separated by walls and were in no way connected, except that the air conditioning unit served both areas and there was a common return-air duct.

Glass began remodeling, and its employees did the work, which included affixing a plastic surfacing material to counters. To fasten the plastic to the counters, the employees purchased glue, with the brand name Stick, that was manufactured by Steel, packaged in a sealed container by Steel, and retailed by Paint Company.

In the course of the remodeling job, one of Glass's employees turned on the air conditioning and caused fumes from the glue to travel from Glass through the air conditioning unit and into Innes's office. The employees did not know that there was common ductwork for the air conditioners. Innes was permanently blinded by the fumes from the glue.

The label on the container of glue read, "DANGER. Do not smoke near this product. Extremely flammable. Contains Butanone, Tuluol and Hexane. Use with adequate ventilation. Keep out of the reach of children."

The three chemicals listed on the label are very toxic and harmful to human eyes. Steel had received no reports of eye injuries during the ten years that the product had been manufactured and sold.

If Innes asserts a claim against Glass, the most likely result is that she will

(A) recover, because a user of a product is held to the same standard as the manufacturer.

(B) recover, because the employees of Glass caused the fumes to enter her area of the building.

(C) not recover, because Glass used the glue for its intended purposes.

(D) not recover, because the employees of Glass had no reason to know that the fumes could injure Innes.

[Q4050]

Answer 43: Choice **(D)** is correct. What we care about here is whether Glass is strictly liable for having carried out an abnormally dangerous activity. The answer is, "no." It's very unlikely the use of the glue here would be considered ultrahazardous, as you can see by considering the four elements that generally make an activity ultrahazardous: (1) the activity involves a high risk of serious harm, (2) there's no way to perform the activity completely safely no matter how much care is taken, (3) the activity is not commonly engaged in in the particular community, and (4) the danger of the activity outweighs its utility to the community. At least element (2) is missing (it's possible to do glueing safely by venting the glue fumes to the outside), and it's doubtful whether element (3) is satisfied either (since remodeling with glue occurs all the time, even if this particular glue brand is not widely used). So the activity isn't ultrahazardous.

Nor were Glass's employees negligent — it's clear from the facts that they did not know about the danger that the fumes would be vented over to Innes, so there's no indication of negligence on their part. And Glass has no strict product liability, because as is further discussed in (A) below, only "sellers" or makers of defective products, not users, have such liability.

(A) is incorrect because it states incorrect law. It is not true that a user of a product is held to the same standard as the manufacturer. That's because a manufacturer is strictly liable for selling a defective product, whereas a user is not. (Even if the use occurs in a business context, and even if the use directly injures a third person because the product being used is "defective" and dangerous, the user will be liable only for negligence.)

(B) is incorrect because even if the employees of Glass caused the fumes, this does not automatically make Glass strictly liable. Unless either the activity was ultrahazardous, or Glass's employees were negligent, Glass would not be liable even though the employees caused the fumes to enter plaintiff's area of the building.

(C) is incorrect because there could be an instance where using a product for its intended purposes still creates liability. For instance, if Glass's use of the product was indeed ultrahazardous, as discussed in the explanation for (D), Glass could have been liable.

B. Requirement that D "carry out" the activity

1. Use of independent contractor

Question 44: Landco purchased a large tract of land intending to construct residential housing on it. Landco hired Poolco to build a large in-ground swimming pool on the tract. The contract provided that Poolco would carry out blasting operations that were necessary to create an excavation large enough for the pool. The blasting caused cracks to form in the walls of Plaintiff's home in a nearby residential neighborhood.

In Plaintiff's action for damages against Landco, Plaintiff should

(A) prevail, only if Landco retained the right to direct and control Poolco's construction of the pool.

(B) prevail, because the blasting that Poolco was hired to perform damaged Plaintiff's home.

(C) not prevail, if Poolco used reasonable care in conducting the blasting operations.

(D) not prevail, if Landco used reasonable care to hire a competent contractor.

[Q2148]

Answer 44: Choice **(B)** is correct. Blasting is considered an ultrahazardous activity, giving rise to strict liability. Where one person hires an independent contractor to perform an untrahazardous activity, the hirer is strictly liable, just as the contractor is, even if the hirer used all due care selecting a careful contractor.

(A) is wrong because Landco is responsible for damages caused by Poolco regardless of whether or not Poolco is Landco's employee. The doctrine of vicarious liability provides that in some special relationships, such as that of employer-employee, the tortious act of an employee may be imputed to his employer. As a result, the latter will be held liable, even though its own conduct may have been completely blameless. An employee is one who works subject to the control of the person who has hired him. If the party that caused the damage is not an employee, but an independent contractor, there will generally not be vicarious liability. However, there is an exception — where the work is such that, unless special precautions are taken, there will be a high degree of danger to others. Rest. 2d, §§ 416, 427. That's clearly true of blasting in a residential neighborhood (which is an "ultrahazardous activity" for which the person carrying it out has strict liability). Therefore, Landco, the hiring party, will be liable for the damage caused by Poolco, despite the fact that Poolco is an independent contractor, and even if Landco didn't retain the right to direct and control Poolco's work.

(C) is wrong because the use of reasonable care is irrelevant in a claim for strict liability for an ultrahazardous activity, as this is. (See the discussion of Choice (A) for more about this.)

(D) is wrong because, as the hiring party, Landco will be vicariously liable for harm caused by Poolco based on the abnormal dangerousness of the activity in which Poolco was engaging. See the more extensive discussion of why this is so, in the treatment of Choice (A).

CHAPTER 11

PRODUCTS LIABILITY

I. NEGLIGENCE

A. Classes of defendants

1. Retailers

a. Consequence

Question 45: Parents purchased a new mobile home from Seller. The mobile home was manufactured by Mobilco and had a ventilating system designed by Mobilco with both a heating unit and an air conditioner. Mobilco installed a furnace manufactured by Heatco and an air conditioning unit manufactured by Coolco. Each was controlled by an independent thermostat installed by Mobilco. Because of the manner in which Mobilco designed the ventilating system, the first time the ventilating system was operated by Parents, cold air was vented into Parents' bedroom to keep the temperature at 68°F. The cold air then activated the heater thermostat, and hot air was pumped into the bedroom of Child, the six-month-old child of Parents. The temperature in Child's room reached more than 170°F before Child's mother became aware of the condition and shut the system off manually. As a result, Child suffered permanent physical injury.

Child, through a duly appointed guardian, has asserted a claim against Seller based solely on negligence. The minimum proof necessary to establish Seller's liability is that the ventilating system

(A) was defective.

(B) was defective and had not been inspected by Seller.

(C) was defective and had been inspected by Seller, and the defect was not discovered.

(D) was defective, and the defect would have been discovered if Seller had exercised reasonable care in inspecting the system.

[Q4043]

Answer 45: Choice **(D)** is correct. As a retailer, Seller will only be liable in negligence due to its own affirmative negligence. Retailers only have a duty to inspect if they have reason to believe the product is likely to be defective, and even if they do have a duty to inspect, they'll only be liable if an inspection undertaken with reasonable care would have uncovered the defect. This choice mirrors these requirements by comparing Seller's conduct to what a retailer in the exercise of due care would have done.

(A) is wrong because, as a retailer defending a *negligence* action, Seller will only be liable for negligence due to its own affirmative negligence. So the fact that the product was defective isn't close to enough. If you chose this response, you were probably thinking of strict product liability, under which proof of the defect would be the lynchpin of Child's claim. However, you're told the suit has been brought only in negligence, and negligence requires some proof of lack of due care on defendant's part.

(B) is wrong because it, like Choice (A), understates the proof Child's negligence claim will require. Since the action is based solely on negligence, Seller will only be liable due to its own affirmative negligence. Retailers only have a duty to inspect if they have reason to believe the product is likely to be defective, and even if they *do* have a duty to inspect, they'll only be liable if an inspection undertaken with reasonable care would have uncovered the defect. Thus, merely proving a defect and a lack of inspection would be insufficient to pin negligence liability on Seller — Child would also have to prove that a reasonable inspection would have uncovered the defect.

(C) is wrong because it, too, understates the proof Child's negligence claim will require. Child must show both that (1) Seller failed to follow the reasonable standard of care of a retailer, and (2) this failure proximately and actually caused the accident. Seller's mere failure to discover the defect during an inspection that actually occurred would not make Seller negligent unless a reasonable inspection would have uncovered the defect (since without the latter showing, Seller's failure to inspect in a reasonable manner didn't change the outcome, and thus wasn't the proximate cause of the accident).

II. WARRANTY

A. Express warranties

1. UCC

Question 46: At a country auction, Powell acquired an antique cabinet that he recognized as a "Morenci," an extremely rare and valuable collector's item. Unfortunately, Powell's cabinet had several coats of varnish and paint over the original finish. Its potential value could only be realized if these layers could be removed without damaging the original finish. Much of the value of Morenci furniture depends on the condition of a unique oil finish, the secret of which died with Morenci, its inventor.

A professional restorer of antique furniture recommended that Powell use Restorall to remove the paint and varnish from the cabinet. Powell obtained and read a sales brochure published by Restorall, Inc., which contained the following statement: "This product will renew all antique furniture. Will not damage original oil finishes."

Powell purchased some Restorall and used it on his cabinet, being very careful to follow the accompanying instructions exactly. Despite Powell's care, the original Morenci finish was irreparably damaged. When finally refinished, the cabinet was worth less than 20% of what it would have been worth if the Morenci finish had been preserved.

If Powell sues Restorall, Inc., to recover the loss he has suffered as a result of the destruction of the Morenci finish, will Powell prevail?

(A) Yes, unless no other known removal technique would have preserved the Morenci finish.

(B) Yes, if the loss would not have occurred had the statement in the brochure been true.

(C) No, unless the product was defective when sold by Restorall, Inc.

(D) No, if the product was not dangerous to persons.

[Q1028]

Answer 46: Choice **(B)** is correct. A seller may expressly represent that her goods have certain qualities. If the goods turn out not to have these qualities, the purchaser may sue for breach of warranty. UCC Sec. 2-313. Had the statement "will not damage original oil finishes" been true, then the loss suffered would not have occurred. In this case, the product is not defective or dangerous to people (it only causes harm to a particular type of furniture). Therefore, a warranty claim is suitable for this kind of case.

(A) is wrong because the fact that no other product would have been safer for use on the furniture is irrelevant when the claim is based on breach of an express warranty, i.e., a warranty stating that the product works on all antique furniture and will not damage original oil finishes. This answer sounds like it's trying to conjure up a design defect claim, where it is relevant that the adoption of a reasonable alternative design is available or not. However, the availability of such a reasonable alternative design is irrelevant here, given the warranty claim.

(C) is wrong because suit for breach of warranty does not require that the product be "defective."

(D) is wrong because the fact that the product is not dangerous to people is irrelevant in this case of breach of warranty.

III. STRICT PRODUCT LIABILITY

A. Bystanders and other non-user plaintiffs

Question 47: In preparation for a mountain-climbing expedition, Alper purchased the necessary climbing equipment from Outfitters. Inc., a retail dealer in sporting goods. A week later, Alper fell from a rock face when a safety device he had purchased from Outfitters malfunctioned because of a defect in its manufacture. Thereafter, Rollins was severely injured when he tried to reach and give assistance to Alper on the ledge to which Alper had fallen. Rollins's injury was not caused by any fault on his own part.

If Rollins brings an action against Outfitters, Inc., to recover damages for his injuries, will Rollins prevail?

(A) No, unless Outfitters could have discovered the defect by a reasonable inspection of the safety device.

(B) No, because Rollins did not rely on the representation of safety implied from the sale of the safety device by Outfitters.

(C) Yes, unless Alper was negligent in failing to test the safety device.

(D) Yes, because injury to a person in Rollins's position was foreseeable if the safety device failed.

[Q1104]

Answer 47: Choice **(D)** is correct. This is a strict liability claim for a manufacturing defect, i.e., a scenario in which the product has departed from its intended design in a way that makes it unsafe. It must be proven that (1) the product was defective, (2) at the time it left the defendant's hands, and (3) the product caused harm. The causation element will be satisfied in this case if it was foreseeable that the failure of the safety device would invite rescue by a third party (and if the rescue was not performed in a grossly careless manner).

(A) is wrong because the retailer will be subject to strict product liability; and, therefore the reasonableness of his conduct is irrelevant.

(B) is wrong because reliance is irrelevant here. One who is in the business of selling a product which turns out to be dangerously defective has strict product liability, and that's true whether the retailer made any implied or express representation of safety (and whether or not the buyer relied on such a representation if one was made).

(C) is wrong because, in the ordinary case, the product user's failure to discover the defect will not be considered negligence. And even if the user's failure to discover the defect *was* negligence (which it isn't), that negligence would only reduce the plaintiff's recovery, not eliminate it. (The choice asks you whether plaintiff would "prevail," and a recovery reduced by plaintiff's percentage of fault would still constitute "prevailing" in everyday usage.)

IV. DESIGN DEFECTS

A. Negligence predominates

1. Reasonable alternative design

Question 48: A 16-year-old student purchased an educational chemistry set made by a manufacturer. The student invited his classmate to assist him in a chemistry project. Referring to a library chemistry book on explosives and finding that the chemistry set contained all of the necessary chemicals, the student and the classmate agreed to make a bomb. During the course of the project, the student carelessly knocked a lighted Bunsen burner into a bowl of chemicals from the chemistry set. The chemicals burst into flames, injuring the classmate.

In a suit by the classmate against the manufacturer, based on strict liability, the classmate will

(A) prevail, if the chemistry set did not contain a warning that its contents could be combined to form dangerous explosives.

(B) prevail, because manufacturers of chemistry sets are engaged in an abnormally dangerous activity.

(C) not prevail, because the student's negligence was the cause in fact of the classmate's injury.

(D) not prevail, if the chemistry set was as safe as possible, consistent with its educational purposes, and its benefits exceeded its risks.

[Q1001]

Answer 48: Choice **(D)** is correct. Products that conform to their design, and essentially do what the consumer expects them to do, yet are by their very nature inherently dangerous, are products that are "unavoidably unsafe." The chemistry set is such a product. The question to be determined is whether such an unavoidably-unsafe product is "reasonably safe" (because if it isn't, it gives rise to strict products liability, and if it is, it doesn't trigger such liability). The Third Restatement applies a risk-utility approach to such products, finding them defective rather than reasonably safe "when the foreseeable risks of harm posed by the product could have been reduced or avoided by the adoption of a reasonable alternative design by the seller...and the omission of the alternative design renders the product not reasonably safe." Rest. 3d (Prod. Liab.) § 2(b). (D) essentially applies this test. That is, the choice turns on whether the set was as safe as possible and its benefits exceeded its risks; if it was, the choice correctly asserts that the classmate would not prevail.

(A) is wrong because the outcome would not turn on whether such a warning was given. The presence or absence of a warning will only determine the outcome of a product-liability case if the warning would have altered the outcome. Here, even if there had been a warning, this would probably not have prevented the knocking over of the Bunsen burner. (Would the student have been less likely to knock over the burner if there had been such a warning and he had read it? Probably not.)

(B) is wrong because when a person manufactures and sells a dangerous product that causes injury post-sale, the act of manufacturing and selling it won't be deemed to be an abnormally dangerous activity. If the explosion had occurred during manufacture, that probably *would* qualify for the abnormally-dangerous-activity form of strict liability (also known as strict liability for "ultrahazardous" activities). But post-manufacture and post-sale, the relevant doctrine is strict product liability.

(C) is wrong because it falsely suggests that the student's negligence would bar the manufacturer's liability to the classmate. There can be multiple causes in fact, and if the chemistry set had been defectively designed (which it wasn't), that defect could (and likely would) have been a cause in fact, just as the student's negligence would also have been. In that scenario, the student's negligence wouldn't even have caused the classmate's recovery from the manufacturer to be reduced, let alone eliminated, because the student's negligence wouldn't have been imputed to the classmate.

V. DUTY TO WARN

A. Unknown and unknowable dangers

1. Check adequacy of warning

Question 49: Peter, who was 20 years old, purchased a new, high-powered sports car that was marketed with an intended and recognized appeal to youthful drivers. The car was designed with the capability to attain speeds in excess of 100 miles per hour. It was equipped with tires designed and tested only for a maximum safe speed of 85 miles per hour. The owner's manual that came with the car stated that "continuous driving over 90 miles per hour requires high-speed-capability tires," but the manual did not describe the speed capability of the tires sold with the car.

Peter took his new ear out for a spin on a straight, smooth country road where the posted speed limit was 55 miles per hour. Intending to test the car's power, he drove for a considerable distance at over 100 miles per hour. While he was doing so, the tread separated from the left rear tire, causing the car to leave the road and hit a tree. Peter sustained severe injuries.

Peter has brought a strict product liability action in tort against the manufacturer of the car. You should assume that pure comparative fault principles apply to this case.

Will Peter prevail?

(A) No, because Peter's driving at an excessive speed constituted a misuse of the car

(B) No, because the car was not defective.

(C) Yes, if the statement in the manual concerning the tires did not adequately warn of the danger of high-speed driving on the tires mounted on the car.

(D) Yes, unless Peter's driving at a speed in excess of the posted speed limit was negligence per se that, by the law of the jurisdiction, was not excusable.

[Q2025]

Answer 49: Choice **(C)** is correct. In product liability cases, the duty to warn is in effect an extra duty. That is, even if the product would not be defectively dangerous if accompanied by the appropriate warning, absence of such a warning may convert the product into a defectively dangerous product for which there is strict product liability. So here, even if a tire tread that can separate at speeds of 85+ would not have been defectively dangerous if properly warned of, the car manufacturer (which "sold" the tires as part of the original car equipment) would be strictly liable if the manual did not contain an adequate warning of the risk. And it's quite plausible that the manual's failure to specify that the tires that came with the car were not the sort of "high-speed-capability tires" that were required for high speeds would be an actionable failure to warn (especially in light of the fact that the car was designed and marketed based on its ability to go 100+ mph).

(A) is wrong because it is not a misuse of a sports car to drive it at a speed in excess of 100 miles per hour when that was a use intended by the manufacturer who designed the car for high-speed driving and who marketed the car with an intended and recognized appeal to youthful drivers.

(B) is wrong because, as discussed in (C), the car might well be "defective" in light of inadequate warnings about the capabilities of the tires sold with it.

(D) is wrong because if Peter was found to be negligent he could still prevail. The facts state that the jurisdiction applies a pure comparative fault system in strict product liability actions. In a pure comparative fault system, the plaintiff is allowed to recover even if his fault is greater than that of the defendant. The plaintiff's recovery is reduced by a proportion equal to the ratio between his own fault and the total fault contributing to the accident. Therefore, Peter's negligence would not bar recovery in this case, but merely reduce his recovery.

CHAPTER 12
NUISANCE

I.   PRIVATE NUISANCE

A.   Interference with use

Question 50: Electco operates a factory that requires the use of very high voltage electricity. Paul owns property adjacent to the Electco plant where he has attempted to carry on a business that requires the use of sensitive electronic equipment. The effectiveness of Paul's electronic equipment is impaired by electrical interference arising from the high voltage currents used in Electco's plant. Paul has complained to Electco several times, with no result. There is no way that Electco, by taking reasonable precautions, can avoid the interference with Paul's operation that arises from the high voltage currents necessary to Electco 's operation.

In Paul's action against Electco to recover damages for the economic loss caused to him by the electrical interference, will Paul prevail?

(A) Yes, because Electco's activity is abnormally dangerous.

(B) Yes, for loss suffered by Paul after Electco was made aware of the harm its activity was causing to Paul.

(C) No, unless Electco caused a substantial and unreasonable interference with Paul's business.

(D) No, because Paul's harm was purely economic and did not arise from physical harm to his person or property.

[Q2035]

Answer 50: Choice **(C)** is correct. Paul can win only on a nuisance theory (not on negligence or strict liability for ultrahazardous activities, as to which see Choice (A) below). So let's analyze whether the requirements for nuisance are satisfied here. A private nuisance is an unreasonable interference with the plaintiff's use and enjoyment of his land. In order to recover for private nuisance, the plaintiff must show (1) that his use and enjoyment of his land was interfered with in a "substantial" way and (2) that the defendant's conduct was negligent, abnormally dangerous, or intentional. The facts state that the effectiveness of Paul's electronic equipment is impaired by electrical interference from Electo's plant. But unless the interference with Paul's business is substantial and unreasonable, Paul cannot prevail.

(A) is wrong because Electo's use of high voltage electricity would not be found to be abnormally dangerous, especially considering the fact that the harm it caused (interference with use of land) was not dangerous. Activities considered "abnormally dangerous" are subject to strict liability. The Second Restatement lists factors to consider when determining whether an activity is abnormally dangerous: (1) it creates a high degree of risk; (2) it poses a risk of serious harm; (3) it cannot be eliminated even by due care; (4) it is uncommon and (5) it is inappropriate at the particular site. Liability is more likely to be imposed where the activity's value to the community is outweighed by its dangerous attributes. Rest. 2d, § 520. Here, factors (3), (4) and (5) cut against liability. Generally, electric utilities are found not to be engaged in an ultrahazardous activity when they maintain power lines.

(B) is wrong because, if the interference with Paul's business was not substantial and unreasonable, then Electo would not be responsible in nuisance for any harm caused to Paul, even that harm of which it was subsequently made aware.

(D) is wrong because there *has* been harm to Paul's property. There has been physical harm to equipment located on his property, from Electo's activity.

B. Unreasonableness

1. Test for unreasonableness

a. Noise and unattractive sights

Question 51: Palmco owns and operates a beachfront hotel. Under a contract with City to restore a public beach, Dredgeco placed a large and unavoidably dangerous stone-crushing machine on City land near Palmco's hotel. The machine creates a continuous and intense noise that is so disturbing to the hotel guests that they have canceled their hotel reservations in large numbers, resulting in a substantial loss to Palmco.

Palmco's best chance to recover damages for its financial losses from Dredgeco is under the theory that the operation of the stone-crushing machine constitutes

(A) an abnormally dangerous activity.

(B) a private nuisance.

(C) negligence.

(D) a trespass.

[Q1077]

Answer 51: Choice **(B)** is correct. A private nuisance is an unreasonable interference with the plaintiff's use and enjoyment of his land. Rest. 2d, § 822. Whereas trespass is an interference with the plaintiff's right of exclusive possession of his property, nuisance is an interference with his right to use and enjoy it. A condition, such as noise, near the plaintiff's property that interferes with his peace of mind would be a nuisance, but not a trespass, since nothing physically entered the property. Palmco might not win on its nuisance theory (the court might hold that the social utility of the beach restoration project outweighs the damage to Palmco's use and enjoyment), but of the theories listed it is the only one that is plausible.

(A) is wrong because, even though operating a stone-crushing machine may very well be an abnormally dangerous activity, and worthy of applying strict liability, the only harm caused thus far is noise. And noise is not the kind of harm that makes using a stone-crushing machine abnormally dangerous (if, indeed, use of such a machine *is* abnormally dangerous).

(C) is wrong because a plaintiff generally cannot recover in negligence for pure economic loss, in the absence of harm to the plaintiff's person or property. No exception to this general rule applies here.

(D) is wrong because trespass liability requires physical entry by the defendant (or by some object under the defendant's control) onto the plaintiff's property. Sound waves are deemed insufficiently physical to give rise to trespass liability.

CHAPTER 13

DEFAMATION

I. DEFAMATORY COMMUNICATION

A. Opinion

1. Multiple possible interpretations

a. Applicable to statement of opinion

Question 52: Doe, the governor of State, signed a death warrant for Rend, a convicted murderer. Able and Baker are active opponents of the death penalty. At a demonstration protesting the execution of Rend, Able and Baker carried large signs that stated, "Governor Doe - Murderer." Television station XYZ broadcast news coverage of the demonstration, including pictures of the signs carried by Able and Baker. If Governor Doe asserts a defamation claim against XYZ, will Doe prevail?

(A) Yes, because the signs would cause persons to hold Doe in lower esteem.

(B) Yes, if Doe proves that XYZ showed the signs with knowledge of falsity or reckless disregard of the truth that Doe had not committed homicide.

(C) No, unless Doe proves he suffered pecuniary loss resulting from harm to his reputation proximately caused by the defendants' signs.

(D) No, if the only reasonable interpretation of the signs was that the term "murderer" was intended as a characterization of one who would sign a death warrant.

[Q1022]

Answer 52: Choice **(D)** is correct. If a statement could be reasonably interpreted only in one way, then that interpretation must in fact be defamatory in order for a plaintiff to prevail in a case of defamation. Here, the answer states that there is only one reasonable interpretation, that "murderer" means one that would sign a death warrant. Therefore, the statement was pure opinion (that one who signs a death warrant is properly classified as a murderer), not provably false fact.

(A) is wrong because there must be an element of disgrace connected with the allegation, not a mere lowering of esteem, in order for the statement to be deemed defamatory. Also, to be defamatory a statement must be a provably false statement of fact, and this isn't (for reasons described in the analysis of (D) above).

(B) is wrong because the foundation for the defamation claim must be laid before the constitutional questions are addressed. It is true that when the plaintiff is a public official there is an additional requirement that the defendant make the accusation with knowledge of falsity or reckless disregard of the truth. *New York Times Co. v. Sulllivan* (1964). However, the common law elements of the claim must be satisfied first. To be defamatory a statement must be a provably false statement of fact, and this isn't (for reasons described in the analysis of (D) above). Therefore Governor Doe would fail in setting out a claim for defamation even before the constitutional issues were addressed.

(C) is wrong because if this is libel, then the plaintiff does not have to show "special harm" of a pecuniary nature, and if it is slander, then it would be categorized as "slander per se." It is unclear whether the sign broadcast on television news would be considered libel (written or printed matter) or slander (oral and all other statements). "Special harm" of a pecuniary nature need not be proven for libelous statements. A statement imputing criminal behavior to the plaintiff that is "punishable by imprisonment" or "regarded by public opinion as involving moral turpitude" is "slander per se" and does not require a showing of special harm either. Rest. 2d § 571. Therefore, however the statement is categorized, pecuniary loss need not be proven in order for the plaintiff to prevail.

II. PUBLICATION

A. Requirement of publication generally

1. Must be intentional or negligent

a. Frequent on MBE

Question 53: Drew, the owner of a truck leasing company, asked Pat, one of Drew's employees, to deliver $1,000 to the dealership's main office. The following week, as a result of a dispute over whether the money had been delivered, Drew instructed Pat to come to the office to submit to a lie detector test.

When Pat reported to Drew's office for the test, it was not administered. Instead, without hearing Pat's story, Drew shouted at him, "You're a thief," and fired him. Drew's shout was overheard by several other employees who were in another office, which was separated from Drew's office by a thin partition. The next day, Pat accepted another job at a higher salary. Several weeks later, upon discovering that the money had not been stolen, Drew offered to rehire Pat.

In a suit for slander by Pat against Drew, Pat will

(A) prevail, because Pat was fraudulently induced to go to the office for a lie detector test, which was not, in fact, given.

(B) prevail, if Drew should have foreseen that the statement would be overheard by other employees.

(C) not prevail, if Drew made the charge in good faith, believing it to be true.

(D) not prevail, because the statement was made to Pat alone and intended for his ears only.

[Q2076]

Answer 53: Choice **(B)** is correct. One of the elements of defamation is "publication," i.e., the fact that the defamatory statement was communicated to at least one person other than the plaintiff. Furthermore, plaintiff must show that defendant acted either negligently or intentionally with regard to publication. So if defendant neither knew nor had reason to know that the statement would be heard and understood by someone other than the plaintiff, the publication requirement has not been satisfied, but if defendant did have reason to anticipate such an overhearing, then the requirement has been satisfied.

(A) is wrong because whether or not Pat was fraudulently induced into the office is irrelevant to the determination of his slander suit.

(C) is wrong. Drew could have been negligent in believing in the charge. If Drew was indeed negligent in not verifying the truth of the theft accusation, his "good faith" (i.e., honest belief in the statement's truth) won't shield him. That is, where, as here, the plaintiff is not a public figure, plaintiff may recover for defamation based on a mere showing of negligence regarding the truth, rather than knowledge of falsity or reckless disregard of the truth (which public-figure plaintiffs have to show, as a constitutional matter under *N.Y. Times v. Sullivan* (1964)).

(D) is wrong because if Drew should have foreseen that his statement would be overheard by another person, then the publication element was satisfied, as discussed in the explanation of Choice (C).

2. Must be understood

Question 54: Able and Baker are students in an advanced high school Russian class. During an argument one day in the high school cafeteria, in the presence of other students, Able, in Russian, accused Baker of taking money from Able's locker.

In a suit by Baker against Able based on defamation, Baker will

(A) prevail, because Able's accusation constituted slander per se.

(B) prevail, because the defamatory statement was made in the presence of third persons.

(C) not prevail, unless Able made the accusation with knowledge of falsity or reckless disregard of the truth.

(D) not prevail, unless one or more of the other students understood Russian.

[Q1015]

Answer 54: Choice **(D)** is correct. In a common law claim for defamation, the plaintiff must show that a (1) defamatory statement (2) regarding the plaintiff (3) was communicated to at least one other person (publication) and (4) that the plaintiff's reputation was damaged. In addition, some degree of fault will usually have to be proven. The issue in this fact pattern is whether the statement was published. Able's statement was made in a foreign language, so although there were other students present, it is not clear whether or not the statement was understood (the fact pattern does not, for instance, indicate that the fellow classmates who heard the statement were in the advanced Russian language course). It is therefore unclear whether the "publication" element has been satisfied, and Baker cannot prevail unless it is determined that at least one of the other students understood Able's statement.

(A) is wrong because even if the statement could be categorized as "slander per se," Baker would still have to prove all the other elements of a defamation case; he still needs to show that the statement was indeed understood by at least one other student in the cafeteria in order to fulfill the "publication" element. To ultimately prevail in a case of slander, the plaintiff must usually show special harm of a pecuniary nature unless the statement is categorized as "slander per se." Rest. 2d § 558. A statement imputing criminal behavior to the plaintiff that is "punishable by imprisonment" or "regarded by public opinion as involving moral turpitude" falls under this category. Rest. 2d § 571. However, even if Baker's alleged crime of taking money would fall under the category of slander per se, Baker would still need to overcome the hurdle of proving the publication element, as discussed in the explanation of (D).

(B) is wrong because the "publication" requirement not only requires that the statement be made in the presence of at least one other person, but that the third person understand it and perceive its defamatory aspects. The fact pattern is vague on this matter. Therefore, in order for Baker to prevail, it must be determined that the statement was understood by a third person, as discussed in the explanation of (D).

(C) is wrong because the requirement that the defendant make the accusation with knowledge of falsity or reckless disregard of the truth applies only when the plaintiff is a public official or public figure. *New York Times Co. v. Sulllivan* (1964). Baker, as a student, clearly doesn't qualify as a public figure or public official.

III. FAULT

A. Constitutional decisions

1. Private figures

a. P must prove at least negligence

i. Serious doubts about statement's truth

Question 55: Allen and Bradley were law school classmates who had competed for the position of editor of the law review. Allen had the higher grade point average, but Bradley was elected editor, largely in recognition of a long and important note that had appeared in the review over her name.

During the following placement interview season, Allen was interviewed by a representative of a nationally prominent law firm. In response to the interviewer's request for information about the authorship of the law review note, Allen said that he had heard that the note attributed to Bradley was largely the work of another student.

The firm told Bradley that it would not interview her because of doubts about the authorship of the note. This greatly distressed Bradley. In fact the note had been prepared by Bradley without assistance from anyone else.

If Bradley asserts a claim against Allen based on defamation, Bradley will

(A) recover, because Allen's statement was false.

(B) recover, if Allen had substantial doubts about the accuracy of the information he gave the interviewer.

(C) not recover, unless Bradley proves pecuniary loss.

(D) not recover, because the statement was made by Allen only after the interviewer inquired about the authorship of the note.

[Q2188]

Answer 55: Choice **(B)** is correct. Even under Supreme Court First Amendment-based restrictions, states are permitted to give a private (i.e., non-public-figure) plaintiff the right to win if the plaintiff can show that the defendant made a defamatory falsehood and behaved at least negligently with respect to the statement's truth. Since Bradley is not a public figure, the fact that the defendant entertained substantial doubts about the truth of the statement is more than enough to prove negligence. (In fact, such doubts probably even establish the "reckless disregard of the truth" variety of "actual malice," which Bradley would have to show if he *were* a public figure.)

(A) is wrong because it is not enough to prove that the statement was false. All states require that some degree of fault be proven on the part of the defendant.

(C) is wrong because special harm need not be proven in this case. A plaintiff may generally establish slander only if he can show that he sustained some special harm, usually required to be of a pecuniary nature. However, there are four kinds of utterances, categorized as "slander per se," which, even though they are slander rather than libel, require no showing of special harm. One of these is an allegation that adversely reflects on the plaintiff's fitness to conduct his business, trade, profession, or office. That kind of utterance occurred in this case.

(D) is wrong because it is irrelevant. A defamatory statement is actionable, despite the fact that it came out in a conversation where the subject matter was being inquired into. The defendant may have a privilege to respond to a reasonable inquiry, but the privilege is a qualified one, which is lost if it is abused by defendant's negligence concerning the truth or falsity of the answer.

Sources of Modified NCBE Questions

The following NCBE-released questions have been modified to more closely mirror the current style and format of MBE questions. They were modified with permission of the National Conference of Bar Examiners (NCBE).

NCBE Publications:
A "Sample MBE" (February 1991), © 1995
B "Sample MBE II" (July 1991), © 1997
C "Multistate Bar Examination Questions 1992," ©1992
D "Sample MBE III" (July 1998), © 2002
E "MBE-OPE 1," © 2006
F "MBE-OPE 2," © 2009

S&T MBE 2 Question Number	NCBE Source (A-F in the above list)	NCBE Question Number
Constitutional Law		
5	B	79
28	A	195
32	B	8
34	B	162
36	A	21
39	B	155
41	A	122
42	A	73
43	D	190
44	A	114
48	B	193
49	B	184
51	A	138
53	B	153
54	A	133
Contracts		
1	A	141
2	B	111
3	B	174
4	B	34
5	A	41
6	D	28
10	B	29

11	A	120
12	B	44
15	B	123
18	A	17
20	A	128
22	D	39
23	A	44
25	A	108
26	B	52
30	B	106
32	D	143
34	A	89
35	B	185
37	B	141
41	D	20
42	A	30
43	A	86
44	D	9
45	B	32
49	D	83
50	A	194
55	A	172
57	A	121
58	B	62
Criminal Law and Procedure		
13	C	182
30	B	81
36	D	68
39	B	143
42	B	144
Evidence		
7	C	305
8	C	320
15	A	49
37	A	5

Real Property		
1	A	63
4	A	173
7	A	107
8	A	200
9	B	187
10	A	151
13	A	47
14	A	90
15	A	66
20	B	21
21	A	29
26	C	32
29	B	107
31	B	81
39	D	65
41	A	132
42	B	114
48	C	58
49	D	123
51	A	54
52	A	123
53	B	163
57	B	157
Torts		
5	C	477
7	C	476
18	A	69
19	B	129
20	A	68
45	C	351
48	A	1